"The love of God has long languished_____. Not only has it not received the sustained attention that it deserves, but it has not always been clear where to locate it: in a discussion of the divine attributes, the Trinity, soteriology, creation, providence, somewhere else, everywhere? Another problem is that the love of God is too often conflated with images of human love. John Peckham rightly takes aim at this mistake and at other popular myths about God's love. Here is a study of God's love, based on the whole canon of God, that I admire even at those points (and there are a few) where I disagree."
Kevin J. Vanhoozer, Trinity Evangelical Divinity School

"Many people talk about how to do 'theological interpretation of Scripture,' but John Peckham actually does it in this book. He does it in a well-informed and thoughtful way, and he helps us gain a clearer—and more biblical—vision of the great love of the Triune God."
Thomas H. McCall, Trinity Evangelical Divinity School

"In view of the universal agreement that love is a crucially important attribute of God, it is astonishing that we so often are content to operate with conceptions of love that are hastily adopted, often from popular culture, without thorough consideration. John Peckham seeks to remedy this state of affairs with a thorough biblical examination of the love of God, bringing the text into dialogue with the multitude of popular conceptions of love. Strongly recommended for all who seek to understand how it is that God loves them."
William Hasker, emeritus professor of philosophy, Huntington College

"What strikes me about *The Love of God: A Canonical Model* is four things: its learning, sophistication, originality and comprehensiveness. Concerning its learning: the author is impressively conversant with almost all of the relevant literature, so far as I can see. Regarding its sophistication: the author displays a subtle and sophisticated grasp of the issues; he is sure-footed in theology, biblical interpretation and philosophical theology. That combination is hard to come by. Concerning its originality: rather than running with the crowd, the author questions common assumptions on a lot of points, on almost all of which, in my view, he is correct. And concerning its comprehensiveness: the author looks at God's love from a large number of different angles; every other treatment that I know of is 'pinched' by comparison. My judgment is that this promises to be a very impressive and influential book."
Nicholas Wolterstorff, Noah Porter Professor Emeritus of Philosophical Theology, Yale University

"Few beliefs about God are more distinctive of Christianity or more appreciated by Christians than the truth that 'God is love.' But not all Christians understand this statement in the same way. John Peckham focuses on God's love in the context of God's relationship with the world, and he describes clearly and carefully the different conceptions of God's love that exist within the church. Though his main text is not difficult to read, the multitude of biblical references cited and the abundance and diversity of his references to the work of other scholars in his footnotes make this a highly valuable resource for further study. Peckham contributes very helpfully to our understanding of God's love through his presentation of the big picture he has constructed from careful theological interpretation of the Bible, viewed as a whole. His foreconditional-reciprocal model of divine love offers a mediating position between the transcendent-voluntarist model of classical theism and the immanent-experientialist model of process panentheism. This is a model in which God's love is volitional, evaluative, emotional, foreconditional and ideally reciprocal. Although I have arrived at a more monergistic model than Peckham has, I benefited from both his exegetical work and his reverent elucidation of how God loves and relates to the world. His book not only stimulated me intellectually; it often prompted me to worship. I commend it heartily to those who want to grow in their love of God through contemplating anew, and more deeply, what God has told us about his loving self in his inspired word and demonstrated to us in his deeds supremely in Christ."

Terrance L. Tiessen, professor emeritus of systematic theology and ethics, Providence Theological Seminary, Canada

"*The Love of God: A Canonical Model* makes an important contribution to issues that are of central concern to both biblical and systematic theology. John Peckham shows mastery of a wide array of biblical and theological literature and has impressively deployed such resources in this well informed and carefully nuanced and hermeneutically sophisticated work. Peckham is clearly committed to the authority of the biblical text and to letting it guide his conclusions. The 'foreconditional-reciprocal' model of God's love in relationship to the world that Peckham defends is a biblically illuminating and theologically attractive proposal that deserves serious consideration and makes a significant contribution to scholarly theological literature."

Jerry Walls, Houston Baptist University

"John Peckham brilliantly reassesses the concept of God's love, which is foundational for the theological framework of the entire Bible. Employing mastery of wide-ranging sources and keen, balanced logic, he shows how layers of philosophical and traditional assumptions and notions have come to filter and obscure the biblical perspective. Implications of this study for major aspects of Christian theology are profound. No doubt some scholars will resist Peckham's challenge to commonly held views, but none can justifiably ignore it."

Roy Gane, professor of Hebrew Bible and ancient Near Eastern languages, Andrews University

"To my knowledge, no other book on the subject of divine love tackles such an all-encompassing range of issues, lays such a solid biblical foundation for the argumentation, dares to question with such insightfulness many long-held assumptions about God's love that need revision, presents such cogent and erudite discussion of relevant philosophical/theological questions, and provides a model for divine love consciously derived from a *sola Scriptura* canonical perspective."

Richard M. Davidson, J. N. Andrews Professor of Old Testament Interpretation, Andrews University

The LOVE of GOD

A Canonical Model

John C. Peckham

IVP Academic
An imprint of InterVarsity Press
Downers Grove, Illinois

InterVarsity Press
P.O. Box 1400, Downers Grove, IL 60515-1426
ivpress.com
email@ivpress.com

©2015 by John C. Peckham

All rights reserved. No part of this book may be reproduced in any form without written permission from InterVarsity Press.

InterVarsity Press® is the book-publishing division of InterVarsity Christian Fellowship/USA®, a movement of students and faculty active on campus at hundreds of universities, colleges and schools of nursing in the United States of America, and a member movement of the International Fellowship of Evangelical Students. For information about local and regional activities, visit intervarsity.org.

All Scripture quotations, unless otherwise indicated, are taken from the New American Standard Bible®, copyright 1960, 1962, 1963, 1968, 1971, 1972, 1973, 1975, 1977, 1995 by The Lockman Foundation. Used by permission.

While any stories in this book are true, some names and identifying information may have been changed to protect the privacy of individuals.

Cover design: Cindy Kiple
Interior design: Beth McGill
Images: © sedmak/iStockphoto

ISBN 978-0-8308-4079-3 (print)
ISBN 978-0-8308-9880-0 (digital)

Library of Congress Cataloging-in-Publication Data

Peckham, John, 1981-
  The love of God : a canonical model / John C. Peckham.
    pages cm
  Includes bibliographical references and index.
  ISBN 978-0-8308-4079-3 (pbk.)
  1. God (Christianity)—Love. I. Title.
  BT140.P38 2015
  231'.6—dc23
                                                                    2015018834

This book is dedicated to my wife, Brenda,

the love of my life and my best friend.

Contents

Acknowledgments — 9

Abbreviations — 11

1 Conflicting Models of Divine Love — 15

2 Toward Addressing the Conflict: A Canonical Approach — 45

3 *Agape* Versus *Eros*? The Biblical Semantics of Divine Love — 69

4 The Volitional Aspect of Divine Love — 89

5 The Evaluative Aspect of Divine Love — 117

6 The Emotional Aspect of Divine Love — 147

7 The Foreconditional Aspect of Divine Love — 191

8 The Reciprocal Aspect of Divine Love — 219

9 Who Is the God Who Loves? — 249

Author Index — 279

Subject Index — 283

Scripture Index — 287

Acknowledgments

Researching the love of God over the course of a number of years has been a richly rewarding privilege. I have been challenged, edified and more than a little surprised by what I have found regarding the complex and beautiful conception of divine love exhibited in Scripture. Through this study I have been brought to an ever-greater appreciation of God's surpassingly great character of love, and I hope that this work will inspire others to a similar appreciation and further contemplation of who God is and the manner in which he relates to humans.

I originally undertook this rewarding task of investigating the nature of divine love as the topic of my dissertation. I am profoundly thankful to Fernando Canale, my dissertation advisor, who inspired me to the task of investigating and articulating a biblical conception of divine love. I am also grateful to Miroslav Kiš and Roy Gane, who provided important guidance and feedback throughout the research and writing process. I would also like to thank the numerous other theologians who read and commented on my work on divine love and encouraged me in various ways in the writing of this new book, especially Jerry Walls.

I am grateful to Andrews University, especially my colleagues in the Theology and Christian Philosophy Department, for providing support and friendship during the writing of this book. It is a privilege and honor to work among such excellent scholars and teachers, and my students have been, and continue to be, a joy to teach, especially as we have pondered together the incomparable love of our great God.

Many thanks are also due to the excellent team at IVP for all of their support and efforts in bringing this project to publication. I would like to thank Gary Deddo for his initial interest in this project, and I am particularly indebted to my editor, David W. Congdon, whose guidance and comments greatly improved this work.

Finally, I would like to express my deepest gratitude to my family. My parents, Ernest and Karen, have provided ongoing encouragement and wisdom. My son, Joel, is my daily source of joy and laughter. Most of all I would like to thank my wonderful wife and best friend, Brenda, whose amazing love, patience, support and encouragement never cease to amaze me.

"We have come to know and have believed the love which God has for us. God is love, and the one who abides in love abides in God, and God abides in him" (1 Jn 4:16).

Abbreviations

AB	Anchor Bible
ABD	*The Anchor Bible Dictionary.* Edited by David Noel Freedman. 6 vols. New York: Doubleday, 1996.
Ages	Thomas Aquinas. *Summa Theologica.* Translated by the Fathers of the Dominican Province. 6 vols. Albany, OR: Ages Software, 1997.
AUSS	*Andrews University Seminary Studies*
BDAG	W. Bauer, F. W. Danker, W. F. Arndt and F. W. Gingrich. *Greek-English Lexicon of the New Testament and Other Early Christian Literature.* 2nd ed. Chicago: University of Chicago Press, 1979.
BECNT	Baker Exegetical Commentary on the New Testament
BSac	*Bibliotheca Sacra*
CBQ	*Catholic Biblical Quarterly*
CD	Karl Barth. *Church Dogmatics.* Edited by Geoffrey W. Bromiley and T. F. Torrance. 14 vols. Edinburgh: T & T Clark, 1936–1969.
DTIB	*Dictionary for Theological Interpretation of the Bible.* Edited by Kevin J. Vanhoozer et al. Grand Rapids: Baker Academic, 2005.
EDNT	*Exegetical Dictionary of the New Testament.* Edited by H. Balz and G. Schneider. Grand Rapids: Eerdmans, 1990–1993.
HALOT	Ludwig Koehler, Walter Baumgartner and Johann Jakob Stamm. *The Hebrew and Aramaic Lexicon of the Old Testament.* Translated and edited under the supervision of M. E. J. Richardson. 4 vols. Leiden: Brill, 1994–1999.
HBT	*Horizons in Biblical Theology*

IDB	*The Interpreter's Dictionary of the Bible*. Edited by G. A. Buttrick. 4 vols. Nashville: Abingdon, 1962.
IJST	*International Journal of Systematic Theology*
JAOS	*Journal of the American Oriental Society*
JATS	*Journal of the Adventist Theological Society*
JBL	*Journal of Biblical Literature*
JETS	*Journal of the Evangelical Theological Society*
JPS	Jewish Publication Society
JRE	*Journal of Religious Ethics*
JRT	*Journal of Reformed Theology*
JSNT	*Journal for the Study of the New Testament*
JSOT	*Journal for the Study of the Old Testament*
JTS	*Journal of Theological Studies*
L&N	*Greek-English Lexicon of the New Testament: Based on Semantic Domains*. Edited by J. P. Louw and E. A. Nida. 2nd ed. New York: UBS, 1989.
LCL	Loeb Classical Library
LW	*Luther's Works*. Edited by Jaroslav Pelikan, Hilton C. Oswald and Helmut T. Lehmann. 55 vols. St. Louis: Concordia; Philadelphia: Fortress Press, 1955–1986.
LXX	Septuagint
MAJT	*Mid-America Journal of Theology*
NAC	The New American Commentary
NIB	*The New Interpreter's Bible*. Edited by Leander E. Keck. 12 vols. Nashville: Abingdon, 1994.
NICNT	New International Commentary on the New Testament
NICOT	New International Commentary on the Old Testament
NIDNTT	*New International Dictionary of New Testament Theology*. Edited by Colin Brown. 4 vols. Grand Rapids: Zondervan, 1986.
NIDOTTE	*New International Dictionary of Old Testament Theology & Exegesis*. Edited by Willem A. VanGemeren. 5 vols. Grand Rapids: Zondervan, 1997.

NIGTC	New International Greek Testament Commentary
NPNF	*Nicene and Post-Nicene Fathers.* Series 1. Edited by Philip Schaff. 14 vols. Buffalo: The Christian Literature Company, 1885–1887.
NTS	*New Testament Studies*
OTL	Old Testament Library
PNTC	Pillar New Testament Commentaries
SBJT	*Southern Baptist Journal of Theology*
SJT	*Scottish Journal of Theology*
TDNT	*Theological Dictionary of the New Testament.* Edited by Gerhard Kittel and Gerhard Friedrich. 10 vols. Grand Rapids: Eerdmans, 1964–1976.
TDOT	*Theological Dictionary of the Old Testament.* Edited by Johannes G. Botterweck and H. Ringgren. 15 vols. Grand Rapids: Eerdmans, 1974–2006.
TJ	*Trinity Journal*
TLNT	Ceslas Spicq. *Theological Lexicon of the New Testament.* 3 vols. Peabody, MA: Hendrickson, 1994.
TLOT	*Theological Lexicon of the Old Testament.* Edited by Ernst Jenni and Claus Westermann. 3 vols. Peabody, MA: Hendrickson, 1997.
TOTC	Tyndale Old Testament Commentaries
TWOT	*Theological Wordbook of the Old Testament.* Edited by R. Laird Harris and Gleason Archer. Chicago: Moody, 1999.
TWTB	*Theological Wordbook of the Bible.* Edited by Alan Richardson. New York: Macmillan, 1950.
UBS	United Bible Societies
VT	*Vetus Testamentum*
WBC	Word Biblical Commentary
ZAW	*Zeitschrift für die alttestamentliche Wissenschaft*
ZNW	*Zeitschrift für die neutestamentliche Wissenschaft*

1

CONFLICTING MODELS OF DIVINE LOVE

Divine love is a central component of God's character, with abundant implications regarding all areas of theology. However, theologians are sharply divided regarding the nature of divine love for the world and the corresponding issues of divine ontology. Considerable semantic and conceptual ambiguity in some treatments of divine love exacerbates the issue.[1] How does one adequately address such an integral, complex and pivotal theological concept? The vastness of the topic precludes an exhaustive overview of the various conceptions of love generally or of divine love in particular. Whereas conceptions of divine love vary widely, the primary features of the contemporary debate over divine love may be illuminated by examination of the differences between two prominent and recent, but irreconcilable, models of divine love, the transcendent-voluntarist and immanent-experientialist models, the former being a descendant of classic theism and the latter representing process panentheism.[2] These models depict mutually exclusive con-

---

[1]"Christian theologians have themselves been somewhat indifferent—inattentive, neutral—with regard to the concept of the love of God, if we are to judge from their often oblique, indistinct, or awkward treatments of the subject" (Kevin J. Vanhoozer, "Introduction: The Love of God—Its Place, Meaning, and Function in Systematic Theology," in *Nothing Greater, Nothing Better: Theological Essays on the Love of God*, ed. Kevin J. Vanhoozer [Grand Rapids: Eerdmans, 2001], p. 1). "Talk of the love of God" is "anything but self-explanatory, despite the ease with which theologians are wont to use familiar phrases" (George M. Newlands, *Theology of the Love of God* [Atlanta: John Knox, 1981], p. 136).

[2]The use of models as an aid to grasping and dealing with major streams of thought is well attested. See Vincent Brümmer, *The Model of Love: A Study in Philosophical Theology* (Cambridge: Cambridge University Press, 1993). Since neither classic theism nor panentheism is a monolithic category (there are numerous other conceptions that fit within classic theism and panentheism), I have identified these models more narrowly by focusing on primary exemplars.

ceptions of both love and divine ontology, amounting to a fundamental impasse. Furthermore, the current theological landscape manifests significant dissatisfaction with these prominent conceptions of divine love.[3]

The sharp conflict and corresponding dissatisfaction regarding competing conceptions of love hinges on answers to five integral questions, which revolve around whether the God-world love relationship is unilateral or bilateral. First, does God choose to fully love only some, or all, or is he essentially related to all such that he necessarily loves all? Second, does God only bestow and/or create value, or might he also appraise, appreciate and receive value? In other words, is divine love only arbitrarily willed, pure beneficence (thematic *agape*), or may it include desire and/or enjoyment (thematic *eros*)?[4] Third, does God's love include affection and/or emotionality such that God is concerned for the world, sympathetically or otherwise? Fourth, is divine love unconditional or conditional? Fifth, can God and humans be involved in a reciprocal (albeit asymmetrical) love relationship?[5]

In order to address these questions, I undertook a biblical investigation by way of a final-form canonical approach to systematic theology, without presupposing the truth or error of existing models.[6] From this research, I have derived a foreconditional-reciprocal model of divine love that addresses the five crucial questions above, explained in the coming chapters. First, however, the theological conflict over the nature of divine love must be understood.

Classic Conceptions of Divine Love and the Process Polemic

The dominant conceptions of divine love throughout the ages of Christian

---

[3]Some have called for an alternative conception altogether. So Thomas Jay Oord, "Matching Theology and Piety: An Evangelical Process Theology of Love" (PhD diss., Claremont Graduate University, 1999), pp. 75-76; Clark H. Pinnock, "Between Classical and Process Theism," in *Process Theology*, ed. Ronald H. Nash (Grand Rapids: Baker, 1987), p. 317.

[4]I use the modifier "thematic" in reference to *agape* and *eros* to distinguish this theological usage of the terms from the considerably different semantic usage of the terms in the Bible and ancient Greek literature.

[5]The responses to these questions are themselves bound up with answers to ontological issues relating to the extent of divine power, issues regarding determinism or indeterminism; the acceptance, rejection or qualification of immutability and impassibility; and the nature of divine perfection and/or self-sufficiency. The positions taken regarding these issues determine whether or to what extent God can be involved in a mutually beneficial relationship.

[6]This methodology is described in chap. 2 (below).

theology are grounded in classic theism. Although classic theism is not monolithic, it generally refers to the classical conception of God as necessary and self-sufficient, perfect, simple, timeless, immutable, impassible, omniscient and omnipotent.[7] In the twentieth century, this view of God was directly challenged by a rising school of natural theology called process theism, a panentheistic system that represents a form of the increasingly popular, though varied and complex, relational theologies.[8] The most prominent form of process theism originated in the writings of Alfred North Whitehead (1861–1947) and was further developed and systematized by Charles Hartshorne (1897–2000).[9] Hartshorne's process theism rejected or redefined each of the previously mentioned divine characteristics of classic theism, positing a conception of divine love directly at odds with the classic tradition. In Hartshorne's view, classical divine ontology fails to maintain meaningful relationship between God and the world such that God is "not an exalted being, but an empty absurdity, a love which is simply not love."[10] In order to evaluate Hartshorne's criticism of classic theism and his alternative model (the immanent-experientialist model), one must first have a basic understanding of the most influential conceptions of God's love in historical theology.[11]

---

[7]For a basic introduction to these elements of classic theism, in contrast to process theism, see Ronald H. Nash, "Process Theology and Classical Theism," in Nash, ed., *Process Theology*, pp. 8-12.
[8]For example, Thomas Jay Oord has recently proposed a panentheistic view of divine love, which he calls essential kenosis theology (*The Nature of Love: A Theology* [St. Louis: Chalice, 2010]). Further, the nonpanentheistic relational theology of open theism launched an alternative to particular aspects of classic theism by affirming some elements, such as omnipotence and divine freedom, but denying divine timelessness, foreknowledge and impassibility (Clark H. Pinnock et al., *The Openness of God: A Biblical Challenge to the Traditional Understanding of God* [Downers Grove, IL: InterVarsity Press, 1994]).
[9]There are other systems of process theology (e.g., that of Pierre Teilhard de Chardin), but the phrase generally refers to the Whitehead/Hartshorne school. Hartshorne was heavily influenced by Whitehead, his teacher, though their systems are not identical. See Whitehead's seminal work, *Process and Reality: An Essay in Cosmology* (Cambridge: Cambridge University Press, 1929). For a discussion of Hartshorne's and Whitehead's differences see Lewis S. Ford, "Hartshorne's Interpretation of Whitehead," in *The Philosophy of Charles Hartshorne*, ed. Lewis Edwin Hahn (La Salle, IL: Open Court, 1991), pp. 313-38. For an introduction to process theology, see John B. Cobb Jr. and David Ray Griffin, *Process Theology: An Introductory Exposition* (Philadelphia: Westminster Press, 1976).
[10]Charles Hartshorne, *Omnipotence and Other Theological Mistakes* (Albany: State University of New York Press, 1984), p. 31. See also Schubert Miles Ogden, *The Reality of God and Other Essays* (New York: Harper & Row, 1966), p. 46.
[11]Given the nature of this study, the historical survey is limited to a few thinkers who exemplify the major issues and have had a large impact on the theology of divine love. For a more detailed historical overview, see Irving Singer, *The Nature of Love*, 3 vols. (Chicago: University of Chicago Press, 1987).

Augustine (354–430). Augustine systematized perhaps the most influential Christian conception of divine love outside Scripture, influenced indirectly by Plato's ontology through Neoplatonism.[12] However, the Platonic ontology of the ultimate being as perfect and immutably self-sufficient, coupled with the Platonic conception of love in terms of desire (*eros*), rendered it impossible for God to love humans, since any desire would require that God be somehow deficient.[13] Whereas Augustine affirmed divine perfection, immutability and self-sufficiency, he broke with Plato by upholding the indispensable tenet of Christianity that God loves humans.[14] Indeed, for Augustine, "love is God."[15] Regarding this apparent paradox he wrote:

> In what way then does He [God] love us? As objects of use or as objects of enjoyment? If He enjoys us, He must be in need of good from us, and no sane man will say that; for all the good we enjoy is either Himself, or what comes from Himself. . . . He does not enjoy us then, but makes use of us. For if He neither enjoys nor uses us, I am at a loss to discover in what way He can love us.[16]

Accordingly, God's love for the world is not acquisitive, evaluative or passible. God can neither desire nor receive any value or enjoyment from the world, since he lacks nothing (aseity).[17] As such, God does not love in the sense of Plato's *eros* (desire) or Aristotle's *philia* (friendship), but divine love is unilateral beneficence (thematic *agape*).

On the other hand, human love toward God is of a different kind than divine love. Whereas divine love is beneficence bestowed downward, proper human love (*caritas*) is directed upward toward God, its only proper object.[18]

---

[12]For an overview and discussion of Augustine's view see John Burnaby, *Amor Dei, a Study of the Religion of St. Augustine* (London: Hodder & Stoughton, 1960).

[13]Notably, divine perfection and self-sufficiency, differently conceived, could be harmonized with divine desire.

[14]Augustine, *Lectures on St. John* 94.5 (*NPNF* 7:542).

[15]Lewis Ayres, "Augustine, Christology, and God as Love: An Introduction to the Homilies on 1 John," in Vanhoozer, ed., *Nothing Greater, Nothing Better*, p. 86.

[16]Augustine, *On Christian Doctrine* 1.31.34 (*NPNF* 2:1109). Significantly, even God's use of humans brings him no advantage because it "has reference only to His goodness" (ibid., 1.32 [*NPNF* 2:1109-10]).

[17]For Augustine, "because of God's self-sufficient perfection, his love for us can in no way be a form of need-love. It is purely gift-love, or *agape*" (Brümmer, *Model of Love*, p. 125). See Augustine, *The City of God* 10.5 (*NPNF* 2:399).

[18]Augustine, *On Christian Doctrine* 1.5.5, 1.22.20 (*NPNF* 2:1090, 1100); Augustine, *On the Morals of the Catholic Church* 20 (*NPNF* 4:86). Yet this does not exclude a proper kind of love for self

Moreover, human love is produced by divine action such that God himself determines who will love him.[19] In this way, Augustine's view excludes a freely reciprocal love relationship between God and humans.

Thomas Aquinas (1225-1274). Aquinas continued along the lines of the Augustinian view of the God-world relationship while adapting it to Aristotelian metaphysics.[20] For Aquinas, God is the perfect, self-sufficient and utterly immutable first mover who remains unmoved and passionless and is thus impervious to desire; pure act with no potentiality.[21] However, in a decisive break from Aristotle's conception wherein God cannot love the world, Aquinas posited friendship love (*amicitia*) between God and humans, in which God is the unilateral benefactor but never the beneficiary.[22] As in Augustine's system, since God lacks nothing, he cannot desire or receive anything for his own benefit.[23] God loves, but "in God there are no passions" (impassibility), such that God's love is a purposive, rational "act of the will," not an act of the "sensitive appetite."[24] Though God loves universally, he does not love all equally. He wills "all some good; but He does not wish every good to them all," and so far as "He does not wish this particular good—namely, eternal life—He is said to hate or reprobate them."[25]

Whereas human love is moved or affected by its object, divine love "in-

---

and for neighbor, in which humans are loved for God's sake, according to the order of love (*ordo amoris*; Augustine, *On Christian Doctrine* 1.27.28 [*NPNF* 2:1105]).

[19]The "grace of God makes a willing man out of an unwilling one" (Augustine, *Contra Julianum opus imperfectum* 3.122, quoted in Anders Nygren, *Agape and Eros*, trans. Philip S. Watson [London: SPCK, 1953], p. 528).

[20]Burnaby, *Amor Dei*, p. 264. See Thomas Aquinas, *Summa Theologica* 2.2.23.5 (Ages 3:264-65). For a defense of Aquinas's conception of divine love, see Michael J. Dodds, *The Unchanging God of Love: A Study of the Teaching of St. Thomas Aquinas on Divine Immutability in View of Certain Contemporary Criticism of this Doctrine* (Fribourg, Switzerland: Éditions universitaires, 1986).

[21]Aquinas, *Summa Theologica* 1.1.3.1-7, 1.1.4.1, 1.1.9.1 (Ages 1:33-44, 48, 92-94).

[22]The possibility for such a friendship between God and humans is predicated on his analogy of being (*analogia entis*), allowing Aquinas to move beyond Aristotle's view that the distance from God to humanity is too great for friendship (ibid., 2.1.65.5 [Ages 2:697]).

[23]God's love does, however, include a qualified kind of desire for the good of others (ibid., 1.1.20.2.3 [Ages 1:282]).

[24]Ibid., 1.1.20.1.1 (Ages 1:278). Accordingly, "sorrow . . . over the misery of others belongs not to God" (ibid., 1.1.21.3 [Ages 1:292]). Compare ibid., 2.2.23.2 (Ages 3:259). For Aquinas, God's love is "willing the good" (benevolence; Vanhoozer, "Introduction: The Love of God," p. 5). See Aquinas, *Summa Theologica* 1.1.20.1.2, 1.37.1 (Ages 1:280, 460).

[25]Aquinas, *Summa Theologica*, 1.1.23.3.1 (Ages 1:313). Here, "God's loving one thing more than another is nothing else than His willing for that thing a greater good: because God's will is the cause of goodness in things" (ibid., 1.1.20.4 [Ages 1:285]).

fuses and creates goodness."[26] Human friendships involve give and take, but God has no reciprocal relations with humankind.[27] Accordingly, human love is derivative from divine love, though Aquinas also maintains that humans who love God love him voluntarily and meritoriously in the sense of enjoying him for his own sake.[28] God thus loves (*caritas*) humans in the sense of beneficence.[29] Aquinas, then, continues the Augustinian emphasis on *caritas* as both the divine essence and that which proceeds from God.[30]

Martin Luther (1483-1546). In Martin Luther's view, divine love is similarly unilateral, nonevaluative, unmotivated and wholly gratuitous beneficence, akin to grace. God's unilaterally determining, irresistible and wholly efficacious will is primary (voluntarism) such that God is entirely self-sufficient, immutable and impassible; the giver who never receives.[31] God's love is thus nonevaluative bestowal: "Rather than seeking its own good, God's love flows forth and bestows good. Therefore, sinners are attractive because they are loved; they are not loved because they are attractive."[32] Simply put, "God is nothing else than love," and his "nature is nothing else but pure beneficence," as manifest supremely at the cross.[33]

---

[26]Ibid., 1.1.20.2 (Ages 1:281-82). Alan Torrance comments that God's love "creates value by giving value to what it loves. It does not desire to receive, or to fulfill itself; it simply gives—and its human object may be worthless and degraded" ("Is Love the Essence of God?" in Vanhoozer, ed., *Nothing Greater, Nothing Better*, p. 130).

[27]Thus Aquinas comments: "A relation of God to creatures, is not a reality in God, but in the creature; for it is in God in our idea only" (*Summa Theologica* 1.1.6.2 [Ages 1:68]).

[28]Ibid., 2.2.23.2 (Ages 3:275). Aquinas thus posits that determinism and "liberty of choice" are compatible (ibid., 1.1.23.3.3 [Ages 1:313]). This allows Aquinas to preserve the power of humans to act in love, and thus gain merit, in accordance with his sacramental soteriology (ibid., 2.2.23.2, 2.2.27 [Ages 3:259, 356-58]).

[29]Humans are not "friends in the active sense (*amantes*)" but "friends in the passive sense of those whom he loved (*amanti*)" (Aquinas, quoted in Liz Carmichael, *Friendship: Interpreting Christian Love* [New York: T & T Clark, 2004], p. 109). See Aquinas, *Summa Theologica*, 2.2.27.8 (Ages 3:358-59).

[30]Aquinas, *Summa Theologica* 2.2.23.2 (Ages 3:260).

[31]LW 33:68. Dennis Ngien comments, "God's 'aseity' consists in the fact that God is *totally* independent of others, and correspondingly absolutely free," willing his own nature (*The Suffering of God According to Martin Luther's Theologia Crucis* [New York: Peter Lang, 1995], pp. 27, 110). Accordingly, "God is not capable of suffering" (LW 38:254).

[32]LW 31:57. Likewise, "God does not love because of our works; He loves because of His love" (LW 30:300). Compare LW 14:106, 22:373. God's love is, then, "free and overflowing bestowal. Indifferent to the worthlessness of its object, it lavishly makes all things good" (Singer, *Nature of Love*, 1:328).

[33]LW 30:300.

For Luther, only divine love (thematic *agape*) is authentic.[34] He vehemently rejected the conception of human love (*caritas*) from Augustine throughout medieval theology, viewing it as a false synthesis inclusive of egocentric love toward God (thematic *eros*). On the contrary, since God is the cause of all authentic love, humans cannot truly love except as passive agents of divine love flowing through them, excluding the possibility of freely reciprocal divine-human love.[35] Thus, whereas Luther breaks significantly from Augustine and Aquinas regarding the value of human love, Luther's view of God's love is generally congruous with both.

Anders Nygren (1890-1978). Anders Nygren's influence as a Christian theologian does not approach the magnitude of Augustine, Aquinas or Luther. Yet Nygren has immensely influenced Christian thinking about divine love via his seminal work, *Agape and Eros,* which fleshes out Luther's view of gratuitous love, *agape*, against *eros*.[36] Nygren posits an absolute dichotomy between *eros* and *agape* such that *eros* is desirous and acquisitive love (vulgar or heavenly), inappropriate to God's perfect and self-sufficient nature, whereas *agape* is the highest love, a unilaterally willed and purely altruistic beneficence that properly describes God's love alone.[37] All other types of love (*eros, philia*, et al.) are not Christian love and should not be conflated or integrated with *agape*.[38] In this view:

1. "*Eros* is acquisitive desire and longing," while "*agape* is sacrificial giving."

2. "*Eros* is an upward movement, man's way to God" while "*agape* is sacri-

---

[34]Because of intrinsic sinfulness, humans are ontologically incapable of love. Thus Luther considers "the very idea that man can love God a dangerous snare of the devil" (Singer, *Nature of Love*, 1:325). See LW 9:85, 21:300, 34:309.

[35]"As water through a tube, humans are passive conduits of divine love" (Luther, quoted in Nygren, *Agape and Eros*, p. 735). Thus "man himself cannot love, but he can receive love and pass it on to his neighbor" (Singer, *Nature of Love*, 1:329).

[36]Gene H. Outka states, "Nygren so effectively posed issues about love that they have had a prominence in theology and ethics they never had before. . . . Whatever the reader may think of it, one may justifiably regard his work as the beginning of the modern treatment of the subject" (*Agape: An Ethical Analysis* [New Haven, CT: Yale University Press, 1972], p. 1). For a recent proponent of Nygren's view, see Colin Grant, "For the Love of God: Agape," *JRE* 24, no. 1 (Spring 1996): 3-21.

[37]Nygren, *Agape and Eros*, p. 92. He contends that *eros* and *agape* "represent two streams that run through the whole history of religion," sometimes "clashing" and "mingling" together (ibid., p. 205). Compare the contrast Heinrich Scholz posits between *agape* and *eros* in *Eros und Caritas: Die platonische Liebe und die Liebe im Sinne des Christentums* (Halle: Max Niemeyer Verlag, 1929).

[38]Nygren, *Agape and Eros*, pp. 75-81, 92.

ficial giving," which "comes down . . . God's way to man."

3. "*Eros* is man's effort," while "*agape* is God's grace."

4. "*Eros* is determined by the quality, the beauty and worth, of its object, it is not spontaneous but 'evoked,' 'motivated,'" while "*agape* is sovereign in relation to its object, and is directed to both 'the evil and the good'; it is spontaneous, 'overflowing,' 'unmotivated.'"[39]

Accordingly, God is the only true agent of love (*agape*), which is spontaneous, unmotivated, indifferent to value, nondesirous and nonemotive, beneficent, gratuitous and sovereign. Humans of themselves are incapable of *agape* such that love is caused only by God's sovereign and unconditional predestination.[40] Nygren's emphasis on need love (thematic *eros*) as opposed to gift love (thematic *agape*) remains influential.[41] However, many have rejected Nygren's dichotomy. Gary Badcock voices a primary line of criticism: "The Bible itself does not actually make the rigid distinction that Nygren presupposes between Christian love, *agape*, and other forms of human love."[42]

The Transcendent-Voluntarist Model of Divine Love

The prominent historical conceptions of divine love above share considerable continuity. Charles Hartshorne's process theism contends that such perspectives prohibit a dynamic, reciprocal God-world relationship. Carl F. H. Henry (1913–2003), one of the strongest recent exemplars of the historical tradition and a contemporary of Hartshorne (1897–2000), responded directly to process thought in his transcendent-voluntarist model. Although classic theism is not monolithic, Henry's perspective provides a sophisticated model that speaks to the questions and criticisms of process and other

---

[39]Ibid., p. 210.
[40]A human loves God only "because God's unmotivated love has overwhelmed him and taken control of him, so that he cannot do other than love God. Therein lies the profound significance of the idea of predestination" (ibid., p. 214).
[41]For instance, these categories were adopted and popularized in C. S. Lewis, *The Four Loves* (New York: Harcourt Brace, 1988), p. 127.
[42]Gary D. Badcock, "The Concept of Love: Divine and Human," in Vanhoozer, ed., *Nothing Greater, Nothing Better*, p. 37. Compare Stephen G. Post, *A Theory of Agape: On the Meaning of Christian Love* (Lewisburg, PA: Bucknell University Press, 1990), pp. 88-89; Reinhold Niebuhr, *The Nature and Destiny of Man: A Christian Interpretation* (New York: Scribner, 1964), 2:84. Although Nygren qualifies his argument as thematic rather than semantic, the biblical data do not bear out the dichotomy thematically or semantically. See chap. 3 (below).

relational theologies.[43] In order to understand the transcendent-voluntarist model of divine love, we will first consider Henry's ontology.

God and the God-world relationship: The ontological framework. The transcendent-voluntarist model emphasizes the sovereignty of God's will and the closely related axiomatic conceptions of transcendence and self-sufficiency, necessity, simplicity, timelessness, immutability, impassibility, omnipotence and omniscience. For Henry, God himself "is a sovereign will."[44] God wills his own life and attributes in absolute freedom (voluntarism).[45] He thus depends on nothing (aseity) and is affected by nothing (impassibility); he "sustains himself in voluntary self-determination." As perfectly self-sufficient, God is simple; his essence, existence and attributes are identical.[46] Accordingly, God is immune to "increase or decrease" and unsusceptible to "ontological change" (immutability).[47] As such, "God is not in time" but not "timeless in such a way as to negate time."[48] Therefore, nothing can affect God or cause him to suffer, being "invulnerable to assault."[49] However, for Henry, divine impassibility does not mean that

---

[43]Ronald Nash cautions that we must "recognize that the relationship between classical theism and Christian theism is a matter of some dispute" ("Process Theology and Classical Theism," p. 3). Henry explicitly differentiates his view from what he calls the Thomistic emphasis on "Greek philosophical motifs" rather than "Judeo-Christian biblical categories" (Carl F. H. Henry, *God, Revelation, and Authority*, 6 vols. [Wheaton, IL: Crossway, 1999], 5:45).

[44]Henry, *God, Revelation, and Authority*, 5:130.

[45]God's "thoughts and acts are shaped neither by external necessity nor by internal limitation except as he is self-determined in what he thinks and does" (ibid., 5:214-15). Thus God's attributes "are virtues that he himself wills in sovereign freedom. They are not external constraints to which God's nature and will must conform" (ibid., 5:215). Compare ibid., 5:69, 319. However, "God's will or nature implies certain limitations on his actions. . . . God will not alter his own nature, that he cannot deny himself, that he cannot lie and cannot sin, that he cannot be deceived, and that, moreover, he cannot die"; such things represent "a logical impossibility" (ibid.).

[46]Ibid., 5:214, 130-32. Simplicity means that, though triune, "God is not compounded of parts; he is not a collection of perfections, but rather a living center of activity pervasively characterized by all his distinctive perfections" (ibid., 5:131).

[47]Ibid., 5:286-87. Compare ibid., 5:65, 292.

[48]Carl F. H. Henry, *Notes on the Doctrine of God* (Boston: W. A. Wilde, 1948), p. 132. Henry maintains the traditional doctrine of timelessness in its essential points and rejects recent conceptions of "everlasting temporality," contending that no "temporal predicates apply" to God, who has no "time-location" (*God, Revleation, and Authority*, 5:270). Compare ibid., 5:271. Nevertheless, Henry holds that this "unchanging and unchangeable God" is "active in temporal processes and historical events, and in the incarnation steps personally into history" (ibid., 5:292). For a recent defense of the traditional view of divine timelessness see Paul Helm, "Is God Bound by Time?" in *God Under Fire: Modern Scholarship Reinvents God*, ed. Douglas S. Huffman and Eric L. Johnson (Grand Rapids: Zondervan, 2002), pp. 119-36.

[49]Henry, *God, Revelation, and Authority*, 5:13.

God is uncaring or "utterly devoid of any feelings."[50] God can feel, but his feelings are purely self-determined.[51]

Since God is impassible, God's relation to the world does not affect him. Rather, God sovereignly determines himself and both the existence and occurrences of the world.[52] God is omniscient in that he perfectly knows his all-inclusive, eternal will, independent of creation.[53] Similarly, the sovereignty of God assumes his omnipotence such that the divine will is always perfectly efficacious.[54] However, in Henry's view, divine determinism and human freedom are compatible; humans are free in the sense that they act voluntarily, but they cannot act otherwise than they do (compatibilism).[55] In all this, God is transcendent, "completely and intrinsically independent" of the world as "voluntary creator" and "preserver," yet also present, active, and "pervasively immanent in it" by "preserving it" and "working out his sovereign purposes in and through it."[56]

Divine love in relation to the world. In the transcendent-voluntarist model,

---

[50]Millard J. Erickson, *God the Father Almighty: A Contemporary Exploration of the Divine Attributes* (Grand Rapids: Baker, 1998), p. 161. For Henry, God is "static" in that he is "unchanging," but not "indifferent" (*God, Revelation, and Authority*, 6:291).

[51]"God cannot undergo passion or suffering; nothing in the created universe can make God feel pain or inflict misery on Him. This does not mean that God has no feelings, but simply that His feelings are not the results of actions imposed on Him by others. His feelings flow from His eternal and unchangeable nature" as "the Unmoved Mover of all else" (Norman L. Geisler, *Systematic Theology*, vol. 2, *God, Creation* [Minneapolis: Bethany House, 2002], p. 112).

[52]Henry, *God, Revelation, and Authority*, 5:223, 13, 69. The "fixed divine decree" of predestination is central to God's sovereignty (ibid., 5:315).

[53]"God's knowledge of what will be is grounded in his knowledge of his eternal purpose" such that "divine omniscience does not imply that God's knowledge is dependent upon his creation" (ibid., 5:269, 277).

[54]Ibid., 5:69, 325. Thus "no one can frustrate God's will" (ibid., 5:318).

[55]Ibid., 6:273. In compatibilism, freedom does not entail the ability to will or act otherwise than one does (libertarianism) but refers to freedom from external compulsion. Compare ibid., 5:282, 6:73. Philosophers distinguish between various kinds of compatibilism. Here and elsewhere (unless otherwise specified), by *compatibilism* I refer to broad compatibilism, the view that determinism is compatible with free will *and* moral responsibility. Some compatibilists favor a narrow form of compatibilism (e.g., semicompatibilism) wherein agents may be determined such that they lack free will but possess moral responsibility. See the essays in Robert Kane, ed., *The Oxford Handbook of Free Will*, 2nd ed. (Oxford: Oxford University Press, 2011), pp. 153-242. For a recent presentation of Christian (broad) compatibilism see Millard J. Erickson, *What Does God Know and When Does He Know It?* (Grand Rapids: Zondervan, 2003). For a view in favor of divine foreknowledge and libertarian freedom see William Lane Craig, *Divine Foreknowledge and Human Freedom: The Coherence of Freedom* (New York: Brill, 1991).

[56]Henry, *God, Revelation, and Authority*, 5:12, 6:35-36. God is unequivocally other—yet not "wholly other"—than the world (ibid., 5:87). As timeless, divine "action" is expressed "in repetitive cosmic processes and events, or in once-for-all acts" (ibid., 6:50).

divine love for the world is sovereignly willed, unconditional, unmotivated, unmerited, freely bestowed beneficence, manifest ultimately in Christ's self-giving, which exemplifies the infinitude of God's self-giving love.[57] Intratrinitarian love is part of God's eternal nature.[58] In keeping with divine aseity and impassibility, the sovereign will of God is the sole origin of God's love, which "presupposes the exclusive voluntary initiative of the sovereign divine being whom no external power can manipulate."[59] God's love for humans, then, is predicated solely on the eternal predestinating divine decree, absent "inner divine necessity" and independent of human action and/or response.[60] Accordingly, while God loves all in some ways, only some are elect unto salvation (election love).[61]

God's love is purely volitional, unmotivated by external factors, neither merited nor elicited by humans but totally gratuitous. Human love toward God does not bring him value, since God lacks nothing and therefore cannot desire or receive value. Thus, "the Lover does not seek to satisfy some personal lack or to remedy an inner need, for God has none, but bestows a benefit on the one he gratuitously loves."[62] Divine love is therefore beneficence, "bestowed not upon a worthy object and not for the personal advantage of the Lover but solely for the benefit of the undeserving recipient."[63]

Further, since God acts but cannot be acted on, divine love is impassible.

---

[57] Ibid., 5:233, 6:356.

[58] Ibid., 6:322. There is an "eternal interchange of holy love between the persons of the self-revealed Godhead" (ibid., 5:172). Compare ibid., 5:155-56, 6:62. Love, however, is not "exhaustive of the totality of God's being, [but] is nevertheless intrinsic to God's very nature" (ibid., 6:348). Since God is simple and his essence equals his existence and all his attributes, divine "love, like all other divine attributes, reflects the whole of his being in specific actions and relationships" (ibid., 6:341). Compare ibid., 5:132.

[59] Ibid., 6:349. Divine love is "not primarily emotional but volitional" (ibid., 6:341).

[60] Ibid., 5:116. Compare Henry, *Notes on the Doctrine of God*, p. 111. As Leon Morris states, "predestination and love go together" (*Testaments of Love: A Study of Love in the Bible* [Grand Rapids: Eerdmans, 1981], p. 191). Accordingly, "God wills to love men and he loves according to his own purpose of election, not according to the actions of men" (ibid., p. 160).

[61] Henry, *God, Revelation, and Authority*, 6:316. This is by no means the only possible view of election love. Compare Karl Barth's view, briefly discussed in chap. 4 (below).

[62] Ibid., 6:343. As such, God's "love emanates from his own character; it is not dependent on the loveliness of the loved, external to himself" (D. A. Carson, *The Difficult Doctrine of the Love of God* [Wheaton, IL: Crossway, 2000], p. 63). So Morris, *Testaments of Love*, pp. 135, 42.

[63] Henry, *God, Revelation, and Authority*, 6:343. "The *agapē* of God confers on the unworthy an undeserved value or boon" (ibid., 6:342). Thus, "*agape* used of God's love means 'benevolence,' a self-less 'sacrificial' love" (Geisler, *Systematic Theology*, 2:367). So Henry, *God, Revelation, and Authority*, 6:344. See chap. 3 (below) regarding this claim.

However, God's love is not devoid of feeling or concern; divine feeling is self-determined.[64] Accordingly, Henry clarifies, "whatever Christian theology means by the impassibility of God, it does not mean that God's love, compassion and mercy are mere figures of speech."[65] Yet, "compassionate response is not induced in God by the distress of creatures, as if they were able to effect a change in the nature of an otherwise uncompassionate being; rather, response is grounded in the living God's essential nature, that is, in his voluntary disposition."[66]

As sovereignly willed, unmotivated and impassible, God's love is unconditionally constant. God "maintains eternal fidelity in love" as "the steadfast God, not a vacillating sovereign."[67] Humans cannot affect God's love for them. Moreover, God's love does not diminish his righteousness or holiness, or preclude his judgment or wrath. Justification from divine wrath is a "voluntary act of mercy" and "does not flow from the justice of God as an inner necessity of God's nature." As such, God's "righteousness" is "coextensive with his love."[68]

THE PROCESS ALTERNATIVE: THE IMMANENT-EXPERIENTIALIST MODEL OF DIVINE LOVE

The transcendent-voluntarist model is categorically rejected by the immanent-experientialist model, which posits that divine love is universal sympathy, the feeling of all others' feelings. In order to understand this conception one must first understand process ontology, which itself describes love. In Hartshorne's panentheistic system, God includes the world via essential relationship and yet is more than the world.[69] As such, God is neither wholly other than the world nor identical with the world (pantheism). In order to better understand this system, I will first summarize Hartshorne's

---

[64]In fact, Henry speaks of "God as having a tender concern for man," even "despite his moral revolt" (Henry, *Notes on the Doctrine of God*, p. 109).

[65]Henry, *God, Revelation, and Authority*, 6:349.

[66]Ibid.

[67]Ibid., 5:13. Morris likewise stresses constancy: "God's love is firm and sure and steadfast, continuing no matter what happens" (*Testaments of Love*, p. 19). Compare ibid., pp. 12, 77, 100.

[68]Henry, *God, Revelation, and Authority*, 6:349, 410, 350. Compare Morris, *Testaments of Love*, pp. 24, 31. See also the chapter "The Holy Love of God," in Henry, *Notes on the Doctrine of God*, pp. 103-13.

[69]God is "in some real aspect distinguishable from and independent of any and all relative items, and yet, taken as an actual whole, includes all relative items" (Charles Hartshorne, *Man's Vision of God and the Logic of Theism* [Hamden, CT: Archon, 1964], p. 89).

process ontology of the world (panpsychism), then his divine ontology (dipolar theism) and the relationship between the two (panentheism), and finally divine love (universal sympathy).

The nature of the world: Panpsychism. For Hartshorne, becoming, the continual temporal process of change, is the basic form of reality.[70] Everything consists of creative minds (even at the subatomic level), and every mind relates to others as both subject (knower) and object (known) within a social process of events (panpsychism).[71] For Hartshorne, to know is to feel, and each mind is thus both feeler (subject) and felt (object) in social relationship.[72] Every mind is always in the process of becoming in relationship because each knower (the subject, feeler) is changed by what it knows (the object, that which is felt). Indeed, according to Hartshorne's panpsychism, to know something is to include that which is known such that what is known is constitutive of the knower (an internal relation), while that which is known is not affected by being known (an external relation).[73] The knower (subject) is thus internally related to what is known (part or the whole of the object) and constituted by it, whereas that which is known (object) is externally related to the knower (subject) and unaffected.[74]

In this manner, each mind is coinherent with other minds, but often only partially so since each mind (except for God) knows only partially, and only that which is known (the relata) is included in the knower (subject). Within this relationship various minds retain "individual distinctness," and each possesses some degree of freedom (creativity) even when acted on.[75] Thus all reality is an indeterministic and interdependent creative synthesis of partially determined and self-determined minds in-

---

[70]Charles Hartshorne, *Reality as Social Process* (New York: Hafner, 1971), p. 17; Hartshorne, "Personal Identity from A to Z," *Process Studies* 2, no. 3 (1972): 211.

[71]Charles Hartshorne, "Panpsychism," in *A History of Philosophical Systems*, ed. Vergilius Ferm (New York: The Philosophical Library, 1950), p. 442. Compare Hartshorne, *Creative Synthesis and Philosophic Method* (London: SCM Press, 1970), p. 272.

[72]Hartshorne, *Man's Vision of God*, p. 223. "That all is psychic means, all is feeling, in reaction with other feeling" (Hartshorne, "Panpsychism," p. 449).

[73]See Hartshorne, *Reality as Social Process*, pp. 70-71; Hartshorne, *The Divine Relativity* (New Haven, CT: Yale University Press, 1964), p. 112.

[74]An external relation is "such that the entity [mind] said to be externally related could have been the same had the relations not obtained" (Hartshorne, *Divine Relativity*, p. 95).

[75]Hartshorne, "Panpsychism," p. 442. Thus, "'within' does not contradict 'other'" (Hartshorne, *Divine Relativity*, pp. 99-100). All minds have "some degree of freedom or self-determination, even in the lowest orders of psyches" (Hartshorne, "Panpsychism," p. 371).

teracting as both subjects (knower, feeler) and objects (known, felt) in continual, relational process.

God and the God-world relationship: Dipolar theism and panentheism. In Hartshorne's ontology of dipolar theism, God is the supreme, all-inclusive mind and therefore the compound individual of the world, not identical or equivalent to the world, but including the world while being more than the world (panentheism). As the supreme mind, God is also subject to the spatio-temporal, indeterministic and interdependent creative synthesis of minds in continual, relational process. God is the universal and supreme subject (knower) and is thereby supremely relative.[76] In this way, God is partially dependent and independent, partially determined and self-determined; the eminently moved mover of all and the all-knowing feeler of all feelings. Yet God is also the universal object, known (in part) by every subject.[77]

God's dipolarity (as universal subject and object), or dual transcendence, refers to God's eminent exemplification of the admirable characteristics of metaphysical contraries.[78] These poles are ontologically distinguishable yet ontically inseparable, such that God is, at once, the absolute-relative, abstract-concrete, potential-actual, necessary-contingent, universal-particular, supreme compound individual (universal object-subject).[79] Just as the subject (knower) includes its object (known), God as the universal subject (concrete and relative) includes the universal object (abstract and absolute).[80] For example, God is absolute in that no other can surpass him and his existence is necessary, yet he is supremely relative in that he is all-inclusive and thus continually in process, ever increasing as the world increases, such that the particularities of his existence are contingent.[81] God is thus the self-surpassing surpasser of all, the transcendental relativity (surrelativism).[82]

---

[76] "To include relations is to include their terms. Hence to know all is to include all" (Hartshorne, *Divine Relativity*, p. 76).
[77] Hartshorne, *Omnipotence*, p. 110.
[78] This raises a significant question, since a given characteristic may be admirable to some but deficient to others.
[79] See Hartshorne, *Reality as Social Process*, p. 168.
[80] The supreme divine mind is both concrete (relative) and abstract (absolute), with the abstract aspect included in the concrete aspect, the former being the abstraction of his essence from his contingent actuality (concrete aspect). See ibid., p. 116.
[81] Hartshorne, *Divine Relativity*, p. 14. This amounts to Hartshorne's important distinction between existence (that an entity is) and actuality (the particularities of the existing entity) (ibid., p. 87).
[82] Hartshorne, *Man's Vision of God*, p. 158. Surrelativism means "to be absolutely guaranteed su-

Since God is the universal subject who exhaustively and immediately knows all minds experientially (omniscience), he includes the world within himself (panentheism) and thereby feels the feelings of all others (universal sympathy) as supremely relative, growing and changing as the world grows.[83] As the universal object, on the other hand, God is known (partially) by every mind (subject).[84] In all this, God is essentially related to the world and thereby dependent on it, needing *some* world to exist.[85] This essential panentheistic relationship, however, does not mean that God and the world are identical. The world is inseparable from and included in God, but God is more than the world. Accordingly, God's relationship to the world might be thought of as analogous to that of a mind and a body or to that of social relativity, though both analogies are imperfect.[86]

God, as universal subject (supreme knower and feeler of all feelings), is dependent on the world and partially determined by it.[87] At the same time, God also maintains a degree of freedom and self-determination and is himself the most influential of all minds as the universal object.[88] In this view, God is not omnipotent but possesses the greatest compossible power.[89] Such power, however, is limited to acting by persuasion since all minds retain some degree of freedom (however slight).[90] The enacting of God's

---

periority to every other individual that comes to exist" (Hartshorne, *Divine Relativity*, p. 21). It refers to the divine relativity as "the reflexivity of its all-surpassingness. It surpasses itself, as well as everything else" (ibid., p. 22).

[83] Hartshorne, *Man's Vision of God*, pp. 14, 259. God is omniscient in that he "knows as actual whatever is actual" but does not know the future since it is not "there to be known" (Hartshorne, *Divine Relativity*, pp. 14-15; Hartshorne, *Man's Vision of God*, p. 98).

[84] God is an object (but not the only object) for every subject (Hartshorne, *Divine Relativity*, p. 70).

[85] Hartshorne, *Man's Vision of God*, p. 108.

[86] Ibid., pp. 348, 177, 86-87, 289; Hartshorne, *Reality as Social Process*, p. 53.

[87] Hartshorne, *Man's Vision of God*, p. 291. "God presumably wills much that we do not will, but he cannot force our will and hence must enjoy and suffer what we enjoy and suffer on the basis of our limited and faulty willing" (David Platt, "Does Whitehead's God Possess a Moral Will?" *Process Studies* 5, no. 2 [1975]: 120). So Hartshorne, *Man's Vision of God*, p. 197.

[88] Thus, "the radical difference between God and us implies that our influence upon him is slight, while his influence upon us is predominant" (Hartshorne, *Divine Relativity*, p. 141). God's "activity lies in *deciding* how to resolve the conflict of interests which he has thus taken into himself" (Hartshorne, *Man's Vision of God*, p. 292).

[89] Hartshorne, *Man's Vision of God*, p. 30; Hartshorne, *Divine Relativity*, p. 138.

[90] Hartshorne, *Divine Relativity*, pp. xvii, 138-39. Persuasion refers to nonunilateral self-determination, which requires other minds to react to God's movement. That is, when God moves himself he thereby creates the necessary condition (but not the sufficient condition) for the effect of the world as the interdependent, creative synthesis of social process.

"will" is severely limited by the nature of social reality.[91] God is thus the most moved mover and the persuasive mover of all, the most important cocreator of the interdependent creative synthesis of social process.

Divine love in relation to the world. Since God is the universal, all-inclusive subject, he feels all the feelings of the world and changes accordingly. This essential relation of God to the world is God's universal sympathy, which is identical to his love.[92] Hence, "love *is* joy in the joy (actual or expected) of another, and sorrow in the sorrow of another."[93] As such, Hartshorne's system is summed up as "love," which, "defined as social awareness, taken literally, is God."[94] God's universal sympathy includes all the joy and suffering of the world according to God's "infinite sensitivity," as well as the desire for the well-being of all the minds that make up the indeterministic, relativistic, spatio-temporalistic panpsychism of social reality.[95]

Since he necessarily feels the feelings of all others, God always loves all others with perfect adequacy (ethical immutability).[96] Nevertheless, as the supremely relative all-inclusive lover, God continually grows and enjoys the ever-increasing value of the world (aesthetic perfectibility).[97] Thus, "God is perfect in love, but never-completed" and "ever growing (partly through our efforts) in the joy, the richness of his life."[98] God's love for others also amounts to self-love since God includes all others. However, since the divine inclusion of all else does not negate the individuality of God or the other

---

[91] Hartshorne, *Man's Vision of God*, p. 293. For Hartshorne, individuals "can only be influenced, they cannot be sheerly coerced" (ibid., p. xvi). David Basinger, however, posits a distinction between "strong" and "weak" coercion, arguing that coercion in the weak sense happens inevitably in human experience (*Divine Power in Process Theism: A Philosophical Critique* [Albany: State University of New York Press, 1988]).

[92] Thus "to love is to sympathize with, and through sympathy to share in, the changes occurring in the persons one loves" (Hartshorne, *Reality as Social Process*, p. 160). Compare Daniel Day Williams, *The Spirit and the Forms of Love* (New York: Harper & Row, 1968), p. 116.

[93] Hartshorne, *Man's Vision of God*, p. 116; emphasis original. Likewise, "Love *is* desire for the good of others, ideally all others, or I have yet to be told what it is" (ibid., p. 14; emphasis original). Compare Charles Hartshorne, *A Natural Theology for Our Time* (La Salle, IL: Open Court, 1967), p. 75.

[94] Hartshorne, *Divine Relativity*, p. 36. Compare Ogden, *Reality of God*, p. 68.

[95] Hartshorne, *Divine Relativity*, p. 76. God is "infinitely more passive" yet not absolutely passive, for "the merely passive, that which has no active tendency of its own, is nothing" (Hartshorne, *Man's Vision of God*, p. 89).

[96] Hartshorne, *Man's Vision of God*, pp. 36, 165. Compare Hartshorne, *Divine Relativity*, p. 125.

[97] Hartshorne, *Reality as Social Process*, p. 51; Hartshorne, *Omnipotence*, p. 119.

[98] Hartshorne, *Reality as Social Process*, p. 156. Compare Hartshorne, *Divine Relativity*, p. 17.

minds, divine love is not *merely* self-love. God is altruistic in desiring the good of all others, yet at the same time all good brings value and enjoyment to God himself; God's only motive is love.[99]

In all this, God as universal subject is the supreme lover of all others, and as universal object he is also the supreme loved one of all others (though not the sole lover or loved one). God's love is absolute in that it is absolutely relative; it always corresponds perfectly to all minds. Thus, God is the eminently relative all-sympathizer, the self-loving lover of all, dynamically relational, emotional and supremely passible.

The Extent of the Conflict and Recent Dissatisfaction

The survey above manifests the irreconcilable difference between the sovereignly willed, unaffected and unenriched, election love of the transcendent-voluntarist model and the all-sympathetic, immanent, affected and enriched, feeling love of the immanent-experientialist model. The crucial points of the conflict may be isolated by way of five integral questions regarding whether the God-world love relationship is unilateral or bilateral. First, does God choose to fully love only some, or love all, or is he essentially related to all such that he necessarily loves all? Second, does God only bestow and/or create value, or might he also appraise, appreciate and receive value? In other words, is divine love only arbitrarily willed, pure beneficence (thematic *agape*), or may it include desire or enjoyment (thematic *eros*)? Third, does God's love include affection and/or emotionality such that God is concerned for the world, sympathetically or otherwise? Fourth, is divine love unconditional or conditional? Fifth, can God and humans be involved in a reciprocal (although asymmetrical) love relationship? These questions are matters of continuing theological debate, as other theologians have increasingly departed from one or both of these models, with many theologians seeking to overcome and/or challenge and transcend some of the binaries posited by these two competing positions.[100]

---

[99]Hartshorne, *Man's Vision of God*, pp. 147, 162. In God there is "perfect agreement of altruism and egoism. For whatever good God may do to any being anywhere he himself, through his omniscient sympathy, will inevitably enjoy" (ibid., p. 161).

[100]Thus the binaries presented for discussion should not be viewed as presenting the only possible options. Note, further, the theologians referenced throughout this work may present similar views on a particular aspect of divine love and yet hold vastly differing perspectives on other aspects of divine love and/or severe disagreements regarding ontology.

Volitional versus essential love for the world. Does God choose to fully love only some, or does he choose to love all, or is he essentially related to all such that he necessarily loves all? In the transcendent-voluntarist model, divine love is freely and sovereignly willed, unmotivated beneficence. God's love originates in his voluntary decision to bestow love on all, but is also limited by his decision as to whom he will love unto salvation (election love). The immanent-experiential model, on the other hand, supposes that divine love does not involve election, being descriptive of an ontologically necessary relation such that divine love is universal as sympathetic, indeterministic relationship.[101]

From Hartshorne's standpoint, the determinism of the transcendent-voluntarist model is unacceptable because it denies meaningful creaturely freedom and thus excludes love.[102] As Daniel Day Williams states, "a will which allows no effective power to any other cannot be a loving will."[103] From Henry's perspective, however, the immanent-experientialist model is unacceptable because it posits the necessity of the God-world relationship and makes God's love for the world the result of nonvolitional relation, in contrast to Henry's affirmation of God's free creation of the world *ex nihilo*.[104] Further, necessary love relationship between God and the world indiscriminately universalizes divine love, in contrast to Henry's exclusivist concept of election love.[105]

Positions taken by other theologians regarding this issue show the extent of the ongoing conflict regarding whether God's love is volitional and/or

---

[101]Divine love does not discriminate, but God is always moved "in a way appropriate to all" (Hartshorne, *Man's Vision of God*, pp. 192-93).
[102]Hartshorne, *Omnipotence*, p. 18.
[103]Williams, *Spirit and the Forms of Love*, p. 128.
[104]Henry, *God, Revelation, and Authority*, 5:12. "If God created out of inner necessity as say process philosophers, why as creatures should we glorify and worship him?" (ibid., 6:289). Bruce McCormack comments that the "thought that creation is, for God, a necessary activity (a thought which is found in virtually all process theologies) might well seem to make God less personal than his free creatures" (Bruce L. McCormack, "The Actuality of God: Karl Barth in Conversation with Open Theism," in *Engaging the Doctrine of God: Contemporary Protestant Perspectives*, ed. Bruce L. McCormack [Grand Rapids: Baker Academic, 2008], p. 187).
[105]Henry, *God, Revelation, and Authority*, 6:289. Concerned that emphasis on divine love might eclipse divine holiness, goodness, justice and judgment, Henry aims to "preclude any promotion of love at the expense of righteousness" (ibid., 6:325). He thus insists that "God is not a vague universal cosmic love but is wrathful toward fallen humanity and needs to be placated" (ibid., 5:303).

essential, elective and/or necessary, particular and/or universal. Many theologians agree with the transcendent-voluntarist model that God loves all in some ways (common love), but only those whom God chooses are loved unto salvation (election love).[106] On the other hand, Thomas Jay Oord believes such a view "sacrifices divine love," thus voicing the question of many: "How can we say that God is loving if God arbitrarily chooses not to elect some to receive salvation?"[107] Oord agrees with the immanent-experientialist model that God necessarily loves all without distinction according to the essential (love) relation of God's nature.

Karl Barth presents an alternative wherein God freely and eternally determines the (derivative) election of all humans *in Christ*, himself the subject and object of election who provides universal atonement.[108] For Barth, God is the one who loves in freedom, and yet there is an "inner necessity of the freedom of God."[109] On some recent readings of Barth's doctrine of election, his perspective transcends any proposed dichotomy between contingency and necessity such that God's free and eternal self-determination to be God for us in Jesus Christ is "contingently necessary."[110]

Many other theologians suggest that God loves everyone freely while granting humans freedom to reciprocate that love or not.[111] In this view, God

---

[106]See the clear exposition of this view in J. I. Packer, "The Love of God: Universal and Particular," in *Still Sovereign: Contemporary Perspectives on Election, Foreknowledge, and Grace*, ed. Thomas R. Schreiner and Bruce A. Ware (Grand Rapids: Baker, 2000), pp. 277-91.

[107]Oord, "Matching Theology," p. 54.

[108]See *CD* II/2, pp. 101-6, 115-18, 123, 166-68, 416, 421. Barth considered election to be "the sum of the Gospel" (*CD* II/2, p. 3). Bruce McCormack considers Barth's doctrine of election to be his greatest contribution to Christian theology ("Grace and Being: The Role of God's Gracious Election in Karl Barth's Theological Ontology," in *The Cambridge Companion to Karl Barth*, ed. John Webster [Cambridge: Cambridge University Press, 2000], p. 92). In Barth's view, "because He who elects is constant and omnipotent and eternal" his "decision" is "independent of all other decisions, of all creaturely decisions. Over and against all creaturely self-determination it is pre-determination—*prae-destinatio*." Grace thus "fully over-rules our human volition and achievement" (*CD* II/2, p. 19). Yet this is no "decretum absolutum," for "there is no such thing as a will of God apart from the will of Jesus Christ" (ibid., p. 115).

[109]*CD* IV/1, p. 195.

[110]Kevin W. Hector, "God's Triunity and Self-Determination: A Conversation with Karl Barth, Bruce McCormack and Paul Molnar," *IJST* 7, no. 3 (2005): 247, 257, 261. However, this reading of Barth is a matter of some dispute. See the discussion in chap. 4 (below).

[111]For example, H. Ray Dunning explains that divine love "is universal rather than selective" such that "none is excluded" (*Grace, Faith, and Holiness: A Wesleyan Systematic Theology* [Kansas City, MO: Beacon Hill, 1988], pp. 196-97). Compare Fritz Guy, "The Universality of God's Love," in *The Grace of God, the Will of Man: A Case for Arminianism*, ed. Clark H. Pinnock (Minneapolis: Bethany House, 1995), pp. 31-49; Thomas C. Oden, *The Living God* (San Francisco: Harper & Row, 1987).

did not need this or any world, yet chooses not to exercise the full extent of his power, manifesting "a form of love that lets the creatures have their own existence."[112] In this sense, Vincent Brümmer contends, "the fact that God allows us as persons to retain the ability to turn away from him, excludes any form of universalism which holds that God's love *must* triumph in the end and cause all to love him."[113] On the other hand, some theologians continue to defend the universalist position that God's love will overcome and finally save everyone.[114] Underlying the controversy regarding these issues is the supposition of many theologians that "love is by definition free," directly related to the conflict between determinism and indeterminism.[115] Debate continues over whether God's love for the world is volitional and/or essential and to what extent.

Disinterested versus evaluative love for the world. Does God only bestow and/or create value, or might he also appraise, appreciate and receive value? In other words, is divine love only arbitrarily willed, pure beneficence (thematic *agape*), or may it include desire or enjoyment (thematic *eros*)? In the transcendent-voluntarist model God, as entirely perfect and self-sufficient, is only the benefactor but never the beneficiary. While God is not "indifferent" since he "realizes value in and through the world" in the sense that "he ascribes worth to the created universe," this involves no "change in God" and thus God *derives* no pleasure or value from the world.[116] Rather, God's love is wholly gratuitous gift love (thematic *agape*) to the exclusion of desirous or receiving love (thematic *eros*); "the love of God is conceived aright" only when "the love of God is discerned in terms of grace."[117]

Conversely, the immanent-experientialist model contends that God feels

---

[112]Wolfhart Pannenberg, *Systematic Theology*, trans. Geoffrey W. Bromiley (Grand Rapids: Eerdmans, 1991), 1:438. Compare Geddes MacGregor, *He Who Lets Us Be: A Theology of Love* (New York: Seabury, 1975).

[113]Brümmer, *Model of Love*, p. 179. So Dunning, *Grace, Faith, and Holiness*, p. 258.

[114]See, for example, the two diverging forms of universalism represented by Thomas B. Talbott, *The Inescapable Love of God* (Parkland, FL: Universal, 1999); and John Hick, *Evil and the God of Love* (London: Collins, 1966). These are discussed further in chaps. 7 and 9 (below).

[115]Brümmer, *Model of Love*, pp. 175, 77. So, among many others, Clark H. Pinnock, *Flame of Love: A Theology of the Holy Spirit* (Downers Grove, IL: InterVarsity Press, 1996), p. 74; Jerry L. Walls and Joseph Dongell, *Why I Am Not a Calvinist* (Downers Grove, IL: InterVarsity Press, 2004), pp. 50-55.

[116]Henry, *God, Revelation, and Authority*, 6:343. Compare ibid., 5:306.

[117]Henry, *Notes on the Doctrine of God*, p. 108.

all feelings (universal sympathy) and thus benefits or suffers along with all joys and sorrows such that the value of his life increases along with the world. Accordingly, the meaning of life is "to serve and glorify God, that is, literally to contribute some value to the divine life which it otherwise would not have." Accordingly, if God "can receive value from no one, then to speak of serving him is to indulge in equivocation."[118] In Hartshorne's view, "to love a being yet be absolutely independent of and unaffected by its welfare or suffering seems nonsense."[119] Furthermore, he claims that "the idea that God equally and solely experiences bliss in all his relations is once for all a denial of the religiously essential doctrine that God is displeased by human sin and human misfortune," and "without such displeasure, the words 'just' and 'loving' seem mockeries."[120] For Hartshorne, "such a God could not love in a real sense, for to love is to find joy in the joy of others and sorrow in their sorrows," but the "wholly perfect could neither gain nor lose."[121]

However, Henry contends that his conception of divine love includes judgment and wrath against evil, whereas the immanent-experientialist model rules out true evaluation, since God himself feels *all* the feelings of others, meaning that he must enjoy the sadism of the sadist and, as such, "God becomes so meshed with historical processes that he internally experiences the quality of evil and is steeped in inner conflict." Further, the thought of God being enriched or appreciating any external value is ontologically unacceptable: "Involvement of God in temporal processes compromises his divine transcendence and portrays him as becoming progressively enriched in experience with the passing of time. The result of Hartshorne's panpsychism is loss of the omniscient and immutable God of the Bible."[122] Moreover, Henry contends that process theology "cannot avoid replacing *agapē* with *eros* as the nature of divine love." In the transcendent-voluntarist model God acts in history "out of self-giving love," whereas in the immanent-experientialist model God acts "to expedite his own fulfillment."[123]

Akin to the transcendent-voluntarist model, many theologians see God

---

[118]Hartshorne, *Divine Relativity*, pp. 133, 58.
[119]Hartshorne, *Reality as Social Process*, p. 40.
[120]Hartshorne, *Man's Vision of God*, p. 195.
[121]Hartshorne, *Reality as Social Process*, p. 156.
[122]Henry, *God, Revelation, and Authority*, 6:272.
[123]Ibid., 6:289-90.

as the giver who creates and bestows value but never receives it. As John Piper explains, "'God is love' is this: it belongs to the fullness of God's nature that he cannot be served but must overflow in service to his creation. The very meaning of God is a being who cannot be enriched but always remains the enricher."[124] In this way, divine love is utterly gratuitous such that, as Millard Erickson puts it, God's "love for us and for his other creatures is completely disinterested."[125] This view is often associated with the dichotomy between desirous "need love" (thematic *eros*) and purely altruistic "gift love" (thematic *agape*).[126] Others, however, reject this dichotomy. For example, Thomas Oden states, "to separate *eros* and *agapē* or to oppose them or set them absolutely off against each other as alternatives (cf. Nygren, *Agapē and Eros*) is to view love incompletely and to fail to understand how one dimension may strengthen the other."[127]

Parallel to this, many theologians, such as Brümmer, reject the concept of love as "pure giving without receiving," contending that such "is not love but mere beneficence" so that God may only be "said to care for us but not about us."[128] Jürgen Moltmann adds that God is capable of receiving value,

---

[124]John Piper, "How Does a Sovereign God Love? A Reply to Thomas Talbott," *The Reformed Journal* 33, no. 4 (1983): 11. This echoes Anders Nygren's assertion that God is altogether "indifferent to value" (Nygren, *Agape and Eros*, p. 210).

[125]Millard J. Erickson, *Christian Theology* (Grand Rapids: Baker, 1998), p. 319. Dunning likewise refers to God's love as "disinterested love," which is "in no way based on the worth of the object" (*Grace, Faith, and Holiness*, p. 195). Similarly, Morris contends, "We do not bring anything valuable to God—in fact, we acquire value only because we are the recipients of his love" (*Testaments of Love*, p. 142).

[126]Nygren's perspective has been the most influential in this regard. Likewise, Emil Brunner contends that, as opposed to *eros*, divine *agape* "does not seek value, but it creates value or gives value." It is "gracious love" (*The Christian Doctrine of God* [London: Lutterworth, 1949], pp. 186-87). Among others, see CD IV/2, p. 747; Donald G. Bloesch, *God, the Almighty: Power, Wisdom, Holiness, Love* (Downers Grove, IL: InterVarsity Press, 2006), p. 146; Erickson, *Christian Theology*, p. 319. See further discussion in chap. 3 (below).

[127]Oden, *Living God*, p. 119. As Catherine Osborne points out, "Both *eros* and *agape* can be used to designate love characterized by *either* generous *or* self-interested concerns" (*Eros Unveiled: Plato and the God of Love* [Oxford: Clarendon, 1994], p. 70). Compare Post, *Theory of Agape*, pp. 17-20, 33; Jürgen Moltmann, *The Spirit of Life: A Universal Affirmation* (London: SCM Press, 1992), p. 261. Martin Cyril D'Arcy also rejects the dichotomy between *agape* and *eros* regarding human love, claiming they are "not enemies but friends," yet maintains that divine love is pure *agape* without *eros* (*The Mind and Heart of Love* [London: Faber & Faber, 1954], p. 304).

[128]Brümmer, *Model of Love*, pp. 132, 240. Likewise, Oord proposes divine love requires "give and take" and the "God whose love is only *agape* (in the sense of *giving*) is a God whose love is incomprehensible" ("Matching Theology," p. 277).

or "an increase of his riches and his bliss."[129] Likewise, Oden states, "God loves all creatures in the twofold sense that God unapologetically enjoys them for their own sake and desires their answering, enjoying love in response to eternally patient, self-sacrificial love."[130] Thus, whether God only bestows value or might also receive enjoyment from the world remains an issue of considerable disagreement, with implications regarding divine self-sufficiency and the supposed altruism-egoism dichotomy.

Impassible versus primarily passive love. Does God's love include affection and/or emotionality such that God is concerned for the world, sympathetically or otherwise? The transcendent-voluntarist model affirms the impassibility of God, yet posits that God does have self-determined feelings. The immanent-experientialist model, in contrast, views God as utterly passible as the universal subject and feeler of all feelings, such that love is identical with his all-encompassing sympathy. Accordingly, Hartshorne harshly criticizes impassibilists: "Using the word 'love,' they emptied it of its most essential kernel, the element of sympathy, of the feeling of others' feelings. It became mere beneficence, totally unmoved (to use their own word) by the sufferings or joys of the creatures. . . . A heartless benefit machine is less than a friend."[131] In his view, impassibility rules out the genuine love of God: "Since love involves dependence upon the welfare of the beloved, and in so far is a passion, God, being passionless, wholly active, is necessarily exempt from it."[132]

In contrast, Henry argues that a suffering, passible God would amount to a deficient, needy deity. In his view, "process theologians err twice over when they league evangelical theism with an immovable and uncompassionate Absolute and when they depict biblical writers as champions of a changing God who in some respects depends upon the universe." For Henry, "God

---

[129]Jürgen Moltmann, *The Trinity and the Kingdom: The Doctrine of God*, trans. Margaret Kohl (San Francisco: Harper & Row, 1981), p. 121. Compare Edward Collins Vacek, *Love, Human and Divine: The Heart of Christian Ethics* (Washington, DC: Georgetown University Press, 1994), pp. 163-71.

[130]Oden, *Living God*, p. 121. Both Moltmann and Oden qualify that this is not out of divine "need," "lack" or "deficiency." Compare ibid.; Moltmann, *Trinity and the Kingdom*, pp. 45, 168. On the other hand, Brümmer states, "If God does not need us, we become infinitely superfluous" (*Model of Love*, p. 242). Compare Sallie McFague, *Models of God: Theology for an Ecological, Nuclear Age* (Philadelphia: Fortress, 1987), p. 134.

[131]Hartshorne, *Omnipotence*, p. 29.

[132]Hartshorne, *Man's Vision of God*, p. 115.

conceived primarily as our 'fellow sufferer' is not the immutable God of the Bible. All talk of the final liberation of man . . . must end in a question mark if God himself is a struggling, suffering deity."[133]

This impasse continues to spark considerable debate. On the one hand, process ontology has been heavily criticized, and many theologians continue to favor divine impassibility, variously defined.[134] Some maintain an unqualified view of impassibility, denying "that God experiences inner emotional changes of state" either "freely from within or by being acted upon from without."[135] On the other hand, Rob Lister affirms a qualified impassibility wherein "God is both invulnerable to involuntarily precipitated emotional vicissitude and supremely passionate about his creatures."[136] A number of other impassibilists similarly affirm that God may have emotional states, but "His feelings are not the result of actions imposed upon Him by others," since "God cannot be acted upon by anything outside of Himself."[137] D. A. Carson also affirms that God is impassible, yet he discourages "attempts to strip God's love of affective content and make it no more than willed commitment to the other's good," claiming that an emotionless God is "profoundly unbiblical and should be repudiated." Yet, "a God who is terribly vulnerable to the pain caused by our rebellion is scarcely a God who is in control or a God who so perfect he does not, strictly speaking, need us."[138]

---

[133]Henry, *God, Revelation, and Authority*, 6:68, 5:292.
[134]See, for instance, Nash, ed., *Process Theology*.
[135]Thomas G. Weinandy, *Does God Suffer?* (Notre Dame, IN: University of Notre Dame Press, 2000), p. 39. Compare Paul Helm, "The Impossibility of Divine Passibility," in *The Power and Weakness of God: Impassibility and Orthodoxy*, ed. Nigel M. de S. Cameron (Edinburgh: Rutherford, 1990), pp. 119, 140. For a far different form of unqualified impassibility, see Friedrich Schleiermacher, *The Christian Faith*, trans. H. R. Mackintosh (Edinburgh: T & T Clark, 1948), p. 206.
[136]Rob Lister, *God Is Impassible and Impassioned: Toward a Theology of Divine Emotion* (Wheaton, IL: Crossway, 2013), pp. 152, 153, 143. Here, God can be "emotionally" affected by creatures, but emotions are defined in way that they remain impassible (e.g., nonpassive, voluntary, self-determined; ibid., pp. 36, 230). Compare Paul L. Gavrilyuk, *The Suffering of the Impassible God: The Dialectics of Patristic Thought* (Oxford: Oxford University Press, 2004).
[137]Norman L. Geisler, H. Wayne House and Max Herrera, *The Battle for God: Responding to the Challenge of Neotheism* (Grand Rapids: Kregel, 2001), pp. 170-71. Compare Morris, *Testaments of Love*, pp. 151, 276; Richard E. Creel, *Divine Impassibility: An Essay in Philosophical Theology* (Cambridge: Cambridge University Press, 1986).
[138]Carson, *Difficult Doctrine of the Love of God*, pp. 46, 48. "If God loves, it is because he chooses to love; if he suffers, it is because he chooses to suffer. God is impassible in the sense that he sustains no 'passion,' no emotion, that makes Him vulnerable from the outside, over which he has no control, or which he has not foreseen" (ibid., p. 60).

Donald Bloesch goes a step further, stating, "The classical idea of perfection as all-sufficiency and completeness had indubitably penetrated Christian thinking and prevented the church through the ages from giving due justice to the biblical idea of God sharing the pain and suffering of his people." Although opposing process theology, he states that "the modern process conception of God who shares our suffering is probably closer to the Biblical view than the Hellenistic conception of a God who is wholly self-contained, who is removed from temporality and exempt from vulnerability."[139] Similarly, Wayne Grudem states, "the idea that God has no passions or emotions *at all* clearly conflicts with much of the rest of Scripture, and for that reason I have not affirmed God's impassibility," for "the opposite is true": God "certainly does feel emotions."[140] In contrast, Karl Barth's view is particularly interesting, affirming divine constancy while eluding the typical framing of impassibility versus passibility.[141] He states that the God of the Bible "can feel, and be affected. He is not impassible," yet "He cannot be moved from outside by an extraneous power" but "is moved and stirred" by "His own free power."[142]

Moltmann, however, unequivocally affirms passible divine love, as he claims that a God incapable of suffering "is poorer than any human" and "a loveless being."[143] Similarly, Williams states, "Impassibility makes love meaningless."[144] Passible love, however, need not exclude volition. As Oord puts it, both intention and feeling are "always present in an expression of love."[145] As many theologians move toward divine passibility, Kevin Van-

---

[139] Donald Bloesch, "Process Theology and Reformed Theology," in Nash, ed., *Process Theology*, pp. 51, 53.

[140] Wayne Grudem, *Systematic Theology: An Introduction to Biblical Doctrine* (Grand Rapids: Zondervan, 1994), p. 166.

[141] Bruce McCormack views Barth as "neither an impassibilist nor a passibilist" and argues that Barth's mature view rejects "divine impassibility," but his view goes "beyond that rather unfortunate set of alternatives," which is part of an "altogether this-worldly dialectic" ("Divine Impassibility or Simply Divine Constancy? Implications of Karl Barth's Later Christology for Debates over Impassibility," in *Divine Impassibility and the Mystery of Human Suffering*, ed. James Keating and Thomas Joseph White [Grand Rapids: Eerdmans, 2009], pp. 184, 185, 182). See discussion in chap. 6 (below).

[142] *CD* II/1, p. 370.

[143] Jürgen Moltmann, *The Crucified God: The Cross of Christ as the Foundation and Criticism of Christian Theology*, trans. R. A. Wilson and John Bowden (New York: Harper & Row, 1974), p. 222. Compare Moltmann, *Trinity and the Kingdom*, pp. 23, 51-52.

[144] Williams, *Spirit and the Forms of Love*, p. 127. So Paul S. Fiddes, *The Creative Suffering of God* (Oxford: Oxford University Press, 1988), p. 50; Oord, "Matching Theology," p. 277.

[145] Oord, *Nature of Love*, p. 30. Compare Stephen G. Post, *Unlimited Love: Altruism, Compassion,*

hoozer comments, "it is becoming increasingly difficult for classical theists to defend the intelligibility of the love of God as an apathetic and unilateral benevolence."[146] Yet there are increasing signs that "impassibilism seems to have begun a miniature resurgence."[147] Thus the conflict over the issue of the possibility or impossibility of divine love continues.

Volitionally unconditional versus essentially unconditional love. Bound up with the questions above is the issue of whether and in what sense divine love is unconditional or conditional, ungrounded or grounded, or something else. For both the immanent-experientialist and transcendent-voluntarist models, divine love is unconditional and cannot be forfeited, yet in very different ways. In the immanent-experientialist model, God's love is ontologically necessary. Divine love cannot be conditional or subject to forfeiture because God is essentially related to and dependent on the world, and this sympathetic "dependence *is* mutuality, is love." Hartshorne thus criticizes the view that "the only really pure—or, at least, the highest—love is that which springs from no 'need' of the beloved, that which 'overflows' from a purely self-sufficient being who derives nothing from any other."[148] In the transcendent-voluntarist model, conversely, God's love is that from a purely self-sufficient being, dependent only on his free sovereign will, and thus God "maintains eternal fidelity in love."[149] Whereas on Hartshorne's view, God needs to love some world, Henry contends that God does not need to love any world, but he does so voluntarily and unconditionally.

Many other recent theologians also view God's love as unconditional. For example, Michael Horton contends that "God's love is unconditioned by

---

and Service (Philadelphia: Templeton Foundation Press, 2003), p. 67; Brümmer, *Model of Love*, p. 160; Moltmann, *Crucified God*, p. 230; Richard Rice, "Process Theism and the Open View of God: The Crucial Difference," in *Searching for an Adequate God: A Dialogue Between Process and Free Will Theists*, ed. David Ray Griffin, John B. Cobb and Clark H. Pinnock (Grand Rapids: Eerdmans, 2000), p. 185; Nicholas Wolterstorff, "Suffering Love," in *Augustine's Confessions: Critical Essays*, ed. William E. Mann (Oxford: Rowman & Littlefield, 2006), p. 136; Dunning, *Grace, Faith, and Holiness*, p. 195.

[146]Vanhoozer, "Introduction: The Love of God," p. 10. Compare Vanhoozer's own recent treatment of impassibility and divine emotion in Kevin J. Vanhoozer, *Remythologizing Theology: Divine Action, Passion, and Authorship* (New York: Cambridge University Press, 2010).

[147]Lister, *God Is Impassible and Impassioned*, p. 148. Compare many of the essays in Keating and White, eds., *Divine Impassibility and the Mystery of Human Suffering*.

[148]Hartshorne, *Man's Vision of God*, pp. 120, 163.

[149]Henry, *God, Revelation, and Authority*, 5:13.

anything in the creature."¹⁵⁰ Likewise, Leon Morris explains that God's love is both "unconditional" and "spontaneous and unmotivated."¹⁵¹ Accordingly, God "will never cease to love" his people since the "constancy of his love depends on what he is rather than on what they are."¹⁵² In Oord's essential kenosis theology, God's love is likewise "unconditional," such that "God loves us no matter what we do."¹⁵³ However, "God loves necessarily" and "cannot not love" humans because "unconditional love refers to God's eternal nature as necessarily including love for creatures," that is, "God's essential nature includes love for the world."¹⁵⁴ From a different perspective, T. F. Torrance believes that God's "self-originating Love" is the ground of his "unconditional love toward" all humankind, such that God "can no more cease loving, or cease to love us, than he can cease to be God or go back on the incarnation and death of his only Son." Yet, while "the love of God remains unchangeably what it was and is and ever will be," humans "may [inexplicably] reject the love of God."¹⁵⁵

Others contend that divine love includes conditions, as apparent in the biblical accounts of the divine-human relationship. For example, D. A. Carson refers to "God's conditional, covenantal love." Indeed, the Scriptures "tell us that Christians remain in the love of God and of Jesus by obedience," and it is therefore "possible for Christians not to keep themselves in the love of God."¹⁵⁶ Is God's love, then, unconditional as many theologians affirm

---

¹⁵⁰Michael Horton, *The Christian Faith: A Systematic Theology for Pilgrims on the Way* (Grand Rapids: Zondervan, 2011), p. 267. Compare Vanhoozer, *Remythologizing Theology*, p. 174.
¹⁵¹Morris, *Testaments of Love*, pp. 31, 137.
¹⁵²Ibid., pp. 77, 12.
¹⁵³Oord, *Nature of Love*, p. 133.
¹⁵⁴Ibid., pp. 129, 133. Yet Oord claims, "God's love is free" in that he chooses among various loving actions (ibid., pp. 139-40). Compare Moltmann, *Trinity and the Kingdom*, pp. 54-55; Paul R. Sponheim, *Love's Availing Power: Imaging God, Imagining the World* (Minneapolis: Fortress, 2011). Most panentheists agree with this perspective, since "divine freedom [with regard to relatedness to the world] is an oxymoron in almost all panentheism" (John W. Cooper, *Panentheism, the Other God of the Philosophers* [Grand Rapids: Baker Academic, 2006], p. 326). However, Phillip Clayton is a notable exception in asserting God's libertarian freedom (*God and Contemporary Science* [Grand Rapids: Eerdmans, 1997], p. 93).
¹⁵⁵Thomas F. Torrance, *The Christian Doctrine of God: One Being Three Persons* (New York: T & T Clark, 2001), pp. 59, 246.
¹⁵⁶D. A. Carson, "Love," in *New Dictionary of Biblical Theology*, ed. T. Desmond Alexander (Downers Grove, IL: InterVarsity Press, 2000), p. 648. For his part, Stephen Post questions "the assumption that God's love is 'unmotivated, unconditional, uncaused, and uncalculating'" (*Theory of Agape*, p. 24). Compare Raymond E. Brown, *The Gospel According to John XIII-XXI*, AB (Garden City, NY: Doubleday, 1979), p. 641.

(although in vastly different manners) and, if so, in what sense(s)?

Unilateral versus reciprocal love. Can God and humans be involved in a reciprocal (albeit unequal) love relationship? On the transcendent-voluntarist model, God is the sole giver, who sovereignly wills love toward humans as pure beneficence (thematic *agape*) and loves some unto salvation (election love).[157] In the immanent-experientialist model, however, love describes the essential God-world relation such that divine love is universal, undifferentiated and necessarily reciprocal. Hartshorne thus rejects Henry's exclusivist election love: "God is held to love all, not just a few; always; not just at times; in all their being, not with neglect of this or that aspect." For Hartshorne, Henry's conception amounts to "metaphysical snobbery toward relativity, dependence, or passivity."[158]

From Henry's standpoint, a mutable being is unworthy of worship, much less worshipful love. Further, Henry contends that "God's absoluteness" is not "incompatible with his real relationship to others." However, "Christian theism disallows intrinsically necessary divine relationships to man and the world, and insists on God's essential independence," in opposition to process theology's position of an indiscriminately universal and "mutual relationship," which "obscures God's causal efficacy in relation to the universe."[159]

Many theologians agree with the view that God's love is akin to unilateral beneficence based on God's sovereign election. For instance, Leon Morris asserts that human love toward God is the work of divine election.[160] In contrast, a number of scholars believe the God-world love relationship involves give and take, whereas a "'one-way' relationship, a giving without receiving," is "strangely inadequate."[161] For Thomas Oden, "God's love for humanity, like all love, is reciprocal. God prizes the world, and values especially human creatures, who have the freedom and imagination to respond to God and to share with God consciousness and compassion."[162] In this view, God seeks freely reciprocal love from humans.[163] Brümmer adds, "love

---

[157]Henry, *God, Revelation, and Authority*, 6:310, 45.
[158]Hartshorne, *Reality as Social Process*, p. 135; Hartshorne, *Divine Relativity*, p. 50.
[159]Henry, *God, Revelation, and Authority*, 6:289, 20.
[160]Morris, *Testaments of Love*, p. 182. Compare D'Arcy, *Mind and Heart of Love*, p. 245.
[161]Burnaby, *Amor Dei*, p. 307.
[162]Oden, *Living God*, p. 121. Yet God's love may be unrequited (ibid., p. 120). Compare Moltmann, *Trinity and the Kingdom*, p. 203.
[163]As James Moffat puts it, "Love seeks love" (*Love in the New Testament* [New York: Harper, 1930],

must by its very nature be a relationship of free mutual give and take, otherwise it cannot be love at all."[164] In E. Ray Clendenen's view, on the other hand, "'divine love' that 'respects human freedom, even to the extent of allowing humanity to be utterly irrational and perverse—that is, to reject the love that has created, sustained, and redeemed it' is a love without arms and legs, that is, not divine at all."[165] From a far different perspective, Oord views give-and-take love relationship as necessary, since "all existence is essentially related and reciprocal."[166]

The conflict regarding the reciprocity of the divine-human love relationship extends to whether God's love is universal, particular or both. As seen above, many theologians contend that God loves all but loves only some unto salvation. For example, J. I. Packer believes that particular love reaches only those whom God has sovereignly elected, while universal love corresponds to God's common grace. Thus God "loves all in some ways," and he loves "some in all ways."[167] However, other theologians suggest that God's love "is universal rather than selective"; God loves "all without discrimination. None is excluded."[168] Some theologians add further nuance, agreeing that God's love does not reach all equally but disagreeing with the view that this is the result of God's unilateral decision. Thus, Thomas Oden states, "All things are loved by God, but all things are not loved in the same way by God, since there are degrees of capacity, receptivity, and willingness among varied creatures to receive God's love."[169]

In this regard, determinists generally contend that God is just in only

---

p. 280). So Oden, *Living God*, p. 119; Post, *Theory of Agape*, pp. 10, 27; Vacek, *Love, Human and Divine*, pp. 188-90; Clark H. Pinnock, "Constrained by Love: Divine Self-Restraint According to Open Theism," *Perspectives in Religious Studies* 34, no. 2 (2007): 149; Pannenberg, *Systematic Theology*, 1:427.

[164]Brümmer, *Model of Love*, p. 155.

[165]E. Ray Clendenen, "Malachi," in *Haggai, Malachi*, NAC (Nashville: B&H, 2004), p. 252, quoting Fritz Guy, "The Universality of God's Love," in *The Grace of God, the Will of Man* (Grand Rapids: Zondervan, 1989), p. 45.

[166]Oord, "Matching Theology," p. 313.

[167]Packer, "The Love of God: Universal and Particular," p. 283.

[168]Dunning, *Grace, Faith, and Holiness*, pp. 196-97. Compare Guy, "The Universality of God's Love," p. 36; Mildred Bangs Wynkoop, *A Theology of Love: The Dynamic of Wesleyanism* (Kansas City, MO: Beacon Hill, 1972); Brümmer, *Model of Love*, pp. 54, 159-60, 75-77; Oord, *Nature of Love*, p. 20; Pinnock, *Flame of Love*, p. 74.

[169]Oden, *Living God*, p. 118. Compare Shawn Floyd, "Preferential Divine Love: Or, Why God Loves Some People More Than Others," *Philosophia Christi* 11, no. 2 (2009): 371.

loving some unto salvation (election love), since all are sinners and rightly deserve punishment. In their view, that God is gracious to some who are undeserving is a quality that should be praised rather than questioned.[170] However, Stephen T. Davis objects with a striking analogy: "Suppose I discover that my two sons are both equally guilty of some wrong—say they both trampled some of my wife's beloved roses in our backyard. And suppose I say to one of them: 'You are guilty and your punishment is that you will be confined to your room.' And suppose I say to the other one: 'You are equally guilty, but as a gift of love, I'm going to let you go without punishment.' Surely it is obvious on the face of it that I have been unfair."[171] Thus there remains considerable disagreement as to whether God's love relationship with the world is unilateral or reciprocal and universal and/or particular.

Conclusion

The transcendent-voluntarist and immanent-experientialist models thus represent mutually exclusive conceptions of divine love that conflict in fundamental ways. Other theologians have increasingly called into question tenets of both models, evidencing an increasing level of dissatisfaction with regard to each. Significant conflict continues over the nature of divine love, especially regarding whether God's love for the world is volitional or essential, evaluative or nonevaluative, passible or impassible, conditional or unconditional, and unilateral or reciprocal. The following chapters seek to address the conflict by way of a canonical approach to systematic theology, explained in chapter two.

---

[170]See the debate between Dave Hunt and James R. White on this issue in *Debating Calvinism* (Sisters, OR: Multnomah, 2004), pp. 255-80.

[171]Stephen T. Davis, "Universalism, Hell, and the Fate of the Ignorant," *Modern Theology* 6, no. 2 (1990): 190.

2

Toward Addressing the Conflict

A Canonical Approach

The transcendent-voluntarist and immanent-experientialist models of divine love depict mutually exclusive conceptions of love and divine ontology, amounting to a fundamental impasse.[1] These and other conceptions of love tend to move from divine ontology to love, the latter being constrained and shaped by the former.[2] The approach explained in this chapter, however, inverts the prevalent order by first investigating the canonical depiction of divine love, while temporarily bracketing out (*epoché*), as much as possible, ontological presuppositions.[3] This final-form canonical

---

[1] This has led to calls for alternative models. For Thomas Jay Oord, "an alternative formal theology appears to be required" in order "to express the love themes central to the Bible and to Evangelical piety more adequately" ("Matching Theology and Piety: An Evangelical Process Theology of Love" [PhD diss., Claremont Graduate University, 1999], pp. 75-76). Clark Pinnock comments, "Unless we construct a model of the divine somewhere between classical and process theism, I fear that we will lose some of our keenest minds to process liberalism" ("Between Classical and Process Theism," in *Process Theology*, ed. Ronald H. Nash [Grand Rapids: Baker, 1987], p. 317).

[2] From a different standpoint, Kevin Vanhoozer notes the "tendency in Western theology to discuss the divine attributes . . . in abstraction from the biblical stories about God's speaking and acting in the history of Israel and Jesus Christ" (*Remythologizing Theology: Divine Action, Passion, and Authorship* [New York: Cambridge University Press, 2010], p. 70). Compare Robert W. Jenson, *Systematic Theology* (New York: Oxford University Press, 1997), 1:60. Vanhoozer asks: "What must God be like in order to do what the Bible depicts him as doing with words: creating, commanding, promising, consoling?" (*Remythologizing Theology*, p. 3).

[3] *Epoché* here refers to temporary suspension of judgment by setting aside *particular* assumptions to examine the phenomena of Scripture in terms of its own system of meaning. In philosophy, *epoché* has broader connotations, relating to the intent to describe phenomena apart from presuppositions toward a "truly descriptive philosophy" (Marvin Farber, "The Ideal of a Presup-

approach to systematic theology affords epistemological primacy to the canon as a whole (*tota Scriptura*), which provides the content for a model of divine love that seeks internal coherence and rigorous correspondence to Scripture, and might illuminate the (implicit) biblical theo-ontology underlying the God-world relationship.

The Final-Form Canonical Approach to Systematic Theology

As the name suggests, the final-form canonical approach accepts the biblical canon as the divinely revealed, inspired and preserved basis of Christian doctrine.[4] The selection of Scripture is admittedly a presupposition, the justification of which is beyond the scope of this work.[5] Notably, however, postmodern epistemology has overcome the strictures of logical positivism. As Kevin Vanhoozer puts it: "Instead of making robust claims to absolute knowledge, even natural scientists now view their theories as interpretations."[6] As such, every system

---

positionless Philosophy," in *Philosophical Essays in Memory of Edmund Husserl*, ed. Marvin Farber [New York: Greenwood, 1968], p. 62).

[4] Here, the *canon* refers to the sixty-six OT and NT books that are recognized most widely throughout Christianity. I believe this canon has been correctly recognized (intrinsic canon) but not determined by the community (community canon), as I have described elsewhere. See John C. Peckham, "The Canon and Biblical Authority: A Critical Comparison of Two Models of Canonicity," *TJ* 28, no. 2 (2007): 229-49; John C. Peckham, "Intrinsic Canonicity and the Inadequacy of the Community Approach to Canon Determination," *Themelios* 36, no. 2 (2011): 203-15. Nevertheless, one need not subscribe to this view of the canon in order to implement this canonical approach.

  A final-form approach means that the canonical text is approached in the extant form(s) available due to the lack of access to a complete, original, final form. Attention is thus directed to the received corpus of canonical texts (according to the best findings of textual criticism) and not to nonmanuscript-based reconstructions. This approach contrasts with the turn toward tradition/community for confessional systematic theology. For a brief discussion of this approach in relationship to and distinction from other canonical approaches such as those of Brevard Childs and James Sanders, see John C. Peckham, "The Analogy of Scripture Revisited: A Final Form Canonical Approach to Systematic Theology," *MAJT* 22 (2011): 43-46. Compare Anthony C. Thiselton, "Canon, Community, and Theological Construction," in *Canon and Biblical Interpretation*, ed. Craig G. Bartholomew et al. (Grand Rapids: Zondervan, 2006), pp. 1-31.

[5] Carl F. H. Henry also adopts Scripture as the ground of theology such that the "legitimacy of what we say about" God "stems solely from the living God who makes himself known and from the divinely inspired Scriptures" (*God, Revelation, and Authority*, 6 vols. [Wheaton, IL: Crossway, 1999], 5:49). For Charles Hartshorne, conversely, nature "is the real 'word of God' concerning the general structure of the cosmos" (*Omnipotence and Other Theological Mistakes* [Albany: State University of New York Press, 1984], p. 73).

[6] Kevin Vanhoozer, *Is There a Meaning in This Text?* (Grand Rapids: Zondervan, 1998), p. 19. Compare Fernando Canale, *Back to Revelation-Inspiration: Searching for the Cognitive Foundation of Christian Theology in a Postmodern World* (Lanham, MD: University Press of America, 2001), p. 9; Kenneth Reynhout, *Interdisciplinary Interpretation: Paul Ricoeur and the Hermeneutics of Theology and Science* (Lanham, MD: Lexington, 2013).

requires the selection of a starting point. This is not to say that all choices are equally adequate or valuable, but rather that it is not necessary to provide a defense of one's epistemological starting point a priori. Therefore, as Fernando Canale states: "If the meaning of the ultimate framework for intelligibility rests on human choice, why not choose divine revelation as available in Scripture?"[7]

This approach to the text as canon includes three notable commitments regarding the nature of Scripture: (1) a high view of the revelation-inspiration of the canon, (2) the dual authorship (divine and human) of the canonical text, and (3) grammatical-historical procedures of exegesis. Although readers need not subscribe to these commitments in order to follow along with my treatment of divine love, a basic explanation of these commitments may assist the reader in understanding my conclusions.

First, I am committed to a high view of the revelation and inspiration of the biblical canon as infallible, meaning that the canon is fully trustworthy and unfailingly accurate in all that it affirms. Accordingly, I believe that divine revelation was accurately inscripturated in the canon via divine inspiration (2 Tim 3:16; 2 Pet 1:20-21) in such a way that the words written by the human authors are the word of God (compare 1 Thess 2:13).[8] In the

---

[7]Canale, *Back to Revelation-Inspiration*, p. 10. The objection that theism should not be selected as a starting point also founders in that, as Thiselton notes, "Non-theism or positivism is no more value-free than theism" ("Canon, Community, and Theological Construction," p. 4).

[8]While I do not pretend to be able to explicate the precise manner of the divine agency and operation regarding the revelation and inspiration of Scripture, I subscribe in large part to the sophisticated and complex model proposed by Fernando Canale, which he calls the historical-cognitive (linguistic) model. See Canale, *Back to Revelation-Inspiration*, pp. 127-60. This model affirms Scripture's own claims to divine revelation and inspiration (the doctrine of Scripture) while also paying close attention to the rich and multifaceted variety (but not incongruity) in the canon (the phenomena of Scripture). On this approach, God condescends to "utilize the modes, characteristics, and limitations of human cognition and language" via various patterns of revelation such as the theophanic (Ex 3:1-15; Jn 1:1-14), writing (Ex 31:18), prophetic (speaking; Ex 20:1), visual representation (Is 6:1-3; Acts 10:9-17), historical (Is 43:18-19) and existential/sapiential patterns (cf. Prov 1:7) (ibid., pp. 148, 134). The process of inspiration whereby revelation is inscripturated in the canon consists of the human author "writing [according to each's own background, personality, location, and literary style] while the divine author supervises the entirety of the process" (ibid., p. 147). The diverse phenomena of Scripture is thus accounted for by a "general historical supervisional pattern of God's inspiration" that "represents a nonintrusive, yet direct overview, of the entire process of the writing of Scripture," with an "occasional direct-remedial-corrective pattern" that ensures the trustworthiness of the entirety of Scripture as "historically constituted" (rather than historically conditioned) but does not "divinize Scripture into an otherworldly level of perfection and accuracy" (ibid., pp. 145, 142, 147). Divine action in revelation-inspiration is thus not reduced to one pattern (and certainly does not correspond to mechanical dictation) but recognizes various patterns and diverse divine

words of Vanhoozer, the "canon" is "Christ's Spirit-borne commissioned testimony to himself."[9]

Second, on this view, the canon is a text with dual authorship (divine and human) that is rendered harmonious (neither monolithic nor self-contradictory) via divine revelation and inspiration.[10] There is, then, a "properly theological unity implicit in the idea that God is the ultimate communicative agent speaking in Scripture," the "divine author" of the canon.[11] My reading of the canon as a unified and internally congruent corpus is undergirded by this view of the Holy Spirit's superintendence of the writing process, including the trustworthy conveyance of the history and worldview that is presented in specific texts and in the canonical text as a whole.[12] As

---

activities alongside the distinctive contributions and limitations of human authors, all of which "account[s] for the richness and manifoldness of biblical revelation" (ibid., p. 134). Compare Vanhoozer's view that the "doctrine of inspiration is what justifies the canonical practice of reading the Bible to hear the Word of God," wherein "inspiration is a matter of the Spirit speaking in and through the canonical Scriptures, coordinating the various human voices [each author contributing, 'in his own way, to the guiding of the whole'] so that, together, they articulate the theo-drama," while "speaking of inspiration does not specify the exact process [or mode of guidance] but emphasizes the result" (*The Drama of Doctrine: A Canonical-Linguistic Approach to Christian Theology* [Louisville: Westminster John Knox, 2005], pp. 230, 231). Thus, "the biblical texts have a 'natural history'" since "they have human authors. Yet these human testimonies are caught up in the triune economy of word-acts and so ultimately become divine testimonies" (ibid., p. 177).

[9]Vanhoozer, *Drama of Doctrine*, p. 194.

[10]As shall be seen below, however, this does not require a naive view regarding the retrieval of authorial intention (e.g., the intentional fallacy).

[11]Vanhoozer, *Drama of Doctrine*, pp. 177, 181. Put differently, "God is the ultimate agent of canonical discourse" (ibid., p. 178). Compare Nicholas Wolterstorff's philosophical proposal regarding the divine authorship of Scripture in *Divine Discourse: Philosophical Reflections on the Claim That God Speaks* (New York: Cambridge University Press, 1995). In this regard, Gerhard Maier contends that "biblical writers seek consciously to recede into the background. They point away from themselves to *God as the author*" (*Biblical Hermeneutics* [Wheaton, IL: Crossway, 1994], p. 22).

[12]In the words of David Yeago, recognizing "the biblical canon as inspired Scripture" means to approach "the texts as the discourse of the Holy Spirit, the discourse therefore of one single speaker, despite the plurality of their human authors," such that "the church receives the canon, in all its diversity, as nonetheless a *single* body of discourse" ("The Bible: The Spirit, the Church, and the Scriptures," in *Knowing the Triune God*, ed. David Yeago and James Buckley [Grand Rapids: Eerdmans, 2001], p. 70). Compare Daniel J. Treier's explanation of canon as a prominent focus of the theological intepretation of Scripture, wherein "interpreters are not shy about relating particular passages to the larger context of the entire Bible. We need not ignore the historical development of words and concepts, engaging in simplistic synthetic connections that obscure the particularities of any given text. But neither should we operate as prisoners of alien standards imposed by academic guilds that tend to reject the unity of Scripture or allow passages to relate only on the narrowest criteria" (*Introducing Theological Interpretation of Scripture: Recovering a Christian Practice* [Grand Rapids: Baker Academic, 2008], p. 201).

Vanhoozer puts it, "we must read the Bible canonically, as one book. Each part has meaning in light of the whole (and in light of its center, Jesus Christ)."[13] Accordingly, the canonical text is the most trustworthy source of theological data such that claims that are properly derived from the canon about God's relationship to the world (and ontological claims implied thereby) are taken as theologically significant.[14] One who does not subscribe to this view may nevertheless appreciate the canonical reading laid out here by allowing something like a new literary-criticism approach to the final-form canon as a unified literary work[15] and/or entertaining the possibility of a final-form canon that was redacted in a way that the community perceived to be sufficiently internally congruent.[16] The implementation of this canonical approach regarding divine love might then serve as an informative case study.

Third, I have used grammatical-historical procedures of exegesis, only the conclusions of which are represented in this manuscript.[17] This means, among other things, that I take the claims made in the text (carefully interpreted exegetically) to be accurate and historical.[18] This approach does not

---

[13] Vanhoozer, *Drama of Doctrine*, p. 178. "That God has spoken and acted in Jesus Christ and that God speaks and acts in the canonical Scriptures that testify to him" is a "core 'evangelical' conviction" (ibid., p. 26).

[14] Compare Vanhoozer's canonical-linguistic approach, wherein the supremely normative "canon—the final form of 'Holy Scripture'" is, among other things, "the charter document of the covenant that stands at the heart of the relationship of God and humankind" (*Drama of Doctrine*, p. 141). As "divine canonical discourse," Scripture is "not merely a record of revelation" but "itself a revelatory and redemptive word-act of the triune God" (ibid., pp. 179, 177).

[15] As Yeago notes, "There is no reason why a purely literary analysis could not take seriously a biblical canon, Jewish or Christian, as a unified whole, received as such by an important community of readers" and with "no rational imperative" to "regard the formation of the canon as less significant than, say, the redaction of the Pentateuch; if the latter can be taken seriously as the composition of a single literary work out of diverse pre-existing parts, so too can the former" (Yeago, "The Bible," p. 71). Compare David Noel Freedman's "master weaver" hypothesis regarding nearly half of the OT, briefly discussed below.

[16] Consider the field of canon criticism, especially the pioneering work of Brevard Childs. Paul R. Noble suggests that "Childs' Canonical Principle of interpretation (i.e., that the meaning of each text should be found through interpreting it in the context of the completed canon) is formally equivalent to believing that the Bible is so inspired as to be ultimately the work of a single Author" (*The Canonical Approach: A Critical Reconstruction of the Hermeneutics of Brevard S. Childs* [Leiden: Brill, 1995], p. 340).

[17] For the larger treatment of the biblical text(s) regarding divine love, see the more detailed exegetical work and engagement with biblical scholarship in John C. Peckham, *The Concept of Divine Love in the Context of the God-World Relationship* (New York: Peter Lang, 2014).

[18] With the exception of those views that are depicted in the canon as themselves false (e.g., the views of Job's friends regarding his suffering). Further, such an approach does not interpret

look "behind" the text to a reconstructed precanonical history but focuses on the text's own claims as they are given in the final-form canon.[19] Taking the canon as accurately representing its own history, this approach considers relevant extant historical materials (e.g., other ancient literature, artifacts) while reserving priority for the canonical text.[20] Here again, one who ques-

---

biblical texts allegorically or mythologically unless there is an internal textual indication of the corresponding genre(s).

[19]Compare the way Richard M. Davidson frames his massive study *Flame of Yahweh: Sexuality in the Old Testament* (Grand Rapids: Baker, 2007), pp. 2-3: "This study specifically analyzes the theology of the final canonical form of OT. It utilizes insights from such widely accepted synchronic methodologies as the new literary criticism and the new biblical theology, which focus upon the final form of the OT text. It will not inquire about the possible precanonical history of the text but seek to understand the overriding theological thrust of Scripture wholistically as it now presents itself in the biblical canon. This canonical, close-reading approach does not ignore, however, the unique settings and theological emphases of different sections of the canonical OT. By focusing upon the final form of the OT text, I believe it is possible that the interests of both liberal-critical and evangelical OT scholarship may merge in seeking to understand what constitutes the canonical theological message of the OT regarding human sexuality." Consider also Vanhoozer's "canonical approach" that "has nothing to do with an ahistorical approach that takes the Bible as a free-floating 'text,' nor with a historicist approach that focuses on the events behind the text," but "takes the whole canon as the interpretative framework for understanding God, the world, oneself, and others" by reading "individual passages and books as elements within the divine drama of redemption" (*Drama of Doctrine*, p. 149). Joel B. Green further points to the "aim of historical work" shifting "from the discovery of meaning embedded in or behind the text to hearing the robust voice of the text as a subject (rather than an object) in theological discourse" (*Practicing Theological Interpretation* [Grand Rapids: Baker, 2011], p. 127). Thus, in Green's view, "theological interpretation of Christian Scripture concerns itself with interpretation of the biblical texts in their final form, not as they might be reconstructed by means of historical-critical sensibilities (i.e., Historical Criticism₁)" (ibid., p. 49).

[20]The historical context of a passage, when ascertainable, may make vital contributions to understanding. However, this approach is wary of taking, for instance, an ancient Near Eastern parallel and then reading it into the biblical text, as has sometimes occurred in the history of biblical interpretation. Consider treatments of ancient Near Eastern parallels regarding so-called covenant love, wherein the supposed meaning of the cognates of the primary OT word for love (אהב) in ancient Near Eastern covenant contexts was imposed on similar forms in the biblical text only to later have many scholars question the supposed meaning in ancient Near Eastern contexts and reject the view that the meaning of such cognates in the ancient Near Eastern texts requires a similar meaning in biblical contexts (see chap. 3 below; compare the extended discussion in Peckham, *Concept of Divine Love*, pp. 197-201). Extrabiblical extant texts and artifacts shed considerable light on the interpretive options of the text but are themselves not determinative for the interpretation of the text because (among other reasons) (1) they themselves must be interpreted and are often underdeterminative with regard to meaning in their own context (we may know considerably less about the extracanonical text/artifact and its context than we know about the biblical text that it is used to interpret); (2) historical correspondence depends on the dating/authorship of the biblical texts, which may be disputed and holds implications regarding whether reuse of a text is present and, if so, which text is reusing the other; and (3) the relationship between the text/artifact and the canonical text, if any, is often unknown. For instance, if a biblical writer is indeed writing after the supposed parallel (which is sometimes unclear), the biblical writer may be aware of and interacting with the extracanonical text/artifact (or with the

tions whether the canon accurately depicts history might suspend judgment and ask what kind of claims (historical and otherwise) the text itself presents and to what theological views those claims lead. Regardless of presuppositions regarding the nature of the text, each reader can ask along with me regarding divine love: (1) what is the theology depicted *in* (rather than *behind*) the text and (2) what does all of the canonical data depict when taken together as a cohesive literary document in its final form?

Canonical correspondence and coherence. Two criteria of adequacy pertain to this canonical approach: correspondence to the canon and internal coherence.[21] Canonical coherence seeks a system with internal consistency and lucidity. This approach subscribes to the canon's own claims to internal coherence and thus entails a sympathetic reading of the canon, seeking the congruity of diverse texts without injury to individual texts and expecting internal consistency (but not simplistic identicality) without dismissing or overlooking areas of perceived or apparent tension.[22] As such, the canon may be approached as a unified composition while recognizing the diversity stemming from human authorship and various historical contexts.[23] Yet some have suggested that, for the sake of legitimate, critical study,

---

trajectory of the view therein as it has affected the writer's horizon), but the writer may be intentionally using but changing (and/or correcting) the trajectory of that text/paradigm. Simply because ostensible contemporaries of biblical authors held a view or interpreted an issue in a particular way (to the extent we understand their view, itself questionable), it does not follow that the biblical authors shared that view or used overlapping material as their contemporaries did. This may seem like a rather obvious point, but it holds considerable implications about how the extant historical materials should be used in interpreting biblical texts. Conclusions regarding such matters are often unclear, and this approach thus urges caution while affording priority to the canonical text.

[21]Compare Grant R. Osborne's criteria of validity according to his critical realism, including the "criteria of coherence, comprehensiveness, adequacy, and consistency" and "durability" (*The Hermeneutical Spiral: A Comprehensive Introduction to Biblical Interpretation*, 2nd ed. [Downers Grove, IL: InterVarsity Press, 2006], p. 398).

[22]Consider Vanhoozer's application of Paul Ricoeur's distinctions (regarding personal identity) between *idem* as a "self-sameness" or "'hard identity,' where hard connotes immutability and permanence," and *ipse* identity, a "'soft' identity" as a "kind of sameness" that "partakes more of narrative than of numeric identity" (*Drama of Doctrine*, p. 127). Vanhoozer proposes that, as divinely authored but not dictated, the canon exhibits a unity of *ipse* identity, which allows for "development" and "growth" and is thus "entirely, and especially, compatible with the pattern of promise and fulfillment" one sees in the OT and NT (e.g., the unity without uniformity that is manifest in the NT typological use of the OT) (ibid., p. 128).

[23]As Vanhoozer puts it: "In reading the Bible as a unified canon, however, we are not only engaging Scripture and its human authors; we are engaging—and being engaged by—God," who "is ultimately the one [triune God] responsible for the way in which the various books of the Bible

any presupposition of the truthfulness of the text should be tabled.[24] However, why not first look for coherence and consistency in the text without uncritically assuming it? As Daniel J. Treier explains, the considerable diversity and polyphony of the canon does not necessarily amount to a disharmonious cacophony of voices; even where "the same vocabulary" and intertextual allusions are used "in markedly different ways" (e.g., Rom 4 and Jas 2 of Gen 15:6), "if each addresses different questions, it is plausible that their voices are complementary rather than contradictory."[25] Accordingly, as I. Howard Marshall notes, where tensions arise there might be an "underlying unity," despite a "different level of perception."[26] Faithful attention to the diversity in Scripture itself points the interpreter back to the text to seek understanding that progressively expands in depth and breadth.

The historical rationale for approaching the canonical text as mutually consistent and complementary, despite its varied authorship and historical contexts, stems from the view that canonical texts were written from within the stream of canon that preceded them such that successive human authors consciously intended faithfulness to preceding canonical writings, by which their preconceptions were shaped and corrected (e.g., Is 8:20).[27]

---

cohere" and who "stands being the canon, ensuring the truth of its testimony" (ibid., p. 178). See the earlier discussion of the divine and human authorship of Scripture (pp. 48-49).

[24]Compare John Barton, *The Nature of Biblical Criticism* (Louisville: Westminster John Knox, 2007).

[25]Daniel J. Treier, "Scripture, Unity of," in *DTIB*, p. 733.

[26]I. Howard Marshall, *New Testament Theology: Many Witnesses, One Gospel* (Downers Grove, IL: InterVarsity Press, 2004), p. 30. Grant Osborne adds: "Critical scholarship in this sense is often more 'literalistic' than are conservative scholars in that it often assumes that any so-called contradiction or difference between biblical writers removes the basis for a deeper theological unity between them" (*Hermeneutical Spiral*, p. 350).

[27]The apparent congruity of the canon has been recognized elsewhere. For instance, David Noel Freedman has explained "demonstrable links" pointing to "the intricate and interlocking character of the Hebrew Bible," which "supports the view that a single mind or compatible group [a Master Weaver or Editor] was at work in collecting, compiling, organizing, and arranging the component parts into a coherent whole" (*The Unity of the Hebrew Bible* [Ann Arbor: University of Michigan Press, 1991], p. 73). Compare Stephen G. Dempster, *Dominion and Dynasty: A Biblical Theology of the Hebrew Bible* (Downers Grove, IL: InterVarsity Press, 2003); Walter C. Kaiser, *Recovering the Unity of the Bible: One Continuous Story, Plan, and Purpose* (Grand Rapids: Zondervan, 2009). Consider also Hans W. Frei's seminal proposal of the unity of narrative, which gathers Scripture as part of an overarching story, a realistic narrative in contrast to referential reading, in *The Eclipse of Biblical Narrative* (New Haven, CT: Yale University Press, 1974). Compare Meir Sternberg, *The Poetics of Biblical Narrative* (Bloomington: Indiana University Press, 1985); Robert Alter, *The Art of Biblical Narrative* (New York: Basic Books, 1981). Consider also Robert Jenson's aim in his systematic theology to interpret "the God identified by the bibli-

As Anthony Thiselton comments, "Intertextual resonances form part of the hermeneutic of the biblical traditions themselves."[28] The theological rationale for such an approach affirms the canonical claim that Scripture is divinely revealed and inspired and is, as such, a unified (though not monolithic) document; it is not merely the words of humans but the word of God (compare 2 Tim 3:16; 1 Thess 2:13), itself containing numerous examples of something like a canonical approach.[29] Vanhoozer thus refers to the "Bible as a unified canonical whole," which should "ultimately count as a divine communicative work" that comprises "the entire length and breadth of the canon."[30]

This canonical approach, then, focuses on textual and intertextual interpretation of the canon as a unified, literary document in accordance with the analogy of Scripture (*analogia Scripturae*), seeking the maximum achievable correspondence to the intention *in* the text, which must be discernible, demonstrable and defensible.[31] The intention *in* the text is the effect of authorial (divine and human) intent. While the text inscripturates

---

cal narrative," thus "follow[ing] the one biblical narrative, to identify the one biblical God" (Jenson, *Systematic Theology*, 1:57-58). In his view, the "unity of Scripture" should be "construe[d] . . . by the identity of this God" (ibid., 1:58).

[28]Thiselton, "Canon, Community, and Theological Construction," p. 5. In Thiselton's view: "Texts can actively shape and transform the perceptions, understandings, and actions of readers" (*New Horizons in Hermeneutics* [Grand Rapids: Zondervan, 1992], p. 31).

[29]The notion of canon in the limited sense of "rule" or "standard" appears often (Is 8:16, 20; Ex 17:14; Deut 31:9, 12; Josh 1:8; 23:6; 1 Kings 2:3; Neh 8:8-18; 9:3; Mt 7:24, 26; Lk 10:26; 24:27; Acts 2:42; 17:11; 24:14; Rom 4:3; Gal 1:8-12; 1 Thess 2:13; 2 Thess 2:15; 3:14; 2 Tim 1:13; 3:16; Tit 1:9; 2 Jn 9-10; Jude 3). Notice especially Christ's use of Moses, the Prophets and the Psalms to explain "the things concerning Himself in all the Scriptures" (Lk 24:27, 44). Vanhoozer makes a case that Philip, in "using Scripture to explain the event of Christ," may have been "initiating his Ethiopian inquirer into" just such "a 'canonical' practice initiated by Jesus Christ, abetted by the Spirit, and instantiated by the rest of the New Testament" (Vanhoozer, *Drama of Doctrine*, p. 120; see Acts 8:26-39). This and other internal evidence of what is sometimes called canonical consciousness provides the necessary condition for a canonical approach that is ultimately grounded in Christ.

[30]Vanhoozer, *Remythologizing Theology*, p. 12. Consider also Nicholas Wolterstorff's suggestion of "unity behind the text," that is, the canon "authorized" as a work ("The Unity Behind the 'Canon,'" in *One Scripture or Many? Canon from Biblical, Theological, and Philosophical Perspectives*, ed. Christine Helmer and Christof Landmesser [New York: Oxford University Press, 2004], pp. 220, 228). See also, among many others, Paul McGlasson, *Invitation to Dogmatic Theology: A Canonical Approach* (Grand Rapids: Brazos, 2006), p. 28.

[31]No method can mechanically distinguish between adequate and inadequate interpretations. Subjectivity as to what qualifies as adequate is unavoidable but should be limited by the attempt to provide discernible, demonstrable and defensible interpretation, continually subjected to the text in a hermeneutical spiral.

authorial intention to some degree, only the effect of that intention (the text) remains an object of investigation.[32] The interpreter's task is to identify the intent that remains discernible in the text and thereby interpret the meaning *in* the text, insofar as possible. As differentiated from reader-response theories, then, Christopher Seitz explains that a canonical reading "shares a concern for the objective reality of the text and for its intentional direction and ruled character."[33] Accordingly, this approach adopts a hermeneutical (critical) realist perspective that determinate meaning in the text exists prior to interpretation,[34] "while recognizing that the interpreter brings his/her own horizon to the text such that explicating the meaning in the text is an imperfect, complex, and continual process" requiring an ongoing hermeneutical spiral.[35] The text as canon thus provides the objective control to which interpretation should conform.

---

[32]Since the author's consciousness at the time of writing is not available for examination, appeal to intent that is beyond or behind the text (that is, not textually discernible) is speculative. So Jean Grondin, *Introduction to Philosophical Hermeneutics* (New Haven, CT: Yale University Press, 1994), p. 73. This canonical approach thus rejects the unfortunate dichotomy between what the text *meant* and what the text *means*. The former is not entirely recoverable but, as cause of the text, grounds the latter such that contemporary meaning in the text should not be separated from the original meaning *in* the text insofar as that can be discovered. See the compelling criticism of this distinction in favor of a canonical biblical theology in Gerhard F. Hasel, "The Relationship Between Biblical Theology and Systematic Theology," *TJ* 5, no. 2 (1984): 113-27. Compare Osborne, *Hermeneutical Spiral*, p. 32.

[33]Christopher Seitz, "Canonical Approach," *DTIB*, p. 100. See also Vanhoozer's approach to the text as a communicative act, based on the speech-act theory of Austin and Searle, in which "the sense of the text" is logically inseparable from "the intention of the author" as ordering agent (Vanhoozer, *Is There a Meaning*, p. 109).

[34]Consider, on the other hand, Hans-Georg Gadamer's seminal view that meaning is not located merely in authorial intent but in a "fusion" of the textual and interpreter's horizons such that the reader cannot fully recover the meaning of the text, since the interpreter's horizon always contributes to the interpretation because of one's historically effected consciousness (*wirkungsgeschichtliches Bewußtsein*). See Hans-Georg Gadamer, *Truth and Method*, trans. Joel Weinsheimer and Donald G. Marshall (New York: Continuum, 2004). While this canonical approach recognizes that one's interpretation is always more than the determinate meaning of the text because of the horizon of the interpreter, it insists that the interpreter's horizon is not a valid contributor to theological meaning but should continually be subjected to the text (on the view that the canonical text is the result of human *and* divine authorship). For an excellent discussion of the various issues involved with regard to intention and the location of meaning, see Vanhoozer, *Is There a Meaning*.

[35]Peckham, "The Analogy of Scripture Revisited," p. 51. Here and elsewhere, I use the term *spiral* to refer to the process of going back and forth between various components (i.e., text and context, interpreter's horizon and the text's horizon) that mutually correct one another, avoiding vicious circularity while moving ever closer to the intended meaning *in* the text. Thus, "continuous interaction between text and system forms a spiral upward to theological truth" (Osborne, *Hermeneutical Spiral*, p. 392).

Accordingly, this canonical approach includes exegesis as a crucial starting point but transcends exegetical limitations, looking beyond (but never overlooking) individual texts toward the theological interpretation of the entire canon.[36] This approach likewise transcends biblical theology in-

---

[36]My canonical approach holds some significant values in common with the theological interpretation of Scripture (TIS), which Gregg Allison describes as "a family of interpretive approaches that privileges theological readings of the Bible in due recognition of the theological nature of Scripture, its ultimate theological message, and/or the theological interests of its readers" ("Theological Interpretation of Scripture: An Introduction and Preliminary Evaluation," *SBJT* 14, no. 2 [2010]: 29). Although there is considerable "vagueness and variety associated with" TIS, in part due to the "'ecclesiastical breadth' of the scholars involved," Daniel J. Treier identifies the common themes of "canon, creed, and culture as the foci by which theological interpretation serves the church" ("What Is Theological Interpretation? An Ecclesiological Reduction," *IJST* 12, no. 2 [2010]: 158, 156, 148). According to Treier: "All advocates of the terminology either highlight or acknowledge the following practices:" (1) "recovering the past," (2) "reading within the Rule(s)" and (3) "reading with others" (ibid., pp. 148-49). See the explanation of these in Treier, *Introducing Theological Interpretation of Scripture*, pp. 39-100.

I share the commitment to the canon of Scripture as a distinctively theological text that should not be read as just another book but as a means to "hear God's word and to know God better" (Vanhoozer, "Introduction: What Is the Theological Interpretation of Scripture?" *DTIB*, p. 22). Compare Treier, *Introducing Theological Interpretation of Scripture*, pp. 202, 204. As Yeago states: "Whatever else it means, theological exegesis deals with the Bible as a word about God and from God" ("The Bible," p. 36). Likewise, I especially resonate with those who affirm what Vanhoozer calls "the ecumenical consensus of the church" that "the Bible should be read as a unity and as narrative testimony to the identities and actions of God and of Jesus Christ" ("What Is Theological Interpretation of Scripture?" p. 19). Compare Treier, *Introducing Theological Interpretation of Scripture*, p. 201.

The relationship between my canonical approach and TIS (broadly speaking) might further be helpfully framed by the relative priority given to that which is (1) behind the text (the past), (2) in the text (the contents of the text itself) and (3) in front of the text (the way readers interpret and respond to the text). Compare Vanhoozer, "What Is Theological Interpretation of Scripture?" p. 19; Joel B. Green, *Seized by Truth: Reading the Bible as Scripture* (Nashville: Abingdon, 2007), pp. 105-22. Put simply, my approach focuses on and gives primacy to what is in the text. Whereas both what is behind and in front of the text hold considerable significance, on my view what is in the text itself should govern one's understanding of what is behind (the precanonical history of the text) and in front (the way individuals and interpretive communities should read the text as canon).

With regard to what is behind the text, I share the dissatisfaction of many practitioners of TIS regarding any reading and/or approach to Scripture that "brackets out a consideration of divine action" (including but not limited to numerous historical-critical procedures; Vanhoozer, "What Is Theological Interpretation of Scripture?" p. 20). Compare Treier, *Introducing Theological Interpretation of Scripture*, pp. 34, 199. I thus resist any historical criticism of the canon that focuses on what is behind the text to the exclusion of what is in the text and/or conflicts with the canon's own claims about itself, history and/or theology proper. Compare Treier, *Introducing Theological Interpretation of Scripture*, pp. 14, 34, 199; Francis Watson, "Authors, Readers, Hermeneutics," in *Reading Scripture with the Church: Toward a Hermeneutic for Theological Interpretation* (Grand Rapids: Baker, 2006), p. 120; Vanhoozer, "What Is Theological Interpretation of Scripture?" p. 22; Green, *Practicing Theological Interpretation*, pp. 46-48, 127. In this regard, however, TIS includes various approaches, just as it does regarding the broader doctrine of Scripture, general

sofar as that discipline refers to the compilation and summary of particular books or themes. Going beyond an outline of biblical data, the canonical approach asks theological questions of the canon, seeking text-based and text-controlled answers, with careful attention to avoid extracanonical presuppositions. The canonical approach thus includes the exegesis and compilation of biblical data but applies them to the quest for the inner logic of the text(s) in relation to the entire canon, without dismissing the complexity of the texts.[37]

Hermeneutical and phenomenological exegesis. This process is further clarified by Fernando Canale's distinction between hermeneutical and phenomenological exegesis.[38] Hermeneutical exegesis refers to the philological and historical dimensions of the exegetical method, while phenomeno-

---

and special hermeneutics, and the relationship to biblical theology. Compare the discussion among four leading proponents in A. K. M. Adam, Stephen E. Fowl, Kevin J. Vanhoozer and Francis Watson, *Reading Scripture with the Church*.

With regard to what is in front of the text (past and present interpretative communities), whereas there are various proposals within TIS regarding the extent of authority of Christian tradition, creeds and the contemporary community, it seems to me that some proponents of TIS may give too much credence to past and present community interpretations, e.g., Fowl; see his *Theological Interpretation of Scripture* (Eugene, OR: Cascade, 2009). My own view is closest to Vanhoozer's "canonical-linguistic approach" that "locates normativity in the divine author's, not the interpretative community's, use of Scripture" while recognizing the appropriate role of the church in "performance of the Scriptures" (*Drama of Doctrine*, p. 181). In my view, further, any "reading within the Rule(s)," including (but not limited to) affirmation of particular creeds and/or confessions, should itself be ruled by the canon (Treier, "What Is Theological Interpretation?" p. 148). Whereas I agree that the Christian tradition should be appreciated and engaged, my worry regards the precise manner of adjudicating between what should be retrieved and what should not (whose tradition, which creeds and which community?). This includes questions about "'recovering the past' by imitating elements of pre-critical exegesis" (which precritical exegesis and/or what postcritical procedures?; Treier, "What Is Theological Interpretation?" p. 149). Compare Treier, *Introducing Theological Interpretation of Scripture*, p. 34. While I agree with the view that reading "Scripture is an act of piety, oriented toward Christ and the church's needs in practice" (ibid.), my canonical approach employs grammatical-historical procedures of exegesis that seek the intention *in* the text and look to the text (individual pericope and canon) itself to control whether and to what extent a text or passage is interpreted figuratively, seeking to avoid (as far as possible, recalling our own situatedness) superimposing an "extratextual grid" on the text. See D. A. Carson, "Theological Interpretation of Scripture: Yes, But . . . ," in *Theological Commentary: Evangelical Perspectives*, ed. Michael Allen (London: T & T Clark, 2011), p. 199.

[37]Canonical primacy includes high regard for textual details. The meaning of individual texts should not be flattened in order to fit a broader system. Compare Treier, "Scripture, Unity of," p. 733. Such a method of analogy could "lead to an overemphasis on the unity of biblical texts," resulting in "'artificial conformity' that ignores the diversity of expression and emphasis between divergent statements in the Bible" (D. A. Carson and John D. Woodbridge, *Scripture and Truth* [Grand Rapids: Zondervan, 1983], p. 361).

[38]See Canale, *Back to Revelation-Inspiration*, p. 149.

logical exegesis refers to interpretation that goes beyond a particular pericope in seeking the canonical horizon that impacts the meaning of the text(s).[39] As such, phenomenological exegesis uses exegetically derived canonical data in order to uncover the ontology implicit in the canon and, in so doing, address the conflict between the interpreter's metaphysical framework and that which is constitutive of the internal logic of the canon by continually subjecting the interpreter's horizon to the canonical horizon.[40] As Vanhoozer explains, "Doctrine is largely a matter of exegesis, of providing 'analyses of the logic of the scriptural discourse.'"[41] Whereas the questions and tools of philosophical analysis may be used, the "data" and "answers" of philosophical systems are not afforded epistemological weight but always subjected to the canon.[42] Accordingly, this approach brackets out (*epoché*),

---

[39]See ibid., p. 148. This phenomenological method differs from the ontological suppositions of Edmund Husserl, particularly his premise that reality is grounded in human perception. Here phenomenological methodology responds to the need to continually criticize and re-form one's preconceived worldview on the basis of engagement with the phenomena of the canonical text.

[40]This view of the "canonical horizon" operates either on (1) a view of divine authorship that brings unity amid the complexity of the text as canon (my view) or (2) a kind of literary- or canon-criticism approach wherein the final form of the canon might be treated as a unified but not monolithic literary document (perhaps on the view of community redaction; see earlier discussion, (p. 49). In either case, the interpreter seeks to uncover minimal ontological claims that appear to be required or implied by a coherent reading of the canonical text. Of course, competing ontological claims might arise from differing textual interpretations. However, this approach attempts to limit such ontological claims to those that might be discernibly and defensibly derived from the text, leaving open (where necessary) the issue of arbitrating between such competing claims, which might be advanced by further evidence and investigation. My own commitment to an internally congruent canonical horizon is undergirded by my belief that the Holy Spirit superintended the writing process and thus the history and worldview that are presented in specific texts and in the canonical text as a whole.

[41]Vanhoozer, *Drama of Doctrine*, p. 20. Vanhoozer's quotation here is from David Yeago, "The New Testament and the Nicene Dogma: A Contribution to the Recovery of Theological Exegesis," in *The Theological Interpretation of Scripture: Classic and Contemporary Readings*, ed. Stephen E. Fowl (Malden, MA: Blackwell, 1997), p. 87.

[42]Canale has criticized the apparent priority given to philosophy "as the main provider of the 'system' or intellectual framework" for much of theology (*Back to Revelation-Inspiration*, p. 53). Similarly, Childs adds, "For systematic theologians the overarching categories are frequently philosophical. The same is often the case for biblical scholars even when cloaked under the guise of a theory of history" (Brevard S. Childs, *Biblical Theology in Crisis* [Philadelphia: Westminster Press, 1970], p. 158). Compare Osborne, *Hermeneutical Spiral*, p. 396. Compare Jay Wesley Richards's contention that the Christian doctrine of God must be derived "not simply from general metaphysical intuitions" but "from unique, contingent things that God has done in history and, in particular, in Jesus Christ" (Jay Wesley Richards, *The Untamed God: A Philosophical Exploration of Divine Perfection, Immutability, and Simplicity* [Downers Grove, IL: InterVarsity Press, 2003], p. 30). This approach seeks a canonical metaphysic, which is rigorously gleaned from the data of Scripture. As Rob Lister states, "metaphysical reflection on scriptural revelation is not, in prin-

as far as possible, the interpreter's (known) preconceptions in favor of the (identifiable) preconceptions required by the text in its pericope as well as the text as canon, thereby seeking to allow the canon to provide its own metaphysical framework.[43] As Canale states, "In this phase of data interpretation, exegetes and theologians cancel out all previously inherited theories that could prove to be hindrances to the understanding of Scripture."[44]

Despite the intent to overcome them, however, preconceptions will remain. As Gerhard Maier puts it, "Every hermeneutic will be grounded in certain metaphysical convictions," but "which presuppositions" and "assumptions" are "justified" and "legitimate"?[45] Consequently, the hermeneutical spiral is never complete, ever moving toward a more adequately canonical metaphysical framework while correcting the interpreter's horizon. While looking at the text hermeneutically to ascertain the textual intent (both divine and human), the canonical approach also uncovers the ontological suppositions that provide the framework for the text's communication. Phenomenological exegesis thus complements hermeneutical exegesis by way of reciprocal interdependence; the former keeps the canonical horizon in view while the latter's focus on individual verses and pericopes contributes to and corrects the interpreter's metaphysical framework in an ongoing spiral that does not subvert the multivalency of the text(s).[46] These

---

ciple, unacceptable" but is actually "unavoidable. Indeed, Scripture does commend a metaphysic (e.g., the Creator/creature distinction)" (*God Is Impassible and Impassioned: Toward a Theology of Divine Emotion* [Wheaton, IL: Crossway, 2013], p. 174). It is crucial, however, to intentionally subject one's own preconception of the content of that metaphysic to the data of Scripture.

[43]Here, the interpreter seeks the answers to metaphysical questions that the text requires, a complex task considering that there may be multiple metaphysical options that could fit, which again magnifies the usefulness of the canonical context as a whole. Accordingly, this approach takes care to avoid the imposition of a "canon within the canon" in favor of *tota Scriptura*.

[44]Canale, *Back to Revelation-Inspiration*, p. 149. Osborne adds: "The key is to 'bracket' out our own beliefs and to allow the other side to challenge our preferred positions. This will drive us to examine the biblical data anew and to allow all passages on the topic to have equal weight" (*Hermeneutical Spiral*, p. 373).

[45]Maier, *Biblical Hermeneutics*, p. 46.

[46]I distinguish between multivalency *in* the text and multivalency that various scholars might perceive *behind* the text. Since this approach is not concerned with the precanonical history of the text, issues regarding perceived multivalency *behind* the text (e.g., multiple cultural contexts and different historical situations) are left for further investigation as needed on a case-by-case basis. This basic delimitation is necessary for the manageability of a canonical approach, which itself then invites dialogue and further investigation of each individual pericope. The multivalency *in* the text, on the other hand, is preserved in this canonical approach by attempting to recognize the complexity of the exegetical upshot(s) of the text(s) (via grammatical-historical

complementary categories of exegesis address the two hermeneutical circles (the text and the interpreter, and the canonical parts and whole) from the standpoint of the epistemological primacy of the final-form canon for systematic theology.[47]

Overall, this final-form canonical approach uses the canon as the source of answers to theological questions, toward the articulation of a coherent system that corresponds to the text as nearly as achievable while continually subjecting the interpreter's horizon to that of the canon in a hermeneutical spiral. Any extracted theological model is by no means the final word but remains secondary to the canonical text, which further corrects the system by way of ongoing canonical investigation. Therefore, the model of divine love sought in this study intentionally avoids prior commitment to ontological systems, in search of rigorous correspondence to the text as canon.[48] This is accomplished by first ascertaining the canonical description of divine love and thereafter asking what must God be like, inverting the prevalent order of presupposing ontology, then reasoning to divine characteristics.[49]

Method of investigation and presentation. This canonical approach was implemented in my investigation by first conducting an inductive reading of the entire canon, which analyzed any texts and/or passages that might address the systematic questions raised by the conflict of interpretations

---

procedures) and do justice to all of it without injury to any of it. Thus any theological model that attempts to do justice to all of the texts must be complex enough to incorporate the canon's complexity. My own theological interpretation is guided by my belief in the inspiration and unity of Scripture such that the theological tensions in the text do not amount to contradictory theological claims. However, I conscientiously attempt to avoid synthetically harmonizing, flattening and/or in any way injuring the apparent exegetical upshot of any particular text/passage. Whether I succeed in this intention is open to review (in this regard, consider my more detailed treatment of the biblical data in Peckham, *Concept of Divine Love*).

[47]Thus, while "phenomenological answers are logically prior to hermeneutical ones, they are actually recognized from within the ongoing, reciprocal, correcting task of interpretation" (Peckham, "The Analogy of Scripture Revisited," pp. 52-53).

[48]This approach does not rule out the possibility that the canonical data may affirm an existing, traditional viewpoint. It merely does not assume the veracity of any particular existing viewpoint.

[49]By inverting the method in this way I propose that the particular economy of God's revelation possesses epistemological priority. Compare Vanhoozer's question, phrased variously throughout his project, "What must God be like if he is actually the speaking and acting agent depicted in the Bible?" (*Remythologizing Theology*, p. 23). Elsewhere, "What must God be in order truthfully to be represented as repenting, grieving, compassionate?" (ibid., p. 50). He also attempts to avoid ontotheology in favor of theo-ontology, that is, to avoid "'bad' metaphysics" that impose "a system of categories on God without attending to God's own self-communication" (ibid., p. 8).

(see chapter one). The data extracted from this investigation were analyzed and grouped in an ongoing spiral that included both narrowing and expansion of the data in accordance with the findings. Although the canonical data were investigated inductively, this book lays out the material deductively by grouping the pertinent content under five aspects of divine love that were garnered from the canon and responsive to the systematic questions (see chapters four through eight).[50] Since the large amount of canonical data precludes an exhaustive presentation of its analysis, the thematic presentation in the following chapters consists of but a survey of the research conducted.

This book does not attempt to produce an exhaustive conception of divine love but is limited to outlining a canonical and systematic model of divine love in the God-world relationship, open to revision based on the implications of ongoing investigation. Thus, rather than addressing the entire concept of love, or even of divine love, this book focuses on divine love in the context of the God-world relationship. As such, intratrinitarian love is addressed only to the extent that it sheds light on the nature of God's love in relationship to the world.

Regarding the treatment of biblical material pertaining to the incarnate Christ's love, a decision is required. Should such passages be used as evidence regarding the nature of divine love? This study operates on the view that Christ was (and is) fully divine and became fully human without divesting himself of divinity.[51] According to the canon, Christ came to reveal God and proclaimed in no uncertain terms: "He who has seen Me has seen

---

[50]In the original investigation, the data were grouped under each of the five aspects and according to the various sections of the canon. Such diacanonical presentation respects the canonical groupings of the text without entering into the speculative field regarding the authorship and dating of specific passages and texts. There is striking continuity (amid diversity) throughout the canon with regard to divine love. Indeed, each of the five aspects of divine love appears in each section of the canon: the Torah, Prophets, Writings, Gospels and Acts, Pauline Epistles, and General Epistles and Revelation. See Peckham, *Concept of Divine Love*.

[51]As Vanhoozer writes: "The incarnation both ratifies and corrects all previous anthropomorphism: the New Testament does not speak of God as though he were like a human being but rather as a human being: Jesus Christ" (*Remythologizing Theology*, p. 65). Compare Eberhard Jüngel's contention that "the Christian faith asserts . . . that God was among men as the man Jesus," requiring a rejection of both "dogmatic" anthropomorphism, which "speaks of God *like* a man" and "symbolic" anthropomorphism, which "forbids speaking of God *as* a man" (*God as the Mystery of the World* [Grand Rapids: Eerdmans, 1983], p. 297).

the Father" (Jn 14:9; compare Jn 1:14; 2 Cor 4:4; Col 2:9; Heb 1:2-3; 1 Jn 4:9).⁵²
I therefore take seriously the manifestation of divinity set forth in the person and work of Christ. Yet how can this be done without collapsing the divine nature into the merely human?

The relevance of examples of Christ's love depends on the manner in which one believes Christ's life corresponds to and/or reveals the divine life. There are many proposals in this regard that may fall within acceptable limits of orthodoxy, and it is beyond the scope of this work to directly address these ongoing debates.⁵³ For the purposes of this study, one need not commit to any particular means of adjudicating these issues/questions beyond recognition of the minimal claim that the single person of Christ was fully divine and fully human, allowing one to affirm at least the possible relevance of the life of Jesus for the conception of God's love proper. Without

---

⁵²Vanhoozer points to the NT "apostolic claim that Jesus is 'the exact representation of God's being'" (Heb 1:3; Jn 14:9; *Remythologizing Theology*, p. 64). As such, "the son's humanity is the ultimate form of God's self-presentation, Jesus is God's definitive word and in his person and history corresponds to what it is that makes God God" (ibid., p. 51).

⁵³To take just a few recent examples, Kathryn Tanner suggests that the "same human features of Jesus' life may be attributed to Jesus as both divine and human [without one either supplementing or replacing the other] since Jesus' divinity, the Word's assumption of his humanity, is the immediate source of his whole human life" such that "Jesus can be said to lead a life both human and divine at the very same time" (*Jesus, Humanity and the Trinity: A Brief Systematic Theology* [Minneapolis: Fortress, 2001], p. 16). Here, "humanity and divinity are attributed to one and the same subject," Jesus who is "both God and human being" (ibid., p. 21). Yet considerable mystery remains: "But what accounts for this unity of subject? Here is a mighty conundrum!" (ibid., p. 22). Consider also Robert Jenson's narrative treatment, which arrives at the conclusion "that the sufferer of the Gospels is, without qualification or evasion, the second identity of God" (*Systematic Theology*, 1:144). As such, he understands the "Crucifixion, precisely as Jesus' human doing and suffering, as itself an event in God's triune life" (ibid., 1:189). In this regard, Bruce McCormack has suggested that "a different set of ontological commitments are needed" to overcome the "problems resident in the nexus of ideas which made the Chalcedonian Formula possible" without "setting aside the theological values" therein of a "single-Subject Christology" that upholds both the "full divinity" and "the full humanity of Jesus Christ" (Bruce L. McCormack, "The Actuality of God: Karl Barth in Conversation with Open Theism," in *Engaging the Doctrine of God: Contemporary Protestant Perspectives*, ed. Bruce L. McCormack [Grand Rapids: Baker Academic, 2008], p. 221). He sets forth his understanding of Barth's contribution that replaces substance ontology with an understanding of essence as "actualized and historicized," rendering "divine timelessness and impassibility . . . completely untenable" (ibid.). On the other hand, Stephen Holmes laments any view wherein "the human career of Jesus of Nazareth is the internal history of God," because he believes this departs from the "Chalcedonian and later conciliar tradition" and requires that "many of the traditional attributes [eternity, impassibility, immutability] must be radically redefined, or completely discarded" or "significantly revised" ("Divine Attributes," in *Mapping Modern Theology*, ed. Kelly M. Kapic and Bruce L. McCormack [Grand Rapids: Baker Academic, 2012], p. 64).

delving into the myriad interpretive issues and disagreements regarding the application of properties to Christ's divine and/or human natures, then, this study operates on the hypothesis that the testimony regarding the person of Christ sheds light on the nature of God's love (without presupposing the precise manner in which it does so).[54]

In this regard, one might entertain a modified view of *communicatio idiomatum* such that, absent compelling canonical reasons otherwise, the data regarding the incarnate Christ's love correspond not only to his humanity but also his divinity.[55] Significantly, this does not entail that the experiences of God in Christ be understood as identical to those of ordinary humans. To ascribe the experiences of Jesus univocally to God would require the conclusion that God becomes hungry, thirsty, tired and so on. On this working approach, however, if one allows the possibility that divinity might condescend in the person of Christ to assume the capacity

---

[54]In keeping with my canonical methodology, I have elected not to presuppose a fully developed Christology, because that would require answering a great deal of questions regarding divine ontology (among others) that are intentionally left for further investigation in order to mitigate ontological presuppositions that necessitate particular conclusions regarding divine love. It does seem to me, however, that Christ's life is part of God's own history. The second person of the Trinity truly became human while remaining fully divine such that the single person Jesus Christ both manifested divinity in relation to humans and modeled how humanity should relate to God. At the same time, with Tanner, I wish to avoid "becom[ing] (mistakenly) preoccupied with fascinating, but ultimately beside-the-point issues concerning the exact relations between Jesus' divine and human qualities" (*Jesus, Humanity, and the Trinity*, pp. 16-17).

[55]Consider Luther's view of the *communicatio idiomatum* wherein the "two natures, the human and the divine, are inseparable," being "so united in one Person that the properties of the one nature are also attributed to the other" (LW 22:492). Accordingly, Luther "ascribe[s] to the divinity, because of this personal union, all that happens to humanity, and vice versa" (ibid., 37:210). Nevertheless, Christ's divine and human natures are not to be confused; one should "identify and recognize each nature properly" (ibid., 24:105-6). Compare McCormack's reading of Barth as holding a communication of attributes on the view of *"genus tapeinoticum"* (literally, the "genus of humility"), the "sharing by the divine in the being of the human such that human attributes are rightly ascribed to the divine," which was the "polar opposite of the Lutheran genus majesticum" (wherein "the hypostatic union made possible a human participation in the divine attributes of omniscience, omnipotence, and omnipresence") ("Divine Impassibility or Simply Divine Constancy? Implications of Karl Barth's Later Christology for Debates over Impassibility," in *Divine Impassibility and the Mystery of Human Suffering*, ed. James Keating and Thomas Joseph White [Grand Rapids: Eerdmans, 2009], p. 175). The *genus tapeinoticum* "creates the possibility that the man Jesus should be the performative agent of all that is done by the God-human in his divine-human unity" (ibid., p. 177). In this way, "what Jesus experiences, God experiences" (ibid., p. 179). Alternatively, one might consider Garrett DeWeese's argument for a contemporary monothelite model in "One Person, Two Natures: Two Metaphysical Models of the Incarnation," in *Jesus in Trinitarian Perspective*, ed. Fred Sanders and Klaus Issler (Nashville: B&H Academic, 2007), pp. 114-53.

to feel (among other things) hunger, thirst, fatigue and so on, then one might have no difficulty taking seriously the view that Christ manifests not merely human love but also divine love, albeit as it operates within the unique situation of the incarnation.[56] However, the provisional nature of such an approach must be emphasized.

On the approach of this study, then, no attempt is made to distinguish which dispositions and/or actions correspond to Christ's divinity and/or humanity; all are (tentatively) taken to properly refer to Christ's person as the supreme revelation of God to humans.[57] Such an approach yields at least two important results. First, this approach takes seriously the claims of Christ that he reveals the Father (e.g., Jn 14:9) and thus takes the canonical data regarding the incarnate Christ as informing the conception of divine love (compare Rom 8:35, 39) while recognizing that the particular forms and manifestations of love by Jesus were limited and shaped by Christ's humanity and historical situation. In the words of Kathryn Tanner, the "love of the Father for us is manifest in what the Son does, in much the same way a ray of light displays the character of its source."[58] Second, this approach recognizes the considerable correspondence between the characteristics of Christ's love and that exhibited by Yahweh

---

[56]That is, God might condescend to assume a form (voluntary, temporary self-limitation) in which such things that are normally alien to God may be experienced (in a manner appropriate to divinity; see the discussion of analogy in chap. 6 below). Anthony C. Thiselton comments: "If the sovereign, transcendent God freely chooses or decrees to allow himself to suffer, this is an enhancement, not a diminution, of his sovereign freedom to choose how he will act" (*The Hermeneutics of Doctrine* [Grand Rapids: Eerdmans, 2007], p. 478). Compare Eberhard Jüngel's view of Christ as the parable of God (*God as the Mystery*, p. 288).

[57]Ascribing Christ's experiences to his human nature alone has a long history in the Christian tradition, playing a significant role in the christological controversies of the fourth century and onward, the issues of which continue to evoke spirited debate and construction. Compare Paul L. Gavrilyuk, *The Suffering of the Impassible God: The Dialectics of Patristic Thought* (Oxford: Oxford University Press, 2004); Keating and White, eds., *Divine Impassibility*. McCormack notes: "Where the sufferings of Jesus are assigned to the human nature alone, there the human nature is being treated as if it were a Subject in its own right—which has to render incoherent the [Chalcedonian] commitment to a single-Subject Christology" (McCormack, "Actuality of God," p. 220). In McCormack's view: "There can be only one Subject of the human sufferings of Jesus, and this Subject is the Logos. That the Logos suffers humanly goes without saying. Suffering is made possible only through the *assumptio carnis*. But it is the Logos who suffers, for there is no other Subject" (ibid., p. 222).

[58]Kathryn Tanner, *Christ the Key* (New York: Cambridge University Press, 2010), p. 151. Thus it may be imprudent to attempt to separate out what is human and what is divine in the life of Christ: "Jesus performs divine works in a human way (saves us by living a human life); and performs human works in a divine way (lives a human life in a way that saves)" (Tanner, *Jesus, Humanity, and the Trinity*, p. 21). Compare ibid., pp. 16, 18-19.

in the Old Testament and ascribed to *Theos* in the New Testament, which reinforces the notion that Christ incarnate manifests divine love.[59] For example, depictions of divine compassion in the Old Testament and New Testament are strikingly similar to that manifested by Christ in the Gospels (compare Lk 1:58).[60] Thus Leon Morris contends that "Christ's action is God's action. Christ's love is God's love."[61] Alan Torrance adds: "There can be no dichotomy between the divine and human *agape* in Christ."[62]

Notably, however, the findings of this study do not hinge on the admissibility of the depictions of Christ's love; the five aspects of God's love are evident apart from the data pertaining to Christ incarnate. Yet the striking correspondence between the depictions of Christ's love and other depictions of God's love throughout Scripture appears to reinforce both the forceonditional-reciprocal model of divine love and the move to take the testimony regarding the person of Christ as illuminating the nature of divine love.[63] As T. F. Torrance proclaims, the Gospels "speak powerfully of the Love of God in its concrete embodiment and manifestation in the self-giving love and compassion of Jesus" such that in Jesus "there is disclosed the very nature of the Love of our Father in heaven for all his children."[64]

Although a brief excursus such as this cannot do justice to the complexity of the issues involved, I trust that this brief treatment of my working approach provides an understandable rationale (if not agreeable to all) for the manner in which I treat passages pertaining to Christ's incarnation. In order to orient the reader for the more detailed explanation of the aspects of divine

---

[59]For example, the love of God and Christ are equated in Rom 8:35, 39 such that G. Johnston comments, "God's love is precisely the same as Christ's love (Rom. 8:28-39)" ("Love in the NT," *IDB* 3:171). Compare Ethelbert Stauffer, "αγαπάω, αγάπη, αγαπητός," *TDNT* 1:49. Thomas Schreiner adds: "No ultimate separation should be erected between Christ's love and God's love"; indeed, to "separate the Father from the Son in the act of self-giving would grossly distort the NT" (*Romans* [Grand Rapids: Baker, 1998], pp. 464, 260). See also Jn 5:20; 15:9; Rom 5:8; Eph 5:1-2; 2 Thess 2:16; 1 Pet 2:3.

[60]W. Günther and H. G. Link write: "The mercy and compassion shown by Jesus reveals the mercy and love of God" ("αγαπαω," *NIDNTT* 2:543).

[61]Leon Morris, *The Epistle to the Romans*, PNTC (Grand Rapids: Eerdmans, 1998), p. 224.

[62]Alan Torrance, "Is Love the Essence of God?" in *Nothing Greater, Nothing Better: Theological Essays on the Love of God*, ed. Kevin J. Vanhoozer (Grand Rapids: Eerdmans, 2001), p. 135.

[63]This correspondence may hold significant implications for further work on Christology, which I hope to undertake in the future.

[64]Thomas F. Torrance, *The Christian Doctrine of God: One Being Three Persons* (New York: T & T Clark, 2001), pp. 57, 58.

love in the coming chapters, I now turn to a brief overview of the foreconditional-reciprocal model of divine love as volitional, evaluative, emotional, foreconditional and ideally reciprocal.

Overview of the Canonical Model of Divine Love in Relation to the World

Divine love in the context of the God-world relationship consists of many aspects that interrelate with considerable complexity, yet striking harmony.[65] Scripture speaks of God's love by means of various terms that point to various features.[66] Accordingly, the term *love* as used in this canonical model refers to a complex concept, including considerable polysemy. At the risk of oversimplification, God's love is virtuous, kind, generous, unmerited, voluntary, faithfully devoted, evaluative, profoundly affectionate and compassionate, intensely passionate, patient and long-suffering, merciful, gracious, just, steadfast, amazingly reliable and enduring but not unalterably constant, preferential but not arbitrarily exclusive, relationally responsive, desirous of reciprocation, and active. God loves qualities like goodness, justice, righteousness; indeed, his love is inextricably bound to such qualities. Divine love is most often directed toward humans and is continually manifested in action that grounds the divine-human relationship itself, including creation, calling and election, covenant, beneficence, deliverance, forgiveness, redemption, restoration, corrective discipline, wrath toward oppressors and evil of all kinds, and many others.[67] Through such providential actions, God's everlasting love persistently draws humans to himself, calling individuals to respond freely to God's love and thus enter into a re-

---

[65]Here I depart from Thomas Jay Oord's contention that "the Bible does not provide an internally consistent witness to love's meaning. Biblical writers talk about love in different ways and give it differing meanings" (*The Nature of Love: A Theology* [St. Louis: Chalice, 2010], p. 12). To be sure, there is great diversity regarding the meaning and usage of *love* within the canon. At the same time, there is a consistent (though not monolithic or simple) canonical view of divine love. I do not believe any single aspect should be selected and declared to be "the meaning of love dominant in the biblical witness" (ibid., p. 13).

[66]See the discussion of the semantics of divine love in chap. 3 (below).

[67]The case can be made that all God's actions are loving, but the presentation and defense of such a case requires consideration of all of the divine actions, which far exceeds the scope of this work. For this reason, I make no attempt to explain in detail the specific actions of God that constitute each of the various types and aspects of love. Suffice it to say that, according to Scripture, God does what is best, righteous and just, always and without fail (e.g., Deut 32:4; Zeph 3:5; Rev 15:3).

ciprocal love relationship of mutual delight.[68] God takes pleasure in those who respond positively to him (his beloved) and enjoys the most profound, intimate friendship with them. Likewise, God's love is intensely emotional, akin to, but exponentially greater than, the compassion of the mother for her infant and the passion of the husband for his wife. While God desires and expects appropriate human response and faithfully seeks reciprocal love, he is often the victim of unrequited love.

The characteristics of divine love in the context of the God-world relationship briefly described here are grouped according to five primary aspects: divine love is (1) volitional, (2) evaluative, (3) emotional, (4) foreconditional and (5) ideally reciprocal. These five aspects are each basic to the biblical understanding of God's love relationship with the world, and they interrelate and support one another while each contributes to the wider view of God's multifaceted love. First, divine love is volitional but not merely volitional. It includes a free, volitional aspect that is neither essential nor necessary to God's being yet also not arbitrary. The divine-human love relationship is neither unilaterally deterministic nor essential or ontologically necessary to God, but bilaterally (though not symmetrically) volitional and contingent. Second, divine love is evaluative. This means that God is capable of being affected by, and even benefitting from, the disposition and/or actions of his creatures (with divine mediation). Third, God's love is profoundly emotional and passible, though not to the exclusion of volitional and evaluative aspects.[69] Fourth, divine love is foreconditional, not altogether unconditional. That is, divine love is prior to all other love and offered to creatures prior to any conditions but not exclusive of conditions.

---

[68]Here and elsewhere in this work the term *reciprocal* refers to love that flows bilaterally but does not assume that such love is symmetrical or equal.

[69]This aspect is significantly affected by decisions regarding the treatment of accommodative language and figurative expressions regarding God. Three guidelines are followed in this canonical approach (justified and explained further in chap. 6 below). First, since all language available to the interpreter is human language, the dismissal of the exegetical force of figurative language of God for this reason would be self-defeating. Second, it is inappropriate from the standpoint of a canonical methodology to assume that the interpreter knows what God is like prior to and/or independent of the biblical data itself and to use such assumptions to qualify and/or dismiss biblical language descriptive of divine pathos. Third, the frequent idiomatic usage of figurative anatomical expressions, with both divine and human agency, suggests that such idioms need not be taken to refer to literal anatomy and are not dependent on the anatomical referent itself. Therefore, the interpreter should not exclude the well-known meaning of an idiom simply because it is in reference to God, without compelling textual data.

Divine love in relation to the world is unconditional with respect to God's volition, but conditional with respect to the ongoing God-world relationship. Finally, divine love is ideally reciprocal. God universally seeks a relationship of reciprocal love but enters into particular, intimate relationship only with those who respond appropriately. While these five aspects may be distinguished, they are not altogether distinct. They overlap considerably, as evidenced by both the semantic and thematic canonical data.[70]

Conclusion

This chapter has described the final-form canonical approach to systematic theology that was employed in investigating the meaning of divine love in light of the contemporary debate, toward a model that is internally coherent and corresponds rigorously to Scripture. Further, I have briefly outlined how this methodology has been employed toward careful interpretation of the canonical data, seeking the canonical perspective on divine love without assuming the accuracy or inaccuracy of other models (with regard to love itself or ontology on the whole). Finally, this chapter has presented a brief overview of the foreconditional-reciprocal model of divine love in order to orient the reader for the more detailed explanation of each aspect in the coming chapters. Overall, God's love is volitional, evaluative, emotional, foreconditional and ideally reciprocal within the context of the God-world relationship. The following chapter introduces the semantic background of divine love before turning to an explanation of each aspect.

---

[70]The overlap between the five aspects is readily apparent by reference to the semantics alone. The primary words for love in the OT and NT collocate with and closely relate to terminology that points to each of the five aspects. For a demonstration of the various semantic overlaps that also supports the various aspects described in this chapter, see the word studies in chap. 3 (below). For instance, the language of *election* and *divine will* relate closely to the language of God's love (see chap. 4 below). God's decision to create, election, and commitment to the covenant relationship initiated (but not unilaterally maintained) by that election exemplify the volitional aspect of God's love. Moreover, this volitional aspect complements both the emotional and evaluative aspects of divine love toward the world. Indeed, evaluation, volition and emotion are all bound up in the language of God's election, good pleasure, delight, etc., by way of both OT and NT terminology, all of which closely correspond to and collocate with the most important words descriptive of divine love. God's evaluation is further seen in various language and descriptions of his delight and joy over his people and, conversely, his displeasure and righteous indignation against evil, all of which are closely associated with the major terminology of love. Closely connected to God's evaluative love is his emotional love, evidenced in various depictions of his compassion and passion. These volitional, evaluative and emotional aspects are assumed by, and necessary for, the foreconditional and ideally reciprocal aspects of love.

3

AGAPE VERSUS *EROS*?

The Biblical Semantics of Divine Love

Agape is gift love, but *eros* is need love. *Eros* desires and acquires, while *agape* is pure giving, never receiving. *Eros* is motivated by self-interest, but *agape* only seeks the good of others, to the exclusion of all self-interest. *Agape* is unmotivated, spontaneous and unconditional, whereas *eros* is motivated, conditional and lasts only as long as its object fulfills its desire. So goes the sweeping and highly influential *agape-eros* distinction, which has had significant influence not only in popular musings on love but even in some serious theological studies. If presuppositions regarding the meaning of biblical terms for love are left unchecked, one might possess this or another preconception of God's love or *agape*, assume that is what is meant by the biblical term *love*, and read that preconception into the text every time terminology of love appears. This chapter seeks to avoid this outcome by a brief overview of the semantics of divine love, challenging the influential *agape-eros* distinction and, in the process, introducing the major biblical terms of love that correspond to the wider foreconditional-reciprocal model.

The terms included in the following brief survey were selected in conjunction with the inductive reading, investigation and analysis of the canonical data. These terms, which directly impinge on the systematic issues regarding divine love, were investigated from the standpoint of a synchronic-canonical approach, recognizing the inherent limitations of semantic studies with regard to systematic investigation.[1] Meanings of words may vary de-

---

[1]Such an approach does not naively hold that words held fixed meaning in various instances over

pending on their context and usage throughout Scripture, similar to the manner in which English words take on various meanings in different usage and over time. Thus the semantic range of a term should not be read into each occurrence (illegitimate totality transfer), and neither should a particular nuance of a word in one location be extrapolated to all other occurrences of that word.[2] Accordingly, the brief semantic overviews below are not intended to reduce the terms to simple, narrow or monolithic definitions.[3] Rather, the survey in this chapter serves to (1) exclude simplistic and/or reductionist definitions that have been attached to various terms and (2) provide an overview of the range of meaning and biblical usage (including polysemy and multivalency) of the most pertinent terms that impinge on the meaning of divine love in order to provide crucial background for engaging the wider canonical model.[4]

The Theological Inflation of *Agape*

Agape *versus* eros. Anders Nygren's influential view that *agape* is uniquely descriptive of the highest love, genuinely exhibited by God alone, is often repeated in print and pulpit alike.[5] Although it has come under considerable criticism, with good reason,[6] the agapist view continues to find sub-

---

the ages. However, this approach dovetails with the diacanonical approach to the text discussed in chap. 2 (above), enabling a grasp of the content as a unified canonical work without entering into the speculative field regarding the authorship and dating of specific passages and texts.

[2]On the common lexical fallacy and illegitimate totality transfer see Grant R. Osborne, *The Hermeneutical Spiral: A Comprehensive Introduction to Biblical Interpretation*, 2nd ed. (Downers Grove, IL: InterVarsity Press, 2006), p. 84.

[3]Purely semantic investigation of these or other terms is not sufficient to construct a model of divine love.

[4]For a more detailed and extensive treatment of these and other terms related to divine love, see John C. Peckham, *The Concept of Divine Love in the Context of the God-World Relationship* (New York: Peter Lang, 2014).

[5]For Nygren, *eros* is acquisitive and desirous love, *philia* denotes reciprocal friendship and attendant emotionality, and *agape* refers to self-sacrificial beneficence toward the unworthy. See the discussion of Nygren's view in chap. 1 (above). While Nygren himself was making a thematic, not a semantic, argument, many of his assumptions (whether dependent on him or not) have spilled over into semantic discussions (explicitly or implicitly). See Ethelbert Stauffer, "αγαπάω, αγάπη, αγαπητός," *TDNT* 1:35-37; W. Günther and H. G. Link, "αγαπαω," *NIDNTT* 2:540, 542; Ceslas Spicq, "αγαπη," *TLNT* 1:9-13.

[6]For example, William Klassen states, "Nygren's thesis has been all but discredited" ("Love in the NT and Early Jewish Literature," *ABD* 4:385). Consider Eberhard Jüngel's engagement with the *agape-eros* dichotomy. He accepts the distinction between an "eros-structure of love, or 'concupiscent love' (*amor concupiscentiae*), or need-love," and "gift-love, or 'benevolent love' (*amor benevolentiae*), or the agape-structure of love," but wisely cautions that one should "not establish

stantial support.⁷ In this view, *agape* is unilateral beneficence, volitional but not emotional love, in direct contrast to acquisitive and desirous love (*eros*).⁸ Whereas *eros* egoistically responds to qualities or actions, *agape* is purely altruistic, nonevaluative love for the unworthy.⁹ Accordingly, *agape* flows unilaterally from God to others but never from others to God. Human "love" is nothing more than God's love flowing through a passive agent.¹⁰ *Agape* is thus unconditional, unilaterally willed, utterly spontaneous and arbitrary, impassible election love.¹¹

However, while ἀγαπάω is the most prominent New Testament word group of love, ἀγάπη is not itself a superior term of divine love.¹² Usage in the LXX and New Testament demonstrates that the word group may convey

---

these different forms as opposing alternatives!" (*God as the Mystery of the World* [Grand Rapids: Eerdmans, 1983], p. 318). In dialogue with what Jüngel takes to be an overly strong contrast between *eros* and *agape* made by Heinrich Scholz (*Eros und Caritas*), Jüngel posits that "Love without some kind of self-relatedness would be" both "an enormous abstraction" and "a falsification of the love from above" while, conversely, "love without the greater selflessness within the self-relationship... would be the opposing abstraction," a "falsification of love from below" (ibid., p. 319n15). Compare ibid., pp. 338-39.

⁷For instance, Leon Morris adopts Nygren's "basic idea of ἀγάπη" as "self-giving love for the unworthy" while allowing that Nygren may have "equated" his distinctions "too narrowly with the use of particular Greek words." Nevertheless, "there is such a love as he describes as *Agape* and that it is the Christian understanding of love seems clear" (*The Gospel According to John*, NICNT [Grand Rapids: Eerdmans, 1995], p. 293). Compare C. S. Lewis, *The Four Loves* (New York: Harcourt Brace, 1988); Colin Grant, "For the Love of God: Agape," *JRE* 24, no. 1 (Spring 1996): 7.

⁸C. E. B. Cranfield contends that ἀγάπη "evidently refers to the will rather than to the emotion" ("Love," *TWTB*, p. 134). Likewise, G. Johnston defines ἀγάπη as "passionless love" ("Love in the NT," *IDB* 3:169). So Richard C. Trench, *Synonyms of the New Testament* (Grand Rapids: Eerdmans, 1948), p. 42. Compare Spicq, "αγαπη," *TLNT* 1:10-14; Ceslas Spicq, *Agape in the New Testament*, 3 vols. (St. Louis: B. Herder, 1963), 1:11-12.

⁹For Morris, divine *agape* "is not a love of the worthy, and it is not a love that desires to possess." We "do not bring anything valuable to God" but "acquire value only" as "recipients of his love" (Leon Morris, *Testaments of Love: A Study of Love in the Bible* [Grand Rapids: Eerdmans, 1981], pp. 28, 142). Compare Stauffer, "αγαπάω, αγάπη, αγαπητός," *TDNT* 1:49; Cranfield, "Love," *TWTB*, p. 135; Spicq, "αγαπη," *TLNT* 1:8.

¹⁰The human is merely "like a vessel or tube through which the stream of the divine blessings must flow without intermission to other people" (Luther, *WA* 10, I, I, quoted in Anders Nygren, *Agape and Eros*, trans. Philip S. Watson [London: SPCK, 1953], p. 735). Morris recognizes that "mutual love can be seen" throughout Scripture but subsumes it under unilateral election, saying, "God produces love in his elect" (*Testaments of Love*, pp. 42, 182). Compare Cranfield, "Love," *TWTB*, p. 136; Stauffer, "αγαπάω, αγάπη, αγαπητός," *TDNT* 1:50.

¹¹Morris comments: "We must clearly recognize that God's love is unconditional" (*Testaments of Love*, p. 31). Compare Stauffer, "αγαπάω, αγάπη, αγαπητός," *TDNT* 1:49-50; Günther and Link, "αγαπαω," *NIDNTT* 2:544.

¹²The word group appears more than 300 times in verbal (ἀγαπάω), noun (ἀγάπη) and adjectival (ἀγαπητός) forms combined, describing divine or human love.

a broad range of meaning from the most virtuous love of affection and generosity (e.g., 1 Cor 13:4-13) to lust that fades quickly after its rapacious selfishness is satisfied. Positively, it may refer to love that is affectionate, warm, concerned with and interested in its object(s); love in the sense of high regard, value and appreciation for its object(s); love that includes enjoyment, pleasure and fondness; preferential love (whether proper or improper); and love demonstrated in action, often of a beneficent nature.[13] Negatively, the word group is used of (1) misdirected love, such as Demas's ἀγαπάω for the evil world (2 Tim 4:10; compare Jn 3:19; 12:43), and (2) rapacious "lust," such as Amnon's ἀγαπάω and ἀγάπη for his half-sister Tamar, whom he raped (2 Sam 13:15 LXX), and Shechem's ἀγαπάω for Dinah, whom he raped (Gen 34:2-3 LXX).

With divine agency, the ἀγαπάω word group only refers to perfect, virtuous love, yet it departs from Nygren's view in many ways.[14] First, divine ἀγαπάω is not arbitrary, unilaterally willed election love.[15] God's love (ἀγαπάω and other terms) is the ground of election but not identical with it (see chapter four). Indeed, divine ἀγαπάω is often explicitly conditional; the Father loves (ἀγαπάω) humans *because* they love (ἀγαπάω) the Son (Jn 14:21, 23; compare Jn 10:17; 15:9-10; 2 Cor 9:7; Jude 21; see chapter seven). Second, although divine ἀγαπάω is often for unworthy objects (e.g., Rom 5:8) and frequently associated with grace, it is nevertheless evaluative. That is, it often takes into account qualities and/or actions of its object or objects.[16] For example, "God loves [ἀγαπάω] a cheerful giver" (2 Cor 9:7; compare Jn 10:17; Heb 1:9).[17] Third, divine ἀγαπάω often exhibits responsive emotionality (Jn 13:1; compare 1 Pet 1:22; 4:8).[18] For instance, Christ is God's "beloved"

---

[13]See "αγαπαω, αγαπη," L&N 1:292. See also "αγαπαω," BDAG, pp. 5-6; Spicq, "αγαπη," *TLNT* 1:12-13.
[14]This response to the agapist claims is limited to an overview; further evidence appears in the following chapters.
[15]I use ἀγαπάω here and throughout this discussion not only to refer to the verb form but as representative of the entire word group.
[16]The many instances of misdirected love assume that love ought to be directed toward appropriate objects (see Mt 6:24; Lk 11:43; Jn 3:19; 12:43; 2 Tim 4:10; 2 Pet 2:15; 1 Jn 2:15; Rev 12:11; cf. 1 Thess 5:13).
[17]Kenneth Wuest contends that ἀγαπάω refers to "love called out of one's heart by the preciousness of the object loved. It is a love of esteem, of evaluation" ("Four Greek Words for Love," *BSac* 116, no. 463 [1959]: 243). Compare James Moffat, *Love in the New Testament* (New York: Harper, 1930), p. 49; "αγαπαω, αγαπη," L&N 1:292; Spicq, "αγαπη," *TLNT* 1:11-12; Gerhard Schneider, "αγαπη," *EDNT* 1:9.
[18]"*Agape* desires response, and desires it passionately" and even "yearns for a loving response"

(ἀγαπητός) in whom he is "well-pleased" (εὐδοκέω; compare Mt 3:17; 17:5).[19] Finally, ἀγαπάω is not unilateral, and neither is God the only proper subject of love.[20] The Father loves humans (Jn 3:16; 14:21; compare Deut 4:37), and humans love God (1 Cor 8:3; Jas 1:12; 1 Jn 5:3; compare Ex 20:6). The Son loves humans (Mk 10:21; Jn 13:1), and humans love the Son (Lk 7:47; Jn 14:21; Heb 6:10).[21] Within the Trinity, the Father loves the Son (Jn 3:35), and the Son loves the Father (Jn 14:31). The ἀγαπάω word group as used in Scripture, then, differs considerably from the agapist conception.

Agape *versus* philos. Like ἀγαπάω, the φιλέω word group may connote affectionate love, fondness, attraction, concern, special interest and/or enjoyment/pleasure or evaluation.[22] It often connotes belonging in friendship or family, or virtually any kind of relationship.[23] However, the agapist perspective claims that *philos* is a deficient love of emotional and reciprocal friendship unsuitable to denote "Christian love."[24] Some have further claimed that φιλέω connotes a reciprocal relationship between equals and is thus inappropriate "for expressing a love that unites God and humans."[25]

(J. A. T. Robinson, "Agape and Eros," *Theology* 48 [1945]: 99). Compare Klassen, "Love in the NT," *ABD* 4:385; William E. Phipps, "The Sensuousness of Agape," *Theology Today* 29, no. 4 (1973): 370-79; "αγαπαω, αγαπη," L&N 1:292; Spicq, "αγαπη," *TLNT* 1:12-13.

[19]Here and elsewhere the ἀγαπάω word group is closely related to the evaluative emotion of delight (e.g., Phil 1:15-16; 2 Tim 4:8). Thus, complementing εὐδοκέω, ἀγαπάω may also mean "take pleasure in" (BDAG, "αγαπαω," pp. 5-6). Compare "φιλεω," L&N, "αγαπαω," 1:300. See the discussion of εὐδοκέω in chap. 5 (below). In the LXX, ἀγαπάω translates אהב in the sense of emotional love (Hos 11:1; Jer 38:3) and evaluative love (Ps 145:8). It is also used to translate a number of terms of delight and/or compassion such as חפץ (Ps 50:8; Esther 6:9), רצה (1 Chron 29:17), משׂושׂ (Jer 30:31), שׁעע (Ps 93:19) and שׁעשׁעים (Is 5:7). Further, the collocation of ἀγαπάω with other word groups in the NT strongly suggests emotionality, including the contrast between love and hate (Mt 5:43-44) and the close association with compassion (Lk 6:36; Phil 2:1), mercy (Eph 2:4), kindness (1 Cor 13:4), comfort (2 Thess 2:16) and patience (Gal 5:22).

[20]See Günther and Link, "αγαπαω," *NIDNTT* 2:543; Schneider, "αγαπη," *EDNT* 1:9.

[21]Human love toward God, Jesus and one another is denoted by both ἀγαπάω and ἀγάπη, excluding the assertion that only the noun ἀγάπη is reserved for divine agency.

[22]The basic meaning of the verb φιλέω (25 NT instances) is to love in the sense of regarding with affection. The noun φίλος (29 NT instances) signifies a loved one or friend, and the noun φιλία (1 NT instance) refers to a relationship between loved ones, e.g., friendship. See Günther and Link, "αγαπαω," *NIDNTT* 2:538; Klassen, "Love in the NT," *ABD* 4:385; "φιλεω," L&N 1:300; Gustav Stählin, "φιλεω, καταφιλεω, φιλημα," *TDNT* 9:117.

[23]Stählin, "φιλεω, καταφιλεω, φιλημα," *TDNT* 9:115. Compare "αγαπαω, αγαπη," L&N 1:292; Günther and Link, "αγαπαω," *NIDNTT* 2:542.

[24]Morris, *Testaments of Love*, pp. 119, 263.

[25]Spicq, "αγαπη," *TLNT* 1:10-11, 13. Compare Irving Singer, *The Nature of Love*, 3 vols. (Chicago: University of Chicago Press, 1987), 1:160; Viktor Warnach, *Agape: die Liebe als Grundmotiv der neutestamentlichen Theologie* (Düsseldorf: Patmos-Verlag, 1951), p. 162n1.

While it is true that the φιλέω word group commonly depicts a reciprocal relationship, it is not true that it assumes an equal or symmetrical relationship. For instance, Christ's "friends" (φίλος) must obey him (Jn 15:14).[26] Many have argued that the ἀγαπάω word group was selected by biblical authors and infused with a new meaning denoting the highest love.[27] For example, Richard Trench asserts that ἀγάπη was "a word born within the bosom of revealed religion."[28] However, many scholars have come to recognize that the relative prominence of ἀγάπη in the LXX and New Testament is the result of a linguistic shift around the time of the writing of the LXX.[29] Accordingly, James Barr states, "In relation to ideas of love, this noun [ἀγάπη] is no more than a nominalization of those same relations and emotions which in verb form were expressed by ἀγαπάν."[30]

---

[26]The technical classical usage (by Aristotle and others), which often refers to utilitarian reciprocity and the maintenance of community status, does not appear in the NT. See Stauffer, "αγαπάω, αγάπη, αγαπητός," TDNT 1:36, 115; Stählin, "φιλεω, καταφιλεω, φιλημα," TDNT 9:114-15, 46. This is especially apparent in Christ's sacrificial love for his friends (φίλος; Jn 15:13).

[27]In support of this view, some point to the fact that while the verb ἀγαπάω and the older noun ἀγάπησις (which appears infrequently in the LXX but never in the NT) appear relatively frequently in Greek from Homer onward, the noun ἀγάπη is not very well represented in extrabiblical Greek literature (if at all). The φιλέω word group, by contrast, appears more frequently in pre-LXX Greek than in biblical Greek. It has been disputed whether the noun ἀγάπη appears at all in pre-LXX Greek, though some instances have been suggested, including the instance of ἀγάπη with regard to Isis in P. Oxy. 1380. See Stauffer, "αγαπάω, αγάπη, αγαπητός," TDNT 1:37-39. Compare Spicq's overview of the instances of pre-LXX ἀγάπη and his reasons for rejecting them ("αγαπη," TLNT 1:14-15). Further, the *eros* word group appears relatively frequently in classical Greek, though never in the NT, but appears in the LXX a number of times. The oft-referred-to fourth Greek term for love, *storgos*, appears in the NT only as part of a compound (Rom 12:10).

[28]Trench, *Synonyms of the New Testament*, p. 43. Spicq also suggests that the colorless ἀγάπη was given a higher meaning in the LXX ("αγαπη," TLNT 1:11). So also Klassen, "Love in the NT," ABD 4:381; Stauffer, "αγαπάω, αγάπη, αγαπητός," TDNT 1:39, 36; Schneider, "αγαπη," EDNT 1:9. Some have suggested ἀγάπη was selected to avoid sexual connotations. So Morris, *Testaments of Love*, pp. 103, 125, 128. However, ἐράω, φιλέω and ἀγαπάω each may "denote sensual love" (Stählin, "φιλεω, καταφιλεω, φιλημα," TDNT 9:115). See 2 Sam 13:15; Lam 1:2.

[29]Robert Joly has compellingly argued that the increase in usage of the ἀγαπάω word group may be accounted for exclusively on the basis of diachronic linguistic shifts. The preference for this group was present in Hellenistic times; the change took place for linguistic reasons from the fourth century B.C. onward. Specifically, *philein* was moving from "love" to "kiss" (due to the disappearance of the older word for kiss—*kunein*), while *agapan* moved from "be content with" to "love," with some overlap with previous meanings (*Le vocabulaire chrétien de l'amour est-il original* [Brussels: Univ de Bruxelles, 1968], p. 33). So Moisés Silva, *Biblical Words and Their Meaning: An Introduction to Lexical Semantics* (Grand Rapids: Zondervan, 1995), p. 96; D. A. Carson, *Exegetical Fallacies* (Grand Rapids: Baker Academic, 1996), pp. 51-52. C. C. Tarelli suggested something similar prior to Joly in "Agapē," JTS 1, no. 1 (1950): 64-67. Compare Moffat, *Love in the New Testament*, p. 47.

[30]James Barr, "Words for Love in Biblical Greek," in *The Glory of Christ in the New Testament*, ed. L. D. Hurst and N. T. Wright (Oxford: Clarendon, 1987), p. 8.

Those who promote a qualitative difference between ἀγαπάω and φιλέω in the New Testament often appeal to John 21:15-17, wherein Jesus asks Peter three times, "Do you love Me?" In the first two instances, Jesus asks, "Do you ἀγαπάω me?" Yet, in the last instance Jesus asks, "Do you φιλέω me?" In all three instances, Peter replies affirmatively that he loves (φιλέω) Jesus. Some assert that in the first two forms of the question, Jesus is asking Peter whether he loves him with the highest, divine love of ἀγαπάω. Peter's response with φιλέω, they claim, suggests that he is unwilling to ascribe ἀγαπάω love to himself and therefore responds with the lesser φιλέω.[31] However, others have asserted that Jesus first asks whether Peter loves him with a weaker form of love (ἀγαπάω) and that Peter is actually asserting that he loves (φιλέω) Jesus with great passion and warmth of affection, which Jesus concedes in his third response.[32] Thus even scholars who suggest difference in the meaning of the terms disagree on the nature of that difference.

Conversely, many scholars conclude that the terms are used as roughly interchangeable terms (here and elsewhere) and that these verses reflect the typical stylistic variation used by John throughout his writings.[33] Thus Peter is upset not because of the language Christ uses but because Jesus repeats the same question three times, which he takes as a rebuke.[34] Commentators offer a number of reasons for this view. First, many believe that Christ would not have been speaking in Greek and thus the variations are John's stylistic rendering.[35] Second, the same verses also reflect stylistic variation of other

---

[31] So B. F. Westcott, *The Gospel According to St. John* (London: J. Murray, 1908), p. 303; Wuest, "Four Greek Words for Love," pp. 246-47; Spicq, *Agape* 3:95-96.

[32] So Trench, *Synonyms of the New Testament*, p. 43. Consider also the Vulgate translation of *diligere* and *amare* for ἀγαπάω and φιλέω in Jn 21.

[33] Johnston, "Love in the NT," *IDB* 3:177; Günther and Link, "αγαπαω," *NIDNTT* 2:542-43; Klassen, "Love in the NT," *ABD* 4:389; Rudolf Bultmann, *The Gospel of John* (Philadelphia: Westminster Press, 1971), p. 711n5; Marie-Joseph Lagrange, *Évangile selon saint Jean* (Paris: J. Gabalda, 1936), pp. 529-30; Moffat, *Love in the New Testament*, pp. 46-47. Kenneth L. McKay, however, argues that the variation is not merely stylistic but builds to a climax ("Style and Significance in the Language of John 21:15-17," *Novum Testamentum* 27 [1985]: 321-23, 332).

[34] Many believe that Jesus asks the question three times to parallel Peter's previous threefold denial and restore him. So D. A. Carson, *The Gospel According to John* (Grand Rapids: Eerdmans, 1991), p. 678; Morris, *Gospel According to John*, p. 772.

[35] So Carson, *Gospel According to John*, pp. 676-77; Morris, *Gospel According to John*, pp. 770-72; George R. Beasley-Murray, *John*, WBC (Dallas: Word, 2002), p. 394; Andreas J. Köstenberger, *John*, BECNT (Grand Rapids: Baker, 2004), p. 596; "αγαπαω, αγαπη," L&N 1:293; Günther and Link, "αγαπαω," *NIDNTT* 2:542-43; Moffat, *Love in the New Testament*, pp. 46-47; Raymond E. Brown, *The Gospel According to John XIII-XXI*, AB (Garden City, NY: Doubleday, 1979), p. 1103.

terms. Jesus says, "tend [βόσκω] My lambs [ἀρνίον]" (Jn 21:15), "shepherd [ποιμαίνω] My sheep [πρόβατον]" (Jn 21:16), and "tend [βόσκω] My sheep [πρόβατον]" (Jn 21:17).[36] Third, Peter answers both times, "Yes, Lord; You know that I love You" (Jn 21:15-16). If a distinction was at work, why didn't Peter say: "No, but I love you less (or more) than you are asking"?[37] Fourth, ἀγαπάω and φιλέω are used interchangeably (or nearly so) throughout the Johannine writings and the wider New Testament.

Even if nuance of meaning is intended in John 21 (which is not obvious but also cannot be conclusively ruled out), the wider usage of the terms suggests that they do not depict higher and lower loves. The meaning of the ἀγαπάω and φιλέω word groups, as used in the New Testament, overlap in nearly every respect. Both are used to describe the Father's love for the Son (Jn 3:35; 5:20), the Father's love for the disciples because of their love for Jesus (Jn 14:21, 23; 16:27), Jesus' love for humans (Rev 3:9, 19), Jesus' love for individuals (Jn 11:5, 36), human love for Jesus (Mt 10:37; Jn 14:21, 23; 16:27), human love for other humans (Jn 15:17, 19) and human love for their own life (Jn 12:25; Rev 12:11), and both terms describe the disciple whom Jesus loves (Jn 20:2; 13:23).[38] Furthermore, both are used of preferential love (Mt 10:37; Jn 11:5; 13:1; 20:2), misdirected love (Mt 23:6; Lk 20:46; 22:15; Rev 22:15; 2 Tim 4:10; compare Is 56:10; Prov 21:17), conditionally reciprocal divine love (Jn 14:21, 23; 16:27; compare Prov 8:17; Jas 4:4), emotion and/or passion (Jn 11:36; 13:1; compare Jas 4:4), pleasure, enjoyment and/or evaluative love (Mt 3:17; 6:5; 17:5; 23:6; compare Gen 27:4, 9, 14), familial (Mt 10:37; Col 3:19; compare Gen 37:3-4) and other insider love (Jn 13:1; 15:14-15), and love that includes discipline (Heb 12:6; Rev 3:19). In many other instances the ἀγαπάω and

---

[36]See Carson, *Gospel According to John*, pp. 676-77; Morris, *Gospel According to John*, pp. 771-72; Beasley-Murray, *John*, p. 394; Köstenberger, *John*, p. 596; "αγαπαω, αγαπη," L&N 1:293; Günther and Link, "αγαπαω," *NIDNTT* 2:542-43; Moffat, *Love in the New Testament*, pp. 46-47. Compare Edwin D. Freed, "Variations in the Language and Thought of John," *ZNW* 55, nos. 3-4 (1964): 192-93.

[37]As J. H. Bernard puts it, "Why should he say 'Yes,' if he means 'No'?" (*A Critical and Exegetical Commentary on the Gospel According to St. John* [New York: C. Scribner's Sons, 1929], 2:704).

[38]The only subject-object relations of love that are not described by the verb φιλέω are human love for the Father and Jesus' love for the Father. With regard to the latter, Jesus' love for the Father is only explicitly stated once in the entire NT. Regarding the former, the compound φιλόθεος does describe "lovers of God" (2 Tim 3:4), and the noun refers to Abraham as the "friend [φίλος] of God" (Jas 2:23; cf. Jas 4:4). Compare the expectation of human φιλέω toward God/Jesus in 1 Cor 16:22.

φιλέω word groups collocate with closely related meanings and share a common Old Testament background and overlapping LXX usage (both translating אהב; see below).[39]

Thus, although the word groups are not identical in every respect, both ἀγαπάω and φιλέω may refer to the highest and noblest aspects of love or to inferior qualities such as misdirected love.[40] As D. A. Carson states, "There is nothing intrinsic to the verb ἀγαπάω (*agapao*) or the noun ἀγάπη (*agape*) to prove its real meaning or hidden meaning refers to some special kind of love."[41] God's love is always perfect, but the terminology of love (whether by ἀγαπάω or φιλέω) does not by itself connote perfect love. As Carson puts it, "Doubtless God's love is immeasurably richer than ours, in ways still to be explored, but they belong to the same genus, or the parallelisms could not be drawn."[42]

The Wider Semantics of Love in Scripture

אהב, *the forerunner of* **ἀγάπη.** אהב is the most prominent Old Testament word for love and overlaps the primary aspects of love that may be denoted by ἀγαπάω, being used to refer to everything from the most virtuous love of affection and generosity to lust that fades quickly after its rapacious selfishness is satisfied.[43] The אהב word group often denotes affection or fondness

---

[39]See Jn 15:13-14, 17-19; 1 Thess 4:9; 1 Pet 1:22. Moreover, Christians are the φίλοι (3 Jn 14) as well as the ἀγαπητός (3 Jn 2, 5, 11). In the LXX, both terms are used to translate אהב, including Jacob's preferential love for Joseph (Gen 37:3-4) and when "wisdom" states "I love [ἀγαπάω] those who love [φιλέω] me" (Prov 8:17; cf. Prov 21:17). Josephus also alternates the terms stylistically.

[40]Many scholars consider the terms synonymous in most cases, while recognizing minor differences in the semantic range. See Carson, *Exegetical Fallacies*, pp. 51-52; Stählin, "φιλεω, καταφιλεω, φιλημα," *TDNT* 9:115-16, 24; Raymond E. Brown, *The Gospel According to John I-XII* (Garden City, NY: Doubleday, 1966), p. 498; William Hendriksen, *The Gospel According to John* (Grand Rapids: Baker, 1953), 2:487, 494-500; Köstenberger, *John*, p. 596; Günther and Link, "αγαπαω," *NIDNTT* 2:543. For example, of personal love the verb φιλέω is always used in the NT within an associative relationship of some commonality, i.e., "insider love," whereas ἀγαπάω may signify both "insider" and "outsider" love (most often the former). However, the φιλέω word group includes love for the other (including the stranger) in the compound terms φιλόξενος and φιλοξενία (1 Tim 3:2; Rom 12:13; Heb 13:2; cf. Mt 11:19; Lk 7:34). Considering the smaller sample size and fallacy of arguments from silence, it would be unwise to draw conclusions from the way a term is *not* used in the NT.

[41]Carson, *Exegetical Fallacies*, p. 32.

[42]D. A. Carson, *The Difficult Doctrine of the Love of God* (Wheaton, IL: Crossway, 2000), p. 48.

[43]The verb אהב appears 215 times in 200 verses, and the noun אהבה 37 times in 34 verses. In the LXX, the verb אהב is translated by ἀγαπάω in the vast majority of the LXX occurrences of ἀγαπάω (over 160 times; φιλέω, φίλος, ἐράω and ἐραστής also translate it in some instances), and the

for its object, whether romance, lust, desire, friendship, preference, acceptance, delight and devotion with corresponding action, among other things.[44] Although אהב does not necessarily refer to positive, noble or appropriate love in and of itself (e.g., Gen 34:3; 2 Sam 13:1, 4, 15), with divine agency the word group always manifests perfect love.

Akin to the agapist view, some scholars have suggested that God's אהב is unilaterally willed, unconditional election love.[45] Eugene Merrill views both love (אהב) and election (בחר) as "technical terms" that are "virtually synonymous" such that "'to love' is to choose, and 'to choose' is to love."[46] Furthermore, some have contended on the basis of parallels to ancient Near Eastern language usage that אהב (at least in Deuteronomy) is a technical term for nonemotional loyalty within a purely legal, covenant relationship.[47] However, the Old Testament use of אהב raises significant questions regarding both of these claims. First, although אהב contains a very significant volitional aspect (e.g., Hos 14:4 [5]) and can be commanded, it is not identical to choice.[48] Love is the basis of election, not its equivalent; *because* God loved the patriarchs, he chose Israel (Deut 4:37; compare Deut 7:7-13; 10:15).[49]

---

noun ἀγάπη is the term used most often to translate the Hebrew noun אהבה (15 times in 14 verses; ἀγάπησις and φιλία are also used numerous times) and is not used to translate anything else in the LXX. A few other terms translate אהב once. It thus "covers all the wealth of the three Greek terms" but, in contrast to ancient Near Eastern cults, never refers to "religious eroticism" (Stauffer, "αγαπάω, αγάπη, αγαπητός," *TDNT* 1:38).

[44]See Ernst Jenni, "אהב," *TLOT* 1:46; P. J. J. S. Els, "אהב," *NIDOTTE* 1:277-99; Arnulf Bergman, A. O. Haldar and Gerhard Wallis, "אהב," *TDOT* 1:99-118.

[45]Norman H. Snaith, *The Distinctive Ideas of the Old Testament* (London: Epworth, 1962), pp. 13, 95, 134; Morris, *Testaments of Love*, p. 31; Pieter A. Verhoef, *The Books of Haggai and Malachi*, NICOT (Grand Rapids: Eerdmans, 1987), pp. 196-97; Els, "אהב," *NIDOTTE* 1:280; Larry R. Walker, "'Love' in the Old Testament: Some Lexical Observations," in *Current Issues in Biblical and Patristic Interpretation*, ed. Gerald F. Hawthorne (Grand Rapids: Eerdmans, 1975), pp. 287-88.

[46]Eugene H. Merrill, *Deuteronomy*, NAC 4 (Nashville: B&H, 1994), p. 132. Compare Cranfield, "Love," p. 132.

[47]William L. Moran, "The Ancient Near Eastern Background of the Love of God in Deuteronomy," *CBQ* 25 (1963): 78. The central premises of this seminal study of אהב in Deuteronomy have been adopted and expanded over the years. See, for instance, Susan Ackerman, "The Personal Is Political: Covenantal and Affectionate Love ('āhēb, 'ahăbâ) in the Hebrew Bible," *VT* 52, no. 4 (2002): 440; Els, "אהב," *NIDOTTE* 1:285-87; Dennis McCarthy, "Notes on the Love of God in Deuteronomy and the Father-Son Relationship Between Yahweh and Israel," *CBQ* 27 (1965): 144-45; J. W. McKay, "Man's Love for God in Deuteronomy and the Father/Teacher-Son/Pupil Relationship," *VT* 22, no. 4 (1972): 426-35; J. A. Thompson, "Israel's 'Lovers,'" *VT* 27, no. 4 (1977): 475-81; Walker, "'Love' in the Old Testament," pp. 283-84.

[48]אהב collocates with בחר, "to choose, elect," in five verses, all with love as the basis of God's election of Israel/Judah (Deut 4:37; 10:15; Is 41:8; Ps 47:4 [5]; 78:68). Compare chap. 4 below.

[49]אהב as the basis of election is widely recognized. See, among others, William A. Dyrness, *Themes*

Further, divine אהב is often explicitly evaluative rather than the result of arbitrary divine choice. Thus God loves the righteous (Ps 146:8) and the pursuer of justice (Prov 15:9; compare Is 61:8; Ps 11:7; 33:5; 37:28).[50] Moreover, although divine אהב is everlasting (Jer 31:3) it is also frequently depicted as conditional and cannot, then, be the product of unilateral election (Deut 7:12-13; Hos 9:15; Ps 146:8; Prov 15:9).[51] While the majority of instances support Susan Ackerman's position that אהב is used one-sidedly since the agent is "typically the hierarchically superior party in the relationship," there are counterexamples such as Ruth to Naomi (Ruth 4:15) and the slave's love of his master (Ex 21:5; Deut 15:16).[52] Further, God himself expects and receives reciprocal (but not symmetrical) love as evidenced in the abundant expressions of divine אהב toward human beings (Deut 4:37; 7:13; 10:15; 1 Kings 3:3; Is 43:4; Ps 146:8) coupled with the many divine commands for humans to love God (Deut 6:5; 10:12; 11:1, 13; 13:3 [4]; 30:6; Josh 22:5; 23:11; Ps 31:23 [24]) and instances of actual human love for God (Ex 20:6; Judg 5:31; 1 Kings 3:3; Ps 97:10; 116:1; 145:20; compare Is 41:8; 2 Chron 20:7).[53]

---

in *Old Testament Theology* (Downers Grove, IL: InterVarsity Press, 1979), p. 59; Gordon R. Clark, *The Word Hesed in the Hebrew Bible* (Sheffield: JSOT Press, 1993), p. 263; Wallis, "אהב," *TDOT* 1:104.

[50]The evaluative aspect is also apparent in the close collocation of אהב with evaluative pleasure and/or delight (חפץ in 1 Sam 18:22; Ps 34:12 [13]; 109:17; רצה/רצון in Prov 3:12; 16:13 and many others; e.g., Zeph 3:17) as well as its contrast with evaluative hatred (שנא; see Is 61:8; Zech 8:17; Amos 5:15) and the frequent attention given to misdirected love (e.g., Ps 4:2; Zech 8:17; Amos 5:15; Hos 3:1; 9:1, 10).

[51]See the discussion of this tension in chap. 7 (below).

[52]Ackerman, "The Personal is Political," p. 447. Ackerman unconvincingly explains the former as Ruth having become the superior by marriage and childbearing and the latter as merely a utilitarian expression. Compare Thompson, "Israel's 'Lovers.'" Other possible counterexamples include the love between David and Jonathan (1 Sam 20:17; 2 Sam 1:26), the love of women toward men in Song 1:3-4, 7; 3:1-4, and ultimately the love from humans toward God (see examples above).

[53]Els notes that the root is "used 27x when God loves persons, as against 24x when persons love God" ("אהב," *NIDOTTE* 1:279). Moreover, אהב often collocates with חסד, "steadfast love" or "lovingkindness," in repeated statements that God reciprocates חסד toward humans who love him (Ex 20:6; Deut 5:10; 7:9; Neh 1:5; Dan 9:4). However, some scholars have marginalized the instances of human love toward God by suggesting that all (or nearly all) are the result of the so-called Deuteronomistic tradition. See Snaith, *Distinctive Ideas of the Old Testament*, p. 133; Claude Wiener, *Recherches sur L'Amour pour Dieu dans L'Ancien Testament* (Paris: Letouzey Et Ane, 1957). However, reduction of religious אהב to the Deuteronomist tradition founders on at least two points. First, not all of the instances are found in writings generally ascribed to the Deuteronomist(s). See Judg 5:31; Ps 5:11 [12]; 69:36 [37]; Jer 2:2; and perhaps even Ex 20:6. See Els, "אהב," *NIDOTTE* 1:283. Second, attribution of writings to the Deuteronomist tradition hinges on disputed, speculative reconstructions, some of which find the "Deuteronomist" nearly

Second, although אהב is often (but not always) covenantal, covenant language is itself grounded in the more basic language of affective kinship relationships. Duane Smith notes that we "must not suppose" that "biblical covenants borrowed their kinship language from the social world of treaties. Both the language of biblical covenant and treaty language developed in a social environment in which kinship was the primary model for understanding all human interaction" such that ancient Near Eastern treaties and covenants "used kinship to describe their content."[54] Thus, "the root [אהב] is first and foremost a kinship term."[55] As R. Laird Harris further explains, "kings borrowed" the word love "from general use to try to render covenants effective. They tried to make the vassal promise to act like a brother, friend and husband. It does not follow that God's love is merely a factor in a covenant; rather the covenant is the sign and expression of his love."[56] Thus, as Jacqueline Lapsley puts it, love language "is imported into the political realm from family life, where it originated," and "its emotional connotation in that context is transferred to the political context in the borrowing."[57]

Hence, covenant contexts do not reduce אהב to nonemotional loyalty. Rather, love is the prior basis of covenant (Deut 4:37; 1 Sam 18:3), and אהב "decidedly involves the emotions."[58] Divine אהב is explicitly emotional in

---

everywhere. See Linda S. Schearing and Steven L. McKenzie, eds., *Those Elusive Deuteronomists: The Phenomenon of Pan-Deuteronomism*, JSOT Supplement (Sheffield: Sheffield Academic, 1999).

[54]Duane Smith, "Kinship and Covenant in Hosea 11:1-4," *HBT* 16 (1994): 49. Moshe Weinfeld adds that the "whole diplomatic vocabulary of the second millennium is rooted in the familial sphere" ("The Covenant of Grant in the Old Testament and in the Ancient Near East," *JAOS* 90, no. 2 [1970]: 194).

[55]Smith, "Kinship and Covenant," p. 43. Scott Hahn has also compellingly demonstrated this in *Kinship by Covenant: A Canonical Approach to the Fulfillment of God's Saving Promises* (New Haven, CT: Yale University Press, 2009). So also Frank Moore Cross, *From Epic to Canon: History and Literature in Ancient Israel* (Baltimore: Johns Hopkins University Press, 1998), p. 5; Leo Perdue, "The Household, Old Testament, and Contemporary Hermeneutics," in *Families in Ancient Israel*, ed. Leo G. Perdue et al. (Louisville: Westminster John Knox, 1989), p. 240.

[56]R. Laird Harris, "חסד," *TWOT*, p. 306. Compare Clark, *Hesed*, p. 128; Richard D. Patterson, "Parental Love as a Metaphor for Divine-Human Love," *JETS* 46, no. 2 (2003): 208. Despite structural similarity, there is significant difference between God's covenant love and that of other ancient Near Eastern treaties. As Ernest W. Nicholson states, it would have been "distasteful and counterproductive to tell the Israelites that God 'loves' them in the same way as a suzerain (e.g. Ashurbanipal or Nebuchadrezzar) 'loves' his vassals and that they are to 'love' Yahweh as vassals 'love' their suzerains" (*God and His People: Covenant and Theology in the Old Testament* [Oxford: Oxford University Press, 1986], p. 79).

[57]Jacqueline Lapsley, "Feeling Our Way: Love for God in Deuteronomy," *CBQ* 65, no. 3 (2003): 355.

[58]Ibid., p. 354. Gottfried Quell adds that אהב "hardly ever loses its passionate note" ("Love in the OT," *TDNT* 1:23). Similarly, Katharine Sakenfeld, "Loyalty and Love: The Language of Human

many instances, including covenantal contexts (Hos 3:1; compare Hos 11:1, 8-9).[59] God passionately loves his people (compare Ex 20:5-6; Deut 4:23-24; Hos 11:1-9) and expects humans to love him wholeheartedly in return (Deut 6:5; 10:13; 11:13; 13:3; 30:6; Josh 22:5).[60] The centrality of love (אהב) to family relationships, on which the covenant framework stands, explains the significant overlap between the metaphors of covenant, marriage and parent-child relationships (Ezek 16:33-37; Hos 3:1; 11:1, 4; 14:5 et al.). Thus divine אהב is not unilateral or purely willed election love, and neither is it a legal commitment devoid of emotion. It is volitional but also evaluative, emotional, conditional and expectant of a reciprocal response. These aspects also appear in various other important biblical terms that relate closely to divine love.

חסד *and New Testament counterparts—steadfast love and mercy.* חסד is one of the most significant descriptors of God's character in the canon; it is a purely relational term that is often translated as lovingkindness, steadfast love, loyalty, goodness, faithfulness and mercy (among others).[61]

Interconnections in the Hebrew Bible," in *Backgrounds for the Bible*, ed. Michael P. O'Connor and David Noel Freedman (Winona Lake, IN: Eisenbrauns, 1987), p. 225; Georg Hentschel, "'Weil der Herr euch liebt . . .' (Dtn 7, 8): Die Liebe im Ersten Testament," *Internationale katholische Zeitschrift* 23, no. 5 (1994): 400-408. This is supported by the close collocation of אהב with language of emotionality, including: the seat of emotions (נפש and לב/לבב; Ps 11:5; 119:167), pleasure and/or delight (חפץ, 1 Sam 18:22; Ps 34:12 [13]; 109:17; רצה/רצון, Prov 3:12; 16:13; חשק, Deut 10:15; cf. Gen 34:3, 8; Ps 119:47 and many others; Zeph 3:17), compassion (חמל; Is 63:9), passion/zeal (קנאה), lovingkindness (חסד, Ex 20:6 et al.), and its frequent contrast with hatred (שנא; Gen 37:4; 2 Sam 13:15; Mal 1:2-3; Eccles 9:6). Edmund Jacob thus speaks of "the sense of ardent and voluntary desire contained in the root *'ahab*," which is confirmed by comparison to other roots such as חפץ, חשק and רצה (*Theology of the Old Testament* [New York: Harper & Row, 1958], p. 109). Compare Wallis, "אהב," *TDOT* 1:102. The intense passion of God's love for his people is further depicted by divine קנא (Ex 20:5-6; Deut 5:9-10; 6:15). See chap. 6 below.

[59]Moshe Weinfeld notes both the "affection and emotion" in the love between God and Israel in the midst of "covenantal overtones" (*Deuteronomy 1-11*, AB 5 [New York: Doubleday, 1991], pp. 351, 369).

[60]Some have struggled with the concept of "love" that can be commanded and have thus divested it of emotion. See McKay, "Man's Love for God in Deuteronomy," p. 426; Quell, "Love in the OT," *TDOT* 1:25. However, Jeffrey H. Tigay rightly clarifies that אהב "covers the whole range of human affection: sexual love, love of friendship, and love for God. It is more than a voluntary expression of the emotions. It can be commanded, and it expresses itself in concrete acts of obedience to law." Further, the "idea of commanding a feeling is not foreign to the Torah, which assumes that people can cultivate proper attitudes" (*Deuteronomy* [Philadelphia: JPS, 1996], p. 76). So Lapsley, "Feeling Our Way," p. 365. God thus despises merely external ritual and outward observance of his commands (e.g., Is 51:16-17, 19). The external action of obedience must correspond to an internal, emotive devotion. So Els, "אהב," *NIDOTTE* 1:286.

[61]חסד occurs 251 times in 245 verses, primarily in noun form. The verb form appears only in identical verses (2 Sam 22:26 = Ps 18:25 [26]).

Throughout the Old Testament, חסד refers to beneficial relational conduct and/or attitude in accord with the highest virtues (love, loyalty, goodness, kindness), which meets and exceeds all expectations (often manifested in mercy and forgiveness), in which the agent (divine or human) is ontologically free to will to act otherwise and is responsive to and/or creates or maintains the expectation (but not hard obligation) of appropriate response from the recipient.[62] At its core, חסד includes voluntary, positive disposition and/or action toward another.[63] Perhaps Donald Gowan puts it best when he writes that חסד "cannot be adequately translated by anything short of a paragraph."[64]

God's חסד manifests his character of love, compassion, goodness, faithfulness and justice.[65] It often appears within the context of covenant relationship, but it is not restricted to covenant or any other formalized relationship.[66] Even within covenant contexts חסד may operate outside as well as above and beyond covenant restrictions.[67] God's חסד both grounds covenant

---

[62]See Hans-Jürgen Zobel, "חסד," *TDOT* 5:44-64; H. J. Stoebe, "חסד," *TLOT* 1:449-64; Harris, "חסד," *TWOT*, pp. 305-7; D. A. Baer and R. P. Gordon, "חסד," *NIDOTTE* 2:211-18; Clark, *Hesed*; Nelson Glueck, *Hesed in the Bible* (Cincinnati: Hebrew Union College, 1967); Katharine Sakenfeld, *The Meaning of Hesed in the Hebrew Bible: A New Inquiry* (Missoula, MT: Scholars Press, 1978).

[63]Many scholars see an emotional aspect as a connotation of חסד. Clark spoke of it as "an emotion that leads to activity beneficial to the recipient" (*Hesed*, p. 267). Zobel also sees חסד as "involv[ing] an emotional element," even early, which becomes clear in its association with רחם ("חסד," *TDOT* 5:53).

[64]Donald Gowan, *Theology in Exodus* (Louisville: Westminster John Knox, 1994), p. 236.

[65]חסד is closely associated and collocates significantly with all the divine virtues, including his love (אהב; Ex 20:6; Jer 2:2; 31:3; Ps 31:23; 37:28), compassion (רחם; Ex 34:6; Is 54:8-10; 63:7; Hos 2:19 [21]; Joel 2:13; Jon 4:2; Ps 25:6; Lam 3:22, 32) and goodness (טוב; Jer 33:11; Ps 69:16; 1 Chron 16:34), which are manifested in his voluntary association with humanity. God's goodness, commitment, reliability, steadfastness and fidelity to the objects of his חסד are further emphasized in the frequent collocations of חסד with אמת (Gen 24:27; Ex 34:6; Ps 85:10 [11]; 89:14 [15]), אמן (Deut 7:9) or אמונה (Ps 36:5; 98:3), all of which connote aspects of truth and faithfulness. Divine חסד is also closely associated with justice, evident especially in collocations with צדק and משפט (Ps 33:5; 89:14 [15]; Is 16:5; Jer 9:23 [24]; Hos 2:19 [21]). Thus חסד overlaps with both mercy and forgiveness, on the one hand, and justice on the other, tying them together (Ps 85:10).

[66]Many scholars recognize that חסד is not restricted to covenant, including Zobel, "חסד," *TDOT* 5:53, 61; Harris, "חסד," *TWOT*, pp. 306-7; Katharine Sakenfeld, "Love in the OT," *ABD* 4:379; Stoebe, "חסד," *TLOT* 1:455, 60; Clark, *Hesed*, p. 192; Thomas M. Raitt, "Why Does God Forgive?" *HBT* 13 (1991): 54; Alfred Jepsen, "Gnade und Barmherzigkeit," *Kerygma und Dogma* 7 (1961): 265; Morris, *Testaments of Love*, p. 69. Contra the mistaken claims in Glueck, *Hesed in the Bible*, p. 102; Snaith, *Distinctive Ideas of the Old Testament*, pp. 94-95, 98. See, for example, Job 10:12.

[67]חסד extends beyond the covenant people in numerous examples, manifesting its universality (Ruth 1:8; Jon 4:2; Ps 33:5; 117:1-2; 119:64; 145:8-9; cf. 2 Sam 15:20). Compare Sakenfeld, "Love in the OT," *ABD* 4:379. Contra Clark, *Hesed*, p. 145.

and consistently goes far beyond responsibilities and reasonable expectations (covenant, moral or otherwise).[68] Human action often warrants the rupture of the divine-human relationship, yet divine חסד grounds forgiveness and thus often connotes mercy (though it is more than mercy). God would have remained entirely just had he withdrawn חסד and compassion from Israel after its egregious golden calf apostasy (Ex 32). Yet God revealed his character as the one "abounding in lovingkindness [חסד] and truth" and "compassionate and gracious, slow to anger" (Ex 34:6), the one "who keeps lovingkindness [חסד] for thousands," the forgiver of all kinds of sin while also upholding justice (Ex 34:7; compare Jer 9:23; Ps 85:10; 89:14). God bestows חסד freely but not arbitrarily. In many instances (such as covenant) God has committed himself to certain voluntary responsibilities (soft obligations) to which his faithfulness is unparalleled. Yet, while such covenants create divine responsibility that calls for חסד (a soft obligation), God is never externally obligated to bestow חסד (a hard obligation).[69] God's חסד is always a manifestation of his free and voluntary association with humanity (Gen 19:19; 24:12, 27; 32:10; 2 Sam 7:15).[70]

Divine חסד is thus unmerited and exceeds all duties, yet it is not altogether unconditional. God's חסד is repeatedly characterized as everlasting (Jer 33:11; Ps 136) on the one hand, and yet it may be forfeited and withdrawn (Jer 16:5; compare Ps 77:8; 88:11; 89:49).[71] Divine חסד is extremely steadfast,

---

[68]This surpassing and superabounding aspect is magnified in the phrases "abundance of חסד" (Ex 34:6; Is 63:7) and "greatness of חסד" (Gen 19:19; Ps 145:8).

[69]A hard obligation is the sort of obligation that is enforceable and, as such, is binding with regard to external factors, while a soft obligation refers to responsibilities that may include expectations but are not enforceable and thus always maintain volitional freedom (e.g., the Israelites' failure to show חסד to Gideon's descendants in Judg 8:35). Thus, as Gerald Larue points out, "passages, such as Ps. 25:6, 7; 106:1, 7, 45; 107:1, 8, 15, 21, 31; 138:8, suggest that Yahweh ought to show *hesed* as a moral imperative to a distressed people or else fall short of moral responsibilities" ("Recent Studies in Hesed," in Glueck, *Hesed in the Bible*, p. 4). Compare Sakenfeld, *Meaning of Hesed*, p. 234.

[70]As such, חסד is not restricted to "mutually obligatory relationship," as Glueck suggests (*Hesed in the Bible*, p. 55). Sakenfeld rightly points out that the request or situational expectation of חסד is always one the potential grantor could deny; חסד cannot "be required or compelled" (*Meaning of Hesed*, pp. 45, 176, 234). Compare Stoebe, "חסד," *TLOT* 1:454-55; Harris, "חסד," *TWOT*, p. 305; Jepsen, "Gnade und Barmherzigkeit."

[71]Zobel suggests חסד is "characterized by permanence and reliability" ("חסד," *TDOT* 5:57). Compare Snaith, *Distinctive Ideas of the Old Testament*, p. 102. However, Baer and Gordon acknowledge that "Numerous texts witness to at least the hypothetical possibility of losing God's חסד or of having it taken away" ("חסד," *NIDOTTE* 2:215). Compare Gen 24:27; Ps 36:10 [11]; 77:8; 88:11; 106:45; 2 Chron 6:42.

reliable and enduring, yet, as Sakenfeld puts it, "God's *ḥesed* is conditional, dependent upon the good repair of the covenant relationship that it is up to Israel to maintain" (compare Deut 7:9, 12; 2 Sam 22:26; 1 Kings 8:23; Ps 25:10; 32:10; 2 Chron 6:14).[72] Thus divine חסד is "from everlasting to everlasting on those who fear Him" (Ps 103:17).

Indeed, חסד (divine or human) presumes relational responsiveness toward or within reciprocal (though often unequal) relationship. חסד may (1) respond to חסד (Gen 21:23; Josh 2:12-14), (2) respond to another previous positive action or preexisting relationship (Gen 20:13; 24:49; 47:29; 1 Sam 20:8, 14-15; 2 Sam 3:8; 9:1, 3, 7), or (3) initiate a relationship, which expects appropriate future response (1 Sam 15:6; 2 Chron 24:22). Thus חסד always operates within a context of relational, voluntary, reciprocal (though often unequal) responsibility. God himself responds with חסד to the thousandth generation of those who love (אהב) him and keep his commandments (Ex 20:6; Deut 5:10; compare Deut 7:9; Neh 1:5; Dan 9:4).

Although some scholars deny the reciprocal nature of חסד, contending that humans never direct חסד toward God, often alongside the supposition that humans cannot benefit God, some cases do exhibit human חסד toward God.[73] For example, God remembers "the devotion [חסד] of your youth, the love [אהב] of your betrothals" (Jer 2:2; compare Is 40:6; Hos 6:4; Neh 13:14; 2 Chron 32:32; 35:26).[74] As an aspect of God's character of goodness, God's

---

[72]Sakenfeld, "Love in the OT," *ABD* 4:379.

[73]Zobel, "חסד," *TDOT* 1:61-63; Clark, *Hesed*, pp. 259, 67; Jepsen, "Gnade und Barmherzigkeit," pp. 268-69. Complementing this objection is the assertion that חסד flows from superior to inferior. So Michael Fox, *Proverbs 1-9*, AB 18A (New York: Doubleday, 2000), p. 144. However, while the majority of instances appear to flow from a superior to inferior (with regard to status), there are many examples in human interpersonal usage of either the request or bestowal of חסד from a societal inferior to a societal superior (Gen 20:13; Josh 2:12-14; 2 Sam 2:5; 3:8; 16:17; 2 Chron 24:22; cf. 1 Sam 20:8, 14-15). Further, the disproportionate number of "instances of *hesed* as a divine characteristic" may skew a conception of חסד as only from superior to inferior, since "*ḥesed*, when used of God, will, by definition, involve relationships of superior and inferior" (Baer and Gordon, "חסד," *NIDOTTE* 2:212).

[74]Numerous scholars recognize examples of human חסד toward God, including Glueck, *Hesed in the Bible*, pp. 56-63; Baer and Gordon, "חסד," *NIDOTTE* 2:213; Snaith, *Distinctive Ideas of the Old Testament*, p. 128; Stoebe, "חסד," *TLOT* 1:458-59. Sakenfeld thinks that human חסד toward God appears in every instance of חסד in Hosea (Hos 2:19 [21]; 4:1; 6:4; 10:12; 12:7; "Love in the OT," *ABD* 4:380). In a number of these and other potential cases of human חסד toward God, the object of חסד is unclear (Mic 6:8; Hos 10:12; 12:6 [7]; Zech 7:9; Prov 3:3-4). That God expects human חסד is apparent in that he laments the people's lack of חסד (Hos 4:1; cf. Hos 6:6). Although it is possible that the object is merely other humans, it seems likely that, in many such

חסד exhibits God's never-failing goodness and steadfast love, which he expects humans to emulate. It is not mere clemency or beneficence but consists of always doing what is best, righteous and just, always and without fail.

The ἐλεέω word group is the closely relating, but not identical, New Testament counterpart of חסד.[75] ἐλεέω may refer to mercy, lovingkindness, heartfelt concern, compassion and/or sympathy of a strongly emotive character, often explicitly manifested in action.[76] It is frequently used of God's wonderful, abundant and enduring, but not thereby unconditional, lovingkindness, compassion and/or mercy (compare Lk 1:50, 58; Ps 102:17).[77] Divine ἐλεέω is undeserved (Tit 3:5), consistently active (Eph 2:4; 1 Pet 1:3) and often manifests emotionality (Lk 1:78; compare Lk 10:33, 37) as well as conditionality—at times the reception of divine mercy is conditional on humans bestowing mercy to one another (Lk 1:50; 1 Tim 1:13; Gal 6:16; Jude 21).[78] The range of this word group thus corresponds with that of loving-

---

instances, both relations with God and fellow humans are in view (cf. Prov 19:17). Elsewhere, idolaters are characterized as those who "forsake their חסד" (Jon 2:8). Since idolatry is a sin against God himself, this text implies that humans ought to maintain their חסד toward him in true worship. Finally, the adjective חָסִיד also appears to be a manifestation of human חסד in relationship to God. For instance, "with the kind" (חָסִיד) God shows himself "kind" (חסד) (2 Sam 22:26 = Ps 18:25 [26]), and the חָסִיד should love God (Ps 31:23 [24]; cf. Ps 37:28; 97:10).

[75]The noun ἔλεος translates חסד over 200 times in the LXX (e.g., Ex 20:6; 34:7; Deut 7:9), and the adjectives of the word group also translate the חסד word group at times (Jer 3:12; Prov 11:17; 20:6; cf. Prov 28:22). ἔλεος also translates the רחם word group (6 times), תְּחִנָּה, favor, supplication (6 times), צְדָקָה, righteousness (3 times) and חן, favor, grace (2 times), as well as a number of other terms once. Conversely, beyond its rendering by ἔλεος, חסד is translated 9 times by the closely related πολυέλεος, "abundant mercy," and 9 times by δικαιοσύνη, righteousness (cf. Gen 19:19), among a number of others once. The verb ἐλεέω most often translates חנן (38 times), often of divine graciousness in collocation with divine compassion (רחם/οἰκτιρμός, Ex 33:19). ἐλεέω also often translates words of compassion רחם (25 times as well as חמל 7 times and רחם 5 times), often of God, and other terms once. The adjective ἐλεήμων translates חסד twice and a number of other terms once but usually translates חנון (12 times), especially in the statements that God is "merciful and gracious" (οἰκτίρμων καί ἐλεήμων; Ex 34:6 et al.).

[76]Spicq calls it "fundamentally a species of love," usually of God ("ελεεω, ελεος," TLNT 1:475). See also H. H. Esser, "ελεος," NIDNTT 2:594; Rudolf Bultmann, "ελεος, ελεεω," TDNT 2:483, 85. In secular Greek usage ἔλεος signified intense emotion, often prompted by the affliction of another for which one feels mercy and/or sympathy. Greek thought considered such emotion (πάθος) inferior, but in the LXX ἔλεος is "exalted" and "becomes a religious virtue and especially a divine attribute" (Spicq, "ελεεω, ελεος," TLNT 1:473). Compare Bultmann, "ελεος, ελεεω," TDNT 2:477-78.

[77]The word group collocates with the ἀγαπάω word group, with significant overlap, in Eph 2:4; 2 Tim 1:2; Jude 2, 21; 2 Jn 3. In the LXX, the terms also collocate in many instances, including as translations of God's lovingkindness to those who love God, the former translated by ελεος and the latter by ἀγαπάω (Ex 20:6 et al.).

[78]The group never explicitly refers to ἐλεέω/ἔλεος from a situationally inferior toward a situation-

kindness (חסד) and overlaps significantly with the Old Testament and New Testament terminology of compassion, to which we now turn.[79]

רחם *and New Testament counterparts—compassionate love.* The רחם word group generally refers to intense, profoundly emotional, compassionate love manifested in beneficent action (when appropriate), most often of God.[80] It is believed to be based on the word for womb (רֶחֶם) and accordingly corresponds to a "womb-like mother love."[81] רחם is often explicitly affected and/or aroused, a "feelings word" that "denotes strong emotion" that is responsive to the actual state of affairs (e.g., Gen 43:30; 1 Kings 3:26; Ps 103:13).[82] It includes mercy but is more than mercy; it is an emotional love, a compassionate affection that God manifests in merciful, nonobligatory action that far surpasses responsibilities and reasonable expectations. Gottfried Quell thus calls it "the strongest word for love that biblical language has."[83]

רחם is fundamental to God's character of compassionate love, which surpasses even a mother's tender feelings for her child (Is 49:15; 63:15; Jer 31:20; Ps 103:13) and is reflected in freely given, unmerited, corresponding action

---

ally superior in the NT, including human mercy toward God—though God desires mercy (Mt 9:13; 12:7, both OT allusions translating חסד). Some instances of expectation of human to human ἔλεος are likely to be understood as indirect ἔλεος toward God (cf. Mt 5:7; Jas 2:13).

[79]The association between the ἐλεέω, οἰκτίρω and σπλαγχνίζομαι word groups is so significant that Esser groups them together in "Mercy, Compassion," *NIDNTT* 2:593. In the NT, the ἐλεέω word group overlaps significantly with the οἰκτιρμος word group, "compassion, pity," especially as it relates to the notion of sympathy for someone else's hardship (Rom 9:15). Rudolf Bultmann goes so far as to say: "There is no palpable distinction between" the word groups in the LXX ("οἰκτιρω, οἰκτιρμος, οἰκτιρμων," *TDNT* 5:160). In the LXX, the two collocate in many significant instances, including Ex 33:19; 34:6 and many other instances where רחם (translated by οἰκτίρω) and חסד (translated by ἐλεέω) collocate. The ἐλεέω word group also collocates once with σπλάγχνον (Lk 1:78) and twice in the LXX (Odes 9:18; Prov 12:10).

[80]The word group appears in the nominal רחמים (37 verses), verbal רחם (43 verses), two forms of adjectival רחום (13 verses) and once as רַחֲמָנִי (Lam 4:10). See Stoebe, "רחם," *TLOT* 3:1225-30; H. Simian-Yofre, "רחם," *TDOT* 13:437-52; Leonard J. Coppes, "רחם," *TWOT*, pp. 841-43; Mike Butterworth, "רחם," *NIDOTTE* 3:1093-95.

[81]See Phyllis Trible, *God and the Rhetoric of Sexuality* (Philadelphia: Fortress, 1978), pp. 31-59. רחמים is "probably in reference to the accompanying physiological phenomena of strong emotion" (Stoebe, "רחם," *TLOT* 3:1226). This connection is widely recognized and also attested in other Semitic languages. See Butterworth, "רחם," *NIDOTTE* 3:1093; Simian-Yofre, "רחם," *TDOT* 13:438. As such, the word group may refer to the seat of emotions or the profound emotions of compassion and/or affection. Compare Coppes, "רחם," *TWOT*, pp. 842-43.

[82]John E. Goldingay, *Daniel*, WBC 30 (Dallas: Word, 1989), pp. 243-44.

[83]Gottfried Quell, "Jesaja 14, 1-23," in *Festschrift Friedrich Baumgärtel*, ed. L. Rost (Erlangen: Universitätsbund, 1959), p. 140. Gowan contends that it "needs to be given a stronger emotional quality than the word 'mercy' usually has" (*Theology in Exodus*, p. 236). רחם and אהב do not collocate in a single verse but do in passages such as Hos 2:25–3:1; 14:3-4 [4-5].

(Ex 33:19; 34:6). Some have suggested that רחם depicts compassion from a superior to an inferior.[84] Although this is true of the majority of cases, the psalmist declares "I love [רחם] You, O LORD" (Ps 18:1 [2]).[85] Further, divine compassion is both particular and universal. God "is good to all, and His mercies are over all His works" (Ps 145:9; compare Jer 12:15). Yet, though God's רחם is amazingly enduring, it may be withdrawn (Jer 16:5); its reception is contingent on the maintenance of an ongoing divine-human relationship (compare Deut 13:17-18; 30:2-3; Is 27:11; 55:7; Jer 42:12-16; Hos 1:6-7; 2:4; 2 Chron 30:9).[86]

The οἰκτίρω and σπλαγχνίζομαι word groups in the New Testament both correspond closely to רחם.[87] The οἰκτίρω word group appears infrequently in the New Testament but with considerable significance, denoting the basic meaning of a highly emotive response to someone's hardship—compassion, sympathy, mercy, tender feeling and/or pity.[88] The σπλαγχνίζομαι word group is closely related to the οἰκτίρω word group and similarly refers to the feeling (or the seat of the feeling) of warm sympathy, pity and/or compassion at someone's misfortune and/or affectionate love, including the "tender [σπλάγχνον] mercy [ἔλεος] of our God" (Lk 1:78; compare Phil 1:8).[89]

---

[84] See the discussion in Stoebe, "רחם," TLOT 3:1227.

[85] This is the only occurrence where רחם is in the *qal* and the only instance of God as the object of רחם. Many have considered this to be a textual corruption or scribal gloss, especially since this phrase does not appear in the parallel in 2 Sam 22:2. However, textual data favor its validity, and the proposed emendations are not very compelling. See Simian-Yofre, "רחם," TDOT 13:444; Stoebe, "רחם," TDOT 3:1227.

[86] Related terms of divine compassion such as חמל and נחם also appear frequently in the OT.

[87] Beyond its rendering by the ἐλεέω word group (see footnote 75 above), the verb רחם is translated 12 times by οἰκτίρω, 4 times by ἀγαπάω and once by παρακαλέω (Is 49:13). Beyond its translation by ἔλεος, רחמים is most often translated by the noun οἰκτιρμός (20 times) and the adjective οἰκτίρμων (7 times) as well as a number of others once. The adjective οἰκτίρμων most often translates רחום (12 times), usually of God being "compassionate [οἰκτίρμων] and gracious [ἐλεήμων]" (Ex 34:6). The verb οἰκτίρω also translates חנן in 10 verses, often of divine compassion (cf. Is 30:18; Ps 101:14). The noun οἰκτιρμός also translates חן once. Whereas the σπλαγχνίζομαι word group appears more frequently in the NT than the οἰκτίρω word group, only the noun of the σπλαγχνίζομαι word group appears in the LXX (only 3 times). The σπλαγχνίζομαι word group appears to have come into common use in post-LXX Jewish literature. See Helmut Köster, "σπλαγχνον, σπλαγχνίζομαι," TDNT 7:552.

[88] See Bultmann, "οικτιρω, οικτιρμος, οικτιρμων," TDNT 5:161; H. H. Esser, "οικτιρμος," NIDNTT 2:598.

[89] The noun σπλάγχνον may refer to the "inward parts" of the body as the "seat of emotions," akin to the functioning of רחמים in the OT, or to the "feeling itself" of great "love" and "affection" (BDAG, p. 938). See Esser, "οικτιρμος," NIDNTT 2:599; E. Dhorme, *L'emploi métaphorique des noms de parties du corps en hébreu et en akkadien* (Paris: Librairie orientaliste P. Geuthner, 1963),

Conclusion

Many other terms shed light on divine love, but this brief survey has provided a glimpse of the most prominent semantics of divine love throughout Scripture and, in so doing, challenged the view that *agape* is purely or uniquely descriptive of God's love. Indeed, the meaning of the ἀγαπάω and φιλέω word groups as used in the New Testament overlap in nearly every respect, including the usage of both to describe God's perfect love. Likewise, אהב conveys a similarly multifaceted picture of love, as do terms of lovingkindness (חסד), mercy (ἐλεέω) and compassion (רחם, οἰκτίρω, σπλαγχνίζομαι). Significantly, the many facets of the various terms that have briefly been surveyed here correspond to the aspects of divine love that will be portrayed individually in the next five chapters.

---

pp. 111-12, 134-35. Whereas the noun is used of God (Lk 1:78; cf. Phil 1:8) but is more often used of humans, the verb σπλαγχνίζομαι is found only in the Synoptics and always with divine agency (usually Jesus), referring to highly emotive compassion. Spicq explains it is "literally a movement of the entrails at the sight"; to "have a visceral feeling of compassion" ("σπλάγχνα, σπλαγχνίζομαι," *TLNT* 3:274-75). See also Köster, "σπλάγχνον, σπλαγχνίζομαι," *TDNT* 7:548-59; H. H. Esser, "σπλάγχνα, σπλάγχνον," *NIDNTT* 2:599-600; "σπλαγχνίζομαι; σπλάγχνα," L&N 1:294. Both the οἰκτίρω and σπλαγχνίζομαι word groups collocate with ἀγαπάω numerous times (see Lk 6:36; Rom 9:13, 15; Phil 2:1; Col 3:12). Both groups also collocate with other major characteristics that relate closely to love, including "kindness," "comfort" and "patience" or "longsuffering." The adjective πολύσπλαγχνος also describes God's abundant compassion (Jas 5:11).

4

THE VOLITIONAL ASPECT
OF DIVINE LOVE

Does God love freely and, if so, what does that mean? If God's love is volitional, is divine love purely a product of the divine will? Does God choose to fully love only some, or does he choose to love all, or is he essentially related to all such that he necessarily loves all? Conversely, are humans free to love God and/or others? As surveyed in chapter one, there is an ongoing conflict of interpretations over how these questions should be answered. The transcendent-voluntarist model submits that divine love is freely, sovereignly willed and unmotivated beneficence. God freely bestows love on all but also decides to love only some unto salvation (election love). The immanent-experiential model, on the other hand, supposes that divine love does not involve election, since it is descriptive of an ontologically necessary God-world relationship. Since God's love for others is essential to him, divine love is universal as sympathetic, indeterministic relationship. Each model, then, explicitly rejects the answer proposed by the other. Other theologians struggle to adequately address these questions and their implications, coming to various conclusions with regard to whether and to what extent God's love is volitional, essential or both.[1]

I investigated the canonical data toward addressing such questions, without presupposing that a particular existing model of divine love, or underlying divine ontology, was correct. This chapter consists of an explication of the volitional aspect of love within the foreconditional-reciprocal model,

---

[1] See the description of the two main models and other perspectives in chap. 1 (above).

derived from the canonical methodology described in chapter two. This model posits that divine love in relation to the world is voluntary and not necessary or essential to God's being, yet also not exclusively volitional, since it is also evaluative, emotional, forecondtional and ideally reciprocal.

God's Love for Creatures Is Volitional

The conviction that God loves humans is central to Christian theology. God loved the world so much that he gave himself (Jn 3:16; Rom 5:8). However, the nature of divine love for the world is a subject of controversy. Is God's love for the world volitional and/or essential, contingent and/or necessary, particular and/or universal? God's love might be purely volitional such that God's love for others is predicated solely on his will, affirming God's absolute sovereignty and self-sufficiency (aseity), as the transcendent-voluntarist model proposes. From this perspective, the God-world relationship is not necessary or essential to God. On the other hand, God's love for creatures might be essential to him such that the God-world relationship is necessary to his being, as in the immanent-experientialist model. From this perspective, any view that denies meaningful creaturely freedom denies love, because freedom in relationship is the only context for authentic love. My canonical investigation supports an alternative view that God's love for the world is volitional but neither necessary nor exclusively volitional.

God's freedom in love. Many theologians have recognized that, as Kevin Vanhoozer states, "God's love is a free act, not a (natural) necessity" such that "God wills to relate in love to those who are not God."[2] In Karl Barth's view of God as the one who loves in freedom, further, God "is no less the One who loves if He loves no object different from Himself."[3] However, whereas the

---

[2] Kevin Vanhoozer, *Remythologizing Theology: Divine Action, Passion, and Authorship* (New York: Cambridge University Press, 2010), p. 151. For Vanhoozer, love "is primarily a covenantal rather than an ontological relation" (ibid.). John W. Cooper adds that God's "creation of the world" is "a genuinely free choice" (*Panentheism, the Other God of the Philosophers* [Grand Rapids: Baker Academic, 2006], p. 325).

[3] *CD* II/1, p. 280. Compare *CD* II/1, p. 257. Barth's mature conception of divine freedom is a matter of dispute among Barth scholars. In Bruce McCormack's seminal but controversial view, Barth's theology radically shifted in 1936 and beyond from "thinking about the being of God" that "still gave expression to a residual commitment to aspects of classical metaphysics" to becoming "more consistently postmetaphysical" ("The Actuality of God: Karl Barth in Conversation with Open Theism," in *Engaging the Doctrine of God: Contemporary Protestant Perspectives*, ed. Bruce L. McCormack [Grand Rapids: Baker Academic, 2008], p. 211). This shift led to Barth's

transcendent-voluntarist model contends that God chose to create love relationship with the world but could have done otherwise, on Kevin Hector's reading of Barth, this traditional dichotomy between the contingency and necessity of the God-world relationship is overcome via a dialectic conception wherein "there is a sense in which humanity is contingently necessary to God."[4] That is, creation is, "in some sense, contingently necessary" such that "God has eternally determined to be God-with-us" and therefore "God has freely *bound* Godself to creating the 'us' with whom God would be."[5] David W. Congdon

---

conception of Jesus as the subject and object of election, which (in McCormack's view) collapses the traditional distinction between the Logos *asarkos* and Logos *incarnandus* and ultimately requires that God's being as triune is itself constituted by divine self-determination. Thus, McCormack offered "a critical correction against Barth" aimed at removing what he "view[s] as an inconsistency in Barth's thought" ("Grace and Being: The Role of God's Gracious Election in Karl Barth's Theological Ontology," in *The Cambridge Companion to Karl Barth*, ed. John Webster [Cambridge: Cambridge University Press, 2000], p. 102). Compare ibid., pp. 92-110; Bruce L. McCormack, *Karl Barth's Critically Realistic Dialectical Theology* (Oxford: Clarendon, 1995), pp. 453-63; McCormack, "Seek God Where He May Be Found: A Response to Edwin Chr. van Driel," *SJT* 60 (2007): 62-79. On the other hand, George Hunsinger lists himself among the "traditionalists ... who contend that Karl Barth, thoughout his *Church Dogmatics*, never changed his mind that the triune life of God was prior to the divine decision of election" ("Election and the Trinity: Twenty-Five Theses on the Theology of Karl Barth," in *Trinity and Election in Contemporary Theology*, ed. Michael T. Dempsey [Grand Rapids: Eerdmans, 2011], p. 91). Compare Paul D. Molnar, "Can the Electing God Be God Without Us? Some Implications of Bruce McCormack's Understanding of Barth's Doctrine of Election for the Doctrine of the Trinity," in *Trinity and Election in Contemporary Theology*, p. 84. In Hunsinger's view, statements like the following (written in 1932) still stand: "God would be no less God if He had created no world and no man. The existence of the world and our own existence are in no sense vital to God, not even as the object of His love. The eternal generation of the Son by the Father tells us first and supremely that God is not at all lonely even without the world and us. His love has its object in Himself" (*CD* I/1, pp. 139-40). In this regard, Hunsinger points to Barth's response to a recorded interview in 1968 wherein he was asked whether he would "still endorse" this quote from 1932, and he replied, "Splendid, isn't it!" (Karl Barth, *Gesprache 1964-1968* [Zurich: Theologischer Verlag Zürich, 1997], p. 286, quoted in Hunsinger, "Election and the Trinity," p. 96).

[4]Kevin W. Hector, "God's Triunity and Self-Determination: A Conversation with Karl Barth, Bruce McCormack and Paul Molnar," *IJST* 7, no. 3 (2005): 247. Thus, "God is free *from* the world in order to be free-*for* it" (ibid., p. 256). Compare *CD* II/1, p. 313. Paul D. Molnar, however, contends that "such an idea already introduces a logical necessity here" ("The Trinity, Election, and God's Ontological Freedom: A Response to Kevin W. Hector," in *Trinity and Election in Contemporary Theology*, p. 58).

[5]Hector, "God's Triunity," p. 261. Hector comments further, "because God has so [eternally] determined Godself ['to be God-with-and-for-us'], 'there is no height or depth in which God can be God in any other way' (*CD* II/2, p. 77)" (ibid., p. 255). Notably, McCormack sees "an instability at the heart of Barth's treatment of the being of God in *Church Dogmatics* II/1" wherein Barth asserts: "Just as there is in God the highest necessity, so there is also the highest contingency. And this highest contingency in the essence of God, that which is limited by no necessity ... is precisely that which He *wills*" (Barth, *Kirchliche Dogmatik* II/1, p. 616, translated and quoted in McCormack, "Actuality of God," p. 238). Compare *CD* II/1, p. 548. McCormack contends, how-

thus explains that Barth's references to freedom in his "later dogmatics" do not suggest that "there are possible worlds in which God could have acted differently."⁶ Rather, Barth refers to an "inner necessity of the freedom of God" rather than a "sovereign *liberum arbitrium*."⁷ Thus, God's "contingent decision is also necessary. God can only will what God in fact does."⁸

On the other hand, George Hunsinger asserts that for Barth, "creation is purely an act of sovereign grace and divine freedom. It is in no way necessary for God, not even 'contingently' (whatever that might mean)."⁹

---

ever: "Barth cannot have it both ways. He has to choose: either necessity (so that power, knowledge, and will in God are limited by his necessary being) or freedom (so that God's essence is *wholly*—not partially—determined by that power and knowledge which find their root in an eternal act of divine will)" ("Actuality of God," p. 238). For McCormack, "God's relation to the world is rightly characterized in terms of an 'omnivolence'" wherein the truly "primal" decision that is "divine election stands at the root of God's being or 'essence'" (ibid., pp. 239, 210). Compare CD II/2, p. 50. However, "the divine 'freedom'" should not "be understood voluntaristically (as a choice among options)" (Bruce L. McCormack, "Introduction: On 'Modernity' as a Theological Concept," in *Mapping Modern Theology*, ed. Kelly M. Kapic and Bruce L. McCormack [Grand Rapids: Baker Academic, 2012], p. 16). Thus, "God's freedom does not consist in a choice between alternatives"; such a view "is far too anthropomorphic" (McCormack, "Election and the Trinity: Theses in Response to George Hunsinger," in *Trinity and Election in Contemporary Theology*, p. 135). "God's freedom is finally the freedom to exist—or not to exist" (ibid., p. 136). McCormack's position is thus thoroughly actualist, that is, the "divine 'essence' is an activity whose purpose is rooted in the divine freedom" without any "metaphysical gap between God's being and acting" (ibid., pp. 125, 135).

⁶David W. Congdon, "*Apokatastasis* and Apostolicity: A Response to Oliver Crisp on the Question of Barth's Universalism," *SJT* 67, no. 4 (2014): 480n40.

⁷*CD* IV/1, p. 195. That is, Congdon explains, God's will is not "a libertarian free will" that is "capable of choosing any possibility," but "God is wholly self-determined. God necessarily is what God has done" (Congdon, "*Apokatastasis*," p. 470). Thus, divine freedom "does not mean that God could have acted otherwise" (ibid.). Compare McCormack's view that Barth had "trespassed against the very core of his methodological commitments" exclusive of speculation by "speaking not only of what God did but of what he could have done" ("Actuality of God," p. 236).

⁸Congdon, "*Apokatastasis*," p. 469. "Necessity and contingency are paradoxically identical within Barth's covenant ontology" such that emphasizing "one at the expense of the other is to miss the dialectical complexity of his theology" (ibid.). There is "necessity within the singularity of the divine decision," but "the necessity of a certain occurrence taking place is not immanent to (or grounded in) the occurrence itself" (ibid.). Congdon thus rejects an "immanent-intrinsic necessity" but accepts a "transcendent-extrinsic necessity" of the God-world relationship, similar to Eberhard Jüngel's distinction between "earthly necessity" and the "eschatological must (δεῖ)" (ibid.). Barth's appeals to divine freedom, then, are "best understood as a way of acknowledging the historical contingencies and particularities associated with the concrete encounter between God and specific human beings" (ibid.).

⁹Hunsinger, "Election and the Trinity," p. 111. He adds: the "idea that creation was 'contingently necessary' for God has nothing to do with Barth, and would in any case be absurd, if it is meant in some pre-temporal way" (ibid.). Similarly, for Molnar, "the idea that creation is 'contingently' necessary for God" is one that "Barth never accepted and never could accept, given his conception of divine freedom" ("Trinity, Election," p. 47).

Rather, Hunsinger contends that Barth consistently saw God as "free not to have created the world."[10] Paul Molnar similarly insists that Barth "always emphasizes both" "God *for* us" and "God's freedom *from* us" such that Barth dialectically "holds both that God loves us with his eternal love and that God is free in that love both in himself and in his actions *ad extra*."[11] Otherwise, he claims, "God will necessarily be related to us and the distinction between Creator and creature would be lost."[12] As T. F. Torrance puts it, God "was perfectly free to create or not to create."[13] Robert Jenson suggests caution, however: "It might not have been so. God might have been the God he is without this world to happen to." Yet, "how God would have described his own being had he been without the world, we cannot even inquire."[14]

Apart from any claim regarding what God *might* have been and/or done, Scripture presents God's love for the world as taking place within a freely voluntary relationship (see below).[15] On my understanding of Scripture,

---

[10]Hunsinger, "Election and the Trinity," pp. 109-110n20. For instance, Barth states, God "does not will Himself without us. In all the fullness of His Godhead, in which He might well have been satisfied with Himself, he wills Himself together with us" (CD IV/2, p. 777).

[11]Molnar, "Trinity, Election," pp. 47, 59. He affirms that God in eternity "determined himself to be God for us" but rejects that God determined himself "to be the triune God" or "that he could not have done otherwise" as "utterly foreign to Barth's thinking" (ibid., p. 58). Note, however, that even on Molnar's reading Barth presents a distinct alternative to the conflict between the transcendent-voluntarist and immanent-experientialist models.

[12]Ibid., p. 55.

[13]Thomas F. Torrance, *The Christian Doctrine of God: One Being Three Persons* (New York: T & T Clark, 2001), p. 237. Torrance refers to the "unlimited *freedom* of God," who, "far from being a static or inertial Deity like some 'unmoved mover,'" is "absolutely free to do what he had never done before, and free to be other than he was eternally," even "to become incarnate as a creature" while "nevertheless remaining eternally the God that he always was" (ibid., p. 208). On the other hand, Friedrich Schleiermacher affirmed God's absolute freedom in creation of the world while maintaining that God was never without the world: "He on Whom everything is absolutely dependent is absolutely free," while maintaining that this does not mean "that God might equally well have not created the world," which would assume "an antithesis between freedom and necessity" and thus place God "within the realm of contradictions" (*The Christian Faith*, trans. H. R. Mackintosh [Edinburgh: T & T Clark, 1948], p. 156).

[14]Robert W. Jenson, *Systematic Theology* (New York: Oxford University Press, 1997), 1:221. Compare McCormack's view that, whereas "'*God* would be God without us'" is "a true statement" that "must be upheld at all costs if God's grace is to be truly gracious," any attempt to "specify precisely what God would be without us" would be "guilty of the abstract metaphysical speculation which was the bane of early church theology" ("Seek God," p. 76).

[15]This regards God's ontological independence from the world but does not intend to address the question of the relationship between God's essence and his will, including the complex question of whether the creation of this (or some) world was inevitable due to God's love (consider the philosophical distinction between inevitability and necessity). The data that I have studied re-

further, God's love relationship with the world is neither (strictly) necessary nor essential to his being such that God did not *need* to create any world.[16] Love relationship existed within the Trinity before the world's beginning (Jn 17:5, 24), yet God freely loves the world.[17] As T. F. Torrance states, "God did not have to create the world. He had no need for others to be able to love."[18] Yet God freely decided to create beings and bestow his love on them, voluntarily opening himself up to relationship with the world while remaining distinct from it.[19] In this way, as Richard Rice states, "the world owes its existence to God's free choice, not to metaphysical necessity," such that "love is a voluntary commitment."[20] Divine-human love relationship could not take place without God's logically, ontologically and chronologically prior decision to create other beings. God is thus the causal origin and prime agent of all relationship.

---

garding divine love appear to me to be underdeterminative on this issue. See the brief discussion in chap. 9 (below).

[16]My inference that God did not *need* to create any world (apart from whether it was inevitable that God would do so) dovetails with the wider evidence regarding the volitional aspect of God's love but also might be grounded in canonical statements that God has no needs (that is, there is nothing external to God that is necessary for his existence). For example, Acts 17:25 refers to the fact that God is not "served by human hands, as though He needed anything, since He Himself gives to all *people* ['people' is absent in the Greek] life and breath and all things." Further, consider statements such as Rev 4:11, where God is praised as the one who "created all things" and "because of [his] will [θέλημα] they existed, and were created" (cf. Prov 16:4; Is 43:7, 10, 19-21; Col 1:15). Here and elsewhere, if moral praiseworthiness entails freedom (as I believe it does, though philosophical debate is ongoing on this issue), then the frequent praise of God for creating (e.g., Ps 148:5-6; 149:2; Rev 4:11 et al.) might indirectly suggest God's freedom to will otherwise. See the discussion of various options regarding the contingency and/or necessity of the God-world relationship later in this chapter.

[17]John 17:24 refers to the Father's love for the Son "before the foundation of the world," and the context confirms the Son's preexistence, sharing glory with the Father "before the world was" (Jn 17:5). Although Jn 17 includes no explicit reference to the Holy Spirit's involvement in the love relationship, I believe the preexistence and the personality of the Spirit can be properly derived from Scripture, and I take inclusion of the Holy Spirit in the eternal intratrinitarian love relationship to be a proper inference from the Trinity doctrine and numerous statements about the Holy Spirit's love (e.g., Rom 5:5; Gal 5:22; 2 Cor 13:14; compare the brief discussion in chap. 8 below).

[18]Torrance, *Christian Doctrine of God*, p. 244.

[19]This presumes that the world is not eternal but came into being via divine creation, which is the explicit canonical view and is among the most basic of biblical metaphysical suppositions. Such a view takes seriously various biblical texts that refer to a "before" the world (e.g., Jn 17:5, 24, among others) suggesting that the God-world relationship is not eternal and, therefore, not essential to God's being.

[20]Richard Rice, "Process Theism and the Open View of God: The Crucial Difference," in *Searching for an Adequate God: A Dialogue Between Process and Free Will Theists*, ed. David Ray Griffin, John B. Cobb and Clark H. Pinnock (Grand Rapids: Eerdmans, 2000), p. 185.

This volitional aspect of God's love for the world extends beyond the act of creation. God's amazing and undeserved commitment to his creatures is demonstrated by his continued love for creatures, even after the fall, manifest supremely in the self-giving love of Christ: "He who did not spare His own Son, but delivered Him over for us all, how will He not also with Him freely give us all things?" (Rom 8:32). While human sin merits death, God has made a way to repair the ruptured relationship and continues to bestow his love even on sinful and undeserving human beings, though he is under no obligation to do so (Rom 5:8). In response to the fall and subsequent disordering of the world, God chose a people through whom he would reach out to all peoples and committed himself to them in covenant relationship for the benefit of all (Gen 12:3; 18:18). God's people, the recipients of election on the basis of God's freely bestowed and undeserved love, were expected to reciprocate God's love through commitment and obedience to him (Deut 7:7-13; 10:15). Volition is thus a crucial element of the covenant relationship. The closely related marriage and parent-child metaphors of divine-human relationship likewise highlight the voluntary aspect of love relationship.[21] Marriage assumes voluntary union and commitment. Likewise, the parental metaphor is often depicted as one of "adoption." God bestowed a special love relationship on Israel by choosing them to be his children, undeservedly (Deut 7:6-8; 10:15).

Within this framework, Scripture consistently displays God's love as freely given. In the aftermath of repeated rebellion by his people, for instance, God declares: "I will heal their apostasy, I will love them freely [נְדָבָה], for My anger has turned away from them" (Hos 14:4 [5]). The adjective נְדָבָה connotes the "determinative . . . element of free will," referring to what is offered "totally voluntarily."[22] In this context, the people don't deserve God's love; indeed, by their egregious rebellion they have forfeited any right to divine compassion, mercy and grace, yet God willingly loves them without any compulsion, moral or otherwise. Likewise, that God's love for creatures is contingent on his will is evident by God's statement after Israel's golden calf rebellion, "I will be gracious to whom I will be gracious, and will show

---

[21]See the discussion of kinship metaphors in chap. 8 (below).
[22]J. Conrad, "נדב," *TDOT* 9:220, 222. The noun form of the root depicts "freewill offering" (Ex 35:29; 2 Chron 31:14).

compassion on whom I will show compassion" (Ex 33:19; compare Rom 9:15-18). Here God voluntarily maintains love relationship with a people who have no right to it. God was under no obligation to show them mercy, but exercised his right to bestow gracious compassion.

The volitional aspect of God's love is also displayed in those instances where God finally withdrew his lovingkindness and compassion, in response to the people's apostasy (Jer 16:5; compare Hos 9:15). Here and elsewhere, divine lovingkindness (חסד) is fundamentally free. חסד is predicated on voluntary association, and God possesses the prerogative to remove it.[23] Since (in some sense) divine love toward creatures can be removed, it cannot be necessary or essential to God. Notably, however, the context of Jeremiah 16:5 shows that the people's actions warranted the removal of lovingkindness long before God did so. Despite repeated rebellion and rejection of his loving overtures, God's lovingkindness persisted far beyond any obligations or reasonable expectations, manifesting his long-suffering character.[24] Time after time, God renewed his love commitment to his people, toward ultimately reclaiming and restoring them to reciprocal divine-human love relationship (Ex 32-34; Neh 9; Ps 78). The removal of lovingkindness, then, is neither automatic nor arbitrary but God's voluntary response to obstinate evil.

God's commitment to love humans reaches its apex in Christ, who manifested the depth and height of God's love by willingly giving himself up for humans (Rom 5:8; Gal 2:20; Eph 5:25). Christ's redemptive work of love is explicitly voluntary as he proclaims, "No one has taken it away from Me, but I lay" down my life "on My own initiative" (Jn 10:17-18). Thus God not only voluntarily created and bestowed love on humans but continued to bestow his love even at the expense of giving himself. "Greater love has no one than this, that one lay down his life for his friends" (Jn 15:13). Despite the enormity of human evil, which had forfeited the benefits of God's love, he has generously showered love on us such that we might be called his

---

[23]See Katharine Sakenfeld, *The Meaning of Hesed in the Hebrew Bible: A New Inquiry* (Missoula, MT: Scholars Press, 1978), pp. 45, 176, 234. It is likewise apparent by other terms that God's love (אהב and ἀγαπάω) and compassion (רחם) are freely given and unmerited and may be forfeited, though they extend beyond all expectations. See chap. 3 above.

[24]The volitional aspect of divine love is similarly evident in God's response to entreaty and God's "repenting" wherein God exercises his freedom to change course, either bestowing or withholding loving actions (e.g., Jer 18:7-10; Jon 3:9; 4:2). See John C. Peckham, "The Passible Potter and the Contingent Clay: A Theological Study of Jeremiah 18:1-10," *JATS* 18, no. 1 (2007): 130-50.

children (1 Jn 3:1). As Karl Barth comments, "God does not owe us either our being, or in our being His love," but "we are debtors to God, without God owing anything to us."[25]

The material above presents only a selection of the biblical data that unambiguously supports the view that God's love for the world is volitionally free, as the transcendent-voluntarist model maintains, and thus departs from the view that divine love for creatures is necessary to his being (e.g., the immanent-experientialist model). However, a number of questions remain with regard to the nature and extent of the volitional aspect, including, is God's love for creatures a product of his volition alone?

God's love is volitional but *not* merely volitional. The controversial question of whether and to what extent divine love is volitional relates directly to the issues of whether divine love for the world is (strictly) contingent or necessary, and universal or nonuniversal.[26] If divine love for the world is essential to his being, it must be universal. Conversely, if divine love for the world is volitional, it must be contingent (in some fashion), leaving open the question of the particularity and/or universality of divine love.[27]

Whereas most Christian theologians have denied universalism, a number of theologians (past and present) have affirmed that God wills to love everyone in such a way that his love will finally overcome and save everyone.[28] Conversely, the transcendent-voluntarist model maintains that God loves all in some ways (common love) but only those whom God chooses are loved unto salvation (exclusivist election love). In this view, the volitional nature of God's love is emphasized such that God's love is contingent on the divine will alone as "sheer gratuity," the gift love of unilateral beneficence (thematic *agape*).[29] In Emil Brunner's words, divine love is "free

---

[25]*CD* II/1, p. 281.

[26]See the earlier discussion of the concept of "contingent necessity," which attempts to overcome the dichotomy of (strict) contingency and necessity in this regard (pp. 91-93).

[27]For an account of universalism that includes particularity, see Tom Greggs, *Barth, Origen, and Universal Salvation: Reclaiming Particularity* (Oxford, Oxford University Press, 2009). Compare Oliver D. Crisp, "Is Universalism a Problem for Particularists?" *SJT* 63, no. 1 (2010): 1-23.

[28]See, for example, the discussion of various forms of universalism in chaps. 7 and 9 (below), including those represented by Thomas B. Talbott, *The Inescapable Love of God* (Parkland, FL: Universal, 1999); John Hick, *Evil and the God of Love* (London: Collins, 1966). See also the discussion of Karl Barth's perspective, which appears to require that all humans will finally be saved (though he refused to embrace universalism as a worldview).

[29]Irving Singer, *The Nature of Love*, 3 vols. (Chicago: University of Chicago Press, 1987), 1:15.

and generous grace."[30] This view magnifies God's aseity and freedom, since God's love for creatures does not depend on anything other than himself.

Thomas Jay Oord, however, contends that such a view "sacrifices divine love," asking: "How can we say that God is loving if God arbitrarily chooses not to elect some to receive salvation?"[31] In his essential kenosis theology, congruent with the immanent-experientialist model in this respect, God necessarily loves all without distinction according to the essential (love) relation of God's nature. Yet Oord maintains that whereas God "loves necessarily" and "cannot not love," "God's love is free" in the sense that God may choose between various loving actions.[32]

Other theologians suggest that God's love relationship with creatures is not essential to him, such that God freely loves everyone but grants humans freedom to accept or reject that love. Thus God truly desires to save all, but some reject his love.[33] Along these lines, the foreconditional-reciprocal model suggests that God's love is volitional but not *merely* volitional. That is, while Scripture presents God's love for the world as freely given and not necessary to his being, such love is not the product of divine volition alone. God's love is also evaluative, emotional, foreconditional and ideally reciprocal (see the further discussion of the universality and particularity of divine love in chapter eight).

For now, let us return to some primary passages in order to examine what manner of volitional love they depict. God's statement, "I will be gracious to whom I will be gracious, and will show compassion on whom I will show compassion," is often used to support the perspective that God's love is exclusively volitional, that God arbitrarily chooses to be gracious to some and not others (Ex 33:19; compare Rom 9:15-18).[34] However, there is compelling

---

[30]Torrance, *Christian Doctrine of God*, p. 185.
[31]Thomas Jay Oord, "Matching Theology and Piety: An Evangelical Process Theology of Love" (PhD diss., Claremont Graduate University, 1999), p. 54. On this question, see chaps. 7 and 8 (below).
[32]Singer, *Nature of Love*, p. 129. Compare Jürgen Moltmann, *The Trinity and the Kingdom: The Doctrine of God*, trans. Margaret Kohl (San Francisco: Harper & Row, 1981), pp. 54-55.
[33]So H. Ray Dunning, *Grace, Faith, and Holiness: A Wesleyan Systematic Theology* (Kansas City, MO: Beacon Hill, 1988), pp. 196-97; Thomas C. Oden, *The Living God* (San Francisco: Harper & Row, 1987); Vincent Brümmer, *The Model of Love: A Study in Philosophical Theology* (Cambridge: Cambridge University Press, 1993), p. 179.
[34]For instance, see Leonard J. Coppes, "רחם," *TWOT*, p. 842; J. A. Motyer, *The Message of Exodus* (Downers Grove, IL: InterVarsity Press, 2005), p. 309.

evidence that this phrase serves to emphasize the divine right to bestow mercy on even those who are egregiously undeserving but does not refer to arbitrary election of some (but not others) to receive mercy. Exodus 33:19 echoes and expands God's self-description in the first call of Moses by way of a parallel *idem per idem* construction, moving from "I AM WHO I AM" (Ex 3:14) to something like "I will proclaim before you the name Lord, and the grace that I grant and the compassion that I show" (JPS).[35] In the context of Exodus 32–34 the thrust of this statement is that God's love is volitionally bestowed; he is under no obligation (moral or otherwise) to be merciful toward Israel in light of its egregious apostasy. However, as Yahweh, he has the right to bestow mercy on the undeserving. Yet even this voluntary and unnecessary bestowal of mercy and compassion is not presented as wholly arbitrary. After the rebellion with the golden calf the people are called by Moses to make a choice, and it is those who refuse to repent who forfeit God's mercy (Ex 32:26). Thus, while Exodus 33:19 presents a striking example of the volitional aspect of God's love, it does not present divine love as *merely* volitional. God's love for this rebellious people is contingent on his will in Exodus 33:19, but it is not contingent *only* on his will.

Likewise, consider once again the kinship metaphors of the divine-human relationship, which depict bilateral voluntary commitment. God expects humans to respond to him with devotion, underscored by his frequent charge of infidelity by his "bride" (Jer 3:8-10, 20; Hos 2–3). Furthermore, although the relationship of adoption originates by parental decision, it is significant that the child's part also includes volition (though not necessarily from the outset), as a child might eventually remove herself

---

[35]G. S. Oden surveys the examples of the *idem per idem* construction and comes to the conclusion that (1) it may express the totality/intensity of the action of the verb, (2) the adverbial locating phrase (אֲשֶׁר) stresses the extent of the verbal action such that termination of argument is only a secondary function of this construction, and (3) the traditional interpretation that the construction refers to God's arbitrary choice is without substance ("Idem Per Idem: Its Use and Meaning," *JSOT* 17, no. 53 [1992]: 107-20). Many other scholars concur that this construction signifies an emphasis on God's attributes of grace and compassion rather than discrimination between objects of God's mercy. See, among many others, Douglas Stuart, *Exodus*, NAC 2 (Nashville: B&H, 2006), p. 708; J. Gerald Janzen, *Exodus* (Louisville: Westminster John Knox, 1997), p. 248; David Noel Freedman, "The Name of the God of Moses," *JBL* 79 (1960): 154; Walter Brueggemann, "The Book of Exodus," *NIB* 1:940; Nahum M. Sarna, *Exodus* (Philadelphia: JPS, 1991), p. 214; Brevard S. Childs, *The Book of Exodus*, OTL (Philadelphia: Westminster Press, 1974), pp. 76, 596; Terence E. Fretheim, *Exodus* (Louisville: John Knox, 1991), p. 305.

from such a relationship and have nothing to do with her parents (Deut 32:10; Jer 3:13-14, 19; Ezek 16:1-6; Hos 11:1). In this way, both metaphors poignantly describe the nature of God's covenant relationship as bilateral voluntary commitment, which is integral to the ideal divine-human love relationship (see chapter eight).

These and other instances of Scripture present God's love as volitional without reducing divine love to volition, as if love relationship is a product of God's will alone. God's love is not only voluntary but is also integrally connected with his very character of love (see chapter nine).[36] God is love and will always be loving, but he does not need to love any world, since God has always enjoyed sufficient love relationship within the Trinity.[37] God's love is volitional in a way that corresponds to his character and complements the evaluative, emotional, foreconditional and ideally reciprocal aspects.

What Is the Nature of the Relationship Between Divine Love and Election?

At the heart of the volitional aspect of divine love stands the biblical concept of election, the understanding of which holds massive repercussions regarding the God-world relationship.[38] God's love is sometimes depicted by theologians as purely volitional "election love," that is, God's arbitrary bestowal of love on only those whom he chooses.[39] In this view, the "love of God implies election," and love itself is simply "the orientation of his 'sovereign will.'"[40] Accordingly, Leon Morris contends that "predestination and

---

[36]In recognizing the volitionally free aspect of divine love, one should be careful not to assume a false dichotomy between the divine will and essence/character such as might be offered by radical forms of voluntarism. See chap. 9 (below).

[37]Compare Barth's view of God as the one who loves in freedom: "God's loving is necessary" as "the essence and nature of God," yet "it is also free from every necessity in respect of its object" (*CD* II/1, p. 280). Vanhoozer adds, "God is already love in himself," so "it is only thanks to a free act that God wills to relate in love to those who are not God" (*Remythologizing Theology*, p. 151).

[38]God's love is closely connected to his will and often associated with election throughout Scripture. See, among others, Deut 4:37; 7:7; 10:15; Ps 47:4; 78:68; Is 41:8; 42:1; 44:1-2; Mt 12:18; Jn 15:19; Rom 9:11-13; 11:28; Eph 1:4-5; Col 3:12; 1 Thess 1:4; Jas 2:5. Compare the discussion of Mal 1 and Rom 9 below.

[39]So, among many others, Leon Morris, *Testaments of Love: A Study of Love in the Bible* (Grand Rapids: Eerdmans, 1981), pp. 159-60; Carl F. H. Henry, *God, Revelation, and Authority*, 6 vols. (Wheaton, IL: Crossway, 1999), 6:106-7; J. I. Packer, "The Love of God: Universal and Particular," in *Still Sovereign: Contemporary Perspectives on Election, Foreknowledge, and Grace*, ed. Thomas R. Schreiner and Bruce A. Ware (Grand Rapids: Baker, 2000), p. 280.

[40]Stauffer, "αγαπάω, αγάπη, αγαπητός," *TDNT* 1:49-50. Stauffer, himself a Christian universalist,

love go together."⁴¹ This echoes Anders Nygren's elevation of *agape* as "purely theocentric love, in which all choice on man's part is excluded."⁴² The foreconditional-reciprocal model, on the other hand, suggests that election is a manifestation of divine love, but neither God's love nor his election is purely volitional. The divine-human love relationship is based on God's free decision to bestow love but also requires human response.

The nature of election. Deciding which of these perspectives, if any, best reflects the canonical data requires careful consideration. To "elect" might mean to choose arbitrarily or to choose evaluatively. That is, divine election might be an entirely subjective act of God's will, or election might require the response of its object(s). In the former view, God unilaterally and unconditionally elects those whom he wills, independently of their characteristics or actions. My canonical research supports the latter view: election is the result of a divine call (sometimes on the basis of evaluation) to which humans freely respond.

In the following evaluation of the relationship of love and election in Scripture, four crucial points will become apparent:

1. Divine love is the basis of election.

2. Both divine love and election are volitionally free but are not the products of volition alone.

3. Divine election often (if not always) includes evaluation (though not necessarily merit) and sometimes corresponding emotion.

4. Divine election is not unilaterally determined but requires appropriate human response and thus may be forfeited.⁴³

At the outset, two kinds of election (vocational and salvific) must be distinguished from each other, though they may overlap. Vocational election refers to God's choice of individuals and/or groups for a specific role in the plan of salvation, often with the purpose of revealing God's character.⁴⁴

---

associates them under "God's unconditional sovereignty in loving and hating, electing and rejecting (R. 9:13, 25)" (ibid.).

⁴¹Morris, *Testaments of Love*, p. 191.

⁴²Anders Nygren, *Agape and Eros*, trans. Philip S. Watson (London: SPCK, 1953), p. 213.

⁴³The third and fourth points are reinforced in chaps. 5-7 (below).

⁴⁴For example, Abraham, Isaac, Jacob, the people of Israel, priests, Saul, David, the Twelve and Paul were vocationally elected.

Salvific election describes those instances in Scripture where those who will ultimately receive salvation are referred to as the "elect" (e.g., Mt 24:24; Mk 13:22).[45]

Divine love as the basis of election. Returning to the issue of the specific relationship between love and election, we have seen that some scholars conflate love and election into a single concept, excluding evaluation and emotion. For example, Eugene Merrill views love and election in the Old Testament as "technical terms" that are "virtually synonymous," such that "'to love' is to choose, and 'to choose' is to love."[46] On the other hand, many scholars maintain that love is not identical to election but the basis of it.[47] As Edmund Jacob comments, "the origin of election is found in love."[48]

The nature of the association between love and election is clarified by three passages in Deuteronomy that directly address this issue, the first instance of which happens also to be the first appearance of divine אהב in Scripture.

1. "Because He [God] loved [אהב] your fathers, therefore He chose their descendants after them" (Deut 4:37).

2. "Not because you were more numerous than all other peoples did Yahweh delight [חשק] in you, therefore he chose you when you were the least of all peoples, because of the love [אהבה] of Yahweh for you, and he kept the oath he swore to your fathers" (Deut 7:7-8).[49]

3. "Yet in your fathers Yahweh delighted [חשק] to love [אהב] them. Therefore he chose their seed after them, even you, from all the peoples as it is this day" (Deut 10:15).[50]

---

[45]I do not intend an absolute or rigid distinction between these kinds of election. One's response to God's vocational election holds salvific implications, and it is not always clear where one begins and the other ends.

[46]Eugene H. Merrill, *Deuteronomy*, NAC 4 (Nashville: B&H, 1994), p. 132. See the discussion of אהב in chap. 2 (above).

[47]See, e.g., P. J. J. S. Els, "אהב," *NIDOTTE* 1:285; Gordon R. Clark, *The Word "Hesed" in the Hebrew Bible* (Sheffield: JSOT Press, 1993), p. 263; Gerhard Wallis, "אהב," *TDOT* 1:104; Henry, *God, Revelation, and Authority*, 6:347.

[48]Edmund Jacob, *Theology of the Old Testament* (New York: Harper & Row, 1958), p. 108. So also W. Günther and H. G. Link, "αγαπαω," *NIDNTT* 2:544.

[49]My translation. I have departed from the NASB, both here and in Deut 10:15, because the translation of חשק as "set His love" or "set His affection" in Deut 7:7 and Deut 10:15, respectively, is potentially misleading, as discussed below.

[50]My translation. In both cases, I have translated *wāw* with בחר as a *wāw* of consequence ("there-

In each of these texts God's choice of Israel is based on his love.⁵¹ Here and elsewhere, God's will, election and his love are closely associated, yet divine love is not identical to election or merely a product of God's will. Rather, divine love is itself the basis of election (and covenant), as many other passages affirm (e.g., Is 41:8; 42:1; Ps 47:4; 78:68; 1 Thess 1:3-4; 2 Thess 2:13-15).

However, divine love does not unilaterally maintain the covenant relationship. God's love for his people includes both evaluative and emotional aspects (see chapters five and six).⁵² Indeed, the use of חשק in Deuteronomy 7:7; 10:15 suggests that God's love for his people includes tender feeling, affection and emotion.⁵³ Elsewhere, God "rejected the tent of Joseph, And did not choose the tribe of Ephraim" (Ps 78:67), but "chose the tribe of Judah, Mount Zion which He loved" (Ps 78:68). The content of these verses shows that Israel was not arbitrarily rejected but provoked God by idolatry such that he was "filled with wrath" and "greatly abhorred Israel" (Ps 78:58-59). Thus, although the status of God's elect is unmerited, it is evaluative and

---

fore he chose") in accordance with the usage in Deut 4:37, where the parallel statement is predicated on "because" (תַּחַת) such that the *wāw* with בְחַר is a *wāw* of consequence. Jacqueline Lapsley translates, "Yhwh became attached to Israel's ancestors in love and chose their seed after them" ("Feeling Our Way: Love for God in Deuteronomy," *CBQ* 65, no. 3 [2003]: 361).

⁵¹Compare Clark, *Hesed*, p. 130; Byron E. Shafer, "The Root *bhr* and Pre-Exilic Concepts of Chosenness in the Hebrew Bible," *ZAW* 89 (1977): 39.

⁵²In Els's analysis, אהב in these verses signifies, among other things, "an emotive event, expressing a divine *feeling* of love" ("אהב," *NIDOTTE* 1:280). This contradicts the once-prevalent view, popularized by William Moran and discussed in chap. 3, that אהב in many (or all) OT covenant contexts is primarily a term descriptive of merely legal, nonemotional loyalty.

⁵³חשק appears in only 13 verses and is very closely related to אהב. The nonpersonal usages of חשק refer to bands in the construction of the sanctuary (Ex 27:17; 38:17, 28), suggesting derivation from a root meaning of bind, adhere, unite or stick together. So Gerhard Wallis, "חשק," *TDOT* 5:261. The personal usages, however, depict emotional clinging, attachment, longing, attraction, desire and/or delight. In Gen 34:8 (Shechem for Dinah) it means "longing" or even "passionate desire." So Els, "אהב," *NIDOTTE* 1:280. In Deut 21:11 חשק depicts a man's desire for a beautiful woman. It is used of other desires as well (1 Kings 9:1, 19; 2 Chron 8:6; Is 38:17). It is also used to describe the one who has "loved" (חשק) God and "therefore" God will deliver him (Ps 91:14). Merrill and others contend that בחר, חשק and אהב are "essentially synonymous as their usage elsewhere clearly shows" (Merrill, *Deuteronomy*, p. 203). Compare Wallis, "חשק," *TDOT* 5:263. However, a comparison of the usage of these terms, including a survey of all the OT usages of חשק, shows that the term does not connote "choice" in the sense of arbitrary election. See John C. Peckham, *The Concept of Divine Love in the Context of the God-World Relationship* (New York: Peter Lang, 2014). Accordingly, many other scholars interpret this term as emotional and often translate it as "delight" or "desire," in line with the etymology and usage of the term throughout the OT. Among many others, see Els, "אהב," *NIDOTTE* 1:280; David Talley, "חשק," *NIDOTTE* 2:318; Robert Alter, *The Five Books of Moses* (New York: Norton, 2005), pp. 917, 33; Lapsley, "Feeling Our Way," p. 360; Jeffrey H. Tigay, *Deuteronomy* (Philadelphia: JPS, 1996), p. 56.

conditional and must be maintained by appropriate human response to God (Deut 7:9, 11-13; 10:16).

On the other hand, those who conflate love and election often appeal to Mal 1:2-3, where God states, "I have loved [אהב] you," but the people respond, "How have You loved [אהב] us?" God answers that, although they were brothers, he "loved [אהב] Jacob" (Mal 1:2) but "hated [שנא] Esau" (Mal 1:3).[54] Some interpret "love" (אהב) and "hate" (שנא) as election and rejection, respectively, often explicitly excluding the evaluative and emotional aspects of one or both.[55] Yet, if one reads "loved" (אהב) as "chosen," God's reply seems to be a superfluous restatement of his earlier declaration, especially when we consider that the complaint against God's love presumes election, implying something like, "You ought to have loved us [as the elect], but you haven't." God's reply also presumes election as context but contends that God has, in fact, manifested love toward his elect, as evidenced by comparing the status of Judah to that of desolate Edom.[56] In this context, *love* does not mean "choose"; the fact of Israel's election is appealed to as the manifestation of God's love, in accordance with the wider usage of the terminology throughout the canon.[57]

The two Abrahamic peoples, descendants of brothers, both deserved de-

---

[54]The foreground of the passages suggests that this refers to Israel and Edom, the descendants of Jacob and Esau (Mal 1:3-5; Obad 10). Scholars disagree on whether this reference also refers to the individuals Jacob and Esau, in large part due to Paul's usage of this passage in Rom 9:13. In my view, the primary emphasis here is on the nations of Israel and Edom, yet the reference to the progenitors of both nations also draws attention to the historical reversal of birthrights, i.e., election (of a vocational nature).

[55]For instance, E. Ray Clendenen considers love and hate "to be figurative, pointing to God's sovereign election in choosing by his grace to form a relationship with some of his creatures" but not others ("Malachi," in *Haggai, Malachi*, NAC [Nashville: B&H, 2004], p. 372). This view is often supported by the supposition that שנא may be used as technical language for divorce (Deut 21:15-17; 22:13, 16; 24:3). However, E. Lipinski shows that while it is a technical term used "in connection with divorce," the use of the term in Hebrew "leaves no doubt that this verb expresses an emotional condition implying the wish for separation or removal from the 'hated' person" ("שנא," *TDOT* 14:169). See Judg 14:16; 15:2; 2 Sam 13:15. Even in the use of שנא toward Leah, Jacob may have felt some animosity toward her due to her part in Laban's deception (Gen 29:31, 33).

[56]Although the precise manner of Edom's downfall is not clear, Edom had become desolate while Israel had been restored from exile.

[57]Consider the word studies of אהב and ἀγαπάω in chap. 3 (above), which show that these terms are nowhere reduced to choice (though volition is an aspect of love that they describe). See also the evaluative nature and emotionality of both divine "love" and "hate" in chaps. 5 and 6 (below). Compare the extended discussion in Peckham, *Concept of Divine Love*, pp. 230-34.

struction (Ezek 25:12-13; Mal 2:11; 3:6), yet only the descendants of the younger remain. The contrast of God's treatment of Judah and Edom concretely shows the manner of divine love toward Judah, while at the same time deconstructing the supposition that Judah deserves divine love. On the one hand, Judah has been specially privileged by God's ongoing love toward them and the election that springs from it, despite their repeated rebellion and slander of his name (Mal 2:11; 3:6). Yet Judah's treatment is not arbitrary. God expects his love to be reciprocated by his people (as seen throughout the remainder of Malachi). Despite Judah's elect status, judgment could and did fall on them (repeatedly), though God was abundantly long-suffering until there "was no remedy" (2 Chron 36:16).

On the other hand, Edom has not been treated unjustly, and neither were they arbitrarily "hated." God had previously shown his great concern for Edom (Deut 2:5) but, because of their evil actions, God was finally "indignant [זָעַם] forever" toward them (Mal 1:4). Notice the evaluation (response to evil) and emotion (indignation) of divine animosity toward Edom. In every other biblical instance, God's hatred (שָׂנֵא) toward humans is prompted by their evil action(s) (e.g., Is 1:14; Jer 12:8; 44:4; Hos 9:15; Amos 5:21; 6:8; Ps 5:5-6 [6-7]; 11:5). The fact that all other instances of divine hatred are not arbitrary but evaluative (and most are also explicitly emotive), alongside a number of intertextual hints suggesting evaluative divine animosity toward Edom (in Malachi and the wider canon), indicates that the instance in Mal 1:2-3 should likewise be interpreted as evaluative hatred rather than mere rejection.[58] As David L. Petersen states, in "Malachi, hate is hate," and this "rhetoric requires that Yahweh hate Edom virulently in order to demonstrate his unmitigated love toward Israel."[59]

---

[58]Indignation and judgment against Edom are often described as "because" of their evil actions. See Ezek 25:12-14; 35:15; 36:5; Joel 3:19; Amos 1:9, 11; Obad 10-14; Lam 4:22. Edom was guilty of doing the things God hates (Deut 16:22; Ps 5:6 [5]; 11:5; 129:5; etc.). Thus, "Edom brought divine judgment upon themselves" (Andrew E. Hill, *Malachi*, AB 25D [New York: Doubleday, 1998], p. 167). Similarly, the former occupants of the promised land were not treated arbitrarily but were dispossessed because of their wickedness (Deut 9:4-5) after hundreds of years of probation (Gen 15:16).

[59]David L. Petersen, *Zechariah 9–14 and Malachi* (Louisville: Westminster John Knox, 1995), p. 170. The term *hate* in Scripture, however, does not necessarily refer to maximal animosity, but the "semantic scope ... reaches from the strongly affective 'to hate'" even "to a somewhat diluted 'to feel aversion for, not want, avoid'" (Ernst Jenni, "שָׂנֵא," *TLOT* 3:1278). The degree of animosity depends on the context (see chap. 5 below).

God's choice of a special people was not to the exclusion of others but toward blessing all nations (Gen 12:2-3).[60] "God's plan for the salvation of the nations was his motive for the election of Israel."[61] God's election of the few ultimately benefits all, since God intends, through Israel, to eventually enter into love relationship with peoples of all nations (Gen 12:3; Deut 10:18; Acts 10:34-35). In this vein, John Walton makes a compelling case that a primary purpose of God's election and covenant was to reveal God's character and the modus operandi of divine-human relationship.[62] If God related to all peoples of the world in precisely the same way, then God's revelation would be merely general, rather than special, revelation. By electing Israel, God's relations with them could function as a microcosm of the God-human relationship. If this understanding is correct, it seems that God bears longer with Israel in order to manifest his character to all peoples; his persevering love toward them is intended to reveal his love to all.[63] God's compassion and grace for Israel is a model of what he will bestow on all sinners who accept his love (Jn 3:16; Rom 10:13; 1 Jn 1:9).

Paul's quotation from Malachi 1:2-3, "Jacob I loved [ἀγαπάω], but Esau I hated [μισέω]" (Rom 9:13), in the midst of his broad discussion of Israel's election, sheds further light on this crucial point. Here again, some take this language as a reference to "election love." Douglas Moo, for instance, comments, "God's love is the same as his election."[64] Conversely, Frédéric Godet contends that these statements "do not signify merely: 'I have preferred the one to the other'" but both are based on a "difference of feeling in God himself," which consists of "moral sympathy" and "moral antipathy."[65] Moo's position is tied to the view that Paul is here affirming double predestination. Yet many scholars make a compelling case that Romans 9–11 is not (pri-

---

[60]God is not playing favorites; with him there is no partiality (Deut 10:17; Acts 10:34; Rom 2:11). As Ronald E. Clements puts it: "God's election does not mean groundless and unmerited favoritism. Were that the case, God would have been shown to flout the very righteousness the covenant declared and upheld" ("The Book of Deuteronomy," *NIB* 2:359).

[61]Lamar Eugene Cooper Sr., *Ezekiel*, NAC 17 (Nashville: B&H, 1994), p. 105.

[62]John H. Walton, *Covenant: God's Purpose, God's Plan* (Grand Rapids: Zondervan, 1994).

[63]This explains God's frequent concern for his "name" (i.e., reputation; see Ex 32:12-13; Ps 109:21; 143:11; Ezek 18:25; 20:9, 14, 22, 44).

[64]Douglas Moo, *The Epistle to the Romans*, NICNT (Grand Rapids: Eerdmans, 1996), p. 587. Compare Morris, *Testaments of Love*, p. 159.

[65]Frédéric Godet, *Commentary on St. Paul's Epistle to the Romans* (New York: Funk & Wagnalls, 1883), p. 350.

marily) about the salvific status of Jacob and Esau individually or their descendants collectively.[66] Rather, Paul demonstrates God's justice in salvation history, specifically the prerogative of God to include believing Gentiles and exclude unbelieving descendants of Abraham. As Robert Mounce comments, Paul is not "teaching double predestination" but that God had not failed to "maintain his covenant."[67] Paul's argument goes something like this: Both Isaac and Jacob had older brothers (Ishmael and Esau, respectively) who were not elect (Rom 9:6-14), and from this it follows that (1) Israel did not merit or earn election, and (2) merely being a descendant of Abraham does not entail election (e.g., Rom 9:6). Just as God had the right to elect Israel, who did not merit it (Deut 9:4), God has the right to "cut off" those who persist in unbelief while including among his elect those who do accept Christ (Rom 11:22-23), offering salvation to all who believe (Rom 3:22; 4:11, 24; 10:9-13).

Paul reinforces this point by referencing the locus classicus of God's manifestation of his character of love (in response to rebellion): "I will have mercy [ἐλεέω] on whom I have mercy, and I will have compassion [οἰκτίρω] on whom I have compassion" (Rom 9:15). As noted earlier, the statement of Exodus 33:19 that Paul quotes here is (in context) not a statement of arbitrary exclusion from mercy but a positive statement that God has the right to bestow mercy on even the most undeserving. By reminding his interlocutors of this historical mercy shown to Israel, the ridiculousness of the claim that others (the Gentiles) should be excluded from divine mercy becomes apparent. That is, if God is able to justly have mercy on Israel after the golden calf rebellion, how much more does he have the right to show

---

[66]So, among others, William S. Campbell, "The Freedom and Faithfulness of God in Relation to Israel," *JSNT* 13 (1981): 39; Gottlob Schrenk, "εκλεγομαι, εκλογη, εκλεκτος," *TDNT* 4:179; J. Eckert, "εκλεκτος," *EDNT* 4:418-19; James D. G. Dunn, *Romans 9-16*, WBC 38B (Dallas: Word, 2002), p. 562. Moo himself recognizes the "strong case" for a "corporate and salvation-historical interpretation" but prefers a deterministic reading on the basis of his adoption of a Calvinistic approach (*Romans*, p. 585). Similarly Thomas Schreiner, *Romans* (Grand Rapids: Baker, 1998), pp. 500-501.

[67]Robert Mounce, *Romans*, NAC (Nashville: B&H, 2001), p. 199. Compare Dunn, *Romans 9-16*, pp. 544-46. In this vein, R. Laird Harris points out that "it does not necessarily follow that Esau [or Edom] was hated before he was born. This statement is quoted from Mal 1:3 which was written long after Esau had lived his predominantly secular life" and, indeed, after Edom was desolate. The election of Jacob over Esau before they were born (Rom 9:11-12) refers back to Gen 25:23 (editor's note in Gerard Van Groningen, "שׂנא," *TWOT*, p. 880).

mercy to the Gentiles? Thus, William Campbell contends: "These words are intended not as proof that the divine election is arbitrary but as proof to the contrary."[68]

Election requires human response. Those who adopt the so-called election love perspective contend that the "elect" are such because of God's "effective love" and they could not do otherwise than respond appropriately to God's love. In Thomas Schreiner's view, "Those whom God calls are powerfully and inevitably brought to faith in Jesus Christ"; this "call of God is extended only to some and is always successful."[69] Others, however, maintain that elect status requires appropriate response: "Never is the implication given that God intends to accept some and to reject others. The New Testament affirms absolutely that it is God's will that all men would come to know him."[70] Along these lines, the foreconditional-reciprocal model interprets the canonical evidence to mean that humans are called (invited) by God to be a part of his elect but that humans possess the God-given ability to accept or reject God's call and, consequently, love relationship with God.

Divine election requires human response and is often, in this and other senses, evaluative.[71] Although God chooses specific individuals or groups

---

[68]William S. Campbell, "The Freedom and Faithfulness of God in Relation to Israel," *JSNT* 13 (1981): 30. So also Joseph A. Fitzmyer, *Romans*, AB 33 (New York: Doubleday, 1993), p. 567; R. C. H. Lenski, *The Interpretation of St. Paul's Epistle to the Romans* (Columbus, OH: Wartburg, 1945), pp. 608-9. Compare F. Staudinger, "ἐλεος," *EDNT* 1:431; H. H. Esser, "Ἔλεος," *NIDNTT* 2:597. I cannot do justice to the rich content of Rom 9–11 here. Suffice it to say that careful examination of Pauline quotations, allusions and use of language suggests indeterminism, regarding both the original context of many allusions/quotations in Rom 9–11 and the terminology and themes elsewhere. For example, Paul's treatment of the potter and the clay is clarified by attention to the explicit conditionality of that metaphor in Jer 18:1-10. Further, Paul's explanation of God's right "to make from the same lump one vessel [σκεῦος] for honorable [τιμή] use and another for common use [ἀτιμία]" (Rom 9:21) should not be taken deterministically, considering the use of the same language elsewhere that suggests conditionality on human volition. Second Timothy 2:20-21 refers to "vessels [σκεῦος] . . . some to honor [τιμή] and some to dishonor [ἀτιμία]," and then adds, "if anyone cleanses himself from these *things*, he will be a vessel [σκεῦος] for honor [τιμή]" (2 Tim 2:20-21; cf. 1 Thess 4:4). See, in this regard, the further treatment of Rom 9–11 and other passages such as Eph 1 in Peckham, *Concept of Divine Love*, pp. 391-98.

[69]Thomas Schreiner, *1, 2 Peter, Jude*, NAC (Nashville: B&H, 2007), pp. 429-30. Likewise, for Moo the divine call is related to God "irresistibly" bringing about "what he chooses" (*Romans*, p. 582).

[70]Barclay Moon Newman and Eugene Albert Nida, *A Handbook on Paul's Letter to the Romans* (New York: UBS, 1994), pp. 166-67.

[71]The primary terminology of election (vocational and salvific) in both the OT (בחר) and NT (ἐκλέγομαι) often depicts evaluation (e.g., Is 48:10) and appraisal of what is distinguished,

to carry out particular aspects of his plan (vocational election), humans may accept or reject God's call initially and/or forfeit it after having received it. Abraham was elected to be the father of Israel, but faith response was required (Heb 11:8). Conversely, both King Saul and Judas were elected by God (1 Sam 10:24; Jn 6:70) but forfeited that status by rebellion (1 Sam 15:23; Jn 17:12).[72] Thus, although divine election is undeserved, it "must find response in the proper behavior of the elect."[73] Thus David counsels Solomon, "if you seek Him, He will let you find Him; but if you forsake Him, He will reject you forever" (1 Chron 28:9; compare 1 Kings 9:2-9; 11:11; 1 Chron 22:13; 28:7; 2 Chron 6:16; 7:17-20; Ps 132:11-14).[74] Likewise, though Israel did not merit election (Deut 7:7-8), appropriate response was expected of them in order to enjoy the benefits of election (Deut 7:9-13; 10:15-16). Similarly, although Christ chose his disciples, they are his "friends" only if they obey him (Jn 15:14, 16, 19).

Accordingly, many passages in the canon explicitly present God's call and election as conditional on response, yet no passages clearly depict either God's call or election as unilaterally effective.[75] For example, Jesus speaks of those "called" (καλέω) to the "wedding feast" who were "unwilling to come," such that "those who were invited [καλέω] were not worthy" and others were therefore invited (Mt 22:3-4, 8-9; compare Lk 14:16-24). As Gottlob Schrenk comments, this "invitation implies obedience.... Nowhere do we read that those invited are forced to refuse. The whole point of the parable is that one does not have to decline or to appear in an unsuitable

---

considered the best and/or excellent. Indeed, "the act of choosing (and thus the words of this group) includes a judgment by the chooser as to which object he considers to be the most suitable for the fulfilment of his purpose. It is not of vital importance whether it be objective criteria, or subjective feelings and considerations which are paramount in making the decision" (L. Coenen, "εκλεγομαι," *NIDNTT* 1:536). Compare "εκλεκτος," L&N 1:360. Compare chap. 5 (below).

[72]God "would have established" Saul's "kingdom over Israel forever" but because of his sin, his kingdom did "not endure" (1 Sam 13:13-14).

[73]H. Wildberger, "בחר," *TLOT* 1:214. That is, "election does not have such permanence that it cannot be called into question by the improper behavior of the elect" (H. Wildberger, "מאס," *TLOT* 2:654).

[74]Sadly, Solomon turns from God, who proclaims, "Because you have done this . . . I will surely tear the kingdom from you, and will give it to your servant" (1 Kings 11:11; cf. 1 Kings 11:33).

[75]I examined every passage that uses the language of calling or election throughout the canon. See the full description of this investigation in Peckham, *Concept of Divine Love*, pp. 378-87.

garment."[76] Notably, the parable is directed at those who were "chosen" but ultimately reject God's will for them. Moreover, this parable immediately precedes Christ's statement that "many are called [κλητός], but few *are* chosen [ἐκλεκτός]" (Mt 22:14).[77]

As such, the "called" are not always "chosen." The "called" are those who may accept or reject God's invitation, while the "chosen" are those who accept the invitation.[78] As Craig Blomberg puts it, "Those responding properly may be said to have been chosen. The elect are the true community of the people God chooses to save, even as Israel had once been so chosen, but those people must freely respond to the Spirit's work in their lives.... Election does not violate free will nor occur irrespective of" response.[79] The divine-human love relationship enjoyed by the elect, then, requires appropriate response (compare Rom 10:9, 12-13; 11:22-23).[80]

---

[76]Schrenk, "εκλεγομαι, εκλογη, εκλεκτος," *TDNT* 4:186. Similarly, R. T. France, *The Gospel of Matthew*, NICNT (Grand Rapids: Eerdmans, 2007), p. 827; John Nolland, *The Gospel of Matthew*, NIGTC (Grand Rapids: Eerdmans, 2005), p. 892.

[77]The "many" likely refers to God's universal invitation (cf. Jn 3:16; 1 Tim 2:4, 6; Tit 2:11), as "the πολλοί is probably to be taken as a universalizing Semitism, which can be translated 'everyone'" (Donald A. Hagner, *Matthew 14-28*, WBC 33B [Dallas: Word, 2002], p. 632). So B. F. Meyer, "Many [= All] Are Called, but Few [= Not All] Are Chosen," *NTS* 36 (1990): 89-97; Craig Blomberg, *Matthew*, NAC 22 (Nashville: B&H, 2001), p. 329. Moo, despite his deterministic view, also recognizes this as "a 'general' call" (*Romans*, p. 530).

[78]The terminology of calling (the καλέω word group) in the NT refers to an invitation that is contingent on acceptance (Mt 22:14; Heb 11:8, as does the OT usage of corresponding terminology, קרא, 2 Sam 15:11; 1 Kings 1:41, 49). Whether the call/invitation has been accepted (or will be accepted) is not indicated by use of the term itself but may be seen at times in the context (Rom 8:28-29). Schreiner contends that κλητός refers to an "effectual" calling that "overcomes human resistance" and "not merely an invitation" since, he believes, "God's unstoppable purpose in calling believers to salvation cannot be frustrated" (*Romans*, pp. 450-51). So also Moo, *Romans*, pp. 530-31, 82. However, I have found no instance of an irresistible call in the canon, despite examination of all usages. See Peckham, *Concept of Divine Love*, pp. 378-87. Compare Karl L. Schmidt, "καλεω," *TDNT* 3:487-536; L. Coenen, "καλεω," *NIDNTT* 1:271-76. For those who view God's "call" as a universal and conditional invitation, see Kenneth Grayston, *The Epistle to the Romans* (Peterborough, UK: Epworth, 1997), pp. 74-75; Lenski, *Romans*, pp. 553-54; Godet, *Romans*, p. 323; W. Sanday and Arthur C. Headlam, *A Critical and Exegetical Commentary on the Epistle to the Romans* (Edinburgh: T & T Clark, 1980), pp. 220-21.

[79]Blomberg, *Matthew*, p. 329. Compare 2 Esdras 8:3, 41. Eckert adds: "A predestinarian misunderstanding of the belief in election is thus rejected.... The elect are those who have followed the invitation into the kingdom of God through Jesus Christ" ("εκλεκτος," *EDNT* 4:417). Likewise, Robert H. Stein comments that the "'chosen ones' designates those who have responded to God in repentance and faith and are thus the recipients of his love and grace rather than to the elect by some kind of predestination" (*Luke*, NAC [Nashville: B&H, 2001], p. 446). This is contra Coenen, who thinks that this is attributed "to the divine choice alone," though he does not provide a compelling rationale for this view ("ἐκλέγομαι," *NIDNTT* 1:540).

[80]For example, "Whoever will call on the name of the Lord will be saved" (Rom 10:13; cf. Rom

Accordingly, Scripture repeatedly refers to those who receive the final reward as "those who love" God. The one "who perseveres under trial" when "approved, he will receive the crown of life which *the Lord* has promised to those who love [ἀγαπάω] Him" (Jas 1:12; similarly, see Rom 8:28; 1 Cor 2:9; compare 1 Cor 8:3; Eph 6:24). The "chosen" (ἐκλέγομαι) are those who "love" (ἀγαπάω) God (Jas 2:5), the "called [κλητός] and chosen [ἐκλεκτός] and faithful" (Rev 17:14).[81] In contrast, those who perish do so "because they did not receive the love [ἀγάπη] of the truth so as to be saved" (2 Thess 2:10).[82] The implication of all this is that those who finally respond to God's call with reciprocal love are God's elect.[83] Accordingly, the "elect" are often referred to as God's "beloved" (compare Rom 1:7; Col 3:12; 1 Thess 1:4; 2 Thess 2:13), who are not only recipients of divine love but also those who appropriately respond (by God's grace). Thus, the "called" and "beloved in God the Father" who are "kept for Jesus Christ" are exhorted: "keep yourselves in the love of God" (Jude 1, 21; compare 2 Pet 1:10; 3:17).[84] Accordingly, those who are finally elect unto salvation are those who love God (and others) in return.

If the interpretation above is correct, the "called" and/or "elect" have not been unilaterally elected or irresistibly called by God. Rather, those who make up the "elect" at Christ's second coming are those who have freely accepted his invitation (call).[85] While such election is offered prior to condi-

---

10:9, 12). Likewise, Rom 11:22-23 shows that the "elect" are not unilaterally so but may forfeit his kindness.

[81] With regard to Rev 17:14, James Moffat comments, these are "those who by their loyalty ratify their calling and election" (*Love in the New Testament* [New York: Harper, 1930], p. 202). Similarly, Robert H. Mounce, *The Book of Revelation*, NICNT (Grand Rapids: Eerdmans, 1997), p. 319; Grant R. Osborne, *Revelation* (Grand Rapids: Baker, 2002), p. 624.

[82] "The causal clause [ἀνθ'ὧν] makes clear that they suffer their fate because they have 'refused to love the truth'" (D. Michael Martin, *1, 2 Thessalonians*, NAC 33 [Nashville: B&H, 2001], p. 246). Compare 2 Thess 2:12, 14. Gordon Fee adds, "They are headed for 'destruction' precisely because they 'were not receptive'" (*The First and Second Epistles to the Thessalonians*, NICNT [Grand Rapids: Eerdmans, 2009], p. 294).

[83] As Schrenk puts it, "those who believe and obey are elected" (Schrenk, "εκλεγομαι, εκλογη, εκλεκτος," *TDNT* 4:187).

[84] In Jude 1 the Textus Receptus has "sanctified" (ἡγιασμένοις) instead of "beloved" (ἡγαπημένοις). The former is widely considered a copyist error, since the latter has overwhelming manuscript support. See Thomas R. Schreiner, *1, 2 Peter, Jude*, NAC 37 (Nashville: B&H, 2007), p. 430.

[85] There are at least two plausible ways to understand the function of the term *elect* when it refers to those who will finally be saved that are in keeping with the evidence that those saved must *freely* respond to God's gracious invitation. First, the "elect" at the second coming of Christ might be understood in the sense of corporate election, meaning that the elect group of believers is in view without reference to the specific individuals who will finally make up that group. Critics

tions, based on God's freely given love (Deut 7:7-8; 9:4-5), human response is required to maintain the special divine-human relationship (Deut 7:9, 11-13; 10:16; Jn 15:14).[86] Such human response, however, is not meritorious. Human response to God's invitation is only made possible by God's prior grace and love (Jn 6:44; 12:32).[87] Election is thus conditional and yet unmerited.[88] This view of divine election (vocational and salvific) as the result of God's call to which humans *freely* respond entails that God grants humans significant freedom, that is, freedom to will otherwise than one does.[89]

LOVE AND BILATERAL SIGNIFICANT FREEDOM

Bilateral significant freedom means that God and humans possess the

---

of this view argue that groups are always made up of individuals. Of course, this is true. However, one might speak of next year's Indianapolis Colts or next term's United States Congress without knowing all of the individuals included therein, thus referring to a corporate group without implying that the individuals who will be in the group *necessarily* make up that group. For an overview of, and argument for, corporate election see William W. Klein, *The New Chosen People: A Corporate View of Election* (Grand Rapids: Academie, 1990). Second, perhaps many (or all) of the biblical instances of the "called" and "elect" presuppose divine foreknowledge such that those who will respond are foreknown by God, while the place of those finally included remains open to the free decisions of the individuals to accept or reject God's invitation. See the brief discussion regarding the ongoing debates over divine foreknowledge and human freedom in chap. 9 (below).

[86]Thus, Peter writes, "brethren, be all the more diligent to make certain about His calling and choosing you; for as long as you practice these things, you will never stumble" (2 Pet 1:10). Richard J. Bauckham comments, "Christ has called the Christian into his kingdom," yet "an appropriate moral response is required if his final salvation is to be guaranteed" (*2 Peter, Jude*, WBC 50 [Dallas: Word, 2002], p. 190). Indeed, if the faith response of the elect were irresistibly determined by God, the numerous exhortations toward the called (Gal 1:6; 5:13; Eph 4:1; 1 Tim 6:11-12; 1 Thess 2:12; 4:7; 2 Thess 1:11; 2:13-15; 1 Tim 6:12; 1 Pet 1:15; 2:9, 21; 3:9; 5:10; 2 Pet 1:3) and elect (Deut 7:11-12; Eph 4:1; Col 3:12; 2 Thess 1:11; 2:13-15; 2 Pet 3:14, 17; Jude 1) would be superfluous.

[87]On the unmerited yet conditional reception of love relationship see the discussion in chap. 7 (below).

[88]"Election is not a logical point of rest" but a "serious responsibility" of "final decision" (Schrenk, "εκλεγομαι, εκλογη, εκλεκτος," *TDNT* 4:188). Compare Gerhard Delling, "Merkmale der Kirche nach dem Neuen Testament," *NTS* 13, no. 4 (1967): 305. For further support for the conditionality of election see William G. MacDonald, "The Biblical Doctrine of Election," in *The Grace of God, the Will of Man: A Case for Arminianism*, ed. Clark H. Pinnock (Minneapolis: Bethany House, 1995), pp. 207-29.

[89]Here and throughout this work I use the phrase *significant freedom* instead of *libertarian freedom* to specify the minimal definition of freedom I use (ability to will otherwise than one does), differentiating it from conceptions of libertarian freedom that make more robust claims as well as from conceptions that do not maintain the freedom to will otherwise than one does. For a brief discussion of my minimal conception of human freedom in relation to God's providence, see John C. Peckham, "Providence and God's Unfulfilled Desires," *Philosophia Christi* 15, no. 2 (2013): 453-62.

The Volitional Aspect of Divine Love

ability to will to act otherwise than they do.[90] God need not have created humans (or any creatures) at all. God's love toward humans is therefore voluntary, not necessary. This volitional aspect of God's love has its counterpart in the divinely bestowed free will of humans to reciprocate or not reciprocate God's love (compare Deut 6:5).[91] Scripture consistently depicts divine and human love as voluntary (Hos 14:4 [5]; Deut 30:15-16, 19-20), whereas instances of causally determined love are absent. Love, whether human or divine, assumes freedom. As Vincent Brümmer puts it, "love is by definition free."[92]

God loves his people "freely" (Hos 14:4 [5]) and, likewise, humans are called to choose to love or not love God. Deuteronomy 30:15-16 states: "See, I have set before you today life and prosperity, and death and adversity; in that I command you today to love the LORD your God." Deuteronomy 30:19-20 continues: "I have set before you life and death, the blessing and the curse. So choose life in order that you may live, you and your descendants, by loving the LORD your God, by obeying His voice, and by holding fast to Him." God's frequent commands of humans to love God (e.g., Deut 6:5; Lev 19:18; Mt 22:37-39) would make little sense if humans are causally determined to love God (or not). Such commands suggest that humans might or might not respond to God's love with reciprocal love and, as such, the God-human love relationship cannot be the result of God's will alone. God's love may be unrequited, and ultimately the benefits of God's love may be forfeited by the lack of appropriate human response.[93] In the words of David Fer-

---

[90]The issue of bilateral significant freedom is among the most controversial in historical and contemporary theology and not easily settled, and I certainly do not presume that it will be settled by the discussion in this book. Readers who are committed to a deterministic perspective such as compatibilism may not be convinced of human significant freedom. However, I encourage consideration of significant freedom as a live option as this book progresses. The following chapters provide additional evidence that supports this premise regarding divine love in the God-world relationship, culminating with a treatment of indeterminism in chap. 9.

[91]The significant freedom of human beings is apparent in numerous instances depicting God's unfulfilled will (e.g., Is 30:15-18; 65:12; 66:4; Lk 7:30). What takes place is not always what God desires (e.g., Lam 3:33; Ezek 33:11; cf. Ezek 18:23, 32; Mt 23:37; Lk 13:34; 2 Pet 3:9; 1 Tim 2:4). See the further discussion in chap. 9 (below).

[92]Brümmer, *Model of Love*, pp. 175, 77. So, among many others, Clark H. Pinnock, *Flame of Love: A Theology of the Holy Spirit* (Downers Grove, IL: InterVarsity Press, 1996), p. 74; Jerry L. Walls and Joseph Dongell, *Why I Am Not a Calvinist* (Downers Grove, IL: InterVarsity Press, 2004), pp. 50-55. Compare James D. G. Dunn, *Romans 1-8*, WBC 38A (Dallas: Word, 2002), p. 481.

[93]This will be explained and further elaborated on in chaps. 7 and 8 (below).

gusson, "the necessary condition of freedom bestowed by the love of God, therefore, is the possibility of our rejecting him."[94]

The divine-human love relationship, then, is neither unilaterally deterministic nor ontologically necessary but mutually (though not symmetrically) volitional and contingent. As Trevor Hart puts it, love is "something contingent upon God's willing to enter into such a relationship in the first place, to place himself under certain relational constraints, to be limited in his freedom by the existence of a genuinely free other."[95] Thus God voluntarily created a world that he remains ontologically independent from, and yet, in creating a world wherein creatures possess genuine freedom, he chooses not to exercise the full extent of his power, manifesting "a form of love that lets the creatures have their own existence."[96] God's will is thus a necessary basis of the divine-human love relationship but does not by itself amount to divine-human love relationship.

Conclusion

This chapter has addressed the question, does God love freely and, if so, what does that mean? The foreconditional-reciprocal model posits that God's love in relation to the world is voluntary but not arbitrary. Divine love for the world is voluntary in that God loves the world freely. Divine love for creatures is neither essential to God's being nor necessary to his existence. Yet God's love for creatures is not the product of his will alone. God's love is closely associated with, but not identical to, God's will and election. God grants humans freedom to love or not love him in return. Thus the love relationship that God desires with human beings is not unilaterally willed but requires the free response of humans to God's freely given love. Thus neither God nor humans love each other by necessity. God freely loves humans and

---

[94]David Fergusson, "Will the Love of God Finally Triumph?" in *Nothing Greater, Nothing Better: Theological Essays on the Love of God*, ed. Kevin J. Vanhoozer (Grand Rapids: Eerdmans, 2001), p. 200.

[95]Trevor Hart, "How Do We Define the Nature of God's Love?" in Vanhoozer, ed., *Nothing Greater, Nothing Better*, p. 109.

[96]Wolfhart Pannenberg, *Systematic Theology*, trans. Geoffrey W. Bromiley (Grand Rapids: Eerdmans, 1991), 1:438. Pinnock believes that God "restrains himself for the sake of the freedom that love requires" (Clark H. Pinnock, "Constrained by Love: Divine Self-Restraint According to Open Theism," *Perspectives in Religious Studies* 34, no. 2 [2007]: 149). Similarly, Oden, *Living God*, p. 75.

calls humans to freely love him in return. God's love for the world, then, takes place within the context of a bilaterally free, volitional relationship.

The volitional aspect of God's love is further supported by consideration of the other aspects of God's love, introduced and explained in the following four chapters. The evidence for the conclusion that love assumes freedom will only become stronger as one considers the many other aspects of love in the following chapters, wherein it will be seen that the voluntary nature of love is not only implied in many passages but required to make sense of the broader conception of the divine-human love relationship as depicted throughout the canon.

5

The Evaluative Aspect of Divine Love

Does God only bestow or create value, or might he also appraise, appreciate and receive value? Is divine love arbitrarily willed, pure beneficence, or may it include desire and/or enjoyment? The transcendent-voluntarist model posits that God, as entirely perfect and self-sufficient, is only benefactor, never beneficiary. God derives no pleasure or value from the world; his love is wholly gratuitous gift love (thematic *agape*), to the exclusion of desirous or receiving love (thematic *eros*). The immanent-experientialist model, on the other hand, contends that God essentially feels all feelings (universal sympathy) and thus always benefits or suffers along with all joys and sorrows such that the value of his life increases along with the world (since God includes the world). Not only do the models contradict each other, but theologians from various other perspectives have been critical of both perspectives.[1]

My canonical investigation suggests that divine love in relation to the world is evaluative.[2] God takes delight in his creatures, and such delight may correspond to his appraisal of humans. However, God's love is not merely sympathy derived from an essential union with creatures. God's love stems from his free decision to love humans (as explained in chapter four).

God's Love Is Evaluative

Does God appreciate value or take joy in the world? On the one hand, if God

---

[1]See the discussion in chap. 1 (above).
[2]In this book, the term *evaluative* refers to the appraisal, appreciation and/or reception of value from external agents.

is unaffected by anything outside himself (impossible), God's love must be such that God does not enjoy, take pleasure in or receive value from creatures. In this view, God's love is purely outgoing. God never receives or enjoys love from creatures but bestows love on the unworthy. On the other hand, God might be related to the world in such a way that he experiences all feelings essentially. In each perspective divine love is nonevaluative in different ways. In the former view, divine love is nonevaluative in that God loves completely independently from appraisal and the reception of value. In the latter view, God's love is nonevaluative in that God indiscriminately and necessarily loves all regardless of evaluation. That is, God enjoys or sorrows in *all* of the experiences of the world. Conversely, the foreconditional-reciprocal model posits that God does appraise, enjoy and receive value from humans, but voluntarily and discriminately according to his perfect evaluation. That is, God delights in what is properly delightful but abhors what is evil; he loves what is upright but hates injustice. God's love is not merely sympathy derived from an essential union with creatures but stems from his free decision, without any deficiency of divine being, to love humans.

Three prominent rationales for the view that God's love is not evaluative frame this discussion. First, it might be presupposed that, by nature, God cannot receive value (the theo-ontological objection). In this vein, John Piper writes: "'God is love' is this: it belongs to the fullness of God's nature that he cannot be served but must overflow in service to his creation. The very meaning of God is a being who cannot be enriched but always remains the enricher."[3] Second, many posit that pure love gives but never receives, such that reception of value or benefits is considered to be selfish and thus inappropriate to divinity (the moral objection).[4] Third, humans are incapable of generating value or eliciting God's delight (the anthropological objection).[5] From this premise, God's love is sometimes equated with love for the unworthy. Each of these rationales will be taken up below.

God's love is consistently evaluative. Throughout Scripture, God

---

[3]John Piper, "How Does a Sovereign God Love? A Reply to Thomas Talbott," *The Reformed Journal* 33, no. 4 (1983): 11.
[4]See Anders Nygren, *Agape and Eros*, trans. Philip S. Watson (London: SPCK, 1953), p. 210.
[5]These three are not the only reasons one might reject the view that God receives value but are sufficient to provide the context of this discussion. Others reason soteriologically in a way that concludes that God only gives but never receives value.

enjoys, delights in, appreciates and finds value in humans.[6] God's love for humans is explicitly linked to evaluative pleasure and/or displeasure semantically and thematically.[7] The primary Old Testament term of love, אהב, frequently overlaps with language of delight, including חפץ,[8] which may connote delight, pleasure or desire, and רצה/רצון,[9] which may connote pleasure in, accept favorably, delight in and so on.[10] Consider

---

[6]Many examples of divine pleasure and delight also point toward the emotional aspect of divine love (see chap. 6 below).

[7]The OT and NT terminology of love often connotes evaluative enjoyment, pleasure and/or delight (see chap. 2 above).

[8]The word חפץ has the basic meaning of "desire" or "delight," often of an emotive nature, which may be manifested in the wish for something or someone or evaluative delight and/or joy in a person or object. For Leon J. Wood, "The basic meaning is to feel great favor towards something" evaluatively and with considerable "emotional involvement." With both divine and human agency it means "to experience emotional delight" ("חפץ," *TWOT*, p. 310). Compare G. Johannes Botterweck, "חפץ," *TDOT* 5:104. David Talley calls it the "direction of one's heart or passion," which "conveys a passionate emotion for an object" ("חפץ," *NIDOTTE* 2:232). In this term, desire (will or purpose) and delight (pleasure or enjoyment) are closely related in that an unfulfilled wish may be seen as a desire, whereas a fulfilled wish may bring delight. Thus the term can depict one's will and often depicts the will of the sovereign, not as a merely subjective expression of the will but an evaluative desire and/or delight. With regard to divine desire, it may refer to various things that God wants to take place, often with a strong sense of what he will accomplish (Is 42:21; 44:28; 46:10; 53:10; 55:11; Ps 115:3). Yet it also at times refers to what God desires to occur but does not occur (Ezek 18:23; 33:11; Is 65:12; 66:4; Ps 51:6 [7]). The two usages of חפץ are complementary, not contradictory, if the underlying meaning of "desire" is kept in mind as something willed, which, when not effectuated, amounts to something wanted.

[9]רצה refers to strong delight in something or someone, often including the connotation of acceptance. The "basic meaning of the verb is best defined as 'be pleased with, find good or pleasant, love, like, wish for,' etc." (H. M. Barstad, "רצה," *TDOT* 13:619). G. Gerleman explains that lexical evidence shows that "the verb was used almost exclusively as an expression of a positive assessment: 'to find something good, be pleased with something'" and "the abstract form רָצוֹן most often indicates the subjective sentiment of pleasure" ("רצה," *TLOT* 3:1259-60). However, many occurrences appear to be, at least partially, rooted in objective qualities and/or actions, though others are ambiguous in this regard. Gerleman adds, "The root finds greatest usage in theological language: to indicate divine pleasure" (ibid., p. 1260). Terence Fretheim contends that the "striking language of God's delighting" by way of this term "demonstrates that feelings are not foreign to his experience of the world" ("רצה," *NIDOTTE* 3:1186). The term sometimes refers to one's desire or will, in some cases describing God's will (Ps 103:21; 143:10; Ezra 10:1). Norman Walker explains that, similar to חפץ, "the root meaning of רָצוֹן is two-sided, namely *will* and *pleasure*" ("Renderings of rāṣôn," *JBL* 81, no. 2 [1962]: 184; emphasis original). The aspect of acceptance appears in the frequent usage of רצה in sacrificial contexts to describe an offering that is pleasing and thus acceptable to Yahweh (conditional on many aspects of the offering itself and ritual performance, Lev 1:3-4; 7:18; 22:19-27), through which its offerer may be reckoned pleasing, "so that [the offerer] may be accepted" by God (Lev 19:5; 22:29; 23:11; cf. Ex 28:37 [38]). This assumes divine responsiveness to humans and appraisal of their actions. Compare the frequent contrast of the term with the negative evaluation of תּוֹעֵבָה ("abomination," e.g., Prov 15:8).

[10]חפץ and רצה / רָצוֹן are very closely associated (e.g., Ps 147:10-11). Gerleman comments, "The

the parallel between divine love and delight in Proverbs 15:8-9:

> The sacrifice of the wicked is an abomination to the LORD,
> But the prayer of the upright is His delight [רְצוֹן].
>
> The way of the wicked is an abomination to the LORD,
> But He loves [אהב] one who pursues righteousness. (compare Prov 11:20; 12:2, 22)

Similarly, "whom the LORD loves [אהב] He reproves, Even as a father *corrects* the son in whom he delights [רצה]" (Prov 3:12). Moreover, consider the exuberant joy that God will one day take in his people: "He will exult [שׂושׂ] over you with joy [שִׂמְחָה], He will be quiet in His love [אַהֲבָה], He will rejoice [גיל] over you with shouts of joy [רִנָּה]" (Zeph 3:17; compare Deut 30:9-10).[11] O. Palmer Robertson calls this verse "a rapturous description of the love of God for his people. . . . Delight, joy, rejoicing, and singing on God's part underscore the mutuality of emotional experience felt by God and the redeemed."[12]

Likewise, the primary New Testament language of love (the ἀγαπάω and φιλέω word groups) is also closely associated with the New Testament

---

two roots are used synonymously to a great extent," though they "have each undergone unique developments in varied directions" ("חפץ," *TLOT* 1:466). Both overlap significantly with love. The close association between אהב and חפץ is manifest in verses like Deut 21:14-15; 1 Sam 18:22; Ps 34:12 [13]; 109:17; compare 1 Kings 10:9; Is 48:14; 2 Chron 9:8. Talley thus suggests that אהב is possibly a "synonym for חפץ" ("חפץ," *NIDOTTE* 2:232). Regarding the close association between אהב and רצה / רָצוֹן see Prov 3:12; 16:13. Likewise, consider the association of אהב with חשק, which connotes attachment, affection and delight (Deut 7:7-8; 10:15; cf. Gen 34:3, 8). Botterweck suggests that דבק, אהב and חשק may be used synonymously ("חפץ," *TDOT* 5:95). See the discussion of חשק in chap. 4 (above) and the survey of each of these and other terms in John C. Peckham, *The Concept of Divine Love in the Context of the God-World Relationship* (New York: Peter Lang, 2014).

[11]Carl Friedrich Keil and Franz Delitzsch suggest: "Silence in His love is an expression used to denote love deeply felt, which is absorbed in its object with thoughtfulness and admiration" (*Commentary on the Old Testament* [Peabody, MA: Hendrickson, 2002], 10:461).

[12]O. Palmer Robertson, *The Books of Nahum, Habakkuk, and Zephaniah*, NICOT (Grand Rapids: Eerdmans, 1990), p. 339. The terms used in Zeph 3:17 further illuminate divine delight: שׂושׂ consistently means "exult" or "rejoice," and in divine usage, the term denotes divine joy, even rejoicing (Is 62:4 [5]; 66:19; Jer 32:41; cf. Jer 49:25; Is 60:15; Lam 2:15). שׂמחה is a very frequent term of joy, gladness and/or delight. It refers not to lasting joy but to a spontaneous emotion of rejoicing, even exuberance (E. Ruprecht, "שׂמח," *TLOT* 3:1273). It mostly refers to human joy but does appear a few times of God in both verbal and nominal forms (Is 9:17 [16]; Zeph 3:17; Ps 104:31). רנן, another prominent term of joy, often of shouting or singing, appears with God as subject only here in Zeph 3:17. Finally, גיל refers to gladness and rejoicing, and appears with divine agency here and in Is 65:19. Wood comments that this root connotes great "emotional involvement" ("חפץ," *TWOT*, p. 310).

terminology of evaluative delight, pleasure, approval and/or acceptance (the εὐδοκέω[13] and δόκιμος[14] word groups, among others).[15] The term "beloved"

---

[13]The εὐδοκέω word group generally denotes desire, pleasure, delight, satisfaction, approval, preference and/or enjoyment of an object or course of action and corresponds closely to the meaning of חפץ and רצה in the OT, both of which it often translates in the LXX. See H. Bietenhard, "ευδοκεω," NIDNTT 2:817; Ceslas Spicq, "ευδοκέω, ευδοκία," TLNT 2:99; "εὐδοκία," "εκλεγομαι," L&N 1:289, 361. The group often connotes evaluation such that the object of preference or desire is considered to be good, something that might bring pleasure, satisfaction or benefit and/or is worthy of selection. Thus ευδοκία may refer to "that which is desired on the basis of its appearing to be beneficial—'desire, what is wished for'" (ibid., p. 289).

The εὐδοκέω word group overlaps with the categories of election and evaluative love. The NT and LXX usage suggests the connotation of evaluative preference such that the element of volitional choice is bound up with the direction toward something that is viewed as worthy or bringing satisfaction or pleasure. Importantly, however, neither the verb nor the noun ever explicitly refers to arbitrary decision or election. As is the case regarding חפץ in the OT, there is a connection between that in which one takes pleasure and that which one desires, wants, wishes for and thus wills. Will (election), emotion and evaluation are closely interrelated in the use of this term (and elsewhere) such that what one wills is, in fact, what is evaluated as preferable and/or brings one pleasure (cf. Heb 10:38). Thus the term "implies strong volition, as well as taking pleasure in" (Gordon D. Fee, *The First Epistle to the Corinthians*, NICNT [Grand Rapids: Eerdmans, 1987], p. 73). As Markus Barth states: "Far from any idea of arbitrariness, [εὐδοκέω] has warm and personal connotations. When God's good pleasure is mentioned, his willingness and joy in doing good are indicated. The happiness that accompanies a radiant good will is implied" (*Ephesians 1-3*, AB 34 [Garden City, NY: Doubleday, 1974], p. 81). Gottlob Schrenk notes that of all such terms "εὐδοκεῖν brings out most strongly the emotional side of the love of Him who elects" ("ευδοκέω, ευδοκία," TDNT 2:740-41).

A strong case can be made that both the divine will and election themselves show evidence of evaluation in NT usage. For example, the primary terminology of will in the NT, θέλω and βούλομαι, often signify desire and/or delight, as is further supported by their frequent translation of the OT terms for desire and delight in the LXX. The θέλω group also collocates frequently with that of ευδοκέω, such that the divine will (θέλημα) is in accordance with God's good pleasure (εὐδοκία; Eph 1:5, 9; cf. Phil 2:13) or in reference to the lack of divine desire (θέλω) for, or pleasure (εὐδοκέω) in, sacrifices (Heb 10:8; cf. Ps 50:18; 146:10). Likewise, the primary OT term of election (בחר) refers to choice or selection, often with the connotation of evaluation and examination (cf. Is 48:10; Prov 10:20). John N. Oswalt comments that the "root idea is evidently 'to take a keen look at' (KB), thus accounting for the connotation of 'testing or examining'" for that which is "best or most serviceable" ("בחר," TWOT, pp. 100-101). H. Seebass likewise points out that "the principles determining the choice can be scrutinized" ("בחר," TDOT 2:75-76). Likewise, as seen in the previous chapter, the corresponding NT ἐκλέγομαι word group refers to choice or selection, often with the connotation of evaluation and appraisal of what is distinguished, considered the best and/or excellent. Thus, "choosing (and thus the words of this group) includes a judgment by the chooser as to which object he considers to be the most suitable for the fulfilment of his purpose" (Coenen, "ἐκλέγομαι," NIDNTT 1:536; cf. "ἐκλέγομαι," L&N 1:360). Selection of an objective nature was often in view by the ἐκλέγομαι group in classical Greek, where the verb is sometimes used of the choice of what is most beautiful, of the best quality or worthy of praise. See Schrenk, "εκλεγομαι, εκλογη, εκλεκτος," TDNT 4:144, 182. See the discussion of the divine will, election, love and evaluation in Peckham, *Concept of Divine Love*.

[14]The δόκιμος word group generally refers to what has been tested, examined or inspected and is found pleasing, acceptable, approved, worthy and/or reliable. See Walter Grundmann, "δόκιμος," TDNT 2:255-60.

[15]The close association between the terminology of love and delight in the NT appears in Mt 3:17;

(ἀγαπητός) itself often conveys evaluative delight, generally denoting "one who is in a very special relationship with another," thus "one who is dearly loved" and/or "prized, valued," "the object of one's affection" and sometimes even one who is worthy of love.[16] For example, Jesus himself is often the worthy object of divine affection and pleasure, the "beloved" (ἀγαπητός) in whom the Father is "well-pleased" (εὐδοκέω; Mt 3:17; 12:18; 17:5; Mk 1:11; Lk 3:22; 2 Pet 1:17).[17]

By these and other terms throughout Scripture, God's evaluative pleasure and displeasure are readily apparent. God loves (אהב) justice (Is 61:8; Ps 33:5; 37:28) and righteousness (Ps 11:7). Likewise, God delights (חפץ) in righteousness, goodness, obedience and lovingkindness (Jer 9:24; Mic 7:18; cf. 1 Pet 3:4) but takes no pleasure in wickedness (Ps 5:4; cf. Deut 12:31; 28:63; Lk 16:15) or in merely external sacrifice (1 Sam 15:22; Is 1:11, 14; Hos 6:6; 9:4; Amos 5:21-22; Mic 6:7-8; Ps 40:6; Heb 10:8).[18] Indeed, "the LORD takes pleasure [רצה] in His people" (Ps 149:4), who are precious and valuable in his sight (Ex 19:5-6; Deut 26:18; Is 43:4; Mt 10:31; 12:12; Lk 12:24).[19] Whereas God "does not delight [חפץ] in the strength of the horse" or "take pleasure

---

12:18; 17:5; Mk 1:11; Lk 3:22; Phil 1:15-16; Heb 12:6 (cf. Prov 3:12); Jas 1:12; 2 Pet 1:17; cf. Heb 12:6. Likewise, in the LXX the ἀγαπάω word group is used to translate a number of terms of delight, such as חפץ (Ps 50:8; Esther 6:9), רצה (1 Chron 29:17), מָשׂושׂ (Jer 30:31), שׁעע (Ps 93:19) and שַׁעֲשֻׁעִים (Is 5:7). Thus Viktor Warnach speaks of ἀγαπᾶν in the LXX as "love in the sense of placing a high value upon some person or thing, or of receiving them with favour" ("Love," in *Encyclopedia of Biblical Theology*, ed. Johannes Baptist Bauer [London: Sheed and Ward, 1970], p. 518).

[16]"ἀγαπητός," BDAG, p. 7; "αγαπαω, αγαπη," L&N 1:293. "It is used above all of an only and precious child" and is thus a strong term of endearment (Stauffer, "αγαπάω, αγάπη, αγαπητός," *TDNT* 1:37).

[17]In this case, "beloved" status is certainly evaluative, since Jesus is the worthy object of divine love. Robert A. Guelich correctly points out that this collocation with ἀγαπητός "underscores the primary motif of affection, delight and pleasure inherent in εὐδοκεῖν" (*Mark 1-8:26*, WBC 34A [Dallas: Word, 2002], p. 34). Similarly, Spicq emphasizes the "affective meaning" such that the "Father's 'pleasure' is the joy of the love that he bears for the Son" and as such "*eudokeō . . . exegete[s] the divine agapē*" ("ευδοκέω, ευδοκία," *TLNT* 2:102). ἀγαπητός thus not only depicts the evaluative aspect of love but is also closely associated with the volitional and emotional aspects (Mt 12:18; cf. Heb 10:38).

[18]Likewise, a just weight (Prov 11:1), the blameless (Prov 11:20), those who deal faithfully (Prov 12:22) and the prayer of the upright (Prov 15:8) are each characterized as God's "delight" (רָצוֹן), in contrast to a false weight (Prov 11:1), lying lips (Prov 12:22) and the sacrifice of the wicked (Prov 15:8), viewed by God as "abominations" (תּוֹעֵבָה).

[19]Elsewhere, God's people may be "delightful" and/or pleasing to him (2 Sam 22:21-28; 1 Kings 10:9; Jer 31:20; Ps 147:10-11; 149:4; Prov 16:7; Dan 9:23; 2 Chron 9:8; Rom 14:18; Col 1:10; 3:20; 1 Thess 4:1; Heb 11:5; 1 Jn 3:22), and human beings are precious and valuable to God (Is 43:4; Mt 10:31; 12:12; Lk 12:6-7, 24) as his special treasure (Ex 19:5-6; Deut 7:6; 14:2; 26:18).

[רצה] in the legs of a man," the "LORD favors [חפץ] those who fear Him, Those who wait for His lovingkindness" (Ps 147:10-11).²⁰ Likewise, God may be "please[d] [ἀρεσκεία] . . . in all respects" when one walks in a manner "worthy of the Lord" (Col 1:10; cf. Rom 14:18; Col 3:20; 1 Thess 2:12; 4:1; 2 Thess 1:5; Heb 11:5).²¹ Again, children who are obedient to their parents are "well-pleasing [εὐάρεστος] to the Lord" (Col 3:20; cf. 1 Tim 5:4).²² On the other hand, God is appropriately displeased, vexed and grieved by humans who practice evil (Is 9:17 [16]; 65:12; 66:4; Eccles 5:4 [3]; 1 Cor 10:5; 1 Thess 2:15).

These texts and others suggest that God's life is enriched by appropriate human response. As Thomas Oden puts it, God "unapologetically enjoys [creatures] for their own sake."²³ Moreover, that God values humans is explicit in that God cares for even the sparrows, but God cares much more for humans who are "more valuable than many sparrows" (Mt 10:31; compare Mt 12:12; Lk 12:6-7).²⁴ Thus, as Jürgen Moltmann states, God is capable of receiving value, or "an increase of his riches and his bliss."²⁵ Gary Badcock

---

²⁰Talley thus suggests that "God's delight, or the lack thereof, revolves around human obedience (cf. Ps 37:22, 28, 34, 38)" ("חפץ," *NIDOTTE* 2:232).

²¹Here, divine pleasure (ἀρέσκω) is explicitly evaluative by collocation with the term *worthy* (ἀξίως). The ἀρέσκω word group refers to what is pleasing or acceptable on the basis of evaluation. See Werner Foerster, "αρεσκω, et al.," *TDNT* 1:456; H. Bietenhard, "ἀρέσκω," *NIDNTT* 2:814-15. Of divine pleasure, see Jn 8:29; Rom 8:8; 1 Cor 7:32; Gal 1:10; 1 Thess 2:4, 15; 4:1; 1 Jn 3:22; possibly also Rom 15:3; 2 Tim 2:4.

²²εὐάρεστος and εὐαρεστέω refer to what is well-pleasing, acceptable and/or delightful, almost always of pleasure and/or acceptability in the sight of God/Christ, often of an explicitly evaluative nature. The verb εὐαρεστέω appears only 3 times in the NT, all with reference to pleasing God (Heb 11:5, 6; 13:16). The adjective εὐάρεστος appears 9 times in 9 verses, all but one instance (Tit 2:9) of what is pleasing and/or acceptable to God. Humans might be exhorted to be "acceptable to God" (Rom 12:1-2; 14:18) or aspire to please him (2 Cor 5:9; cf. Eph 5:10; Heb 13:21) or are, in fact, "well-pleasing to God" (Phil 4:18; cf. Col 3:20). The evaluative sense is also explicit outside the NT, referring to "the experience of being pleased because of what another does" ("εὐαρέστησις," BDAG, p. 403). Compare Foerster, "αρεσκω, et al.," *TDNT* 1:456-57; Bietenhard, "αρεσκω," *NIDNTT* 2:814-15. The ἀγαπάω word group collocates with the ἀρέσκω word group in a single verse only in the LXX Apocrypha, where it is said of Enoch: "There was one who pleased [εὐάρεστος] God and was loved [ἀγαπάω] by him" (Wis 4:10; cf. Heb 11:5). The word group overlaps with the δόκιμος word group in four instances, all with theological significance (Rom 12:2; 14:18; Eph 5:10; 1 Thess 2:4).

²³Thomas C. Oden, *The Living God* (San Francisco: Harper & Row, 1987), p. 121.

²⁴The term for "more valuable," διαφέρω, means to be superior or worth more. Compare William Foxwell Albright and C. S. Mann, *Matthew*, AB (Garden City, NY: Doubleday, 1971), p. 127.

²⁵Jürgen Moltmann, *The Trinity and the Kingdom: The Doctrine of God*, trans. Margaret Kohl (San Francisco: Harper & Row, 1981), p. 121. See also Gary D. Badcock, "The Concept of Love: Divine and Human," in *Nothing Greater, Nothing Better: Theological Essays on the Love of God*, ed. Kevin J. Vanhoozer (Grand Rapids: Eerdmans, 2001), p. 45; Edward Collins Vacek, *Love, Human and Divine: The Heart of Christian Ethics* (Washington, DC: Georgetown University Press, 1994),

adds that God's love "can be affronted by my disobedience or confirmed and even deepened by my obedience and faithfulness."[26]

The evaluative nature of divine love is perhaps most explicit in that God loves (אהב) the righteous (Ps 146:8) and loves (ἀγαπάω) the "cheerful giver" (2 Cor 9:7; cf. Heb 13:16).[27] However, God hates (שׂנא) those who do iniquity (Ps 5:5 [6]; compare Ps 11:5; Prov 11:20; Rev 2:6). Divine love, then, is not indiscriminate but includes appraisal. However, Leon Morris cautions, "It is going too far to suggest that [such] passages teach that the righteous are so meritorious that they win the love of an otherwise unloving God."[28] To be sure, humans never deserve or merit divine love. However, this recognition should not lead us into a false dichotomy. Divine delight may be evaluative without amounting to winning or meriting God's love or transforming God from unloving to loving. God's pleasure and delight are evaluatively responsive to their objects yet distinct from the scale of evaluation that humans may employ (see the discussion below). Divine pleasure or displeasure in humans is (partially) predicated on human disposition and/or action such that God's love for individuals may be increased and/or decreased according to their disposition and/or actions. As Oden puts it, "All things are loved by God, but all things are not loved in the same way by God, since there are degrees of capacity, receptivity, and willingness among varied creatures to receive God's love."[29]

Does God love only the righteous and hate all others? The examples above demonstrate that there is an evaluative aspect of divine love. However, they also raise significant questions. First, does God love only some and not others? Specifically, does God reserve his love only for the "righteous," such as the "cheerful giver"? Second, since the canon elsewhere states that all have

---

pp. 163-71; Catherine Osborne, *Eros Unveiled: Plato and the God of Love* (Oxford: Clarendon, 1994), p. 65; Vincent Brümmer, *The Model of Love: A Study in Philosophical Theology* (Cambridge: Cambridge University Press, 1993), p. 240.

[26]Badcock, "Concept of Love," p. 41.

[27]Murray J. Harris takes 2 Cor 9:7 to affirm God's "special love" and "special pleasure" in the cheerful giver (cf. Heb 13:16; *The Second Epistle to the Corinthians*, NIGTC [Grand Rapids: Eerdmans, 2005], p. 636). Peter C. Craigie speaks of "a confident expression of the love of a righteous God for a righteous person" (*Psalms 1-50*, WBC 19 [Dallas: Word, 2002], p. 134). Thus, "God's judgment follows his evaluation of people" (Duane A. Garrett, *Proverbs, Ecclesiastes, Song of Songs*, NAC 14 [Nashville: B&H, 1993], pp. 126-27).

[28]Leon Morris, *Testaments of Love: A Study of Love in the Bible* (Grand Rapids: Eerdmans, 1981), p. 95.

[29]Oden, *Living God*, p. 118.

sinned and no one is righteous (Ps 143:2; Rom 3:10, 23), does God actually love none of us? Regarding the second question, God loves unworthy human beings due to his gracious decision to partially and temporarily suspend judgment after the fall. As such, God's positive appraisal of creatures is only partially evaluative. Humans are not worthy of positive evaluation, but God's negative judgments are significantly tempered (though not nullified) by his long-suffering mercy and grace (see the explanation later in this chapter). Regarding the first question, Scripture elsewhere teaches that God loves everyone (Jn 3:16).[30] Therefore, these passages should not be taken to suggest that God loves only the "righteous" but that he loves the "righteous" and the "cheerful giver" in a special, evaluative sense. He delights in, takes pleasure in, approves of and enjoys those who do good, while being displeased by evil.

Yet divine hatred holds serious and significant implications for understanding divine love. As referenced earlier, God is said to actually hate (שׂנא) some humans, particularly those who have rejected God and love evil instead (Jer 12:8; Hos 9:15; Ps 5:5 [6]; 11:5; compare Amos 6:8; Ps 106:40; Prov 11:20; Rev 2:6). As Tony Lane points out, the cliché "God hates the sin but loves the sinner" is self-contradictory if it rules out any animosity toward the person. "It is incoherent to say that God is displeased with child molestation but feels no displeasure toward child molesters."[31]

The Old Testament and New Testament terminology of divine hatred, the antonym of love, depicts the most prominent form of negative divine evaluation, which is often also explicitly emotive (e.g., Is 61:8; Ps 45:7 [8]).[32] For

---

[30]Regarding God's universal love, see chap. 8 (below).

[31]Tony Lane, "The Wrath of God as an Aspect of the Love of God," in Badcock, ed., *Nothing Greater, Nothing Better*, p. 155. In one sense God does hate the sin while loving the sinner in that his long-suffering and amazingly enduring love for the sinner may continue alongside animosity. However, the statement is untrue if it is taken to mean that God entirely separates an unrepentant individual from their sins such that their evil does not affect God's disposition toward them.

[32]שׂנא, hate, is the most prominent term of negative divine evaluation, the antonym of אהב. The root most often refers to the emotional feelings of disdain or hatred for something or someone. It "expresses an emotional attitude toward persons and things which are opposed, detested, despised and with which one wishes to have no contact or relationship. It is therefore the opposite of love" (Groningen, "שׂנא," *TWOT*, p. 880). E. Lipinski adds that the verb "refers to an emotional condition of aversion that OT anthropology locates 'in the heart' [לֵבָב] or in the soul (נֶפֶשׁ)" ("שׂנֵא," *TDOT* 14:164). See Lev 19:17; 2 Sam 5:8; Ps 11:5. In the NT, the ἀγαπάω and φιλέω groups frequently function as the antonym of hatred (μισέω), likewise demonstrably evaluative. See Mt 6:24; Lk 6:13; 23:12; Jn 12:25; 15:19; Jas 4:4. In the LXX love and hate collocate in Gen 37:4; Eccles 3:8; Prov 14:20; compare Prov 27:6; Lam 1:2.

instance, God is not one "who takes pleasure [חָפֵץ] in wickedness" but "hate[s] [שָׂנֵא] all who do iniquity" and "abhors [תעב] the man of bloodshed and deceit" (Ps 5:4-6 [5-7]).[33] Divine hatred is likewise evaluative and emotional in Psalm 11:5, where God "tests [בחן] the righteous and the wicked, And the one who loves violence His soul [שׂנא] hates." Evaluation is evident by reference to examination (בחן), and intense emotionality is manifest by the reference to the soul (נֶפֶשׁ), an idiomatic reference to the seat of emotions.[34] This negative evaluation corresponds to the positive evaluation in Psalm 11:7: God "loves righteousness," and the "upright will behold His face" (compare Prov 15:8-9).[35] The evaluative and emotive contrast between divine love and hate is likewise apparent when James states that "friendship [φιλία] with the world is hostility [ἔχθρα] toward God" and thus "whoever wishes [βούλομαι] to be a friend [φίλος] of the world makes himself an enemy [ἐχθρός] of God" (Jas 4:4). Rejection of friendship with God (compare Jn 15:14; Jas 2:23) thus includes both volition (βούλομαι) and hostile emotion (i.e., enmity, ἔχθρα).[36]

It is crucial to recognize that God's displeasure is never described as arbitrary in Scripture but is in every case prompted by evil (e.g., Jer 12:8; Hos 9:15).[37] Significantly, even those among God's "elect" may become the object of divine displeasure (Hos 8:13; Mal 1:10), while the "outsider" may be accepted by God (Acts 10:35). Thus God was not "well-pleased" (εὐδοκέω)

---

[33] תעב is an emotive term, as demonstrated by its usage throughout the OT. Likewise, as seen earlier, חפץ may connote evaluative and emotive pleasure and/or delight.

[34] בחן means to "scrutinize," implying "testing, proving, assaying" (Craigie, *Psalms 1-50*, p. 33). The evaluative nature and emotional intensity of divine displeasure are further apparent when God declares that he has no "pleasure" (חפץ) in the blood of sacrifices (Is 1:11), his soul "hates" (שׂנא) the festivals and feasts (Is 1:14). J. A. Motyer points out: "*My soul hates* is equivalent to 'I hate with all my heart'" (*Isaiah*, TOTC [Downers Grove, IL: InterVarsity Press, 1999], p. 47).

[35] This provides further evidence that divine love and hatred should not be conflated with choosing and rejecting, respectively (see chap. 4 above). They both may connote volition, evaluation and emotional affection.

[36] Douglas Moo sees this against the background of the OT marriage analogy. Here, then, God is the scorned lover by those who choose "friendship with the world." As such: "'Enemy,' especially in light of the OT background . . . must involve hostility of God toward the believer as well as that of the believer toward God" (*The Letter of James*, PNTC [Grand Rapids: Eerdmans, 2000], p. 187).

[37] With regard to arbitrary or unjust hatred, Scripture laments that Jesus was "hated . . . without cause," the implication being that it is unjust to arbitrarily hate someone (Jn 15:25; cf. Ps 35:19; 69:4).

with those of the elect who rebelled in the wilderness (1 Cor 10:5).[38] As D. A. Carson states, "God's wrath is [not] arbitrary or whimsical" but is the "righteous response of his holiness to sin."[39] Indeed, as Tony Lane states, God's "wrath against a particular sinner is demanded by his love for that particular sinner," as well as all others.[40] At the same time, God's righteous indignation is tempered by his amazing mercy and grace; otherwise we could not even exist. Divine hatred, then, does not necessarily refer to maximal negative emotion, as the term *hate* in English generally connotes. The intensity of the divine feelings of hatred and/or displeasure depends on the context and can vary from the most intense loathing to mild aversion.[41]

Moreover, God may (temporarily) love and hate the same object(s) simultaneously, in different respects. For example, God may come to hate his people evaluatively (Hos 9:15) but still continue to long for a particular, love relationship with them and work toward that end (Hos 14:4). As Lane comments, "God loves sinners, not in the sense that he does not hate them along with their sin, but in the sense that he seeks their salvation in Christ."[42] Eventually, however, absent appropriate human response, evaluative hatred will become permanent, and the benefits of God's love will be forfeited (see

---

[38]Notably, it says "with most of them" he was not "well-pleased," implying also that there were some (a remnant) with whom he was pleased. Of the others, Schrenk contends that this "can only imply rejection" ("εὐδοκέω, εὐδοκία," *TDNT* 2:741). Similarly, Bietenhard, "εὐδοκεω," *NIDNTT* 2:819. As such, divine pleasure and election may be forfeited. Fee comments on their "forfeiture of election—despite their privileges," noting that "the vast majority of them experienced God's judgment and failed the prize" (*1 Corinthians*, p. 450).

[39]D. A. Carson, "Love," in *New Dictionary of Biblical Theology*, ed. T. Desmond Alexander (Downers Grove, IL: InterVarsity Press, 2000), p. 647. In Friedrich Schleiermacher's view, in contrast, divine holiness neither approves nor disapproves of evil, because such approval or disapproval would entail a passivity in God that must be rejected if God is the absolutely simple divine causality. See Schleiermacher, *The Christian Faith*, trans. H. R. Mackintosh (Edinburgh: T & T Clark, 1948), pp. 344-45.

[40]Lane, "Wrath of God," p. 164. God hates evil because, among other reasons, it affects everyone negatively. In other words, his love for all must logically result in the response of hatred toward certain states of affairs and even specific persons who perpetrate evil.

[41]"The gamut of feelings of dislike are included in the scope of שׂנא; it may express the most intense hatred of the enemies of God (Ps 139:21-22), or that of a violent enemy (25:19), but it may simply express that which is to be avoided, such as serving as a guarantor for a debt (Prov 11:15), the feelings of aversion for a poor man (19:7), or the aggravation of a neighbor who visits too often (25:17)" (A. H. Konkel, "שׂנא," *NIDOTTE* 3:1257). Thus the "semantic scope" ranges "from the strongly affective 'to hate'" even "to a somewhat diluted 'to feel aversion for, not want, avoid'" (Ernst Jenni, "שׂנא," *TLOT* 3:1278). See the discussion in Peckham, *Concept of Divine Love*, pp. 250-56.

[42]Lane, "Wrath of God," p. 155.

chapter seven). In the meantime, God longs for the day when his people will be his delight, when he will declare "My delight is in her" for "the LORD delights [חפץ] in you," even "*as* the bridegroom rejoices [שוש] over the bride, So your God will rejoice [שוש] over you" (Is 62:4-5). Likewise, the day will come when God himself "will rejoice [שוש] over them to do them good and will faithfully plant them ... with all [his] heart and with all [his] soul" (Jer 32:41; compare Is 65:19; Ezek 20:39-42; Mal 3:12),[43] even as the father rejoiced over his prodigal son who returned home (Lk 15:20-24; compare Zeph 3:17).[44]

The theo-ontological objection revisited. In the above examples, the evaluative nature of divine love is unmistakable. One might attempt to evade the apparent exegetical meaning of these and similar biblical passages by suggesting that the speech is merely metaphorical or otherwise accommodative. This kind of objection will be taken up in the following chapter, with regard to divine impassibility (which impinges on this question). Here, suffice it to say that from the standpoint of a canonical methodology such as the one adopted in this work, the burden of proof is on the interpreter to (1) provide a sufficient canonical rationale that would overturn the apparent exegetical meaning of these passages and (2) explicate what these and other similar canonical statements convey about God if, in fact, God is incapable of evaluative delight and/or enjoyment in his creatures.[45] I concur with Nicholas Wolterstorff's view: "The fact that the biblical writers speak of God as rejoicing and suffering over the state of creation is not a superficial eliminable feature of their speech. It expresses themes deeply embedded in the biblical vision."[46] If this view is correct, God's love for humans is at least partially contingent on appraisal. God does take evaluative joy and pleasure in his creatures, and this means that God is affected by, and intensely interested in, the lives of humans.[47]

---

[43]Note the intensity added by the phrase "with all My heart and with all My soul" (Jer 32:41), denoting God's cognitive and emotive personality.

[44]God delights when even one lost person is found. See Ezek 34:10-11, 13; Mt 18:13; Lk 15:7, 10, 24.

[45]Of course, one might reject the canonical method employed here. Even in that case, however, one might nevertheless evaluate whether the claim that I make in this regard is properly derived on that method. See chap. 2 (above).

[46]Nicholas Wolterstorff, "Suffering Love," in *Augustine's Confessions: Critical Essays*, ed. William E. Mann (Oxford: Rowman & Littlefield, 2006), p. 136. This should not be taken to imply that the only two options are taking Scripture literally and eliminating its language. See the further discussion in chap. 6 (below).

[47]Wolterstorff suggests: "To act out of love toward something other than oneself is to value that

This stands in stark contrast to the position that God cannot take joy in the world, being altogether "indifferent to value," as Anders Nygren puts it.[48] Some proponents of this theo-ontological objection seem to be invested in upholding God's self-sufficiency and majesty, fearing that allowing for an increase or decrease in God's joy or his experience of value in the world would jeopardize God's independence from the world or require a conception of God as somehow deficient or ontologically dependent on the world.[49] This is indeed one danger of process panentheism and other conceptions of God's love that posit divine need.[50] However, in the foreconditional-reciprocal model, these implications are avoided, since the evaluative aspect of divine love is integrally linked with the volitional aspect. God need not be interested in the world, but he has voluntarily bound his interests to the best interests of his creatures (see the discussion below). That God can appreciate and take joy in the world does not require that he is ontologically deficient; divine delight in creatures is not due to any "need or lack of something in himself."[51] Since God does not need this or any world, he is not es-

---

thing and certain states of that thing" (ibid., p. 135). That God can enjoy human action makes truly meaningful reciprocal love between God and humans possible (see chap. 8 below).

[48]See Nygren's notion of "pure love" as wholly altruistic and self-abnegating, exclusive of all self-interest and self-regard (*Agape and Eros*, pp. 100-101, 130-31, 210). Carl F. H. Henry, however, contends that God is not "indifferent" in the sense that God "realizes value in and through the world" and "he ascribes worth to the created universe." But this involves no "change in God" or that God actually gains something (*God, Revelation, and Authority*, 6 vols. [Wheaton, IL: Crossway, 1999], 5:292, 306). For Millard J. Erickson, similarly, God merely enjoys himself: "God loves us on the basis of that likeness of himself which he has placed within us. He therefore in effect loves himself in us. This likeness to him, however, is not our own doing, but is present in us because of his unselfish, giving, nature" (*Christian Theology* [Grand Rapids: Baker, 1998], p. 320).

[49]Others might object not on ontological grounds but on the fear that such a view inappropriately projects human characteristics onto God. See the discussion of this in chap. 6 (below). Of course, another approach might treat such language as myth from a more primitive religious age. In this regard, consider my discussion in chap. 2 (above) of my hermeneutical commitments regarding the revelation and inspiration of Scripture, which conflict with a view that the writers of Scripture conveyed primitive theological views. Even one who does not accept my hermeneutical commitments in this regard, however, might nevertheless temporarily suspend judgment regarding what should or should not apply to God (on one's view of the nature of God and/or Scripture) and consider what the canon appears to claim regarding God.

[50]For example, Brümmer believes, "Only by needing us can God bestow value on us and upon our love for him. If God does not need us, we become infinitely superfluous" (*Model of Love*, p. 242). Compare Sallie McFague, *Models of God: Theology for an Ecological, Nuclear Age* (Philadelphia: Fortress, 1987), p. 134.

[51]Oden, *Living God*, p. 121. Both Moltmann and Oden, among others, are careful to note that although God can and does enjoy his creatures, this is not out of divine need, lack or deficiency (ibid.; Moltmann, *Trinity and the Kingdom*, pp. 45, 168).

sentially dependent on any value in the world for his own being, and neither is his majesty or goodness growing as the world progresses (contra process panentheism).

In my view, conceiving of God as one who cannot appreciate beauty or rejoice in the love of creatures conflicts with the grand narrative of Scripture as the story of God's love relationship with his people and appears to depict God as morally, personally and aesthetically ambivalent, impervious to good and evil, joy and suffering, beauty and discord. As Gary Badcock states, "Were it true to say that God is simply indifferent to its goodness or its rebellion, or that his beneficence in relation to the world takes no account of the events that take place in it, then it would not be possible to say of him that he loves the world."[52] Accordingly, Nicholas Wolterstorff states, "God's love for his world is a rejoicing and suffering love. The picture of God as Stoic sage, ever blissful and nonsuffering, is in deep conflict with the biblical picture."[53] In this way, the canonical data point away from the supposition of an ontological restriction on divine evaluation and enjoyment and point toward God's appropriate appraisal of the world.[54]

GOD'S LOVE INCLUDES SELF-INTEREST VOLUNTARILY BOUND TO THE BEST INTERESTS OF OTHERS

Is God selfish? God's evaluative love entails that God derives pleasure from the positive disposition and actions of humans but is displeased at sin and evil of every kind. Yet does that mean God is selfish? Many posit that pure love is wholly self-sacrificial. That is, love that receives value or benefits is considered to be selfish (the moral objection).[55] From this standpoint, God's love is "purely gratuitous," a love that gives but never receives.[56] As Millard Erickson puts it, God's "love for us and for his other creatures is

---

[52]Badcock, "Concept of Love," p. 46. Catherine Osborne likewise comments: "To suggest that God did not delight in such things [as worship of himself, contrite hearts, uprightness, mercy, etc.], or did not take any interest in such matters at all, would already imply that God was aloof and careless of humanity" (*Eros Unveiled*, p. 65).
[53]Wolterstorff, "Suffering Love," p. 136.
[54]See chap. 6 (below) on divine impassibility, and the further discussion of the theo-ontological implications of divine love in chap. 9 (below).
[55]See, for example, Nygren, *Agape and Eros*, p. 210.
[56]Ceslas Spicq, *Agape in the New Testament*, 3 vols. (St. Louis: B. Herder, 1963), 1:53. Compare Nygren, *Agape and Eros*, pp. 77-78, 157; Alan Torrance, "Is Love the Essence of God?" in Vanhoozer, ed., *Nothing Greater, Nothing Better*, pp. 130, 32.

completely disinterested."[57] Conversely, Thomas Jay Oord argues, "Defining love exclusively in terms of self-sacrifice is not biblical" because "biblical authors affirm self-love."[58] Similarly, Stephen Post astutely notes that "the western tendency to idealize selfless love devoid of even the slightest iota of self-concern is an aberration from the valid ideal of unselfishness in fellowship."[59]

One can understand why anyone who believes that receiving requires deficiency or manifests improper self-interest would deny that God takes pleasure in the world. However, what if such a conception is predicated on a false dichotomy of altruism and egoism? What if God manifests a proper self-interest that is not in conflict with other interest but itself includes the best interests of all of his creatures? For example, consider God's apparent self-interest in many instances of concern for his name (e.g., Ps 106:8; Is 48:9-11; Ezek 20:9, 14, 22; compare Ps 79:9; 143:11), which might be understood as a proper end in itself (since God is the appropriate object of praise, worship, exaltation and love) yet also as a means to an other-directed end—the revelation of his character of love toward evoking human love in response (see chapter eight).

Whereas love may be manifest in self-sacrifice, Scripture does not restrict the concept of love to pure altruism. On the contrary, the Bible recognizes appropriate self-love and self-interest that does not exclude other-interest, in contrast to selfishness and self-centeredness.[60] For example, God commands, "love your neighbor as yourself" (Lev 19:18; Mt 22:39; Rom 13:9 et al.). Likewise, the golden rule states: "treat people the same way you want them to treat you" (Mt 7:12; compare Lk 6:31).[61] Both of these axioms

---

[57]Erickson, *Christian Theology*, p. 319. H. Ray Dunning likewise refers to God's love as "disinterested love," which is "in no way based on the worth of the object" (*Grace, Faith, and Holiness: A Wesleyan Systematic Theology* [Kansas City, MO: Beacon Hill, 1988], p. 195).

[58]Thomas Jay Oord, *The Nature of Love: A Theology* (St. Louis: Chalice, 2010), p. 27.

[59]Stephen G. Post, *A Theory of Agape: On the Meaning of Christian Love* (Lewisburg, PA: Bucknell University Press, 1990), p. 12. Compare Gene H. Outka, *Agape: An Ethical Analysis* (New Haven, CT: Yale University Press, 1972), p. 275.

[60]Here I use *selfishness* to refer to improper self-interest over and against the proper regard for God and others. While God has proper self-interest, he is never selfish. Human beings, on the other hand, are selfish by nature.

[61]John Nolland rightly contends that far from utter self-disregard, the "text assumes positive self-regard and the care for oneself that goes with this" such that "even love for God . . . should not be seen, despite all the rigours of discipleship, as extinguishing the significance of our own well-being (cf. Mt. 7:12; Eph. 5:29)" (*The Gospel of Matthew*, NIGTC [Grand Rapids: Eerdmans,

presuppose appropriate self-regard that is inclusive of regard for others. Likewise, the husband is "to love his own wife even as himself" (Eph 5:33; compare Eph 5:28). Peter O'Brien comments: "The husband's obligation to love his wife as his own body is not simply a matter of loving someone else just like he loves himself. It is, in fact, to love himself."[62] The biblical mandate toward other-interest, then, does not exclude all self-interest.[63] Accordingly, many theologians throughout the ages have recognized a proper place for self-love.[64]

God in Christ is the model of both proper self-love and profound other-love.[65] God rightly commands and receives worship and glory, and enjoys and delights in relationship with his people. However, divine self-interest does not exclude other-interest. Rather, by God's free decision to create, sustain and invest his love in the world, God's self-interest includes the *best*

2005], p. 912). Among others, Craig Blomberg also recognizes that while this is "not a call to self-love," it "does presuppose it" (*Matthew*, NAC 22 [Nashville: B&H, 2001], p. 335). Accordingly, at least some kind of self-love is appropriate. However, self-regard is not to be the ultimate object of one's love. Thus Jesus also states "He who loves his life loses it, and he who hates his life in this world will keep it to life eternal" (Jn 12:25). Importantly, this text does not command one to hate oneself but specifically to hate one's "life in this world." As such, the emphasis is on that selfishness that values one's own human existence above the things of God, thus loving the world (through self) rather than God (cf. 2 Tim 3:2-4).

[62]Peter O'Brien, *The Letter to the Ephesians*, PNTC (Grand Rapids: Eerdmans, 1999), pp. 426-27. So Markus Barth, *Ephesians 4-6* (AB 34A; Garden City, NY: Doubleday, 1974), p. 636; Gregory W. Dawes, *The Body in Question: Metaphor and Meaning in the Interpretation of Ephesians 5:21-33* (Leiden: Brill, 1998), pp. 153-54.

[63]I do not mean to imply that these texts by themselves suggest divine self-love but merely that they show that self-love (of at least some kind) may be appropriate.

[64]See, for example, Augustine, *The Trinity* 15.19.37 (*NPNF* 3:423-24); Thomas Aquinas, *Summa Theologica* 2.2.26.4 (Ages 3:326); Post, *Theory of Agape*, pp. 17-20; Osborne, *Eros Unveiled*, p. 72; Oord, *Nature of Love*, p. 13.

[65]Here I do not mean to imply that intratrinitarian love should be applied in a direct manner as a model of human relationships. As Kathryn Tanner notes: "No matter how close the similarities between human and divine persons, and between a human society and the unity of the trinity, differences always remain—God is not us—and this sets up the major problem for theologies that want to base conclusions about human relationships on the trinity. The chief complication is how to move from a discussion of God to human relationships, given those differences" (*Christ the Key* [New York: Cambridge University Press, 2010], p. 221). Thus, "much of what is said about the trinity simply does not seem directly applicable to humans" in light of our "essential finitude" (ibid., p. 224). Further, I agree with Tanner's concern regarding the considerable danger of extrapolating from what we suppose we know about the Trinity and projecting that onto human society. As Tanner states, "unless one purports to know much more about relations among the trinitarian persons than is probably warranted, one is still left with very vague recommendations" regarding social goods that leave a great deal up to the "ingenuity of the theologian arguing on other grounds" such that political recommendations "amount to little more than what the theologian already believes" (ibid., p. 223).

interests of all others. For example, in Ephesians 5 the church is presented as analogous to Christ's bride *and* his own body: "Husbands, love your wives, just as Christ also loved the church and gave Himself up for her.... So husbands ought also to love their own wives as their own bodies. He who loves his own wife loves himself; for no one ever hated his own flesh, but nourishes and cherishes it, just as Christ also *does* the church, because we are members of His body" (Eph 5:25, 28-30).[66] In these parallel metaphors of love, the giver (Christ) receives by giving. This is far from the selfishness that 1 Corinthians 13:5 excludes by stating that love "does not seek its own." It is appropriate self-interest that includes other-interest. The self-sacrificial love of Christ in dying for the church that she might be redeemed as his bride is bound up with his self-love, that is, his love for his metaphorical body, the church. Torrance sees God's giving of Christ for us (in Rom 8:32) as striking evidence that "God loves us more than he loves himself."[67]

While process thinkers might see in this passage an example of panentheism, the fact that the two metaphors of wife and body are mutually exclusive, if applied literally, rules this notion out. Such language should not be taken to refer to an essential relation between Jesus and human beings any more than a man and a woman form an essential relation when they are married and "become one" (Gen 2:24; 1 Cor 6:16). Indeed, God's self-love, as understood by the foreconditional-reciprocal model, is quite different from that proposed by the process panentheist view that God is internally related

---

[66]Note that this passage refers not only to Christ's earthly life but also to the risen Christ, who remains fully God. I take this passage to be a valid example of a kind of divine, other-inclusive self-love, in the person of Christ, on the basis of my commitment to the minimal claim that, in becoming fully human in the incarnation, Christ was and is no less than fully divine. See the discussion of this in chap. 2 (above). At the same time, as fully human, the earthly life of Jesus "exhibits" and thus models "the sort of relations that humans, in the image of the Son, are to have with Father and Spirit," but "in his relations with other people, Jesus also shows how those relations with Father and Spirit are to work themselves out in community with other people" (Tanner, *Christ the Key*, p. 236).

[67]Thomas F. Torrance, *The Christian Doctrine of God: One Being Three Persons* (New York: T & T Clark, 2001), p. 244. Compare Eberhard Jüngel's view that "love is not identical with absolute selflessness" (*God as the Mystery of the World* [Grand Rapids: Eerdmans, 1983], p. 318). Rather, "love is that still greater selflessness within such great self-relatedness" as it is in "reference to the God who gives up what is most authentic for him in the person of the Crucified One" (ibid., p. 374). Here, "God is the one who loves himself" via an "irremovable differentiation within himself," and, sending the Son, "subjects himself to lovelessness in the beloved" (ibid., p. 327). Compare ibid., p. 385.

to all others such that "promoting their welfare contributes to his own."[68] First, God identifies with the interests of others volitionally, not essentially. Second, God identifies with the *best* interests of his creatures, which must be distinguished from what humans might consider their own interests. God does not identify with evil "interests," and in this way God's interest in the interests of others is evaluative rather than essentially indiscriminate.

Thus God's own enjoyment is both evaluative *and* voluntarily tied to the joy of his creatures, akin to a loving parent's joy in his or her child's happiness. Is the loving parent selfish for taking delight in the joy of his or her children? Certainly not. However, the loving parent also doesn't take joy in self-destructive "pleasure." Likewise, while God has proper self-interest, he is never selfish. God's life is intimately affected by the lives of his children because he has made their best interests his own; the joy of others is integral to God's own joy, but voluntarily and evaluatively, not essentially. As such, Gordon D. Fee is correct when he states that God really does take delight in his creatures, not in the sense that he is "a self-gratifying being after all," but rather, "all that God does he does for his pleasure; but since God is wholly good, his doing what pleases him is not capricious, but what is wholly good for those he loves. God's pleasure is pure love, so what he does 'for the sake of his good pleasure' is by that very fact also on behalf of those he loves. After all, it delights God to delight his people."[69] Whereas selfish humans often place their own interests above those of others, God experiences no such conflict of interests because his will is perfectly directed toward the best good of all. In this manner, God models, affirms and prescribes an unselfish self-interest and a non-self-abnegating other-interest.[70]

Is divine love essentially self-sacrificial? It is commonly believed that divine love is essentially self-sacrificial.[71] Indeed, "many Christians rec-

---

[68]Charles Hartshorne, *Man's Vision of God and the Logic of Theism* (Hamden, CT: Archon, 1964), p. 147.

[69]Gordon D. Fee, *Paul's Letter to the Philippians*, NICNT (Grand Rapids: Eerdmans, 1995), pp. 239-40.

[70]Humans may rightly be called to abnegate "self" if "self" refers to one's selfish sinful nature. God's "self," however, includes no such selfishness. Nevertheless, if abnegation is taken in a weaker sense, then one might affirm T. F. Torrance's comment that "our salvation is grounded immutably in the self-abnegating Love of God" (*Christian Doctrine of God*, p. 254). That Torrance does not mean to suggest something like absolute self-abnegation is apparent in that he also speaks of "the love of the eternally self-affirming and self-giving God" (ibid., p. 246).

[71]For example, Norman L. Geisler suggests that "*agape* used of God's love means 'benevolence,'

ommend a complete and unreserved sacrifice of self as the highest ideal" of love.[72] This view is often associated (though not necessarily so) with the dichotomy between "need love" that desires and/or enjoys (thematic *eros*) and "gift love" (thematic *agape*) that is purely altruistic; it "does not seek value, but it creates value or gives value."[73] On the other hand, Thomas Oden contends that "to separate *eros* and *agapē* or to oppose them or set them absolutely off against each other as alternatives (cf. Nygren, *Agapē and Eros*) is to view love incompletely and to fail to understand how one dimension may strengthen the other."[74] Indeed, as seen in chapter three, "both *eros* and *agape* can be used to designate love characterized by *either* generous *or* self-interested concerns."[75]

To be sure, Christians are called to outgoing love, to place the needs of others above our own (1 Cor 13:5; Phil 2:3-4). Christ himself modeled the greatest love in giving his own life that others might live (Jn 15:13). Nevertheless, although many situations demand love manifest in self-sacrifice, love is not itself essentially self-sacrificial. Christ's self-sacrifice was needed because of the intrusion of evil.[76] In a perfect world, there is no need for utter self-sacrifice; all creaturely interests will be in accord with God's will and thus part of an unceasingly harmonious, cosmic symphony of "mutual flourishing."[77] As such, self-sacrifice is only temporary and

---

a self-less 'sacrificial' love" (Norman L. Geisler, *Systematic Theology*, vol. 2, *God, Creation* [Minneapolis: Bethany House, 2002], p. 367). So Henry, *God, Revelation, and Authority*, 6:344. Compare chap. 3 (above).

[72]Vacek, *Love, Human and Divine*, p. 184. Compare Reinhold Niebuhr, *The Nature and Destiny of Man: A Christian Interpretation* (New York: Scribner, 1964), 2:82.

[73]Emil Brunner, *The Christian Doctrine of God* (London: Lutterworth, 1949), p. 186. See the discussion of Nygren's *agape-eros* dichotomy in chaps. 1 and 3 (above).

[74]Oden, *Living God*, p. 119.

[75]Osborne, *Eros Unveiled*, p. 70; emphasis original.

[76]While the view that Christ became incarnate because of the fall (infralapsarian Christology) has been the majority view throughout Christian history, numerous theologians (e.g., Friedrich Schleiermacher, Isaak Dorner and Karl Barth, among others) have suggested that the incarnation is not "only a divine countermeasure against sin" but also that Christ became incarnate for other reasons (supralapsarian Christology) (Edwin Chr. van Driel, *Incarnation Anyway: Arguments for a Supralapsarian Christology* [New York: Oxford University Press, 2008], p. 164). T. F. Torrance comments, in this regard, "While clapping our hands upon our mouth, without knowing what we say, we may nevertheless feel urged to say that in his eternal purpose the immeasurable Love of God . . . would have become incarnate within the creation even if we and our world were not in need of his redeeming grace" (*Christian Doctrine of God*, p. 210). Compare Robert W. Jenson, *Systematic Theology* (New York: Oxford University Press, 1997), 1:73.

[77]Tanner, *Christ the Key*, p. 235.

therefore cannot be essential to love or exhaustive of its meaning.[78]

Self-sacrifice is virtuous in the appropriate circumstances, but "as a universal principle, self-sacrifice is self-contradictory."[79] Imagine a world where every individual *always* acts self-sacrificially. When two people arrive at the same door, they would both insist on holding the door open for the other and, consequently, neither would ever enter.[80] If everyone always gives but never receives, then there would be no one to receive what is given. As Stephen Post observes, "Self-less, purely one-way love may be an understandable exaggeration of unselfishness, but its impact is essentially negative in that it undermines the circular flow of giving and receiving in which *agape* is sustained and supported."[81] Further, Gene Outka warns: "The feature of self-sacrifice in itself would appear to provide no way of distinguishing between attention to another's needs and submission to his exploitation and no warrant for resisting the latter."[82]

Christ is himself the perfect model of self-sacrificial love, yet he does not view others as superior to himself (Phil 2:3). He could not do so without falsehood. Christ voluntarily lowered himself for the good of all (Phil 2:5-8), but he is to be exalted (Phil 2:9-11). In this way, viewing others as better than oneself (Phil 2:3) cannot be a universal principle but might be understood as a corrective principle that applies in this sinful world, over and against the selfishness of human nature and in light of the recognition that each human is undeserving of God's love (Rom 3:23). God, on the other hand, is neither selfish nor self-serving but desires the best interests of all creatures as well as the glory and exaltation that rightfully belong to him. Only a false elevation of tragedy suggests that God's own joy should be excluded from his interests. As Eberhard Jüngel puts it, a "love story which is only a story of suffering and wants to be only that would contradict the essence of love."

---

[78]Self-denial in the sense that one does not elevate one's own interest above or to the exclusion of others will remain as an eternal principle, but that is not the same as self-sacrifice. Consider Tanner's suggestion that "loss in giving to others on the human plane is a function of a world in disarray and not a necessary consequence of simple finitude." The world might be "arranged in ways that make giving to others a benefit to oneself" (ibid., p. 228). The kingdom is thus to be one of "mutual flourishing" and thus "like the trinity in that" it is "a community of mutual fulfillment in which the good of one becomes the good for all" (ibid., p. 235).
[79]Vacek, *Love, Human and Divine*, p. 184. So Oord, *Nature of Love*, p. 27.
[80]This analogy is a paraphrase of that found in Vacek, *Love, Human and Divine*, p. 184.
[81]Post, *Theory of Agape*, p. 12.
[82]Outka, *Agape*, p. 275.

Thus, the New Testament "does not tell the passion story" of Christ "as a lamentation."[83] The tragedy of the cross, then, is not an end in itself, but a means to the greater end of God's reconciliation with his beloved creatures. Christ "endured the cross," according to Hebrews 12:2, "for the joy set before Him" (compare Jn 15:11; 17:13).[84] Christ's role as servant rather than the one being served, while denying immediate self-gratification in the face of evil, contributed to Christ's ultimate delight, the salvation of his beloved and the enjoyment of a bilateral love relationship with them. Self-sacrifice cannot be the *ultimate* end of divine interest, since it cannot possibly serve as an *ultimate* end of other-interest. If God were to sacrifice his very existence, then no others would exist, since all existence is dependent on God. Thus the suggestion that God's love is *essentially* sacrificial is ontologically impossible.

Some might nevertheless argue that any self-interest detracts from the purity of God's love. However, proper self-interest makes God's sacrificial love even more profoundly amazing.[85] If God has no self-interest by nature, then he has no interests to sacrifice. That is, if nothing can actually add to or subtract from God's happiness, in what sense can sacrifice be made by God? In such a view, God does not seek his own interests, simply because he has none. Likewise, but from a vastly different premise, the process view arrives at the conclusion that "God can make no sacrifices" because of God's es-

---

[83]Jüngel, *God as the Mystery*, p. 374. Tanner adds: "Here is a God who works unswervingly for our good, who puts no value on death and suffering [in and of itself], and no ultimate value on self-sacrifice for the good, a God of gift-giving abundance struggling against the forces of sin and death in the greatest possible solidarity with us—that of incarnation" (*Christ the Key*, p. 261).

[84]Christ's joy is, here again, inclusive of the joy of others. As F. F. Bruce comments, "'The joy set before him' is not something for himself alone, but something to be shared with those for whom he died as sacrifice and lives as high priest" (*The Epistle to the Hebrews*, NICOT [Grand Rapids: Eerdmans, 1990], p. 339).

[85]Scripture manifests that, at the cross, both the Son and the Father "sacrifice" for us in vastly different ways. Although "our Lord Jesus Christ . . . was rich," for our "sake He became poor" (2 Cor 8:9; cf. Phil 2:5-8). Accordingly, we "know love" in that the Son "laid down His life for us" (1 Jn 3:16; cf. Jn 10:17-18; Eph 5:2; Heb 9:26) and undergoes forsakenness (Mt 27:46), while the Father gives his beloved Son out of love for the world: "By this the love of God was manifested in us, that God has sent His only begotten Son into the world so that we might live through Him. In this is love . . . that He loved us and sent His Son *to be* the propitiation for our sins" (1 Jn 4:9-10; cf. Jn 3:16; Rom 8:32). The person of Christ, being fully human but no less than fully divine (see chap. 2 above), manifests divine love in his self-giving sacrifice in a manner unique to his situatedness as incarnate, but the Father also makes a sacrifice that manifests divine love in his own manner. T. F. Torrance suggests further that "[b]ehind the cry of Jesus on the cross there is a mysterious movement in the divine Triunity, a counterpoint between the *pathos* in the crucified Jesus and the *pathos* in God" (*Christian Doctrine of God*, p. 251).

sential relation to all.⁸⁶ However, Scripture depicts God as voluntarily binding his own happiness (but not his existence) to that of his creatures, culminating in the ultimate manifestation of God's love at the cross (Jn 3:16; Rom 5:8). Understood in this way, God's self-sacrifice is magnified, not reduced. If this understanding is correct, the supposition that purely altruistic love (thematic *agape*) is the only true kind of "Christian" love, excluding other aspects such as attraction, enjoyment, pleasure and responsive affection, is unwarranted.⁸⁷

THE PARTIAL AND TEMPORARY SUSPENSION OF THE EFFECTS OF DIVINE EVALUATION

This brings us to the third rationale often used against the evaluative nature of love: Even if God could receive value and it was not selfish to do so, humans are incapable of generating value or eliciting God's delight (as totally depraved and/or otherwise). In this way, God's love is sometimes equated with love for the unworthy. Leon Morris thus states that divine love "is not a love of the worthy" but "a love for the completely undeserving" and "entirely unworthy."⁸⁸ He adds, "We do not bring anything valuable to God—in fact, we acquire value only because we are the recipients of his love."⁸⁹ Likewise, Carl F. H. Henry considers love as beneficence "bestowed not upon a worthy object and not for the personal advantage of the Lover but solely for the benefit of the undeserving recipient."⁹⁰ On the other hand, Edward Collins Vacek suggests that "*agape* is not oriented only to the neediness or incompleteness of others."⁹¹

---

⁸⁶Hartshorne, *Man's Vision of God*, p. 161.

⁸⁷D. A. Carson likewise holds that love is more than altruism, pointing to Paul's contention that even the greatest kinds of giving are possible without love (1 Cor 13): "This surely demonstrates that the love he has in mind is more sweeping than mere altruism, than mere commitment to the good of the other, however self-denying" ("Love," p. 646).

⁸⁸Morris, *Testaments of Love*, pp. 128, 271, 382. Elsewhere Morris allows that the "fact that it denotes a spontaneous, unmotivated love does not mean that it can be directed only toward the unworthy" (ibid., p. 138). To be consistent, then, he must mean that God's love is *sometimes* spontaneous and unmotivated.

⁸⁹Ibid., p. 142. Accordingly, "God delights in this people simply because he chooses to do so" such that there is not "something in them that delights him" (ibid., p. 93). This claim that divine delight is self-determined wholly apart from its object does not accord with the frequent biblical depictions of divine delight as explicitly evaluative.

⁹⁰Henry, *God, Revelation and Authority*, 6:343.

⁹¹Vacek, *Love, Human and Divine*, p. 163.

God's love for the worthy and unworthy. Because we encounter God's love from the human perspective as undeserving recipients, it is not surprising that some view love as essentially love for the undeserving. Indeed, most of the instances of divine love throughout Scripture depict love for the unworthy, since Scripture focuses on God's love for sinners. However, although God loves unworthy humans, God's love itself cannot be *essentially* love for the unworthy, since his love has always been directed toward the entirely worthy Son and Spirit (Jn 17:24). Christ is supremely worthy, excellent, valuable, precious, choice and lovable. Thus the Father declares: "This is My beloved [ἀγαπητός] Son, in whom I am well-pleased [εὐδοκέω]" (Mt 3:17).[92] The Father's love for the Son is not unmotivated or spontaneous but grounded in the reality of who Jesus is *and* what he does.[93] The Father is not only pleased with Christ as his "Son" but loves Christ "because" he lays down his life (Jn 10:17).[94] Accordingly, the Father's love toward the Son depicts volition (election), evaluation and emotion as complementary. He is the "choice" (best) one, the worthy (Mt 12:18).[95] Such election is neither arbitrary nor spontaneous but evaluative; none other could be chosen in his place.[96] He is well-pleasing, for in all his actions he elicits delight; he is "beloved," that is, the Father loves the Son and in such a way that recognizes

---

[92]See also Is 42:1; Mt 3:17; 12:18; 17:5; Mk 1:11; 9:7; Lk 3:22; 9:35; Jn 8:29; Heb 1:9; 10:38; 1 Pet 2:4, 6; 2 Pet 1:17; Rev 5:9, 12.
[93]On the explicitly evaluative delight connoted in many such instances see Spicq, *Agape*, 1:49-50, 53.
[94]R. T. France, among others, sees the declarations as "God's pleasure" in "obedience" and also "more fundamentally" Jesus' "own relationship with God" (*The Gospel of Matthew*, NICNT [Grand Rapids: Eerdmans, 2007], pp. 122-23). So Nolland, *Matthew*, p. 158. Some, however, place the emphasis on God's past evaluative choice (e.g., Joel Marcus, *Mark 1-8*, AB 27 [New York: Doubleday, 2000], p. 163), while others view the statement as one of present, evaluative approval. See discussion in Robert G. Bratcher and Eugene Albert Nida, *A Handbook on the Gospel of Mark* (New York: UBS, 1993), p. 31. Approval toward Christ's obedience on earth would complement the narrative of the wilderness testing, which follows in Matthew and Mark.
[95]Indeed, the various statements of the Father's delight in the beloved and chosen Son (Mt 3:17; 17:5; Mk 1:11; Lk 3:22; cf. Mk 9:7; Lk 9:35) highlight the strong association between ἀγαπητός, εὐδοκέω and (to a lesser extent) ἐκλέγομαι (Mt 12:18). On this close association consider the discussion earlier in this chapter.
[96]If Christ's status as God's beloved, well-pleasing and elect one is taken to derive from arbitrary and nonevaluative election, it calls into question Christ's intrinsic status as preexistent, altogether worthy and very God, and may leave the door open for some form of adoptionism, which is ruled out in the Gospels (see Mt 2:15; Lk 1:32-35; 2:49; cf. Jn 1:1-3; 8:58; Col 2:9 et al.). That Jesus' election was evaluative is likewise apparent in that Jesus was anointed by God because he has "loved righteousness and hated lawlessness" (Heb 1:9; cf. 1 Pet 2:4).

that the Son is worthy to be loved (compare Rev 5:2, 4, 9, 12). Therefore God is manifestly capable of appreciating value and loving the lovable.[97]

Regarding sinful humans as objects of divine love, however, there is a tension between God's evaluative love and the fact that no mere human has ever remained worthy of love. God loves the righteous (Ps 146:8), yet "there is none righteous, not even one" (Rom 3:10; Ps 143:2). All our righteousness is but filthy rags (Is 64:6). Without God's intervention, fallen humans are incapable of bringing anything valuable to God and are thus unworthy of divine love.[98] Yet God has graciously and mercifully made a way by partially and temporarily suspending the consequences of evaluation (e.g., Acts 17:3).[99] That is, because of God's voluntary and undeserved steadfast love, manifested in mercy and grace, the otherwise immediate eradication of evil is temporarily suspended so that all who will respond to God's loving overtures might be reconciled to him (compare 2 Pet 3:9; Ezek 18:32; 33:11).[100] It is only by God's freely bestowed grace that humans were created in the first place and continue to exist after the fall, let alone remain the objects of God's love. Here again, the evaluative aspect of divine love is complemented by its volitional aspect.[101] As T. F. Torrance puts it, in love God "has irrevocably

---

[97]Notably, even Nygren "finds in John the concept of a love that is motivated by the inherent worth of the Son. This at once denies his own definition of *agape* as a love freely outflowing and unmotivated" (G. Johnston, "Love in the NT," *IDB* 3:177). Nygren does not allow this to defeat his view, however, by claiming that the Johannine conception of love is deficient. Compare Nygren, *Agape and Eros*, p. 158.

[98]Nevertheless, although humans cannot generate value without mediation, all humans possess intrinsic value, not deservedly or of their own making, but because God has invested value in each one whom he "fearfully and wonderfully made" (Ps 139:14) in his own image (Gen 1:26-27).

[99]This suspension of the effects of evaluative judgment is "partial," since God still executes some judgment at all times but, presently, his positive appraisal of sinful humans is only partially evaluative, since no creaturely objects are themselves worthy of positive appraisal, and his negative judgments are significantly tempered (but not nullified) by his long-suffering mercy and grace. Therefore, the word *righteous* is used of sinful humans in a qualified sense, a partial righteousness corresponding to the partial suspension of the effects of judgment.

[100]Mercy and grace themselves entail the suspension of some effects of evaluative judgment.

[101]What about the command to "love your enemies" (Mt 5:44)? The call to love others, even enemies, does not nullify evaluation but applies to this particular evil world. While no creatures in this postfall world are worthy of love, on the fruition of the plan of salvation and the eradication of evil all creatures will once again be perfectly lovable. In the meantime, God bestows his universal love on the just and the unjust and commands Christians to do likewise (Mt 5:44-45; Lk 6:35-36). Time remains for those who are now enemies to accept God, and thus everyone should be shown the kind of love that temporarily suspends condemnation (1 Cor 4:5), just as all humans have been the beneficiaries of this temporary suspension (cf. Deut 10:18-19; Mt 7:1-2; 18:26-33; Lk 6:37). Yet, even in Mt 5 it is clear that the effects of evaluation are suspended

committed his Being to relationship with us" and thus "freely seeks and creates fellowship with us, utterly undeserving sinners though we are."[102]

God's prevenient action and mediation. Prior to glorification, humans may bring value to God only through (1) the divine initiative of prevenient grace and foreconditional love and (2) the mediation of Christ. First, God voluntarily bestows prevenient grace and foreconditional love, which create the possibility of appropriate human response. God's prevenient grace is that grace which is bestowed prior to any human response and itself enables human response.[103] God's foreconditional love is that love which he freely grants to all humans prior to, but not exclusive of, conditions (see chapter seven). Prior to any human action, God has loved humans and draws them to himself (Jer 31:3) such that human love is predicated on, and responsive to, prior divine love (1 Jn 4:19). Second, Christ's mediation makes up for the deficiencies of those who are "in Christ" by faith (Rom 8:1). That is, God values the human intention and motivation (itself impossible without God's prior action) and adds to that intention and motivation the ongoing mediation of Christ that makes up for human deficiencies (compare 1 Pet 2:5).

The manner in which this partial and temporary suspension of judgment operates is displayed in the Old Testament by way of the sanctuary system, in which priests mediated the acceptability of humans before God. The sacrificial system typified Jesus Christ the righteous, who gave himself as "an

---

but not nullified in that God promises eschatological reward for those who love their enemies (Mt 5:45-6:6; Lk 6:31-37), being indirectly love toward God. Thus, as Jerry Walls puts it, "To sacrifice such goods for the sake of others is to trust that Trinity is ultimate reality, that giving is reciprocal and mutual in the end" (*Heaven: The Logic of Eternal Joy* [New York: Oxford University Press, 2002], p. 191). The command of "enemy love" and God's love for those who now reject him thus do not contradict God's evaluative love, and neither do they rule out a special kind of love reserved for those within the context of a particular, love relationship. This issue of insider and outsider love is taken up in chap. 8 (below).

[102]Torrance, *Christian Doctrine of God*, p. 5.

[103]Here and elsewhere I use the terminology of *prevenient grace* in the minimal sense that may be derived from this textual evidence of God's initiative to reach out to humans and actively seek to draw humans to himself prior to any human decision (cf. Ezek 34:11, 16; Lk 19:10; Jn 1:9; 6:44; 12:32; 15:16; 1 Jn 3:1; 4:9-10, 19). This is compatible with more developed accounts of prevenient grace but does not require their validity. Compare Thomas Oden's definition of prevenient grace as "the grace that begins to enable one to choose further to cooperate with saving grace," through which "the person then may freely and increasingly become an active, willing participant in receiving the conditions for justification" (*John Wesley's Scriptural Christianity: A Plain Exposition of His Teaching on Christian Doctrine* [Grand Rapids: Zondervan, 1994], p. 243). Compare Roger E. Olson, *Arminian Theology: Myths and Realities* (Downers Grove, IL: IVP Academic, 2006), pp. 163-64.

offering and a sacrifice to God as a fragrant aroma" (Eph 5:2; compare Ezek 20:39-42; 2 Cor 2:14-15) and through whom mediation is truly accomplished.[104] Jesus is thus the worthy object of divine delight as the truly "acceptable sacrifice to God."[105] He "is the primary and exemplary elect" through whom others may be elected (Eph 1:4-6), God's beloved Son in whom others may be adopted as God's beloved children (Rom 8:15-17).[106] Further, "through Jesus Christ," who is "choice and precious in the sight of God," humans may "offer up spiritual sacrifices acceptable to God" as chosen (1 Pet 2:4-5, 9) and thus be "pleasing in His sight" (Heb 13:21; compare Rom 12:1-2; Heb 12:28; 13:15-16; 1 Jn 3:21-22).[107]

Under this umbrella of divine mercy and mediation, God accepts even the most meager human offerings as valuable and pleasing. The evaluative elements of divine love may have been overlooked by some theologians due to the fear of ascribing merit or works-based righteousness to humans. Yet Christ's mediation resolves the apparent tension between divine evaluation, appreciation and pleasure in human beings and the soiled filthiness of human "righteousness." I can never merit God's love. I have nothing of my own to give him; all that I have has been given to me (1 Cor 4:7). However, I can, through faith in Christ, itself evoked by God's prevenient love, respond in ways that please God, similar to the way that a human father is pleased when his son brings him a gift that is otherwise worthless but is priceless in his eyes because his beloved offers it to him freely in love. Thus, while it is correct that God does not *need* anything from us and we cannot give him anything that we have not received, it does not follow that God cannot appreciate our positive response to his love. God takes pleasure in even the smallest appropriate response to his love (compare Mk 9:24; 2 Cor

---

[104]The phrase "fragrant aroma" (ὀσμὴν εὐωδίας) corresponds to the OT phrase רֵיחַ הַנִּיחֹחַ ("soothing aroma") and is used to translate it 37 times in the LXX (including twice in the OT Apocrypha). The OT idiom refers to God's acceptance of the offering as pleasing. In the NT, it appears only here and in Phil 4:18, where it refers to gifts sent to Paul that are "an acceptable sacrifice" and "well-pleasing to God."

[105]F. F. Bruce, *The Epistles to the Colossians, to Philemon, and to the Ephesians*, NICNT (Grand Rapids: Eerdmans, 1984), p. 368. Compare Heb 10:5-10.

[106]Markus Barth, *Ephesians 1-3*, p. 86. Thus, "the Elect (Christ) bears the elect" (Schrenk, "εκλεγομαι, εκλογη, εκλεκτος," *TDNT* 4:175).

[107]Thus, "even the worship and praise of the Christian is dependent on the work of Christ for its acceptability" (Peter H. Davids, *The First Epistle of Peter*, NICNT [Grand Rapids: Eerdmans, 1990], p. 88). Compare the mediating work of the Holy Spirit in Rom 8:26.

8:12). In this way, God truly loves the "righteous," those who conscientiously respond to God's loving overtures in good faith, while there is no mere human who is presently wholly righteous.

Eschatological evaluation. The suspension of some effects of divine evaluation does not nullify final judgment. Scripture repeatedly points to God's evaluation of humans (Jer 11:20; Ps 7:9 [10]; 2 Cor 10:18; 13:5-7; 1 Thess 2:4), including eschatological judgment (1 Cor 3:13; 2 Cor 5:9-10; 1 Pet 1:7; 4:12). Jesus refers to "those who are considered worthy to attain to that age and the resurrection from the dead" (Lk 20:35; compare Acts 5:41; 2 Thess 1:5).[108] Thus the call for prayer "that our God will count you worthy [ἀξιόω] of your calling [κλῆσις], and fulfill every desire [εὐδοκία] for goodness" (2 Thess 1:11; compare 1 Tim 2:2-4) and frequent exhortation of Christians to "examine" (δοκιμάζω) themselves to see where they stand (2 Cor 13:5-6) and to be "approved" (δόκιμος) rather than "unapproved" (ἀδόκιμος; 2 Cor 13:7; compare Rom 12:2; 1 Cor 11:28).[109] Further: "Be diligent to present [παρίστημι] yourself approved [δόκιμος] to God" (2 Tim 2:15).[110] Ultimately the "quality of each man's work" will be tested (δοκιμάζω) by fire (1 Cor 3:13), and God is himself the examiner (1 Thess 2:4).[111] Thus Peter refers to the "proof" (δοκίμιον) of "faith, *being* more precious [πολύτιμος] than gold which is perishable, even though tested [δοκιμάζω] by fire," which will "result in praise and glory and honor at the revelation of Jesus Christ" (1 Pet 1:7; compare 1 Pet 4:12).[112] Accordingly, Paul proclaims it the Christian am-

---

[108]This is almost surely a divine passive; God is the agent of evaluation.

[109]δόκιμος means "'approved by testing' and indicates that the person in question, being pleasing to God, has survived the test" (Leon Morris, *The Epistle to the Romans*, PNTC [Grand Rapids: Eerdmans, 1998], p. 489). Compare Grundmann, "δόκιμος," *TDNT* 2:255-60. The corresponding verb δοκιμάζω refers to proving the quality, acceptability or worth of something by careful examination and/or testing (e.g., 1 Cor 3:13; 1 Tim 3:10).

[110]To present (παρίστημι) oneself sometimes appears in the sense of "offering oneself as a sacrifice" (Rom 12:1; Col 1:22) and sometimes in the sense of "presenting someone before a judge" (Col 1:28; Rom 6:13; 2 Cor 4:14) (Philip H. Towner, *The Letters to Timothy and Titus*, NICNT [Grand Rapids: Eerdmans, 2006], p. 520).

[111]This test "*discloses definitive approval (or otherwise)* in the sense of a disclosure of all the factors which contribute to God's definitive verdict," including "whether the person concerned shares the rightwised (justified) status of those who are in Christ; but it will also disclose the extent to which their work has produced some lasting effect in God's sight" (Anthony C. Thiselton, *The First Epistle to the Corinthians*, NIGTC [Grand Rapids: Eerdmans, 2000], p. 313; emphasis original). The human response to the divine initiative, faith, cannot be separated from faithfulness, which God appreciates.

[112]"The focus here is on the value of genuine faith in God's sight on the day of judgment . . . es-

bition "to be pleasing" (εὐάρεστος) to God, for "we must all appear before the judgment seat of Christ, so that each one may be recompensed for his deeds in the body, according to what he has done, whether good or bad" (2 Cor 5:9-10).

Abundant evidence suggests that divine pleasure includes evaluation of humans, including evaluative judgment. However, pleasing God is only possible because of Christ's mediation and through "faith" that God "is a rewarder of those who seek Him," without which "it is impossible to please [εὐαρεστέω] Him" (Heb 11:6).[113] Douglas Moo astutely notes, "Some Christians have a difficulty with rewards, objecting that our obedience to Christ should be pure and disinterested, unmotivated by any such crass consideration as future reward." However, "the contemplation of heaven's rewards is found throughout the NT as a spur to our faithfulness in difficult circumstances here on earth."[114] Thus, if anyone follows Jesus, "the Father will honor [τιμάω] him" (Jn 12:26).[115]

In the eschaton, the temporary and partial suspension of the effects of evaluation will be over. God will resurrect unto eternal life those who accept God's love and are thus accounted worthy through Christ's mediation (Lk 20:35; 2 Thess 1:5) and transformed into his likeness (1 Cor 15:51-56; 1 Jn 3:2). Conversely, those who reject God's love will be judged accordingly; evil will finally receive its just reward.[116] "Blessed is a man who perseveres under trial;

---

chatological reward will be given to them because of the genuineness of their faith, which is proved by the sufferings they endure" (Schreiner, *1, 2 Peter, Jude*, p. 68). Peter elsewhere makes reference to the "imperishable quality of a gentle and quiet spirit," which is "precious [πολυτελής] in the sight [ἐνώπιον] of God" (1 Pet 3:4). "Such virtue" is "valuable to God" (ibid., p. 154). The adjective πολυτελής means "very precious," "of great worth" (John Elliott, *1 Peter*, AB 37B [New York: Doubleday, 2000], p. 568). Notice also the phrase "in the sight of" (cf. Rom 3:20; 1 Tim 2:3; 5:4), which suggests coming before one for evaluative judgment. In the LXX, this divine evaluation is rendered by the term ἐναντίον, "in the judgment of, before" (Gen 6:8, 11; 7:1; Ex 5:21; 15:26; Lev 1:3; Deut 6:18, among many others). See H. Krämer, "ἐντυγχάνω," *EDNT* 1:461-62.

[113]The precise nature of the reward is uncertain, but it likely refers to the ultimate eschatological reward in light of Heb 12:23. This stands in contrast to Schleiermacher's view that, since all actions flow from the divine causality, "from our own religious consciousness" one "can know only of God's punitive justice; His rewarding relatively to ourselves we must simply leave out of account" (*Christian Faith*, pp. 346-47).

[114]Moo, *James*, p. 71.

[115]τιμάω generally means "to estimate, fix the value" and is thus an evaluative term.

[116]As Henry states, "love does not intercept God's final punishment of evil"; indeed, "self-cancelling justice is not only unbiblical, it also implies amoral love" (*God, Revelation, and Authority*, 6:353-54).

for once he has been approved [δόκιμος], he will receive the crown of life which *the Lord* has promised to those who love [ἀγαπάω] Him" (Jas 1:12; compare Jas 2:5; 1 Jn 5:2; Rom 8:28; 1 Cor 2:9; 8:3).[117]

Conclusion

This chapter has addressed the crucial question, does God only bestow or create value, or might he also appraise, appreciate and receive value? According to the foreconditional-reciprocal model, God evaluatively delights in, takes pleasure in and enjoys creatures while, in response to negative circumstances, God may be displeased, vexed and grieved.[118] This contrasts with the view that, by nature, God cannot be affected by or enjoy anything outside himself. Further, while many contend that pure love should be wholly altruistic, to the exclusion of self-interest, the Bible recognizes proper self-love. Indeed, God has voluntarily bound his own interests to the best interests of all others such that the joy of others is integral to God's own joy, demonstrating beyond doubt the unselfishness of his love in Christ's self-giving for his beloved. Although humans of themselves have no value to offer, God enables humans to respond to his prior and enabling action and mediates their meager offerings through Christ such that sinful humans may bring value to God. In this way, God can appreciate and enjoy the gifts that humans offer, even though they are imperfect. The evaluative aspect of divine love relates closely with what was seen in the previous chapter regarding the volitional aspect. The following chapter will take up the emotional aspect of divine love, which overlaps considerably with the evaluative aspect and likewise complements the volitional aspect.

---

[117]The one who "endures to the end, then at last, winning final approval, he will receive the final reward, the crown of life" (James B. Adamson, *The Epistle of James*, NICNT [Grand Rapids: Eerdmans, 1976], p. 67). Compare Spicq, *Agape*, 2:4. Ultimately, "to be pleasing to God means that they will be vindicated and saved at the final judgment" (Thomas Schreiner, *Romans* [Grand Rapids: Baker, 1998], p. 741).

[118]This means that God does not love all equally, a point taken up in chap. 8 (below).

6

THE EMOTIONAL ASPECT OF DIVINE LOVE

Does God's love include affection and/or emotionality such that God is concerned for the world, sympathetically or otherwise? Is divine love emotionally responsive to humans? Underlying these questions is the broad issue of whether God can be affected by the actions of humans. In other words, is God passible? The transcendent-voluntarist model supports the view that God is impassible, yet God has self-determined emotions. Divine love is not elicited or influenced by anything external to God (since God cannot be acted on) but is predicated solely on God's eternal predestinating divine decree. The immanent-experientialist model, conversely, views God as the supremely passible universal subject of all the experiences of the world, the feeler of all feelings. Here, love is identical with sympathy, which describes God's essential relation to the world. In recent years, many scholars have rejected divine impassibility, whereas others have mounted renewed defenses of this traditional doctrine.[1] My investigation of the canonical data points to the view that divine love for the world is profoundly emotional but not merely emotional. God's love includes deeply responsive emotions that complement the important aspects of volition and evaluation (chapters four and five).

GOD'S LOVE IS DEEPLY EMOTIONAL AND PASSIBLE

Scripture consistently displays God's intensely passionate and profoundly

---

[1]See chap. 1 (above).

emotional love for his people. Yet considerable debate ensues over whether God, properly speaking, can actually experience emotions or passions. Much of this debate hinges on the definition of emotionality. For our purposes, emotion will be defined as conscious feeling(s) affected by and responsive to external stimulation. In this view, an emotion is a passible, affective response to the external world.[2] Those who adopt the view that God is passible have no problem saying that God experiences emotions so defined.[3] However, as shall be seen, the biblical portrayal of divine emotionality departs significantly from that of many passibilists.

Conversely, many impassibilists contend that God is not emotionally affected by the world.[4] As Leon Morris states, "God's love is not an emotion conditioned by the kind of people we are," and thus, "passion" does not constitute "Christian love."[5] Some impassibilists assert that God does have emotions but not passible emotions. Divine "feelings" are the result of God's unilaterally effective will, as opposed to "passions."[6] In this view, biblical material that appears to depict divine passibility is interpreted as accommodative imagery (anthropopathisms), not to be taken as passible emotions.

In order to evaluate these competing claims, at least two questions must be addressed. First, does Scripture depict God's love as emotional in a passible sense (meaning that God is affected by the world)? If so, should we take such

---

[2] It is beyond the scope of this work to broach the ongoing conflict of interpretations in the field of psychology and philosophy regarding the definition and nature of emotion. However, the foreconditional-reciprocal model does appear to complement the aspects of some cognitive (but not exclusively cognitive) theories of emotions that give weight to an evaluative component wherein emotion is a response to an agent's evaluation of the state of affairs. See the brief discussion in Nicholas Wolterstorff, "Suffering Love," in *Augustine's Confessions: Critical Essays*, ed. William E. Mann (Oxford: Rowman & Littlefield, 2006), p. 123.

[3] Unless otherwise qualified, *passibility* refers to being affected by and responsive to the external world. However, passible emotions are not necessarily determined by external stimulus to the exclusion of other mental factors, including volition, evaluation, etc.

[4] *Divine impassibility* may be defined in a variety of ways, with considerable implications depending on the definition. Throughout this book, unless otherwise qualified, I use it to refer to the notion that God cannot be affected by anything outside himself. On various possible understandings of impassibility see David Bentley Hart, "No Shadow of Turning: On Divine Impassibility," *Pro Ecclesia* 11 (2002): 186-95.

[5] Leon Morris, *Testaments of Love: A Study of Love in the Bible* (Grand Rapids: Eerdmans, 1981), pp. 151, 276. This dovetails with the view that *agape* refers "to the will rather than to the emotions" (C. E. B. Cranfield, "Love," *TWTB*, p. 134). See chap. 3 (above).

[6] The definition of "passions" varies from theologian to theologian, and thus some may ascribe "passions" to God in a qualified sense. See below.

biblical depictions to mean that God's love is emotional in a passible sense, or is there some compelling reason(s) to apply the supposition of divine impassibility and reinterpret such depictions of passibility accordingly?

God's compassionate love. Regarding the first question, Scripture consistently displays God's deeply compassionate love and profound concern. Indeed, the most prominent terms of love in the Old Testament and New Testament often connote emotional affection. The אהב word group may depict intense affection and passionate emotion, delight, rejoicing and favor, often with the connotation of devotion with corresponding action(s).[7] Edmund Jacob notes "the sense of ardent and voluntary desire contained in the root" אהב.[8] Gottfried Quell adds that אהב "hardly ever loses its passionate note."[9] Likewise, the ἀγαπάω group (in the LXX and New Testament) may denote much the same meaning as the אהב root does in the Hebrew, including love that is affectionate, passionate, warm, compassionately concerned with and interested in its object(s); love in the sense of high regard, value and appreciation for its object(s); and love that includes enjoyment, pleasure and fondness.[10] The ἀγαπάω word group includes volition but also often denotes emotionality (Col 3:19; 1 Thess 2:7; 1 Pet 1:22; 4:8), including divine emotionality (Mt 12:18).[11] Jesus deeply loved his followers: "He loved [ἀγαπάω] them to the end" (Jn 13:1).[12] Likewise, when a

---

[7]See Gerhard Wallis, "אהב," *TDOT* 1:101-18; P. J. J. S. Els, "אהב," *NIDOTTE* 1:277-99; Ernst Jenni, "אהב," *TLOT* 1:45-54. The word group often collocates significantly with language that depicts emotionality, such as compassion, pleasure, delight, passion/zeal, lovingkindness, the seat of emotions, and its frequent contrast with hatred. See the discussion in chap. 3 (above).

[8]Edmund Jacob, *Theology of the Old Testament* (New York: Harper & Row, 1958), p. 109. Jacqueline Lapsley likewise contends that the term "decidedly involves the emotions" ("Feeling Our Way: Love for God in Deuteronomy," *CBQ* 65, no. 3 [2003]: 354).

[9]Gottfried Quell, "Love in the OT," *TDNT* 1:23.

[10]The verb thus may mean "to regard with affection, loving concern" or "to take pleasure in" ("αγαπαω, αγαπη," L&N 1:292). Compare William E. Phipps, "The Sensuousness of Agape," *Theology Today* 29, no. 4 (1973): 370-79. Accordingly, the ἀγαπάω word group is closely associated in NT usage with many emotive terms. Likewise, in the LXX the word group translates a number of terms of delight and compassion. See chap. 3 (above).

[11]J. A. T. Robinson contends that "*Agape* desires response, and desires it passionately," thus, "Love yearns for a loving response" ("Agape and Eros," *Theology* 48 [1945]: 99). G. Lloyd Carr adds that "*agape*, at least in the Old Testament, is not to be limited to self-giving, non-sensual 'love.' It is a word filled with all the Hebrew concepts of passion, sexual attraction, friendship, obedience, loyalty, duty, and commitment to the other person" (*The Song of Solomon*, TOTC [Downers Grove, IL: InterVarsity Press, 1984], p. 63).

[12]Profound love is connoted by the expression "to the end," likely connoting both intensity and endurance. Herman N. Ridderbos renders it "love to the last breath" and "love in its highest

man approaches Jesus asking him how to inherit eternal life, Jesus, "looking at him... felt a love [ἀγαπάω] for him" (Mk 10:21).[13] Finally, the φιλέω word group also connotes affectionate love, fondness, attraction, concern, special interest and/or enjoyment/pleasure in or valuing of someone or something (Mt 6:5; Jn 11:36; Jas 4:4).[14]

The vigor of God's love (אהב) is manifest in divine joy over humans. God "will exult" over his people "with joy, He will be quiet in His love, He will rejoice over you with shouts of joy" (Zeph 3:17). God delights in goodness, takes pleasure in righteousness and is joyous over every person who responds to his loving overtures (Ps 149:4).[15] The emotionality of divine love is especially striking when it is described as analogous to familial love. God's love is often depicted as the passionate love of a husband for his wife (e.g., Is 62:4; Jer 2:2; 3; Ezek 16; 23; Hos 1–3; Zech 8:2; compare 2 Cor 11:2). Likewise, God's love is repeatedly likened to the tender affection of a parent who adopts and cares for a child.[16] Thus God "loved" Israel and called his "son" out of Egypt (Hos 11:1). God taught "Ephraim to walk," took him in his arms, cared for him (Hos 11:3-4), and "carried" his people "just as a man carries his son" (Deut 1:31; compare Is 63:9). God loves his people even as "one whom his mother comforts [נחם]" (Is 66:13) and has compassion (רחם) on his beloved even as "a father has compassion [רחם] on *his* children" (Ps 103:13).

Divine compassion is exponentially greater than the love of a mother for her newborn child, as God proclaims, "Can a woman forget her nursing

---

intensity" (*The Gospel According to John* [Grand Rapids: Eerdmans, 1997], p. 452). Further, Christ's love is here described as "for his own" (ἴδιος), a "term of endearment to near relations" in some ancient Near Eastern literature.

[13]Such love is here depicted as prompted by sight, a possible reaction corresponding to the frequent instances where Jesus' compassion is prompted by sight (see below). Joel Marcus sees this as "fatherly affection ('moved with love for him')" (*Mark 8-16*, AB 27A [New York: Doubleday, 2000], p. 727).

[14]Consider the LXX use of the term in the sense of what is especially liked and/or brings pleasure (Gen 27:4, 9, 14; Hos 3:1). Compare W. Günther and H. G. Link, "αγαπαω," *NIDNTT* 2:538; William Klassen, "Love in the NT and Early Jewish Literature," *ABD* 4:385; Gustav Stählin, "φιλεω, καταφιλεω, φιλημα," *TDNT* 9:117; "φιλεω," L&N 1:300.

[15]Compare many other examples of God's delight in chap. 5 (above).

[16]On God's love being likened to paternal affection, see Ex 4:22; Deut 8:5, 16; Prov 3:11-12. Although some scholars point to ancient Near Eastern parallels as an explanation for such language, Lapsley points out: "No parallel presents itself for the paradox of a god who is sovereign over the cosmos" but holds "affection for a powerless group of ragtag slaves. It is not unreasonable, therefore, to suggest that God's love for others might also spring from genuine feeling, and not simply from adherence to an abstract idea" ("Feeling Our Way," p. 362).

child And have no compassion [רחם] on the son of her womb? Even these may forget, but I will not forget you" (Is 49:15). The רחם word group denotes compassionate love and tender feelings, including mercy but more than mercy, apparently based on the term "womb" (רֶחֶם) and, accordingly, may refer to a "womb-like mother love."[17] J. Gerald Janzen describes it as "the feeling a mother has for the children whom she carries and feels in her womb, then carries in her arms and nurses at her breast, and afterward continues in faithful compassion toward them."[18] Elsewhere it displays the depth of the divine emotions of compassion by way of the physiological idiom of churning "innards" (Is 63:15; Jer 31:20). Divine רחם, then, is not merely a willed affection but an emotion that is stirred and roused, responsive to the actual state of affairs. As John Goldingay notes, it is a "feelings word" that "denotes strong emotion," the "strong feelings of love and concern" that result in "action."[19]

The New Testament counterparts of רחם, the closely related οἰκτίρω and σπλαγχνίζομαι word groups, likewise depict the profundity of God's emotional, compassionate love, including likening it to the tender affection of a loving parent.[20] The σπλαγχνίζομαι word group, which is the more prominent of the two in the New Testament, refers to the feeling (or the seat of the feeling) of warm sympathy, pity and/or compassion at someone's misfortune, emotion bound up with affectionate love.[21] With such language, the depth of

---

[17] See Phyllis Trible, *God and the Rhetoric of Sexuality* (Philadelphia: Fortress, 1978), pp. 31-59. The noun is "probably in reference to the accompanying physiological phenomena of strong emotion" (H. J. Stoebe, "רחם," *TLOT* 3:1226). Compare *HALOT*, pp. 1217-18; Mike Butterworth, "רחם," *NIDOTTE* 3:1093. Donald Gowan explains that the terminology "needs to be given a stronger emotional quality than the word 'mercy' usually has" (*Theology in Exodus* [Louisville: Westminster John Knox, 1994], p. 236). Compare chap. 3 (above).

[18] J. Gerald Janzen, *Exodus* (Louisville: Westminster John Knox, 1997), p. 252.

[19] John E. Goldingay, *Daniel*, WBC 30 (Dallas: Word, 1989), pp. 243-44. Motyer adds that it "is a heart-love: compassion," that is "emotional, passionate, personal" (*Isaiah*, TOTC [Downers Grove, IL: InterVarsity Press, 1999], p. 386).

[20] Some scholars have suggested that, since ἀγαπάω is relatively infrequent in the Gospels, both word groups therein function in its place. See Helmut Köster, "σπλάγχνον, σπλαγχνίζομαι," *TDNT* 7:555-56. The οἰκτίρω word group is the primary terminology that translates the רחם word group in the LXX, but appears infrequently but significantly in the NT, denoting the basic meaning of a highly emotive response to someone's hardship; compassion, sympathy, mercy, tender feeling and/or pity. The σπλαγχνίζομαι word group appears to have come into common use in post-LXX Jewish literature, largely replacing the οἰκτίρω word group (ibid., p. 552). Compare H. H. Esser, "σπλάγχνα, σπλάγχνον," *NIDNTT* 2:599.

[21] The noun σπλάγχνον may refer to the "inward parts" of the body as the "seat of emotions," depicting visceral emotionality (human or divine) akin to the functioning of רחמים in the OT.

God's compassion is symbolized by a father's passionate and joyous love for his prodigal son who had forfeited any right to his father's compassion by disowning his father and squandering his inheritance. Yet, when the father saw his son, "still a long way off," he "felt compassion [σπλαγχνίζομαι] *for him*, and ran and embraced him and kissed him" (Lk 15:20). Jesus frequently manifests this same profoundly emotional love when he sees people in need and is moved with compassionate (σπλαγχνίζομαι) love for them (Mt 9:36; 14:14; Mk 1:41; 6:34; Lk 7:13; compare to ἀγαπάω in Mk 10:21).[22] Christ's compassion is thus regularly prompted by the sight of someone in distress, describing passible response.[23] Other than the frequent depictions of Christ's compassionate feelings (e.g., Mt 15:32; 20:34; Mk 1:41; 8:2; compare Mk 9:22), the verb occurs only in Christ's symbolic narratives, descriptive of divine compassion (Mt 18:27; Lk 10:33; 15:20). As such, "the verb σπλαγχνίζομαι has become solely and simply an attribute of the divine dealings."[24]

Accordingly, "God is a compassionate [רַחוּם] God" (Deut 4:31) whose "mercies are great" (2 Sam 24:14; 1 Chron 21:13; compare Lk 1:78) and whose "lovingkindnesses never cease" and "compassions never fail" (Lam 3:22).[25] He

---

As such, it often depicts the "seat and source of love, sympathy, and mercy" or the "feeling itself" of great "love" and "affection" ("σπλάγχνον," BDAG, p. 938). So also Esser, "σπλαγχνα, σπλαγχνον," *NIDNTT* 2:599; Köster, "σπλαγχνον, σπλαγχνίζομαι," *TDNT* 7:548-49; "σπλαγχνίζομαι; σπλαγχνα," L&N 1:294. See also E. Dhorme, *L'emploi métaphorique des noms de parties du corps en hébreu et en akkadien* (Paris: Librairie orientaliste P.Geuthner, 1963), pp. 111-12, 134-35.

[22] The verb σπλαγχνίζομαι refers "literally [to] a movement of the entrails at the sight," to "have a visceral feeling of compassion" (Spicq, "σπλαγχνα, σπλαγχνίζομαι," *TLNT* 3:274-75). It is thus descriptive of a "gut response" (R. T. France, *The Gospel of Matthew*, NICNT [Grand Rapids: Eerdmans, 2007], p. 373). This "compassion involves so identifying with the situation of others that one is prepared to act for their benefit" (John Nolland, *The Gospel of Matthew*, NIGTC [Grand Rapids: Eerdmans, 2005], p. 407). In ten of twelve appearances it is passive; the other two are middle (Mt 15:32; Mk 8:2).

[23] Christ is able to "sympathize [συμπαθέω] with our weaknesses" (Heb 4:15; cf. Heb 2:18; 5:8). The word, from which the English *sympathy* is derived, literally means to feel something with someone. Compare Mk 3:5; Jn 11:33-38.

[24] Köster, "σπλαγχνον, σπλαγχνίζομαι," *TDNT* 7:553. This supports taking emotions exhibited by Christ as truly divine emotions (Jn 14:9). The correspondence between the emotions of Christ and those of Yahweh here and elsewhere in the canon presents a compelling argument that such emotions are divine rather than merely human. Thus the mercy and compassion shown by Jesus "reveals the mercy and love of God" (Günther and Link, "αγαπαω," *NIDNTT* 2:543). So N. Walter, "σπλαγχνιζομαι," *EDNT* 3:265. Yet, even if one were to exclude the emotions of Christ (on christological or other grounds), the emotionality of divine love is readily apparent apart from these instances (compare chap. 2 above).

[25] The adjective רַחוּם appears 13 times, and in every instance but the likely exception of Ps 112:4 God is the agent. The close association of God's compassion and graciousness is evident in that

is sympathetic (Is 63:9; Heb 4:15), deeply affected by the sorrows of his people (Judg 10:16; Lk 19:41), willing to hear, answer and comfort (Is 49:10, 15; Mt 9:36; 14:14), "rich in mercy" and "great love" (Eph 2:4; compare Lk 1:78; 2 Cor 1:3).[26] We are to cast our cares on him "because He cares for" us (1 Pet 5:7). Despite repeated rebellion, God proclaims that he will "surely have mercy [רחם]" and his "heart [מֵעֶה] yearns [המה]" for his people, whom he calls "My dear son" and "delightful child" (Jer 31:20; compare Is 63:15). This language depicts profoundly passible and intense emotionality, evidenced by the Hebrew idiom "heart yearns" (מֵעֶה + המה), which literally refers to turbulent or roaring internal organs and here "depicts God's stomach being churned up with longing for his son."[27] John N. Oswalt comments: "It is significant that the attribute of God to which the OT returns again and again is his compassion: his tenderness and his ability to be touched by the pain and grief of his people."[28]

God frequently responds to supplication and/or entreaty, being moved to compassion in his great love and relenting from the execution of judgment in reaction to human entreaty and/or appropriate response (Joel 2:13-14; Jon 3:9-10; 4:2; compare Mt 18:27).[29] For example, God is "moved to pity [נחם] by" his people's "groaning" (Judg 2:18),[30] "could bear the misery of Israel no

---

11 of the 13 instances are paired with words from the root חנן. See Ex 34:6; 2 Chron 30:9; Neh 9:17, 31; Ps 86:15; 103:8; 111:4; 145:8; Joel 2:13; Jon 4:2.

[26]Compare many other references to the greatness of God's compassion, lovingkindness and mercy in Is 63:7; Ps 51:1; Neh 9:19, 31; Dan 9:18; Jas 5:11. Of God's compassion manifest in active beneficence see Ps 51:1; Mt 15:32; Lk 1:54, 78; Eph 2:4; Tit 3:4-5; 1 Pet 1:3.

[27]J. A. Thompson, *The Book of Jeremiah*, NICOT (Grand Rapids: Eerdmans, 1980), p. 575. Patrick Miller describes this as "the deep feeling of God, the parental compassion that is moved to care and tenderness in the presence of the pain of the child (cf. 31:20)" ("The Book of Jeremiah," *NIB* 6:808). The collocation of מֵעֶה and המה or הָמוֹן—"murmur," "roar," sometimes meaning "arouse"—appears five times, always of intense emotional feeling, whether of God (Is 63:15; Jer 31:20) or humans (Is 16:11; Jer 4:19; Song 5:4). מֵעֶה literally refers to internal organs, inward parts, bowels, belly, and is often used in the sense of womb and stomach. It is used in instances of intense physiological pain (Job 30:27; Ps 22:15) but more frequently to denote intense emotions (Is 16:11; Jer 4:19; Lam 1:20; 2:11). Stoebe thus correctly sees this as "expanded parallelism" that "approximate[s] *rahamim*" ("רחם," *TLOT* 3:1226).

[28]John N. Oswalt, *The Book of Isaiah: Chapters 40-66*, NICOT (Grand Rapids: Eerdmans, 1998), p. 299.

[29]See also Gen 18:22-32; Ex 32:1-14; 33:12–34:10; Is 30:19; Ps 69:16 [17]; 102:17; 119:132; Neh 9:27; Dan 9:18; 2 Chron 7:14; compare Deut 32:10-11; 1 Pet 5:7.

[30]The term for "groaning" appears with a causative *mêm* (מִנַּאֲקָתָם), "because of their groaning," indicating the causal relation between God's hearing of Israel's pain and his feelings of compassion for them. See Daniel I. Block, *Judges, Ruth*, NAC 6 (Nashville: B&H, 1999), p. 130. This usage "signifies sorrow at the hurt or pain of another and a desire to come to the victim's aid" (Dennis T. Olson, "The Book of Judges," *NIB* 2:756).

longer" (Judg 10:16),³¹ and is "moved by prayer" for the land (2 Sam 21:14; compare 2 Sam 24:25; 1 Kings 8:50-53). God is eager to relent (נחם) if only his people will repent (נחם) (Jer 18:7-10).³²

Although divine compassion is deeply emotional and responsive, however, it is not merely emotional or passive response. God's love is emotional *and* volitionally free and evaluative. God repeatedly meets human apostasy with undeserved forbearance, grace and compassion. For example, when Israel abandoned God in favor of debased worship of the golden calf, deserving to be cut off, God *freely* bestowed compassion and mercy on those who repented (Ex 32:26-30; 33:19; compare Rom 9:15-16).³³ In doing so he revealed his character as "compassionate and gracious, slow to anger, and abounding in lovingkindness and truth; who keeps lovingkindness for thousands, who forgives iniquity, transgression and sin" (Ex 34:6-7).³⁴ "God would have

---

³¹This is a statement of profoundly passible affection. Literally, "his soul was shortened at the trouble of Israel" (Judg 10:16). In the only other three instances where the syntagm נֶפֶשׁ + קָצַר appears it refers to humans who have grown weary or become impatient (Num 21:4; Judg 16:16; Zech 11:8). See Robert D. Haak, "A Study and New Interpretation of *Qsr Nps*," *JBL* 101, no. 2 (1982): 161-67.

³²נחם may take on various meanings depending on its context and form, which include to comfort or have compassion, be comforted, or comfort oneself, to mourn or be sorry, and to relent/change one's mind. The common theme throughout its usage is that נחם often appears in a situation that prompts intense grief or regret and connotes the emotion and/or active response to that situation. Thus the feeling of sorrow or regret is associated with the action of relenting or changing action accordingly. Thus H. J. Stoebe groups the meaning into two categories, "'be comformed' and 'be sorry' in the broadest scope" ("נחם," *TLOT* 2:734). With divine agency נחם often refers to comfort and/or compassion. In nominal forms, the root may refer to "comfort" given by God (Is 57:17-18; cf. Zech 1:13) or to the presence or absence of divine compassion, which is demonstrably emotive (Hos 11:8; 13:14). In the *piel*, the verb refers to divine comfort toward the people (or the lack thereof), which may result in compassion and the turning away of anger (Is 12:1; 49:13; cf. Is 51:3, 12, 19; 52:9; 61:2; 66:13; Jer 31:13; Zech 1:17; Ps 23:4; 71:21; 86:17; 119:76, 82). In the *pual*, it refers to those comforted or not comforted (Is 54:11; 66:13). In *hitpael* various meanings are presented in a small number of occurrences. First, it is declared that God "will have compassion on His servants" (Deut 32:36; Ps 135:14). In another instance it refers to God being "appeased" (Ezek 5:13). In still another, God is contrasted with humans, specifically that he is not "man, that He should repent" (Num 23:19). The term may also refer to profound, visceral, divine emotions akin to the compassion signified by רחם (Hos 11:8). With God as subject, the verb most often appears in the *niphal*, which may denote divine sorrow and/or grief (Gen 6:6-7; 1 Sam 15:11, 35), being "moved to pity" or "feeling sympathy for" (Judg 2:18; cf. Ps 90:13), and/or relenting or changing course in action (Ex 32:12, 14; 2 Sam 24:16; Is 57:6; Jer 26:19; Joel 2:13-14; Jon 3:9-10; 4:2; Amos 7:3, 6; Ps 106:45; 1 Chron 21:15; cf. Is 1:24). On divine relenting, see the further discussion later in this chapter. Regarding Jer 18, see John C. Peckham, "The Passible Potter and the Contingent Clay: A Theological Study of Jeremiah 18:1-10," *JATS* 18, no. 1 (2007): 130-50.

³³See the discussion of this text in chap. 4 (above).

³⁴Likewise, see Joel 2:13; Jon 4:2; Ps 86:15; Neh 9:17, 31, among others. God's emotional com-

been 'just' in putting an end to these rebellious people. Yet he kept on loving, guiding, and delivering them (Ex 32:10; 33:5)."[35] Even though God's people repeatedly betrayed and forsook him (Judg 10:13; 1 Sam 8:8; 1 Kings 11:33; 2 Kings 22:17; Jer 1:16), God continued to patiently bestow compassion beyond all reasonable expectations (Neh 9:7-33), manifesting the depth of his compassion and exceedingly long-suffering and surpassingly merciful love.[36]

Yet, God's response to entreaty is not automatic; he may not relent (1 Sam 15:29; Jer 4:28; 15:6; compare Mal 1:9-10). As abundant as God's compassion is, God is never compelled to be gracious and may reject human repentance and/or refuse compassion, though he does not do so without good reason, such as when "the people have become so corrupt and disloyal at their core that no hope for true and sustained repentance seems possible," and they proffer only "shallow repentance," which is not "heartfelt."[37] Humans may so persistently reject God that he withdraws his "lovingkindness and compassion" (Jer 16:5; compare Is 63:15; Jer 11:15; 14:10; Hos 9:15; Ps 89:49).[38] Likewise, God's "mercy is upon generation after generation toward those who fear Him" (Lk 1:50; compare Mt 5:7; Ps 103:13), but "judgment *will be* merciless to one who has shown no mercy" (Jas 2:13).[39] Thus divine compassion toward humans is conditional within genuine, historically significant interrelationship and may be forfeited (Is 9:17 [16]; 27:11; Jer 15:1; Ezek 5:11; Mt 18:27, 33, 35; Rom 11:22; Heb 8:9).

God does everything he can to avoid this outcome (Is 5:1-7), repeatedly calling to his people in his "compassion," but they continually "despised His words" even "until there was no remedy" (2 Chron 36:15-16; compare 2 Kings

---

mitment to his people is apparent in his חֶסֶד (lovingkindness), which is often associated with his compassion in the OT and in some aspects closely related to the NT concept of mercy. See chap. 3 (above). Norman Snaith suggests that in חֶסֶד there is "inherent in the word" something of "eagerness, ardour" and "intense devotion" of the "love of God" (*The Distinctive Ideas of the Old Testament* [London: Epworth, 1962], p. 106).

[35]Mervin Breneman, *Ezra, Nehemiah, Esther*, NAC 10 (Nashville: B&H, 1993), p. 241.

[36]Thus one of God's core characteristics is his long-suffering, signified by the idiomatic expression that God is "long of nose" (אֶרֶךְ אַפַּיִם). The length of nose idiomatically referred to the length of time it would take for one to become angry (think of one's nose turning red). See Walter Brueggemann, "The Book of Exodus," *NIB* 1:946. Compare the description of God's anger as the "heat of my nostrils" in Ex 32:10, 12.

[37]Olson, "Book of Judges," *NIB* 2:826.

[38]The conditionality of divine love is explained in chap. 7 (below).

[39]Although God's compassion is conditional in this way, it is never merited (cf. Ex 33:19; Dan 9:18; Tit 3:5).

22:17). Thus Christ lamented how he greatly desired to save his people, but they "were unwilling" (Mt 23:37). Whereas God "longs to be gracious" and "waits on high to have compassion" (Is 30:18; compare Hos 2:19 [21]; Joel 2:18-19; Heb 8:12) in response to his people (Is 30:19), he "will by no means leave *the guilty* unpunished" (Ex 34:6-7). God is thus willing to forgive, but not to the exclusion of justice, and neither in the ultimate absence of love relationship with his people. God's compassionate love is thus emotionally responsive to human action but is also (1) volitional, in that God may maintain or withdraw it from humans and willingly maintains it beyond reasonable expectations; (2) foreconditional, in that it is given freely but may be forfeited; and (3) evaluative, in that its withdrawal is never arbitrary but always responds to human evil (see chapters four, five and seven).

God's intense, but always appropriate, passion. In God's character, compassion is complemented by passion. God is both a "compassionate God" (אֵל רַחוּם; Deut 4:31) and the jealous, or "impassionate," God (אֵל קַנָּא; Deut 4:24; compare Ex 20:5; 34:14; Deut 5:9; 6:15; Josh 24:19; Nah 1:2).[40] As E. Reuter points out, "if jealousy is a critical element of the name of Yahweh," then "our attention must turn at once to the relationship between Yahweh and his worshipers."[41] Indeed, the close association of God's name with both compassion and passion point to God's relationally responsive character, since both compassion and passion as depicted in Scripture are responsive and passible emotions.

The קנא word group denotes the very strong emotions of ardor and intense passion, related to a basic sense of zeal, passion or jealousy for what belongs to one, or (with human agency) envy for what belongs to someone else.[42] Divine jealousy (קִנְאָה) refers to God's passionate and "arduous love"

---

[40]Moshe Weinfeld, *Deuteronomy 1-11*, AB 5 (New York: Doubleday, 1991), p. 207.
[41]E. Reuter, "קנא," *TDOT* 13:54. Interestingly, the emotion of jealousy is associated with love and the "flame of Yahweh" in Song 8:6 (cf. Deut 32:21-22). Although some commentators have seen the use of "Yah" as a superlative, primarily because the divine name is avoided elsewhere (so Tremper Longman III, *Song of Songs* NICOT [Grand Rapids: Eerdmans, 2001], p. 213), it is more likely that it is indeed intended as a reference to the divine name. See the extended discussion in Richard M. Davidson, *Flame of Yahweh: Sexuality in the Old Testament* (Grand Rapids: Baker, 2007), pp. 621-32.
[42]The corresponding NT term, ζηλόω, is almost always used throughout the LXX to translate קנא and likewise refers to passion for someone or something, which may take the form of negative jealousy or positive zeal. See Albrecht Stumpff, "ζῆλος, ζηλόω," *TDNT* 2:886.

The Emotional Aspect of Divine Love 157

for his people or for his name.⁴³ God's passion may be directed in favor of his beloved people and against those who abuse and oppress them, prompting divine deliverance (compare Is 26:11; Joel 2:18; Zech 1:14-17; Heb 10:27). Divine jealousy, however, lacks the negative connotations of human jealousy. It is a virtuous aspect of his love that is never envious of any other beings but is always directed at what rightfully belongs to him.⁴⁴ As spouses ought to be dedicated to each other in exclusive relationship, God rightfully expects and desires exclusive and undiluted love relationship. However, God is often depicted as a scorned husband, the unrequited lover of an unfaithful wife (see Is 62:4; Jer 2:2; 3:1-12; Ezek 16; 23; Hos 1–3; Zech 8:2; compare 2 Cor 11:2). Accordingly, God is repeatedly provoked to jealously by his people's unfaithfulness (Deut 32:21; Ps 78:58). As Paul House explains, "most marriage partners" are instead "justifiably protective of an exclusive sexual relationship." Here, "jealousy is a good and normal trait. God's jealousy is equally positive." It "is no character flaw" but "magnifies God's righteousness, concern, and covenant loyalty."⁴⁵ Divine קנא is thus "the fire of divine passion, Yahweh's enthusiasm for his covenant relationship with Israel," which arises "out of the profundity of his covenant love" (e.g., Ex 20:5-6; Deut 5:9-10; 29:20 [19]; Num 25:11).⁴⁶

God's love, then, appropriately manifests itself not only in positive emotions but also in negative emotions, which are always responsive to evil. In Gen 6:6-7, for example, God is deeply "grieved in His heart" and "sorry" (נחם) because of humanity's evil. This displays the "emotional response of

---

⁴³Leonard J. Coppes, "קנא," *TWOT*, p. 802. Compare Pierre Buis, *Le Deutéronome* (Paris: Beauchesne, 1969), p. 59. Weinfeld comments, "The basic meaning of *qn'*, which is 'jealousy,' applies also to passionate love. Love causes jealousy, and jealousy brings anger that burns like fire (Deut 4:22; 23:21-22)" (*Deuteronomy 1-11*, p. 296). God's passion for his "name" relates not only to self-interest but also to God's concern for creatures, since an accurate picture of his character is more likely to draw people to respond to his passionate love. See Ezek 39:25; Jn 2:17.

⁴⁴The combination of ב + קנא suggests the latter negative emotion of envy (e.g., Prov 3:31) and is never used of God, whereas the construction of ל + קנא suggests the former, an appropriate passion or righteous ardor with action on behalf of its object, used of humans (e.g., 1 Kings 19:10) and of God (e.g., Zech 8:2). See Reuter, "קנא," *TDOT* 13:49. For this reason, H. G. L. Peels believes the "translation 'jealous' is" often "inadequate" ("קנא," *NIDOTTE* 3:939). Compare H. A. Brongers, "Der Eifer Des Herrn Zebaoth," *VT* 13 (1963): 280. Divine passion stands in contrast to depictions of other gods in the ancient Near East who may be envious of one another, whereas no deity manifests "zeal in relation to his worshiper" (G. Sauer, "קנא," *TLOT* 3:1146). Moreover, God's love and passion never refer to sexual desires or activity.

⁴⁵Paul House, *1, 2 Kings*, NAC 8 (Nashville: B&H, 1995), p. 194.

⁴⁶Daniel I. Block, *The Book of Ezekiel: Chapters 1-24*, NICOT (Grand Rapids: Eerdmans, 1997), p. 211.

God" in "God's fervent passion," and his "wounded 'heart' filled with pain" and "emotional anguish."[47] Throughout Scripture, humans repeatedly provoke, grieve, vex and anger God:

> How often they rebelled against Him in the wilderness
> And grieved Him in the desert!
> Again and again they tempted God,
> And pained the Holy One of Israel. (Ps 78:40-41; compare Is 63:10; 1 Cor 10:5)[48]

Peter Craigie comments, "The behavior of the Israelites vexed God; he had a fatherly concern for them as his sons and daughters, so that to see them rejecting his love caused him not only anger, but also pain," because "a loving Father finds it hard to look on while his children invite disaster by their sinful behavior."[49]

God's emotional response to evil appropriately includes displeasure, wrath, jealousy and, when pressed, even hatred, abhorrence and loathing.[50] For example, God proclaims regarding the "beloved" of his "soul" (Jer 12:7): "She has roared against Me; Therefore I have come to hate her" (Jer 12:8; compare Hos 9:15).[51] Likewise, "Jesus himself had loved and hated keenly—hated because he loved, hated intensely whatever challenged, misrepresented, and thwarted the divine purpose on earth."[52] The contrast between divine love and hate, affection and animosity, strikingly portrays both the emotive and evaluative aspects of love.[53] In all this, Scripture "speaks un-

---

[47]Kenneth A. Mathews, *Genesis 1-11:26*, NAC 1A (Nashville: B&H, 1995), pp. 341-42.

[48]עצב and תוה are both in the *hiphil*, denoting humans causing God grief and pain and thus depicting passible emotions. Scripture often depicts God as "provoked ... to anger" (כעס; Deut 32:16) or some other emotion. Human apostasy brings real pain and vexation (כעס) to God, a recurring theme throughout the OT (see, among many others, Deut 4:25; Judg 2:12; 1 Kings 14:9; 2 Kings 21:6, 15; Is 65:3; Jer 7:18-19; Ezek 8:17; 16:26; 20:28; Hos 12:14 [15]; Ps 78:58).

[49]Peter Craigie, *The Book of Deuteronomy*, NICOT (Grand Rapids: Eerdmans, 1976), p. 383.

[50]See K. D. Schunck, "חמה," *TDOT* 4:464. See Is 63:10; 65:3; Hos 9:15; Ps 78:58-59; 95:9-11; Mk 3:5; 1 Cor 10:5; Heb 3:8-10.

[51]The language "beloved of my soul" is intensely emotive, which suggests that the parallel antonym of hatred is as well. Miller comments, "The pathos of the whole section is caught up in that one sentence" of "the beloved of my heart" ("Book of Jeremiah," p. 679).

[52]James Moffat, *Love in the New Testament* (New York: Harper, 1930), p. 54.

[53]Gerhard Wallis points out that the emotive nature of the term אהב "seems to be supported at least by the fact that this emotional feeling which flows out of one's perceptions is contrasted with hate" ("אהב," *TDOT* 1:102). Compare Eccles 9:6; 2 Sam 13:15; Jas 4:4. See the discussion of divine hatred in chap. 5 (above).

ashamedly of Yahweh's passion, presenting him as an intense and passionate Being, fervently interested in the world of humans."[54]

God's wrath-surpassing, compassionate love. Some consider God's negative emotions unpalatable and thus view God's wrath as something to be explained away. However, what kind of "love" would not be angered at the abhorrent suffering that humans inflict on one another? Imagine a mother watching her three-year-old daughter playing at the playground, and then suddenly a man attacks her daughter. Should she not be infuriated? Is not God also righteous in his indignation against evil? Throughout Scripture, humans persistently perpetrated immense atrocities, including child sacrifice and all kinds of debauchery (compare 2 Chron 33:6). *Because* God loves intensely, such evil provokes him to intense, but always appropriate, anger.[55] As Gordon Wenham puts it, God exhibits "the anger of someone who loves deeply."[56]

God's wrath thus stems from his righteous love, which requires appropriate response against evil. Consider Christ's righteous indignation against those who were treating God's temple as common and using it to take advantage of widows, orphans and the poor (compare Mt 21:13). This is the proper reaction of ardent love.[57] As D. C. K. Watson puts it, "Unless God detests sin and evil with great loathing, He cannot be a God of Love," since true love requires justice.[58] "God is passionately concerned about the lives of human beings and whether justice takes place among them."[59] God's loving concern for all (Jn 3:16) requires that he mete out justice and finally eradicate evil.

As explained in chapter five, God's negative emotions are never arbitrary but always evaluative and appropriately responsive to evil; divine "wrath and punishment are never unmotivated."[60] Indeed, "the anger of God is an

---

[54]Bruce Baloian, "Anger," *NIDOTTE* 4:380.
[55]On God's allowance of evil, see chap. 9 (below).
[56]Gordon Wenham, *Genesis 1-15*, WBC 1 (Dallas: Word, 1987), p. 146.
[57]Gerald Borchert comments that, though some are troubled by Jesus' anger, "spineless love is hardly love," while "anger and judgment can in fact be the obverse side of the coin of love" (*John 1-11*, NAC 25A [Nashville: B&H, 2001], p. 164).
[58]D. C. K. Watson, *My God Is Real* (London: Falcon, 1970), p. 39. So Carl F. H. Henry, *God, Revelation, and Authority*, 6 vols. (Wheaton, IL: Crossway, 1999), 6:325.
[59]Baloian, "Anger," *NIDOTTE* 4:381.
[60]Daniel Day Williams, *The Spirit and the Forms of Love* (New York: Harper & Row, 1968), p. 22.

awesome and terrible thing exactly because it follows from a rejection of the equally pervasive love of God."[61] God's negative emotions, then, are not essential to divine love, since, absent sin and evil, their negative aspect would not be. As D. A. Carson states: "Where there is no sin, there is no wrath, but there will always be love in God."[62] Accordingly, God's compassion and mercy far surpass his negative emotions, both in intensity and duration. God's anger lasts but a moment in contrast to his favor, which lasts a lifetime (Ps 30:5; compare Ex 34:7; Is 54:7-10). Thus, as Patrick Miller understands it, the "Lord of Israel is not a Janus-faced God, a God of wrath and a God of love. The wrath of God is always subordinated to the love of God."[63]

God does not want to bring punishment; he "does not afflict willingly," but "if He causes grief, Then He will have compassion" (Lam 3:32-33; compare Judg 10:16; Is 30:18; Lk 13:34). Accordingly, God willingly "restrained His anger" in long-suffering and patience, often postponing and mitigating the execution of divine judgment (Ps 78:38). Indeed, the striking tension between God's profound love and justice is evident in God's angst over his people who have rejected him in Hosea 11:8-9 (see below). As Daniel Simundson comments, "there is a constant tension between justice and mercy. God is a righteous God and will not tolerate evil," and neither will he "abandon God's own standards of justice. And yet, God is constantly pulled in the direction of forgiveness and mercy. God is also in pain when people disobey, and God can see the terrible consequences awaiting them. God wants to forgive and move on to better things if people will give at least some hint of repentance."[64]

In response to infidelity, then, God disciplines his people, but such discipline is itself grounded in his passionate love for them with the hope of ultimate reclamation (2 Pet 3:9; Rev 3:19). For this reason, God disciplines his people "just as a man disciplines his son" (Deut 8:5) "to do good" for them "in the end" (Deut 8:16). "For whom the LORD loves He reproves, Even as a father *corrects* the son in whom he delights" (Prov 3:12; compare Heb 12:6). Accordingly, "God is passionately concerned about us and the thought that

---

[61]Craigie, *Deuteronomy*, p. 384.
[62]D. A. Carson, *The Difficult Doctrine of the Love of God* (Wheaton, IL: Crossway, 2000), p. 67.
[63]Miller, "Book of Jeremiah," p. 814.
[64]Daniel Simundson, "The Book of Micah," *NIB* 7:589.

we should corrupt and destroy ourselves stirs him to the depths. How much better a father who knows what his child is doing to himself or herself and is angry about it than the one who neither knows nor cares what is happening."[65] The unfathomable depth of divine love is manifested in God's giving of his own Son, his supremely beloved, for undeserving humans (Jn 3:16).[66] The entire Godhead desires the reconciliation of creatures to themselves so much that they made the ultimate sacrifice. There is no greater love than this (Jn 15:13).

Passible or Impassible Emotions?

In light of this sample of striking depictions of God's love as deeply emotional and responsive, let us return to the question of divine impassibility. God is presented throughout Scripture as ever involved and invested in the world that he created, being affectionate, loving, devotedly interested in and intimately concerned with humans and exhibiting profound compassion and intensely passionate love. As Rob Lister puts it, "the biblical portrayal of divine emotion is both powerful and pervasive. One cannot read Scripture and come away with the conclusion that God is affectionless."[67]

This brings us to our second question. Should we take the biblical presentation to mean that God's love is deeply emotional *and* passible, or is there some compelling reason to apply the ontological supposition of divine impassibility and reinterpret the biblical data as conveying something other than what they exegetically appear to claim? Consider Hosea 11:8-9,

> How can I give you up, O Ephraim?
> How can I surrender you, O Israel?
> How can I make you like Admah?
> How can I treat you like Zeboiim?
> My heart is turned over within Me,
> All My compassions are kindled. (compare Is 30:15, 18-19; Jer 3:1-12)

---

[65]Oswalt, *Isaiah: Chapters 40-66*, p. 421.
[66]"Surely, to see his son die in such a cruel fashion would break any father's heart—much more so that of our heavenly Father" (Andreas J. Köstenberger, *John*, BECNT [Grand Rapids: Baker, 2004], p. 129).
[67]Rob Lister, *God Is Impassible and Impassioned: Toward a Theology of Divine Emotion* (Wheaton, IL: Crossway, 2013), p. 195. Lister, however, adopts what he calls a qualified impassibilist perspective, further discussed below.

This is passionate, gut-wrenching language that depicts God as experiencing intense emotions that are prompted by his people's rebellion, that is, passible emotions.[68]

Two primary rationales for excluding divine pathos in the interpretation of such passages are frequently offered by some impassibilists. First, the language of Scripture is human language that accommodates human thought patterns and thus should not be taken to correspond to God as he is.[69] Second, God is impassible, and thus biblical language suggesting passibility must not actually be meant to correspond to God as he is.[70] John Calvin displays both of these in his commentary on Hosea 11:8-9: "God, we know, is subject to no passions, and we know that no change takes place in him. What then do these expressions mean, by which he appears to be changeable? Doubtless he accommodates himself to our ignorances whenever he puts on a character foreign to himself." Further, Calvin contends that "the same mode of speaking after the manner of men is adopted; for we know that these feelings belong not to God; he cannot be touched with repentance, and his heart cannot undergo changes."[71] Accordingly, many interpreters label such texts as anthropopathic, that is, they use accommodative language to metaphorically ascribe human emotions to God that are not appropriate to him. Thus Paul Helm rejects "the passibilist understanding of divine

---

[68]The "heart" being turned over is an idiom akin to similar language that is still common today ("gut-wrenching") to describe emotional feelings. The description of God's compassions (נִחוּמִים) as "kindled" (כמר, niphal) is also a striking description of emotionality, as כמר is elsewhere used to describe the most intense of human emotions, such as the mother who appears before Solomon being "deeply stirred [כמר, niphal, + רַחֲמִים] over her son" when he gives the command to divide the child (1 Kings 3:26). Similarly, see Joseph's emotions over his brothers (Gen 43:30). Compare Butterworth, "רחם," NIDOTTE 3:1093; Stoebe, "רחם," TLOT 3:1226.

[69]Others have suggested that such language is not the result of intentional accommodation but depicts a primitive understanding of God from the time of its writing. As noted before, such a view conflicts with my hermeneutical commitments regarding the revelation and inspiration of Scripture (see chap. 2 above). However, one who views such descriptions of divine emotionality as primitive language may nevertheless find this to be a useful explication of the conception of God that would derive if such language (carefully interpreted via the grammatical-historical procedures of exegesis) is taken to adequately (yet analogically) refer to God.

[70]Related to this is the further criticism that passages that appear to ascribe passible emotion to God often utilize anatomical imagery. See the discussion of this below.

[71]John Calvin, *Commentaries on the Twelve Minor Prophets*, trans. John Owen (repr., Grand Rapids: Eerdmans, 1950), pp. 400-401. Consider John W. Cooper's more recent statement that "Scripture presents God as acting and responding in ways that are analogous to humans," but such "biblical assertions of God's reactions are anthropopathic" (*Panentheism, the Other God of the Philosophers* [Grand Rapids: Baker Academic, 2006], pp. 322-23).

emotion," claiming that "the metaphysical or ontological or strictly literal data must control the anthropomorphic and anthropopathic data, and not *vice versa*. The alternative is quite unacceptable, namely, a theological reductionism in which God is distilled to human proportions."[72]

To be sure, the language used in Hosea 11:8-9 accommodates human understanding (see the discussion of analogical language below).[73] However, how would one determine what language in reference to God is, in Helm's words, "metaphysical or ontological or strictly literal" as opposed to "anthropomorphic and anthropopathic"? Why could Hosea's language not be thought of as theopathic and thus hold ontological implications?[74] All language to which any interpreter is privy is human language and therefore accommodative. As such, it does not make sense to exclude the exegetically derived emotional meaning of such imagery *because* it is accommodative human language. Indeed, as G. B. Caird states: "We have no other language besides metaphor with which to speak about God."[75] How, then, does the interpreter know which "human" language accurately corresponds to God

---

[72]Paul Helm, "The Impossibility of Divine Passibility," in *The Power and Weakness of God: Impassibility and Orthodoxy*, ed. Nigel M. de S. Cameron (Edinburgh: Rutherford, 1990), p. 131. Other examples of this interpretive maneuver abound; only a few will be mentioned here. Millard Erickson refers to some passages that "are to be understood as anthropomorphisms and anthropopathisms," being "simply descriptions of God's actions and feelings in human terms, and from a human perspective" (*Christian Theology* [Grand Rapids: Baker, 1998], p. 304). So Henry, *God, Revelation, and Authority*, 5:301-4; Phillip R. Johnson, "God Without Mood Swings," in *Bound Only Once: The Failure of Open Theism*, ed. Douglas Wilson (Moscow, ID: Canon Press, 2001), p. 116; Marvin R. Wilson, "נחם," *TWOT*, pp. 570-71. Martin Luther took a similar position with regard to divine grief in Gen 6:7, stating, "Such an emotion is attributed to God, not as though He were thus moved, but the holy prophets, Moses, and Noah conceived of Him in this way" (LW 17:358). From a vastly different conception of God and methodological approach, Friedrich Schleiermacher stated that "no religious emotion shall be so interpreted, and no statement about God so understood, as to make it necessary to assume alteration in God of any kind" (*The Christian Faith*, trans. H. R. Mackintosh [Edinburgh: T & T Clark, 1948], p. 206). Thus, "the anthropomorphic element, to be found more or less in all" Christian theologies is to be rooted out (ibid., p. 195).

[73]I take this language to be the result of divine accommodation to human language on the view that the biblical text is revealed and inspired in such a way that these words of the human authors are also the word of God (cf. 1 Thess 2:13). See the discussion in chap. 2 (above).

[74]Lister contends that, while they are "truth-bearing," the "many narrative depictions of divine emotional involvement with creation . . . cannot serve as straightforward proof-texts of an archetypal, metaphysical understanding of the divine emotive capacity" (Lister, *God Is Impassible and Impassioned*, p. 173). Yet, what texts can/should be taken as such?

[75]G. B. Caird, *The Language and Imagery of the Bible* (Philadelphia: Westminster Press, 1980), p. 174. So John C. L. Gibson, *Language and Imagery in the Old Testament* (Peabody, MA: Hendrickson, 1998), p. 26.

and which does not?⁷⁶ Because all available language is human language, the accommodative language rationale is not a sufficient argument to exclude the divine pathos that appears to be conveyed in texts such as Hosea 11:8-9.⁷⁷ For many (but by no means all), this rationale is supported by the further supposition of divine impassibility.⁷⁸

The supposition of divine impassibility itself, however, requires either compelling canonical evidence or extracanonical knowledge of what God is actually like.⁷⁹ The latter subverts a canonical approach to theology (see chapter two), which would require compelling canonical data in order to overturn the apparent exegetical meaning of texts like Hosea 11:8-9. However, some would argue that the supposition of divine impassibility is grounded in the canon such that passages that appear to describe divine passibility must be interpreted in light of other texts that assert divine immutability (and hence impassibility).⁸⁰ In my view, there is no biblical evidence for divine impassibility of the kind that would amount to the exclusion of God

---

⁷⁶This question is taken up from the perspective of the foreconditional-reciprocal model later in this chapter.

⁷⁷Duane Garrett comments that here God is "distraught . . . like a father who is at wit's end over what to do with a wayward child, Yahweh is here at a loss as he tries to resolve his compassion for Israel and the punishment demanded by their sin. One may of course regard this as metaphor, as language that somehow puts divine love into terms that a human can understand, even though God himself does not really experience self-doubt and anxiety over issues of justice and mercy." He goes on, "While accepting the fact that God transcends our metaphors and that theological doctrines about the impassability and foreknowledge of God should never be jettisoned, texts such as this should be allowed to speak to us in the power of their raw emotion. It is precisely in texts such as this that the love of God becomes a vivid reality and not a barren abstraction" (*Hosea, Joel*, NAC 19A [Nashville: B&H, 1997], p. 227). I agree with Garrett that the texts must be allowed to speak yet, on that basis, question whether divine impassibility coheres with such texts.

⁷⁸A number of theologians, however, reject divine impassibility while also seeing such biblical language of divine emotionality as anthropopathic. For example, Eberhard Jüngel states that the "biblical texts present the problem of *anthropomorphism*, and do so drastically," appearing to ascribe "predicates [such as anger or jealousy] to God in an almost naïve unconcern," which "poorly fit into the context of an essence which is infinitely superior to all that exists" (*God as the Mystery of the World* [Grand Rapids: Eerdmans, 1983], p. 258). Yet he also maintains that "the word of the cross makes plain that the true God is not apathetic. His capacity for suffering is already witnessed to in the passion of God documented in the Old Testament" (ibid., p. 373n21).

⁷⁹Kevin Vanhoozer, *Remythologizing Theology: Divine Action, Passion, and Authorship* (New York: Cambridge University Press, 2010), p. 60.

⁸⁰For example, Calvin, as many who follow his view, believed Scripture depicted God as immutable in such a way that required the exclusion of divine pathos. Lister notes, however, that Calvin was "prone to shift 'negative' emotional terminology into categories of volition" (Lister, *God Is Impassible and Impassioned*, p. 121).

being affected by the world.⁸¹ Conversely, there is an abundance of biblical testimony that depicts God experiencing passible emotions, only a sample of which appears in this chapter.

For this and other reasons, the supposition of divine impassibility has come under considerable scrutiny, especially by those who contend that impassibility is a vestige of classical Greek ontology and is not grounded in Scripture.⁸² Conversely, this contention (the so-called Hellenization hypothesis) is increasingly rebutted by impassibilists, to the extent that many are eschewing this claim as a misreading of historical philosophy and theology.⁸³ Indeed, "impassibilism seems to have begun a miniature

---

⁸¹The texts usually used to support this view, such as Mal 3:6 and Num 23:19, do not assert immutability or impassibility such that God is unaffected by the world. Rather, they are situated within a canonical context where God is affected and responsive and thus appear to refer to God's constancy of character rather than ontological impassibility. See the word study of נחם earlier, the discussion of Num 23:19 later in this chapter and the further discussion in chap. 9 (below).

⁸²See, for example, John Sanders, "Historical Considerations," in Clark Pinnock, Richard Rice, John Sanders, William Hasker and David Basinger, *The Openness of God: A Biblical Challenge to the Traditional Understanding of God* (Downers Grove, IL: InterVarsity Press, 1994), pp. 59-91.

⁸³See Paul Gavrilyuk's extended and influential treatment in *The Suffering of the Impassible God: The Dialectics of Patristic Thought* (Oxford: Oxford University Press, 2004), pp. 21-63. Thomas Weinandy likewise argues that the Fathers did not "abandon the God of Israel for the God of the Greeks" (*Does God Suffer?* [Notre Dame, IN: University of Notre Dame Press, 2000], p. 108). Compare ibid., pp. 83-113; Gerald L. Bray, "Has the Christian Doctrine of God Been Corrupted by Greek Philosophy?" in *God Under Fire: Modern Scholarship Reinvents God*, ed. Douglas S. Huffman and Eric L. Johnson (Grand Rapids: Zondervan, 2002), pp. 105-18; Lister, *God Is Impassible and Impassioned*, pp. 41-122. Lister contends that while some (Justin Martyr, Clement of Alexandria) presented impassibility as "hyper-transcendent," the traditional mainstream "understanding of a negative term like *impassible* did not prohibit the application of emotionally laden characteristics to God" (*God Is Impassible and Impassioned*, pp. 95, 103). Likewise, "Patristic theology is falsely credited with a bleak view that God is apathetic, uncaring, unconcerned about the world, emotionally withdrawn, and in this sense impassible" (Paul L. Gavrilyuk, "God's Impassible Suffering in the Flesh: The Promise of Paradoxical Christology," in *Divine Impassibility and the Mystery of Human Suffering*, ed. James Keating and Thomas Joseph White [Grand Rapids: Eerdmans, 2009], p. 135).

At the same time, Bray notes, "There is no doubt that the early Christians were influenced by the philosophical currents surrounding them" in order to address their contemporaries ("Has the Christian Doctrine of God Been Corrupted," p. 112). Likewise, Lister comments, "it is obvious to all that the Patristic theologians borrowed Greek language and made use of Greek concepts," though this does not necessarily mean that "biblical authority has been compromised in the attempt to express biblical truth through borrowed terminology" (*God Is Impassible and Impassioned*, p. 61). It is overly simplistic, then, to reduce the issues involved in this historical debate to all or nothing. One might consider some Christian theologians (past and/or present) to be unduly influenced by philosophical presuppositions of their age without baldly accusing them of uncritically appropriating non-Christian worldviews. Yet Bruce McCormack notes the temptation "to regard all modern objections to impassibility as standing somehow in the shadow

resurgence."[84] Nevertheless, a variety of passibilist views continue to garner a significant hearing. For example, the process view, which harshly criticizes the view that God is impassible and "passionless," remains popular in some circles. In this view, "to love a being yet be absolutely independent of and unaffected by its welfare or suffering seems nonsense"; it divests love of "its most essential kernel, the element of sympathy."[85] Similarly, Daniel Day Williams states, "Impassibility makes love meaningless."[86] Jürgen Moltmann contends that a God incapable of suffering "is poorer than any human . . . he is also a loveless being."[87] Paul Fiddes adds: "To love is to be in a relationship where what the loved one does alters one's own experience."[88] Thomas Jay Oord has recently suggested a variant form of panentheism, which he calls essential kenosis theology, in which love "necessarily involves both intention and sympathy/empathy," thus leaving room for passion and volition in divine love.[89] Open theism has likewise proposed that divine love is possible but

---

of Adolf von Harnack's Hellenization thesis" ("Divine Impassibility or Simply Divine Constancy? Implications of Karl Barth's Later Christology for Debates over Impassibility," in *Divine Impassibility and the Mystery of Human Suffering*, ed. James Keating and Thomas Joseph White [Grand Rapids: Eerdmans, 2009], p. 150).

The ongoing debate regarding the correct interpretation of impassibility in the Christian tradition is highly interesting and informative. However, the question that impinges on this study is not to what extent theologians (past and present) have borrowed or been influenced by Greek (or any other) philosophy, as important as that is. To assert that a theological system is wrong *because* it has been influenced by extrabiblical thought exemplifies the genetic fallacy. The crucial question from a canonical methodology is whether a view corresponds rigorously to all of Scripture while maintaining internal coherence. When a large degree of dependence on extrabiblical thought is apparent, it is appropriate to scrutinize whether that view genuinely derives from the canon.

[84]Lister, *God Is Impassible and Impassioned*, p. 148.

[85]Charles Hartshorne, *Reality as Social Process* (New York: Hafner, 1971), p. 40; Hartshorne, *Omnipotence and Other Theological Mistakes* (Albany: State University of New York Press, 1984), p. 29.

[86]Williams, *Spirit and the Forms of Love*, p. 127.

[87]Jürgen Moltmann, *The Crucified God: The Cross of Christ as the Foundation and Criticism of Christian Theology*, trans. R. A. Wilson and John Bowden (New York: Harper & Row, 1974), p. 222. For Moltmann, "God's being is in suffering and the suffering is in God's being itself, because God is love" (ibid., p. 227). However, God does not suffer in the sense of internal relatedness but in voluntary identification. God "opens himself to the suffering which is involved in love" (ibid., p. 230). Compare Moltmann, *The Trinity and the Kingdom: The Doctrine of God*, trans. Margaret Kohl (San Francisco: Harper & Row, 1981), pp. 51-56; Marcel Sarot, *God, Passibility and Corporeality* (Kampen, The Netherlands: Kok Pharos, 1992).

[88]Paul S. Fiddes, *The Creative Suffering of God* (Oxford: Oxford University Press, 1988), p. 50.

[89]Thomas Jay Oord, *The Nature of Love: A Theology* (St. Louis: Chalice, 2010), p. 30.

without proposing that God's love relationship to the world is essential to him.[90] From a different perspective, Eberhard Jüngel adds, "the God who is love must be able to suffer and does suffer beyond all limits in the giving up of what is most authentically his for the sake of mortal man."[91] Many others, from varying theological worldviews, have offered similar criticisms of divine impassibility.[92] In light of criticisms such as these, Kevin Vanhoozer comments that "it is becoming increasingly difficult for classical theists to defend the intelligibility of the love of God as an apathetic and unilateral benevolence."[93]

Wayne Grudem, a proponent of an evangelical version of classic theism, has explicitly denied the concept of divine impassibility, stating, "The idea that God has no passions or emotions *at all* clearly conflicts with much of the rest of Scripture, and for that reason I have not affirmed God's impassibility," for "the opposite is true," since God "certainly does feel emotions."[94] Similarly, Donald Bloesch comments, the "classical idea of perfection as all-sufficiency" has "prevented the church through the ages from giving due justice to the biblical idea of God sharing the pain and suffering of his people."[95] Although no proponent of process theology, he even concedes that "the modern process conception of God who shares our suffering is probably closer to the Biblical view than the Hellenistic conception of a God who is wholly self-contained, who is removed from temporality and exempt

---

[90]See Richard Rice, "Process Theism and the Open View of God: The Crucial Difference," in *Searching for an Adequate God: A Dialogue Between Process and Free Will Theists*, ed. David Ray Griffin, John B. Cobb and Clark H. Pinnock (Grand Rapids: Eerdmans, 2000), p. 185.

[91]Jüngel, *God as the Mystery*, p. 373.

[92]See, among many others, Vincent Brümmer, *The Model of Love: A Study in Philosophical Theology* (Cambridge: Cambridge University Press, 1993), pp. 160, 227; H. Ray Dunning, *Grace, Faith, and Holiness: A Wesleyan Systematic Theology* (Kansas City, MO: Beacon Hill, 1988), p. 195; Abraham Heschel, *The Prophets* (New York: Perennial, 2001), p. 286; Edward Collins Vacek, *Love, Human and Divine: The Heart of Christian Ethics* (Washington, DC: Georgetown University Press, 1994), pp. 160-62; Nicholas Wolterstorff, "Suffering Love," in *Augustine's Confessions: Critical Essays*, ed. William E. Mann (Oxford: Rowman & Littlefield, 2006), p. 135.

[93]Kevin J. Vanhoozer, "Introduction: The Love of God—Its Place, Meaning, and Function in Systematic Theology," in *Nothing Greater, Nothing Better: Theological Essays on the Love of God*, ed. Kevin J. Vanhoozer (Grand Rapids: Eerdmans, 2001), p. 10.

[94]Wayne Grudem, *Systematic Theology: An Introduction to Biblical Doctrine* (Grand Rapids: Zondervan, 1994), p. 166. Similarly, see John S. Feinberg, *No One Like Him: The Doctrine of God* (Wheaton, IL: Crossway, 2001), p. 277; John R. W. Stott, *The Cross of Christ* (Downers Grove, IL: InterVarsity Press, 2006), pp. 320-23.

[95]Donald Bloesch, "Process Theology and Reformed Theology," in *Process Theology*, ed. Ronald H. Nash (Grand Rapids: Baker, 1987), p. 51.

from vulnerability."[96] For Bloesch, however, "the notion of impassibility can be retained so long as it does not mean that God is impassive and unfeeling."[97] Karl Barth's view, however, goes beyond the typical dichotomy of impassibility and passibility. He states that the God of the Bible "can feel, and be affected. He is not impassible," yet "He cannot be moved from outside by an extraneous power" but "is moved and stirred" by "His own free power."[98] Bruce McCormack has recently interpreted Barth as "neither an impassibilist [in the strict sense of nonaffectivity] nor a passibilist," arguing that Barth's mature view of divine constancy actually rejects any "doctrine of divine impassibility" and that his "position would take us beyond that rather unfortunate set of alternatives."[99]

The complexity of this issue is exacerbated by the presence of competing definitions of impassibility, even among impassibilists.[100] Richard Creel as-

---

[96] Ibid., p. 53. See also John Frame's rejection of impassibility insofar as it refers to the absence of divine emotion (*The Doctrine of God* [Phillipsburg, NJ: P & R, 2002], pp. 609-15).

[97] Donald Bloesch, *God, the Almighty: Power, Wisdom, Holiness, Love* (Downers Grove, IL: InterVarsity Press, 2006), p. 94. Compare T. F. Torrance's view that "in Christ God both suffered and did not suffer: through the eternal tranquility of his divine impassibility he took upon himself our passibility." Torrance thus excludes "any thought of God as impassible in the Greek or Stoic sense, and any thought of God as passible in the way human beings are" (*The Christian Doctrine of God: One Being Three Persons* [New York: T & T Clark, 2001], p. 251). Further, Michael Horton contends that he has "revised" impassibility to refer to "incapacity for being overwhelmed by suffering, not inability to enter into it" (*Lord and Servant: A Covenant Christology* [Louisville: Westminster John Knox, 2005], p. 195).

[98] *CD* II/1, p. 370.

[99] McCormack, "Divine Impassibility or Simply Divine Constancy?" pp. 184, 185. Compare *CD* II/1, pp. 495-96. According to McCormack, "impassibility and passibility constitute an altogether this-worldly dialectic," and the "truth is that God transcends this dialectic" (ibid., p. 182). On his reading, "*Barth is able to advance an understanding of divine immutability which is no longer controlled by the further thought of impassibility.* If becoming human, suffering and dying, and so forth, are the content of the eternal decision in which God gives himself his being, then no change is introduced into the being of God when this becoming and so forth take place in time. And if God is immutably determined for suffering, then the concept of immutability has been cut loose from impassibility" (McCormack, "The Actuality of God: Karl Barth in Conversation with Open Theism," in *Engaging the Doctrine of God: Contemporary Protestant Perspectives*, ed. Bruce L. McCormack [Grand Rapids: Baker Academic, 2008], p. 223 [emphasis original]). For his part, McCormack does "not believe that impassibility is a biblical doctrine" ("Election and the Trinity: Theses in Response to George Hunsinger," in *Trinity and Election in Contemporary Theology*, ed. Michael T. Dempsey [Grand Rapids: Eerdmans, 2011], p. 136).

[100] Confusion regarding impassibility is increased by ambiguity regarding the related terms *suffering* and *passion*. Some understand these terms to entail embodiment and maintain that "God is not subject to passion because he is incorporeal" (Gilles Emery, "The Immutability of the God of Love and the Problem of Language Concerning the 'Suffering of God,'" in Keating and White, eds., *Divine Impassibility and the Mystery of Human Suffering*, p. 66). This follows Aquinas, *Summa Theologica* 1.20.1.1. Compare Weinandy, *Does God Suffer?* pp. 38-39. Throughout the

serts, "That which is impossible is that which cannot be affected by an outside force. Hence, impossibility is imperviousness to causal influence from external factors."[101] Paul Helm accordingly refers not to divine emotions but to "themotions," defined as that which is "as close as possible to the corresponding human emotion X except that it cannot be an affect."[102] In a similar vein, Thomas Weinandy rejects the "notion of passibility—that God experiences inner emotional changes of state ... whether freely from within or by being acted upon from without."[103] Thus God is not "capable of freely changing his inner emotional state in response to and interaction with the changing human condition and world order," and God does not have something "analogous to human feelings."[104]

Rob Lister, however, considers this a "more extreme version of divine impassibility than is biblically required or historically warranted," contending that both Scripture and tradition promote a qualified impassibility wherein "God is *both* invulnerable to *involuntarily* precipitated emotional vicissitude *and* supremely passionate about his creatures'" actions and expe-

---

history of theology, such terms also have often held negative connotations, connoting defects or faults. See Gavrilyuk, "God's Impassible Suffering," p. 142. For Paul Helm, "'passion' suggests irrationality and the response of one who has been overwhelmed" ("B. B. Warfield on Divine Passion," *Westminster Theological Journal* 69 [2007]: 102). However, neither *suffering* nor *passion* needs to refer to irrationality, defect or deficiency. To suffer may simply refer to receptivity of either positive or negative experiences (voluntary or involuntary), the broader sense of "undergoing or enduring the action of another upon oneself." Similarly, passion may have "the more generic sense of 'being acted upon by another'" (Gary Culpepper, "'One Suffering, in Two Natures': An Analogical Inquiry into Divine and Human Suffering," in Keating and White, eds., *Divine Impassibility and the Mystery of Human Suffering*, p. 82).

[101]Richard E. Creel, *Divine Impassibility: An Essay in Philosophical Theology* (Cambridge: Cambridge University Press, 1986), p. 11. For Creel, God is impassible with regard to nature, will and feelings, but partially passible and impassible with regard to knowledge such that God genuinely loves in the sense of his predetermining love "presponses" to all possible creaturely actions (ibid., pp. 22, 204). Unlike most impassibilists, he rejects exhaustive foreknowledge and creation *ex nihilo*. Creel has more recently come to the conclusion that "an adequate conception of God must include the notion that God is touched by our sufferings and joys, victories and defeats—though not necessarily in the same ways that we are" ("Immutability and Impassibility," in *A Companion to Philosophy of Religion*, ed. Philip L. Quinn and Charles Taliaferro [Malden, MA: Blackwell, 1997], p. 318). Yet, in the same article, he maintains that divine "impassibility means that it is logically impossible for God to be affected by anything" (ibid., p. 314).

[102]Helm, "Impossibility of Divine Passibility," p. 140. Impassibility follows from Helm's divine ontology: "(1) God is timelessly eternal. (2) Whatever is timelessly eternal is unchangeable. (3) Whatever is unchangeable is impassible. (4) Therefore, God is impassible" (ibid., p. 119).

[103]Weinandy, *Does God Suffer?* p. 39.

[104]Ibid.

riences; God is both "impassible and impassioned."[105] On this view, God is emotionally "affected by his creatures" but "in ways that accord rather than conflict with his will" such that he is transcendently and voluntarily "responsive, but never passive" or "manipulated, overwhelmed, or surprised."[106]

Some impassibilists do not make this distinction so precisely, speaking of divine impassibility as the property of not being affected by the world while also affirming that God possesses voluntary feelings. In this view, God may have emotional states, but "His feelings are not the result of actions imposed upon Him by others" since "God cannot be acted upon by anything outside of Himself."[107] D. A. Carson further maintains that an emotionless God is "profoundly unbiblical and should be repudiated" but nevertheless argues for some form of impassibility in order to preserve God's sovereignty and not "strengthen the hands of Arminians, semi-Pelagians" and "Pelagians."[108] Many

---

[105]Lister, *God Is Impassible and Impassioned*, pp. 152, 153, 143. He distinguishes between "extreme impassibilists," who promote(d) a "hyper-transcendent" perspective that excludes God's being affected by creatures (e.g., Justin Martyr, Clement of Alexandria) and thus "proved an impediment to accounting for divine involvement with creation," and "qualified impassibilists," who dually affirm "divine impassibility and divine passion," affirming "voluntary affections" but excluding unexpected or "involuntary passions" (ibid., pp. 95, 101, 122). Gavrilyuk similarly contends that it was the heretical "Docetists, Arians, and Nestorians" who all "deployed divine impassibility in an unqualified sense, as a property that categorically excluded God's participation in any form of suffering," whereas "the Church Fathers defended the reality of Christ's suffering against the Docetists, the fullness of the incarnate Son's divinity against the Arians, and the unity of his person against the Nestorians" ("God's Impassible Suffering," p. 143). Both Lister and Gavrilyuk suggest that the mainstream tradition should be understood along the lines of a "qualified divine impassibility" (ibid., p. 131).

[106]Lister, *God Is Impassible and Impassioned*, pp. 36, 230. Lister notes that this view might make him a passibilist under Creel's definition (ibid., p. 150). Notably, Helm also speaks of a fully self-controlled impassionate state in reference to the strength of divine commitments, analogous to a "scientist's passion for truth" such that God does not have "passions" and is not a "suffering God" but is "utterly impassioned in all that he does" ("B. B. Warfield on Divine Passion," pp. 102-3). However, Lister distinguishes this from his own position in that Helm views God as entirely atemporal such that God is never "actually re-sponsive" (*God Is Impassible and Impassioned*, p. 230). Weinandy also affirms both divine impassibility and that, as "subsistent relations fully in act [*actus purus*], the persons of the Trinity are completely and utterly passionate in their self-giving to one another" (*Does God Suffer?* p. 119). However, Lister contends that whereas Weinandy's view correctly excludes divine "passivity," it incorrectly precludes divine response (*God Is Impassible and Impassioned*, p. 157).

[107]Norman L. Geisler, H. Wayne House and Max Herrera, *The Battle for God: Responding to the Challenge of Neotheism* (Grand Rapids: Kregel, 2001), pp. 170, 171. Likewise, Cooper contends that "God's pleasure and anger are not passions or emotions caused in him." That is, "classical theism denies that God's feelings are the *effects* of creaturely *causes*" (*Panentheism*, p. 332; emphasis original).

[108]Carson, *Difficult Doctrine of the Love of God*, pp. 48, 22. Carson struggles further with this issue when he questions how one is to reconcile a love "which is clearly a vulnerable love that feels

others make a similar case.¹⁰⁹ As such, God's emotions are unilaterally self-determined, excluding evaluative and emotive aspects insofar as they entail divine response to external stimulus that was not itself causally determined by God. Many impassibilists thus speak of God's impassible emotions.

INTERPRETING LANGUAGE OF DIVINE EMOTIONALITY

In light of the canonical evidence, the foreconditional-reciprocal model agrees with the view that God's love is best understood as emotional in a (qualified) *passible* sense. The foreconditional-reciprocal model thus agrees with those impassibilists who say God does have emotions; the divergence regards whether such emotions are passible or not and in what way. Those who maintain that God's feelings are impassible often promote the admirable goal of preventing God from being thought of as essentially immanent, passive, ontologically vulnerable, or worse, an erratic, vindictive, cosmic basket case.¹¹⁰ Accordingly, a long tradition has excluded divine passibility in part as a reaction against the "anthropomorphic" gods that were so common in ancient religions.¹¹¹ In our age, an equally strong and parallel

---

the pain and pleads for repentance?" (ibid., p. 59). He answers by denying that God is "vulnerable from the outside" (ibid., p. 60). For Carson, "If God loves, it is because he chooses to love; if he suffers, it is because he chooses to suffer. God is impassible in the sense that he sustains no 'passion,' no emotion, that makes Him vulnerable from the outside, over which he has no control, or which he has not foreseen" (ibid.). Compare D. A. Carson, "How Can We Reconcile the Love and the Transcendent Sovereignty of God," in Huffman and Johnson, eds., *God Under Fire*, pp. 308, 345. See Henry's wrestling with this issue in *God, Revelation, and Authority*, 6:345, 349.

[109]Thus Millard Erickson contends that God's impassibility does not mean that God is uncaring or "utterly devoid of any feelings" (*God the Father Almighty: A Contemporary Exploration of the Divine Attributes* [Grand Rapids: Baker, 1998], p. 161). Compare Morris, *Testaments of Love*, pp. 11, 276; Bruce A. Ware, *God's Greater Glory* (Wheaton, IL: Crossway, 2004), pp. 144-47.

[110]Consider Carson's concern about divine passibility: "A God who is terribly vulnerable to the pain caused by our rebellion is scarcely a God who is in control or a God who is so perfect he does not, strictly speaking, need us" (*Difficult Doctrine of the Love of God*, p. 60). "If the love of God is exclusively portrayed as an inviting, yearning, sinner-seeking, rather lovesick passion," then "the cost will be massive," perhaps stealing "God's sovereignty from him and our security from us" (ibid., p. 22). Yet he notes that "Christian love cannot be reduced to willed altruism" (ibid., p. 28).

[111]Thus, "by calling the Christian God impassible the Fathers sought to distance God the creator from the gods of mythology" (Gavrilyuk, *Suffering of the Impassible God*, p. 48). Compare ibid., pp. 47-63; Weinandy, *Does God Suffer?* p. 89. Antianthropomorphic tendencies are apparent in the LXX, which often downplays the portrayal of divine emotions (e.g., Jer 31:20 [LXX 38:20]). For a discussion of many examples, see Charles T. Fritsch, *The Anti-Anthropomorphisms of the Greek Pentateuch* (Princeton, NJ: Princeton University Press, 1943), pp. 17-18. Compare Gavrilyuk, *Suffering of the Impassible God*, pp. 39-46. Albrecht Stumpff explains that, although the LXX

rationale is the avoidance of Feuerbachian criticisms of theology as merely human projection.[112]

Scripture presents God as the omnipotent Creator, ontologically distinct from creation, both transcendent and immanent (see chapter nine). Thus, whatever else we say about God's emotions, we must keep in mind that divine emotions are not identical to human emotions and thus should not be ascribed to God univocally. However, humans were created in the image of God (Gen 1:26-27), and Scripture uses the same language to describe both divine and human emotions (see the discussion below).[113] Interpreting the biblical language of divine emotion as entirely unlike that of humans would amount to utter equivocation. All language available to us is human language, and thus to say anything meaningful about God there must be some likeness. This canonical approach, then, employs an analogical understanding of language about God.

In theological literature, there are various understandings of the relationship of analogical predication to univocity and equivocity such that some mean by *analogical* a great deal of dissimilarity and a minimum of similarity, or vice versa.[114] It is thus crucial to understand at this juncture

---

depicts passion as a positive divine attribute, out of "fear of any kind of anthropomorphising" the idea of passion or jealousy came to be considered inappropriate to God among some Jewish scholars ("ζῆλος, ζηλοω," *TDNT* 2:879-80). Compare Philo's presentation of divine impassibility in "On the Unchangeableness of God," in *The Works of Philo*, trans. C. D. Yonge (Peabody, MA: Hendrickson, 1996), 113.60-61, p. 163. See also Edwin M. Yamauchi, "Anthropomorphism in Ancient Religions," *BSac* 125, no. 497 (1968); Edwin M. Yamauchi, "Anthropomorphism in Hellenism and in Judaism," *BSac* 127, no. 507 (1970).

[112]See Vanhoozer, *Remythologizing Theology*, pp. 21-23. Compare Jüngel, *God as the Mystery*, p. 316.

[113]The degree of correspondence posited by the *imago Dei* is variously understood and not entirely clear in the canonical data, but it does suggest that humans are not totally unlike God. Lister agrees that "in view of both the Creator/creature distinction and the human status as *imago Dei*, there must be both similarity and dissimilarity in how the same emotional terminology applies to God and men" (*God Is Impassible and Impassioned*, p. 36).

[114]Jüngel notes that *analogy* has traditionally been used to refer to similarity within the greater context of dissimilarity. Thus, "Erich Przywara cited as the basic law of analogy . . . 'greater dissimilarity in so great a likeness'" (Przywara, "Metaphysik, Religion, Analogie," in *Analogia entis; Schriften* [Einsiedeln: Johannes Verlag, 1962], III, p. 334, quoted in Jüngel, *God as the Mystery*, p. 283n6). Compare Kant's view that analogy "does not signify (as is commonly understood) an imperfect similarity of two things, but a perfect similarity of relations between two quite dissimilar things" (Kant, *Prolegomena*, quoted in ibid., p. 261). Jüngel, however, aims at a "theological use of analogy which corresponds to faith in the incarnation of God" (ibid., p. 280). For him, analogy thus refers to "the difference of a still greater similarity between God and man in the midst of a great dissimilarity," and "the incarnation" is itself "the unique, unsurpassable instance" thereof in which "God has shown himself to be human in the execution

that I employ (1) *univocal* to mean that words or concepts apply to God and creatures in *exactly* the same way,[115] (2) *equivocal* to mean that words or concepts hold *entirely different* meaning when applied to God than they do when applied to creatures,[116] and (3) *analogical* to mean that there is *some degree* of similarity and dissimilarity of the meaning of words and concepts when applied to God and creatures.[117] That is, any predication that is not univocal (identical meaning) or equivocal (entirely different meaning) falls within the broad spectrum of analogy (similar and dissimilar meaning).[118]

---

of his divinity" (ibid., p. 288).

[115]Thomas Williams states in this regard: "Notwithstanding the irreducible ontological diversity between God and creatures, there are concepts under whose extension both God and creatures fall, so that the corresponding predicate expressions are used with exactly the same sense in predications about God as in predications about creatures" ("The Doctrine of Univocity Is True and Salutary," *Modern Theology* 21, no. 4 [2005]: 578). William P. Alston believes that "we may be able in some cases to use terms univocally of God and creature so far as the *res significata* [a property signified by a predicate term] is concerned, even though the mode of signification will misrepresent the divine being." Yet he also admits that "it may be that no creaturely terms, as they stand, can be so applied" ("Aquinas on Theological Predication: A Look Backward and a Look Forward," in *Reasoned Faith*, ed. Eleonore Stump [Ithaca, NY: Cornell University Press, 1993], p. 178).

[116]As Jordan Wessling puts it: "Theological equivocation is the opposite of univocity," that is, "the view that there are no concepts under whose extension both God and creatures fall; the same term has an altogether different meaning when applied to either God or creature" ("Colin Gunton, Divine Love, and Univocal Predication," *JRT* 7 [2013]: 95-96).

[117]Wessling suggests that "analogy is the doctrine that the relevant predicates have different but related senses" (ibid., p. 95).

[118]The distinction between the univocal, analogical and equivocal use of language has a long history. Consider Thomas Aquinas's usage of Aristotle's distinction between three kinds of naming. He notes that "a term is predicated of different things in various senses. Sometimes it is predicated of them according to a meaning which is *entirely the same* [emphasis mine], and then it is said to be predicated of them univocally, as animal is predicated of a horse and of an ox. Sometimes it is predicated of them according to meanings which are entirely different, and then it is said to be predicated of them equivocally, as *dog* is predicated of a star and of an animal. And sometimes it is predicated of them according to meanings which are partly different and partly not (different inasmuch as they imply different relationships, and the same inasmuch as these different relationships are referred to one and the same thing), and then it is said 'to be predicated analogously,' i.e., proportionally, according as each one by its own relationship is referred to that one same thing" (Thomas Aquinas, *Commentary on Aristotle's Metaphysics* 4.1.535, trans. John P. Rowan [Notre Dame, IN: Dumb Ox Books], p. 198). Compare *Summa Theologica* 1.1.13. See Alston's summary account of Aquinas's use of analogy, wherein he suggests that, for Aquinas, "the divine sense of the predicate 'wills that P', for example, is something like 'does something of the same sort as what we call willing by creatures, except that it is in a higher mode'" ("Aquinas on Theological Predication," p. 161). Notably, my use of the categories and terminology here should not be confused with an endorsement of the manner in which Aquinas employs them in his view of the *analogia entis* (the analogy of being) and/or his defense of divine simplicity.

Analogical predication might thus be adopted as a way to assuage the fears that (1) univocal predication would rob God of his transcendence (collapsing the Creator-creature distinction) and (2) equivocal predication (as defined above) would render us unable to speak intelligibly of God. Whereas (pure) equivocation, amounting to the negation of all predicates relative to God, does not appear to be a live option for most theologians, a number of theologians do offer robust arguments in favor of the univocity of theological language.[119]

In one such defense of univocity, Jordan Wessling distinguishes between "pure univocity," where "the concepts embedded in a predicate share [exactly] the same meaning or sense when applied to God and creature," and "partial univocity," where "a predicate shares the same sense when applied either to God or creature, only this predicate might have either additional or abridged meaning when applied to one of its referents."[120] On this definition, partial univocity entails that there is a common conceptual core, and from this, Wessling reasons, one could "(at least in principle) pinpoint the conceptual commonality" of the term *wise* that applies to both God and Solomon, then "strip away the non-univocal features" such that the term "can be used in a purely univocal way concerning God and Solomon."[121] However, suppose one agrees with Wessling that there *is* a common conceptual core. It does not seem to follow from this that "we can *in principle* find a conceptual core" (emphasis original) and succeed in stripping away

---

[119]Williams, for example, contends that the oft-supposed "three options" of "equivocity, analogy, and univocity" actually "reduce to two: either unintelligibility or univocity" ("Doctrine of Univocity," p. 578). In his view, "*either* the doctrine of univocity is true or . . . everything we say about God is in the most straightforward sense unintelligible—that is, that we literally do not know what we are saying when we say of God that he is good, just, wise, loving, or what have you" (ibid., pp. 579-80). Compare William P. Alston, *Divine Nature and Human Language: Essays in Philosophical Theology* (Ithaca, NY: Cornell University Press, 1989), pp. 17-117. However, might one not say instead that we do, in fact, know what *we mean to say* of God when we claim that he is good, but we do not know the extent to which our conception of good applies to God as he is? It seems to me that the burden of proof lies with those who claim to know the extent of the correspondence (or lack thereof) between our language of God and God as he is.

[120]Wessling, "Colin Gunton, Divine Love," p. 94. Compare William Alston's argument for "partial univocity" of "divine and human action," by which he means there is "a partial overlap between concepts of divine and human action" such that there is "some commonality between our thought of human and divine action and motivation" ("Divine and Human Action," in *Divine and Human Action: Essays in the Metaphysics of Theism*, ed. Thomas V. Morris [Ithaca, NY: Cornell University Press, 1988], pp. 258, 266, 273).

[121]Wessling, "Colin Gunton, Divine Love," pp. 94-95.

"non-univocal features."[122] Whereas a common conceptual core could be found by one who possessed adequate knowledge to do so, it does not follow that we, in fact, possess this requisite adequate knowledge.

Nevertheless, as a faith claim grounded in a high view of revelation-inspiration, I do believe that there is a common conceptual core of the exegetical upshot of the theological language in Scripture. However, I do not believe that I possess adequate knowledge of the divine being to precisely identify that common core. Whereas Wessling allows that "apprehending the exact univocal component of our terms will sometimes" elude "our best efforts," I suggest that such precise apprehension *may* in every case elude even "our best efforts" (at least, prior to glorification).[123] Accordingly, whereas I agree that there is a common conceptual core, I also recognize that there may be considerable difference between what I think is most likely the common conceptual core and the actual common conceptual core.[124] Thus, "one might claim that God and Samson are both 'strong,' maintaining that while it is literally true that God is strong, no one is able to precisely delineate what aspects of human conceptions of strength apply to God."[125]

For those (like myself) who doubt whether an "exact univocal component" or components of a term or concept can be identified with confidence, it seems that partial univocity either fails (if it entails such confidence) or is

---

[122]Ibid., p. 95. Wessling suggests "knowledge of the most moral and propitious courses of action" as a possible "conceptual core of 'wise'" common to "both God and Solomon" that might enable "us to use the term purely univocally of God and Solomon" (ibid.). However, this potential common core appears to presuppose some common core of the terms encapsulated in it (namely *knowledge, moral, propitious*, etc.). Would we not also need to then identify the common conceptual cores of each of these terms and then of the terms used in those descriptions and so on *ad infinitum* in order to claim univocity? As Wilhelm von Humboldt states: "No one when he uses a word has in mind exactly the same thing that another has, and the difference, however tiny, sends its tremors throughout language" (Wilhelm von Humboldt, *Humanist Without Portfolio* [Detroit: Wayne State University Press, 1963], p. 235).

[123]Wessling, "Colin Gunton, Divine Love," p. 95. Compare Alston, "Aquinas on Theological Predication," pp. 153-54.

[124]This satisfies Wessling's parameters that to "avoid the pitfall of equivocity" the defender of analogy "must do something to link together the meanings of God-directed and creature-directed uses of the relevant predicates," whereas to avoid univocity the defender "must not link these meanings together in such a way that we are able to specify the conceptual commonality between God-directed and creature-directed uses of a term" ("Colin Gunton, Divine Love," pp. 95, 96). Both equivocity and univocity are avoided on my view of analogy in that it affirms (by faith) that there is a common conceptual core without claiming to be able to precisely identify that common conceptual core.

[125]Ibid., p. 96.

itself a species of analogy, albeit one that locates the extent of the correspondence of biblical (or other) language to God (as he is) far toward the univocal side of the spectrum.[126] Indeed, if analogy is taken in the broad sense I am using, it appears that partial univocity would be a species of analogy (because it entails *some* similarity and dissimilarity) that falls near the univocal side of the broad spectrum of analogy between (pure) univocity (identical meaning) and (pure) equivocity (entirely different meaning). On the other hand, conceptions of analogy as similarity within the greater context of dissimilarity (that is, analogy falling near the equivocal side of the spectrum) might be qualified in a similar fashion as partial equivocity. My own canonical approach attempts no overarching claim with regard to the degree of similarity or dissimilarity of theological language. Rather, I maintain that one may properly make (tentative) claims regarding what the canon seems to affirm about divine emotions (to the best of one's interpretive ability) while making no claim that such language fully corresponds to God as he is and/or that one can isolate with confidence the conceptual common core that applies to God precisely.[127]

The canonical approach employed here thus gives priority to the canonical language, affirming and using such language as applying to God unless there is a canonically derived rationale not to do so, with the crucial proviso that such language is unavoidably analogical, and thus one must always remain cognizant of the Creator-creature distinction.[128] Nevertheless, such unavoidable uncertainty should not dissuade one from making every effort to explicate the exegetical upshot of biblical language and apply it seriously (but humbly and tentatively) to our theological models, as inade-

---

[126]Over and against Alston's view of partial univocity, Philip A. Rolnick argues: "Unless Alston is prepared to specify what the meaning is to God, he can hardly claim to have depicted 'a core of common meaning'" ("Realist Reference to God: Analogy or Univocity?" in *Realism & Antirealism*, ed. William P. Alston [Ithaca, NY: Cornell University Press, 2002], p. 234). In his view, "Alston has misunderstood analogy as keeping God and humankind too far separated" (ibid., p. 236).

[127]Although on this approach, biblical language of God is affirmed and used in a similar fashion to the way one affirming (partial or modified) univocity might do, the crucial difference is the continual recognition that *all* language about God is analogical. By faith, I believe the canonical language possesses a sufficient extent of similarity to speak meaningfully of him (humbly and tentatively) and be confronted by and respond to Scripture's claims.

[128]That is, on the belief that all theological language falls somewhere within the broad spectrum of analogy, it stands to reason that, if Scripture is the revealed and inspired word of God (see chap. 2 above), Scripture is the most accurate source of theological data.

quate as they may turn out to be.[129] As 1 Corinthians 13:12 states, "now we see in a mirror dimly, but then face to face; now I know in part, but then I will know fully just as I also have been fully known."

However, some impassibilists emphasize the dissimilarity in their supposition of God's *impassible* passion and/or feelings. Consider Weinandy's assertion that God, as pure act, is never emotionally responsive to the world (even voluntarily) yet "utterly passionate" with regard to trinitarian relations.[130] Gary Culpepper remarks that this is an "indeterminate attribution of 'passion' to the life of the eternal God," wherein it is "not at all clear what the term 'passionate' adds" to "God as purely actualized love."[131] Indeed, since Weinandy dismisses the possibility that God's passion is "analogous to human feelings," it appears that he uses the term *passionate* in an equivocal manner.[132] To take another example, Creel maintains that "divine impassibility means that it is logically impossible for God to be affected by anything," which appears to make his claim that "God is [analogically] touched by our sufferings and joys, victories and defeats" rather empty.[133] Lister notes that the assertion of God being "touched" appears "to be at odds with" Creel's "more forceful definition of impassibility."[134] How one should understand God to suffer or be "touched" yet unaffected by external stimuli is not clear, especially if one, like Henry, wishes to avoid reducing "God's love, compassion and mercy" to "mere figures of speech."[135]

Beyond this, it is questionable whether maintaining divine impassibility *and* the ability of God to "feel" does justice to the apparent meaning of the many biblical passages that seem to depict God as experiencing *responsive* emotions, many of which do not merely ascribe emotions to God but situate

---

[129] In much the same way that epistemological certainty is beyond my reach, but that does not dissuade me from theological convictions, the view that theological language is analogous need not deter from theological convictions (though recognition of both should engender humility).

[130] Weinandy, *Does God Suffer?* p. 119. That is, "God simply loves himself and all things in himself in the one act which he himself is" (ibid., p. 127). This dovetails with Keating and White's view that according to God's "pure actuality," "Divine *apatheia* is not apathy, but a characteristic of the plenitude of the divine nature as unblemished love" ("Introduction: Divine Impassibility in Contemporary Theology," in Keating and White, eds., *Divine Impassibility and the Mystery of Human Suffering*, p. 14).

[131] Culpepper, "One Suffering, in Two Natures," p. 83.

[132] Weinandy, *Does God Suffer?* p. 39.

[133] Creel, "Immutability and Impassibility," pp. 314, 318.

[134] Lister, *God Is Impassible and Impassioned*, p. 153.

[135] Henry, *God, Revelation, and Authority* 6:349.

those emotions within the context of give-and-take relationship wherein divine emotions respond to the actual state of affairs and are, therefore, passible.[136] For example, the biblical language of *compassion* explicitly depicts "suffering along with," akin to sympathy/empathy, that is, responsive feeling of emotion along with and for the object of compassion (compare Is 49:15; Jer 31:20).[137]

Following Aquinas, Gilles Emery maintains that passions like compassion "are attributed to God due to the effects they denote" such that "God is affected by the misery of his creatures, admittedly not in himself, but in the effects of his merciful love," that is, "not according to a passion which is suffered" or "some form of divine pain."[138] In other words, God does not feel compassion but "acts" in a way that might analogously be deemed compassionate. However, as has been seen, Scripture depicts not only God's compassionate action but also his genuinely responsive affection and sympathy/empathy. Tellingly, Emery approves of Jacques Maritain's view that mercy in God is "in distinction" from "what we call suffering or sadness," "something for which we have no idea or concept, no name which might be properly applicable to God," except that he claims "we can indeed name it" as "the plenitude of divine charity" while "its mode of existence and its reality in God remain incomprehensible for us."[139]

Lister's qualified impassibility moves beyond this seemingly equivocal treatment of biblical language, maintaining that God is affected by the world, though always voluntarily and in a way appropriate to his transcendence as Creator. Thus "impassibility" is used "to set limits on how God's emotions" are "understood" rather than "deny[ing] their existence altogether."[140] This dovetails with Gavrilyuk's contention that "divine impassibility qualifies the manner in which God endures suffering" and is

---

[136]Consider God's negative emotions such as loathing/hatred. In every instance of Scripture, these are evaluative, being prompted by evil, and thus passible at least in that sense.
[137]See Butterworth, "רחם," *NIDOTTE* 3:1093; Stoebe, "רחם," *TLOT* 3:1226. See also the discussion of רחם in this chapter and chap. 3 (above).
[138]Emery, "Immutability of the God of Love," pp. 67, 56. See Aquinas, *Summa Theologica* 1.21.3. Accordingly, "spiritual or intellectual affections (affections without passion) are employed in proper discourse concerning God," whereas "'sensible affections' cannot be attributed to God properly, but by metaphor" (Emery, "Immutability of the God of Love," p. 67).
[139]Emery, "Immutability of the God of Love," pp. 57-59. See Maritain, "Quelques reflexions sur le savoir theologique," *Revue Thomiste* 69 (1969): 17.
[140]Lister, *God Is Impassible and Impassioned*, p. 21.

"affected" by it, with "perfect control over emotional states" rather than "emotional impotence and indifference."[141]

Whereas I also wish to maintain important distinctions between divine and human emotions (see below), I do not think there is sufficient reason to label God as impassible. The canonical data simply do not cohere with the oft-maintained understanding of impassibility as God's imperviousness to being affected by the world, and using a term prone to such misunderstanding (including among impassibilists) is inefficient and potentially misleading. As Robert Jenson states, despite the "subtle qualifications and real insights involved in the tradition's sophisticated massaging of the notion of impassibility . . . in any sense of impassibility perceptible on the face of the word, it will not do as an attribute of the God of Scripture and dogma."[142] Other theological terms that are also often misunderstood (such as *love* itself) are justifiably maintained in theological discourse by either being canonical terms or by providing sufficient explanatory benefit of the canonical data as a whole.[143] However, *impassibility* is neither referred to in Scripture (semantically or conceptually) nor provides explanatory value that is not already efficiently conveyed by other theological concepts (e.g., creation, transcendence, omnipotence, omniscience).[144] In its extreme sense,

---

[141] Gavrilyuk, "God's Impassible Suffering," pp. 143, 137. He maintains that, for the patristics, "divine impassibility is primarily a metaphysical term, marking God's unlikeness to everything in the created order, not a psychological term denoting (as modern passibilists allege) God's emotional apathy" (ibid., p. 139). Thus Gavrilyuk is willing to say that God is "impassible inasmuch as he is able to conquer sin, suffering, and death; and God is also passible (in a carefully qualified sense) inasmuch as in the incarnation God has chosen to enter the human condition in order to transform it" (ibid., p. 146).

[142] Robert Jenson, "Ipse Pater Non Est Impassibilis," in Keating and White, eds., *Divine Impassibility and the Mystery of Human Suffering*, p. 120. He adds, if indeed "'one of the Trinity' suffered in the flesh,' then the God here referred to by 'the Trinity' is not impassible, in any use of the adjective that would occur to a native user of Greek, Latin, or English—or at least not to any such user who had mastered the relation of subject and predicate" (ibid., p. 119). Jenson maintains that God (including the Father himself) "is not-impassible" but "neither can we say that the biblical God is passible" (ibid., p. 120). He finally suggests that Scripture depicts God "as the subject of his total history with us" as "impassible" yet, in particular instances such as "happening upon a lost sheep," as "passible" (ibid., p. 123). Compare Robert W. Jenson, *Systematic Theology* (New York: Oxford University Press, 1997), 1:125, 144, 234.

[143] Compare the term *Trinity*, which, though not a biblical word and also prone to confusion, helpfully and concisely conveys the canonical depiction of God's triune nature.

[144] Indeed, as Lister notes, "Scripture never makes a direct assertion of a metaphysical doctrine of divine impassibility" and "does not supply" this "theological category," though he claims that "it does instruct us as to this kind of divine invulnerability" and is canonical via "second-order theological reflection on Scripture's first-order statements" toward a model that provides a

then, *impassibility* is either vacuous or directly contradicts the canonical portrayal of divine emotionality, whereas in its qualified form it appears to be superfluous. Suffice it to say, then, that God's emotions are not identical, but analogous, to humans, with similarity and dissimilarity.

Nevertheless, the foreconditional-reciprocal model finds considerable agreement with the qualified impassibilist effort to maintain the Creator/creature distinction, divine transcendence, ontological invulnerability, omnipotence, omniscience and the fact that God is not involuntarily vulnerable. As shall be further explained in chapter nine, the foreconditional-reciprocal model agrees that God is not *essentially* passible or vulnerable in relation to the world, thus departing significantly from extreme passibilist conceptions. God need not have created any world, and thus God's passibility in relation to the world is voluntary. God is not involuntarily vulnerable to the effects of others, "manipulated, overwhelmed, or surprised," and thus experiences emotions in a manner that is entirely flawless and, in this way and others, differs from humans.[145]

At the same time, the foreconditional-reciprocal model maintains that God's emotions may be affected by and responsive to the significantly free actions of creatures. Thus God feels emotions responsive to creaturely actions that he does not causally determine, many of which (grief, anger) he does not ideally desire, experiencing both positive and negative emotions that are evaluatively responsive to human disposition or action.[146] Accordingly, God is

---

"comprehensive theory sufficient to account for all the relevant data" (i.e., "retroduction"; *God Is Impassible and Impassioned*, pp. 190, 173, 174). I agree, in principle, with the valid role of theological reflection on Scripture toward canonical theo-ontology (see chaps. 2 and 9) but do not believe *impassibility* has sufficient explanatory value as Lister uses it to outweigh the confusion. On the other hand, I use *passibility* in a qualified sense because it is both biblical (see the earlier canonical data of divine emotion) and conveys the explanatory value that God may be emotionally affected and responsive. Outside of discussion of the passibility/impassibility debate it might be more precise to simply refer to divine emotionality as theopathic.

[145]Lister, *God Is Impassible and Impassioned*, p. 36. The element of surprise is not necessary to genuinely responsive emotions, because foreknowledge is not identical to experience. One may possess theoretical and certain knowledge of something without thereby having experienced it. Moreover, profound emotions may be felt even when one knew prior to an experience what would in fact happen (compare the feelings one experiences upon rereading a particularly moving story, absent surprise). See the brief discussion of divine foreknowledge in chap. 9 (below).

[146]This contrasts with the determinism that is crucial to many impassibilist readings, David Bentley Hart's being a notable exception (see chap. 9 below). For example, Lister frames God's emotional responsiveness along (compatibilist) deterministic lines such that God "ordained all

passionate toward humans, delighting in goodness but suffering in response to the actions of creatures, experiencing pain evoked by evil (which God does not causally determine).[147] In all this, God, by freely creating this world, voluntarily opened himself up to being affected by creatures yet remains ontologically free to remove himself from such passible relationship with the world while electing to remain constantly committed to that relationship.

However, does a passibilist interpretation of divine emotionality as proposed by the foreconditional-reciprocal model assume a naive, simplistic and/or univocal approach to the biblical text? Some might worry that attributing emotions to God in the way that Scripture appears to do amounts to a collapse of the Creator-creature distinction, among other things. For instance, what are emotions for a being without a cerebral cortex? It seems to me that we must confess that we do not know with precision in this regard (hence the importance of continual recognition that our language regarding God is unavoidably analogous). However, suppose we ask the parallel question of how a being without a cerebral cortex might possess a will. The vast majority of Christian theologians (past and present) seem to have little or no difficulty with the claim that God wills (again, typically understood analogically).[148] Even as the ascription of "will" to God does not require thinking of God as an elevated creature, ascribing passible emotions to God need not require a collapse of the Creator/creature distinction.[149]

---

that has taken place, the nature of his responsive engagement included" (*God Is Impassible and Impassioned*, p. 183). See the discussion of God's ideal and effective wills in chap. 9 (below).

[147]Although *suffer* can refer more broadly to receptivity of the actions of others, here and elsewhere I use it in its contemporary sense of psychological pain or grief. On the other hand, I use passion here and elsewhere (unless otherwise qualified) in the everyday sense of strong responsive emotion. Passibility, again, refers to being emotionally affected such that suffering and passion are subcategories thereof. None of these terms necessarily implies anything with regard to the issue of divine corporeality, since it is possible to conceive of emotions, passions and even suffering coherently alongside incorporeality, just as it is possible to conceive of incorporeal cognition, volition and so on, despite the fact that, for humans, those operations assume a physical brain.

[148]See Vanhoozer's suggestion, in dialogue with Alston's work, that we predicate "'being an agent' [without bodily movement] and 'being a speaker' [without vocal chords] of God analogically" (*Remythologizing Theology*, p. 58).

[149]Although the language of *analogy* itself is not biblical language, I do believe the canon includes a minimal concept of analogy. Scripture presents (at least some) language descriptive of God as analogical (in the minimal sense of similarity *and* dissimilarity), such as when anger (among other emotions) is ascribed to God alongside the proviso that God is "not man, the Holy One in your midst" (Hos 11:9; cf. Is 55:8). See the discussion later in this chapter.

As mentioned earlier, all available language is human language, and therefore our language of God will fail to correspond to him perfectly. Yet, if this is the case, how does one decide which "human" language accurately corresponds to God and which does not? The foreconditional-reciprocal model is derived from a high view of Scripture (see chapter two) positing that the biblical language is the best presently available data regarding the divine nature while recognizing that such language is analogical. That is, there is both similarity and dissimilarity between what the canonical language conveys and God as he actually is. However, we do not have direct access to God and lack the mental capacity to know with specificity the extent of this similarity and dissimilarity. With Vanhoozer, I aim to avoid overestimating "the adequacy of human language and thought" and also avoid underestimating "the importance of responding to the provocations of God's self-revelation."[150]

It seems, then, that one modest way forward is to attempt to remain at the level of Scripture as canon, competently and carefully interpreted in light of its entire canonical context and the details of individual texts.[151] This approach takes the language in its exegetical sense in light of the entire canonical data, while recognizing that the outcome of this procedure will nevertheless unavoidably produce an imperfect conception of God (as is true of all God-talk).[152] Wolterstorff contends, in this regard, "an implication of accepting Scripture as canonical is that one affirm, as literally true, Scripture's representation of God unless, on some point, one has good reason not to do so."[153] My approach recognizes, at the same time, that even language that is properly taken as literal is nonetheless analogical (in the sense previously described).[154] Moreover, not all biblical language is intended literally,

---

[150]Vanhoozer, *Remythologizing Theology*, p. 16.
[151]Recall my final-form canonical methodology (chap. 2 above). Compare John C. Peckham, "The Analogy of Scripture Revisited: A Final Form Canonical Approach to Systematic Theology," *MAJT* 22 (2011): 41-53.
[152]Here and elsewhere, I seek to exegete the intention that is apparent *in the text* while recognizing that the authorial intent itself is not an available object of investigation. See chap. 2 above. Compare Kevin Vanhoozer, *Is There a Meaning in This Text?* (Grand Rapids: Zondervan, 1998).
[153]Nicholas Wolterstorff, "Could Not God Sorrow If We Do?" in *The Papers of the Henry Luce III Fellows in Theology*, ed. Christopher I. Wilkins (Atlanta: Scholars Press, 2002), p. 140.
[154]Consider Vanhoozer's use of William Alston's distinction between literal and univocal: "Two things are 'univocal' if they have the same meaning. To use a term 'literally,' by contrast, is to use it in its conventional rather than figurative sense. God literally speaks and acts, but because

and one must therefore be sensitive to metaphor and idiomatic expression. As Terence Fretheim comments, "Metaphors do reveal an essential continuity with the reality which is God."[155] However, the danger is "either interpreting metaphors literally in every respect or (more commonly today) denying any essential relationship between the metaphor and God."[156]

In this regard, consider the close association between anatomical imagery and divine emotions. Some point to the anatomical imagery in Hosea 11:8-9 and other passages (compare Jer 31:20) as evidence that such language is anthropomorphic (and thus also anthropopathic). However, it will not do to appeal to divine incorporeality as a reason to dismiss language that is based on anatomical imagery, since the same or similar anatomical imagery

---

God does so in his own way, these terms are only partially univocal when applied to God and human beings" (Vanhoozer, *Remythologizing Theology*, p. 211n118). Vanhoozer prefers "to say the two terms ['speaks' and 'acts'] are 'literal and analogical' rather than [Alston's preference for] 'partially univocal.' The key is to remember that 'univocal' pertains to the mode of God's acting, 'literal' to the kind of action done" (ibid.). Compare William P. Alston, "How to Think About Divine Action," in *Divine Action*, ed. B. Hebblethwaite and E. Henderson (Edinburgh: T & T Clark, 1990), pp. 52, 68-69. Compare Merold Westphal's view that "we need two distinctions, one between literal and metaphorical and the other between analogical and univocal." The theist can then say, "'God speaks' is a literal but analogical claim. It is analogical because divine discourse is both like and unlike human discourse; but this is not metaphor, because the performance of illocutionary acts belongs properly and primarily to God and only derivatively" to humans ("On Reading God the Author," *Religious Studies* 37, no. 3 [2001]: 273).

[155]Terence Fretheim, "The Repentance of God: A Key to Evaluating Old Testament God-Talk," *HBT* 10, no. 1 (1988): 51. Lister commends Fretheim's "commitment to analogical interpretation" but correctly criticizes his wider approach that subjectively favors certain metaphors as "controlling metaphors," leading to a "canon within the canon" and seeming to give interpretive priority to human experience rather than taking "all of the analogies together" (*God Is Impassible and Impassioned*, pp. 132, 141).

[156]Fretheim, "Repentance of God," p. 51. In this book, *literal* and *figurative* are used as shorthand terms to distinguish between what is conventionally presumed to be the strict, primary sense of a word or phrase and the use of figures of speech (e.g., metaphors, metonyms, idioms, etc.) wherein the literal meaning (as defined above) of the word or words is nonsensical or untrue. Metaphor has often been defined as a kind of figurative language (though it may also be used broadly as a near synonym of figurative) that compares two unlike things that have some point(s) of commonality. On the cognitive-linguistic view, however, metaphor uses the terms of one conceptual domain to understand another (e.g., life as a journey), whether or not there is obvious similarity between them. The nature of metaphor (and figurative language more broadly) and how it is to be understood and related to or distinguished from the literal sense of language has been (and continues to be) the subject of complex, protracted debate. For an introductory discussion of perspectives on metaphor see William G. Lycan, *Philosophy of Language: A Contemporary Introduction*, 2nd ed. (New York: Routledge, 2008), pp. 175-90. Adequately addressing these issues is beyond the scope of this work. However, the very recognition of the complex issues involved in defining and understanding the nature, meaning and operation of literal and figurative language strengthens the approach advocated here that aims toward remaining close to the language and patterns of Scripture itself.

is consistently used of human emotion without referring to literal human anatomy.[157] For example, the anatomical language in Hosea 11:8-9 is demonstrably idiomatic, since the same anatomical idioms of "heart" (לֵב) and "nose" (אַף) are also used of human agents to convey intense emotions without denoting human anatomy. For example, the idiom "long of nose" (אֶרֶךְ אַפַּיִם) is used of both humans (Prov 14:29) and of God (Ex 34:6) to refer to a long-suffering disposition.[158] In a similar fashion, the "turning" (הָפַךְ) of one's "heart" (לֵב) does not denote the physical movement of anatomy, whether in reference to humans (Lam 1:20) or to God (Hos 11:8). An abundance of other anatomical idioms are used of both God and humans alike but in an apparently figurative manner.[159] As G. B. Caird puts it, "only captious pedantry or childish humour will find it necessary to remark that the eye of a needle cannot see or a tongue of land speak."[160] Why, then, should references to divine agency be divested of the well-understood, grammatical meaning of idiomatic phraseology?

Again, I readily affirm that God does not have "human" emotions, but that does not require that he does not have passible emotions. The foreconditional-reciprocal model takes the exegetical meaning of such idiomatic language, in light of the wider canonical information, as applying to God analogically, that is, as neither entirely similar nor dissimilar to the same language of humans. The wider data of Scripture provide some interpretive controls that assist in the interpretation of such imagery without precisely specifying

---

[157]Such idioms are believed to have been derived from associated physical phenomena (and/or that which was believed to be associated physical phenomena when the idioms originated) such that there is an evident "proclivity" in Semitic languages "to utilize anatomical terms in the creation of new idioms" (Jeffery D. Griffin, "An Investigation of Idiomatic Expressions in the Hebrew Bible with a Case Study of Anatomical Idioms" [PhD diss., Mid-America Baptist Theological Seminary, 1999], p. 39). Compare Dhorme, L'emploi métaphorique des noms de parties du corps en hébreu et en akkadien. Caird suggests this is true of all languages (*Language and Imagery of the Bible*, pp. 172-73).

[158]Of לֵב, "heart," see Hos 11:8; Jer 4:19; Gen 6:5-6.

[159]Consider the idioms of inclining one's ears (2 Kings 19:16; Prov 5:1), favor in one's eyes (Gen 6:8; 32:5), words in one's mouth (Deut 8:3; 2 Sam 14:19), "face" as idiom of presence and hiding one's face as idiom of displeasure (Ex 33:14; 10:11; Deut 31:17-18; Is 53:3), deliverance into one's hand (Gen 14:20; 49:24), strength or power denoted by arms (Ex 6:6; Job 40:9), and murmuring innards in reference to intense compassion (Jer 4:19; 31:20), all used of God and humans. In each case, the idiomatic expressions are widely understood to be independent of the literal anatomical references. On these and many other examples, see Griffin, "Investigation of Idiomatic Expressions," p. 111.

[160]Caird, *Language and Imagery of the Bible*, p. 173.

the extent of similarity or dissimilarity. For instance, within Hosea 11:8-9 itself, God states, "I am God and not man" (compare Is 55:8). It is therefore apparent in the passage itself that the imagery of divine emotionality should not be applied to God univocally. Likewise, divine repentance (נחם) is explicitly differentiated from human repentance in Scripture. For "the Glory of Israel will not lie or change His mind [נחם]; for He is not a man that He should change His mind [נחם]" (1 Sam 15:29; compare Num 23:19; Mal 3:6).[161] Yet Scripture "nowhere indicates that the idea that God does not repent is a universal principle, but always with relation to a specific event or situation."[162] Indeed, God is frequently depicted as exhibiting נחם, including twice in 1 Samuel 15 where God "regrets," or better, "is grieved by," the outcome of his election of Saul (1 Sam 15:11, 35).[163] Moreover, prior to the flood God is "sorry" (נחם) (Gen 6:6), and many times elsewhere God either declares or exhibits his willingness to relent (נחם) in response to humans (Jer 18:7-10; Jon 3:10; 4:2; etc.).[164] However, whereas humans repent of wrongdoing, "God is never said to have committed any sin of which God needs to repent."[165] Thus, God does "relent" (נחם) but in a way that differs from human נחם.[166]

---

[161]First Samuel 15:29 and Num 23:19 have sometimes been taken to mean that God cannot relent. However, both of these occurrences use נחם to contrast with one who would not keep his word, thus implying that the declaration emphasizes the surety and irrevocability of God's decision in that specific instance. First Samuel 15 twice states that God was "sorry" (נחם; 1 Sam 15:11, 35). This is an apparent contradiction unless one understands that contextually the meaning in 1 Sam 15:29 appears to relate to the finality of God's rejection of Saul, not the nature of God. This kind of finality of divine decision appears in God's declaration: "I have spoken, I have purposed, And I will not change My mind" (Jer 4:28; cf. Jer 20:16; Ps 110:4; Zech 8:14; Ezek 24:14). That this is not a blanket policy or an ontological claim is apparent in that later God declares that he will indeed relent in response to human repentance (Jer 18:1-10 et al.). Indeed, several texts suggest that "to repent concerning [threatened/real] calamity" is "fundamental to the divine nature" (Block, *Judges, Ruth*, p. 131).

[162]John T. Willis, "The 'Repentance' of God in the Books of Samuel, Jeremiah, and Jonah," *HBT* 16 (1994): 168.

[163]H. Van Dyke Parunak points to the underlying conception of comfort, consolation or compassion and asserts that נחם entails both "change" and "sorrow" "in the sense of emotional pain" and (at times) sympathy, but no "suggestion of regret" ("A Semantic Survey of Nhm," *Biblica* 56 [1975]: 513, 532).

[164]See Peckham, "Passible Potter," pp. 130-50.

[165]See Fretheim, "Repentance of God," p. 50. For a discussion of some passibilist hermeneutical approaches to language of divine pathos, including that of Fretheim, see Matthew R. Schlimm, "Different Perspectives on Divine Pathos: An Examination of Hermeneutics in Biblical Theology," *CBQ* 69, no. 4 (2007): 673-94.

[166]Similarly, God is depicted as being "wearied" (יגע) by his people (Mal 2:17) or "weary" (לאה)

Similarly, careful examination of divine jealousy, or passion (קָנָא), in the Hebrew Bible demonstrates that one way in which it differs from human jealousy is that it exhibits none of the flawed characteristics of human jealousy, such as envy.[167] God's קָנָא is his always appropriate, passionate love for what rightfully belongs to him.[168] E. Reuter contends in this regard that, in many classical interpretations, the dismissal of divine jealousy as a so-called anthropopathism stemmed from the "notion of divine impassibility, which is inconsistent with the biblical understanding of God but is often espoused nevertheless by both Christian and Jewish theology, creating problems of exegesis."[169] Similarly, whereas humans may hate arbitrarily and unjustly, divine displeasure is always accurately evaluative and appropriate.[170] Human judges may be corrupted (1 Sam 8:3), but God always judges righteously (Gen 18:25). Finally, human love may fail, even that of a mother for her infant, but God's exceeds all expectations (Is 49:15); human lovingkindness is transient (Hos 6:4), but God's is everlasting (Ps 100:5).

Thus the canonical data themselves provide *some* controls with regard to the interpretation of the language used of God and often shed light on *some* of the ways it differs from the same or similar language used of humans.[171] Accordingly, absent textual evidence that suggests otherwise, language of passible divine emotion may be treated as analogically descriptive of God without leading to absurd theological implications. God is depicted throughout the canon as having emotions that are analogical to human emo-

---

of bearing feasts and festivals that are merely for show (Is 1:14), yet elsewhere Scripture states that God does "not become weary [יָעַף] or tired" (Is 40:28). One might then think of the former instances as expression of God's emotional displeasure and disappointment without attributing to God the fatigue that is excluded in Is 40.

[167]See the earlier discussion of קָנָא (pp. 156-57).

[168]This does not support the application of the so-called way of eminence. Whereas one might extrapolate from the apparently theologically sound principle that, used of God, such things only apply in their positive aspects, such a principle is incapable of objective usefulness since different interpreters will find different characteristics "good."

[169]Reuter, "קָנָא," *TDOT* 13:53. Compare Jeffrey H. Tigay, *Deuteronomy* (Philadelphia: JPS, 1996), p. 66; Nahum M. Sarna, *Exodus* (Philadelphia: JPS, 1991), p. 110. Wilhelm Vischer adds: "The LORD is a jealous God, whether this anthropomorphism pleases us or not" ("Words and the Word: The Anthropomorphisms of the Biblical Revelation," *Interpretation* 3, no. 1 [1949]: 13).

[170]Likewise, whereas human anger may overreact, God restrains his anger, despite provocation (Ps 78:38, 58).

[171]Presumably, there are numerous other dissimilarities (not limited to qualitative ones) that may not be included in the canon, due (at least in part) to the limitations of human language, cognition and space (cf. Jn 21:25), but I do not presume to be able to identify them.

tions but wholly good, appropriate and without fault (among other differences).[172] Absent a compelling exegetically and canonically sound argument that emotive language in Scripture is not intended to apply to the conception of God proper, the literary thrust of the biblical text(s) is taken seriously, in conjunction with intertextual canonical controls, concluding that divine love is possible (in a qualified sense). This affords no asylum to a proof-texting approach that falls into a "naïve [pure] univocism" and "fails to reckon seriously with the place of analogy in scriptural God-language."[173] All language of God must be understood as analogical; the interpreter must remain vigilantly cognizant of the limitations of human understanding and the unavoidable inadequacy of human language in reference to God. Yet, where a canonical indication regarding the extent of similarity or dissimilarity regarding divine emotive language is absent or unknown, it seems prudent to err toward the univocal end of the analogical spectrum, in deference to the divinely revealed and inspired words of Scripture.[174]

God's Love Is Not Merely Emotional

According to Scripture, then, God both transcends human emotionality *qua* human emotionality yet experiences emotions divinely (theopathically).[175] God's love for humans is ardent and profoundly emotional. God is intensely interested in and affected by humans, and may be pleased or displeased by their response to him such that the quality of his life is affected by the state of affairs in the world. God enjoys goodness and abhors evil, delights in his creatures but is grieved by their rebellion. His deep compassion is intensely passionate, assiduous but not unconditionally constant, highly emotive but not beyond divine control.

---

[172]This is not an extracanonical presupposition but is derived from the frequent, canon-wide axiom that God is always, and in all things, good (omnibenevolent; Ps 100:5).

[173]Lister, *God Is Impassible and Impassioned*, p. 140. My own treatment of the canonical data has been careful to avoid a simplistic hermeneutical approach. See, in this regard, my extensive engagement with the data and exegetical scholarship in John C. Peckham, *The Concept of Divine Love in the Context of the God-World Relationship* (New York: Peter Lang, 2014).

[174]Recall that, on my usage of *analogical* (as explained earlier), both language that is taken as *closer* to the univocal side of the spectrum (but not identical) and that which is taken as *closer* to the equivocal side (but not entirely different) are properly spoken of as analogical.

[175]As Vanhoozer puts it, "perhaps the Bible's depiction of divine suffering is less a matter of anthropopathic projection than it is a case of human suffering being theopathic (God-like)" (Vanhoozer, *Remythologizing Theology*, pp. 77-78).

As such, the foreconditional-reciprocal model posits that divine love is passible, yet departs in crucial ways from various other passibilist conceptions. For example, the foreconditional-reciprocal model must be distinguished from every form of panentheism. First, divine passibility is not a product of ontological necessity. God is ontically discrete, distinct from the world he created. God chose to create other beings and voluntarily consider their best interests as his own (chapters four and five). Thus divine love is to be sharply distinguished from any conception of sympathy that amounts to ontological dependency or posits that God *must* be (or remain) committed to creatures, emotionally or otherwise. While God's compassion is grounded in his loving character and extends beyond all reasonable expectations, love is voluntarily and evaluatively bestowed (not undifferentiated sympathy). Further, whereas Scripture consistently depicts divine love as passible, God's love is not passive. God's love is extremely active, including God's exercise of power in ways that contradict the panentheism of Hartshorne and others. God is affected by creaturely actions, but he is not acted on in a way that requires weakness or ontological vulnerability.

In this way, God's love for creatures includes deep affection and personal concern that complements its volitional and evaluative aspects. The evaluative aspect is apparent in that divine displeasure and the removal of compassion are always prompted by the appropriate evaluation of evil, while the volitional aspect appears in God's freedom and moral right to remove compassion from the unrepentant long before he does so. As such, it must be emphasized that divine emotions are affected but not determined by external stimulus to the exclusion of other mental factors such as volition and evaluation. The claim that love cannot be emotional if it is volitional subscribes to a false opposition of volition, evaluation and emotion.[176] Indeed,

---

[176]Morris believes "it is nonsense to be commanded to generate a passionate *eros*" (*Testaments of Love*, p. 189). Thus, "we must not confuse love with passion or sentimentality," because love must be volitional rather than emotional (ibid., p. 187). However, emotional love is commanded throughout Scripture. The love God bestows and requires is to be wholehearted, including both volition and emotion (cf. Deut 6:5; Mt 22:37). See chap. 3 (above) and Wallis, "אהב," *TDOT* 1:110. Consider also C. Stephen Evans's view that "some emotions are ones that we have some control over, at least over time" ("Can Love Be Commanded? Kierkegaard's View of Neighbor Love," in *Visions of Agapé: Problems and Possibilities in Human and Divine Love*, ed. Craig A. Boyd [Aldershot, UK: Ashgate, 2008], p. 76). As Tigay notes, "The idea of commanding a feeling is not foreign to the Torah, which assumes that people can cultivate proper attitudes" (*Deuteronomy*, p. 76). Compare Lapsley, "Feeling Our Way," p. 365.

the love in a healthy marriage should include voluntary commitment, enjoyment of each other and emotional affection. Likewise, in Scripture, these aspects of love are complementary and mutually supportive (compare Deut 6:5; Mt 22:37; Mk 1:41), each grounded in God's character of love (see chapter nine). Thus, as Stephen Post contends, "an even balance or co-primacy between emotion and reason is the fitting alternative to those who would diminish the importance of either capacity."[177] The complementary nature of the volitional, evaluative and emotional aspects as coprimary aspects of divine love avoids overemphasis of divine volition on the one hand, or passible emotion on the other.

CONCLUSION

This chapter has presented and explained the profoundly emotional nature of divine love as depicted in the canon, in response to these questions: Does God's love include affection and/or emotionality such that God is concerned for the world, sympathetically or otherwise? Is divine love emotionally responsive to human disposition and/or action? Scripture presents God as affectionate and loving, devotedly interested and intimately concerned about humans, affected by the world in feeling joy and delight in goodness, yet sorrow, passion and intense anger at evil, alongside profound compassion and the desire to redeem humans. While none can overpower God, he is affected by worldly events because he has willingly opened himself up to reciprocal love relationship with creatures. Thus God's love is emotional but not merely emotional, that is, passible (in a qualified sense) yet also volitional and evaluative. Complementing chapter five, then, this chapter has suggested that God enjoys and is deeply affected by reciprocal (though asymmetrical) relationship with humans. The nature of this mutual love relationship as forconditional and ideally reciprocal is further explained in chapters seven and eight.

---

[177]Stephen G. Post, *Unlimited Love: Altruism, Compassion, and Service* (Philadelphia: Templeton Foundation Press, 2003), p. 67. Likewise, Rice explains that "love involves profound sensitivity" yet "love is a voluntary commitment" (Rice, "Process Theism and the Open View of God," p. 185). Compare Oord, *Nature of Love*, p. 30.

7

THE FORECONDITIONAL ASPECT OF DIVINE LOVE

Is divine love for the world unconditional or conditional, unmotivated or motivated, ungrounded or grounded, or something else? Can humans forfeit divine love, or is it unilaterally constant? For both the immanent-experientialist and transcendent-voluntarist models, divine love is unconditional and cannot be forfeited, but in very different ways. In the immanent-experientialist model, God's love is ontologically necessary, since divine love is descriptive of God's essential sympathetic relation to the world. In this view, God cannot do otherwise than feel the feelings of all others. In the transcendent-voluntarist model, conversely, God is purely self-sufficient such that his love depends only on his sovereign will. Thus, although they disagree sharply with regard to divine ontology, both models agree that God's love is unconditional and cannot be forfeited by humans, sharing a view that is widespread in both scholarly and popular literature.[1] My investigation of the canonical data led to the view that God's love in relation to the world is foreconditional. I have coined the term *foreconditional* in order to concisely convey that God's love is freely bestowed prior to any conditions but not exclusive of conditions. Accordingly, some elements of God's love are unconditional, while God's love is in other ways conditional.

---

[1] See chap. 1 (above).

Conflicting Views Regarding the Conditionality of Divine Love

The view that God's love is unconditional is common among theologians from various standpoints. Many ground God's love in God's free and sovereign will such that it is not conditioned on any external factor. For example, Leon Morris contends that God's love is "unconditional" and "spontaneous and unmotivated."[2] Likewise, Michael Horton explains that "God's love is unconditioned by anything in the creature."[3] Similarly, for Karl Barth, "God's love is not merely not conditioned by any reciprocity of love. It is also not conditioned by any worthiness to be loved on the part of the loved."[4] Other statements purporting the unconditionality of divine love abound.[5] If divine love is unconditional in every respect, the object of God's love can do nothing to inhibit, decrease or forfeit such unilaterally constant love.[6] Thus Morris proclaims that God "will never cease to love" his people, since the "constancy of his love depends on what he is rather than on what they are."[7] Likewise, Carl F. H. Henry states that God "maintains eternal fidelity in love. He is the steadfast God, not a vacillating sovereign."[8] God's love is thus spontaneous, unmotivated, ungrounded and unconditional.

---

[2] Leon Morris, *Testaments of Love: A Study of Love in the Bible* (Grand Rapids: Eerdmans, 1981), pp. 31, 137. Morris qualifies that God's "spontaneous and unmotivated" love "does not mean that he may not also respond to the love men show to his Son" (ibid., p. 264). However, this would mean that divine love is not altogether "spontaneous" or "unmotivated" but, at least in some cases, evaluative and responsive.

[3] Michael Horton, *The Christian Faith: A Systematic Theology for Pilgrims on the Way* (Grand Rapids: Zondervan, 2011), p. 267.

[4] *CD* II/1, p. 278.

[5] For Norman H. Snaith, divine love (אהב) is "arbitrary" and "depends solely on the will of the agent," meaning "it is unconditioned by anything outside the Nature of God" (*The Distinctive Ideas of the Old Testament* [London: Epworth, 1962], p. 138). Compare Anders Nygren, *Agape and Eros*, trans. Philip S. Watson (London: SPCK, 1953), p. 210. Similar references to God's "unconditional" love frequently appear in theological dictionaries and biblical commentaries. See Ethelbert Stauffer, "αγαπάω, αγάπη, αγαπητός," *TDNT* 1:49; Andreas J. Köstenberger, *John*, BECNT (Grand Rapids: Baker, 2004), p. 423; Pieter A. Verhoef, *The Books of Haggai and Malachi*, NICOT (Grand Rapids: Eerdmans, 1987), pp. 196-97, 200-201; P. J. J. S. Els, "אהב," *NIDOTTE* 1:280; Edmund Jacob, *Theology of the Old Testament* (New York: Harper & Row, 1958), p. 110.

[6] Accordingly, it is frequently asserted that God's love is "permanent" and "cannot be withdrawn" (Daniel L. Akin, *1, 2, 3, John*, NAC 38 [Nashville: B&H, 2001], p. 133). Compare Geoffrey Grogan, "A Biblical Theology of the Love of God," in *Nothing Greater, Nothing Better: Theological Essays on the Love of God*, ed. Kevin J. Vanhoozer (Grand Rapids: Eerdmans, 2001), p. 56.

[7] Morris, *Testaments of Love*, pp. 77, 12.

[8] Carl F. H. Henry, *God, Revelation, and Authority*, 6 vols. (Wheaton, IL: Crossway, 1999), 5:13. Compare ibid., 5:116, 6:340.

The process panentheism of Hartshorne and others also requires that divine love is altogether unconditional, but here the constancy of divine love is a logical consequence of the view that God is internally and essentially bound to the world and God's love is descriptive of that necessary relation. While God does not need *this* world, he does need *some* world.[9] As such, divine love cannot be conditional or subject to forfeiture, because God is necessarily dependent on others, and this sympathetic "dependence *is* mutuality, is love."[10] Thomas Jay Oord's essential kenosis theology also views God's love as "unconditional" such that "God loves us no matter what we do."[11] For Oord, "God loves necessarily" and "cannot not love" humans.[12] Accordingly, God's love relationship with the world is ontologically necessary, since "unconditional love refers to God's eternal nature as necessarily including love for creatures" and "God's essential nature includes love for the world."[13] Most panentheists agree, since "divine freedom is an oxymoron in almost all panentheism."[14]

However, others believe that divine love does include conditionality, as apparent in the biblical accounts of the divine-human relationship. For example, D. A. Carson refers to "God's conditional, covenantal love."[15] Indeed, he states, the Scriptures "tell us that Christians remain in the love of God and of Jesus by obedience," and it is therefore "possible for Christians not to

---

[9]Charles Hartshorne, *Man's Vision of God and the Logic of Theism* (Hamden, CT: Archon, 1964), p. 164.

[10]Ibid., p. 120.

[11]Thomas Jay Oord, *The Nature of Love: A Theology* (St. Louis: Chalice, 2010), p. 133.

[12]Ibid., p. 129. Compare Jürgen Moltmann, *The Trinity and the Kingdom: The Doctrine of God*, trans. Margaret Kohl (San Francisco: Harper & Row, 1981), pp. 54-55.

[13]Oord, *Nature of Love*, p. 133. Compare Paul R. Sponheim, *Love's Availing Power: Imaging God, Imagining the World* (Minneapolis: Fortress, 2011).

[14]John W. Cooper, *Panentheism, the Other God of the Philosophers* (Grand Rapids: Baker Academic, 2006), p. 326. Phillip Clayton provides an exception, asserting God's libertarian freedom: "A free creation remains free; any effect the world subsequently has on God is a consequence of the initial free decision rather than a sign of eternal necessity" (*God and Contemporary Science* [Grand Rapids: Eerdmans, 1997], p. 93). Oord claims that though God loves necessarily, "God's love is free," by which he means God is free to choose among various loving actions (*Nature of Love*, pp. 139-40).

[15]D. A. Carson, "Love," in *New Dictionary of Biblical Theology*, ed. T. Desmond Alexander (Downers Grove, IL: InterVarsity Press, 2000), p. 648. Consider also Gary D. Badcock's exploration of the "possibility that God's love for the world is of the sort that *is*, in fact, conditioned in some sense by the actions of his creatures" ("The Concept of Love: Divine and Human," in Vanhoozer, ed., *Nothing Greater, Nothing Better*, p. 40).

keep themselves in the love of God" (Jude 21).[16] In a similar vein, the foreconditional-reciprocal model posits that divine love is neither entirely unconditional nor entirely conditional but foreconditional, that is, prior to but not exclusive of conditions.

GOD'S LOVE IMPOSES CONDITIONS

Divine love is conditional. Scripture repeatedly depicts divine love as conditional on human response.[17] In a number of instances, God promises lovingkindness (חֶסֶד) to those who love (אהב) him (Ex 20:6).[18] God is "the faithful God, who keeps His covenant and His lovingkindness [חֶסֶד] to a thousandth generation with those who love Him and keep His commandments" (Deut 7:9) yet "repays those who hate Him to their faces" (Deut 7:10). Therefore Israel is to "listen" to, "keep" and "do" all of God's commands (Deut 7:12). "Then it shall come about, because [עֵקֶב] you listen to these judgments and keep and do them, that the LORD your God will keep with you His covenant and His lovingkindness [חֶסֶד] which He swore to your forefathers. He will love [אהב] you and bless you and multiply you" (Deut 7:12-13).[19] Notably, even what God had promised (swore) is presented as explicitly conditional on the ongoing relationship.[20]

Perhaps most striking, Jesus himself states, "he who loves [ἀγαπάω] Me will be loved [ἀγαπάω] by My father, and I will love [ἀγαπάω] him" (Jn 14:21), and "If anyone loves [ἀγαπάω] Me . . . My Father will love [ἀγαπάω] him" (Jn 14:23). Likewise, Christ later proclaims, "the Father Himself loves [φιλέω]

---

[16]Carson, "Love," p. 648. Likewise, see Raymond E. Brown, *The Gospel According to John XIII-XXI*, AB (Garden City, NY: Doubleday, 1979), p. 641.

[17]Conditionality should not be confused with merit. See the discussion below.

[18]Compare 1 Kings 8:23; Ps 103:11, 17-18; Dan 9:4. Elsewhere, God's lovingkindness (חֶסֶד) demonstrates the relational responsibility, conditionality and expectation of appropriate response such that the ongoing reception of lovingkindness is tied to fidelity to God. God is willing to be the continual benefactor of lovingkindness but requires *willing beneficiaries*. So Katharine Sakenfeld, "Love in the OT," *ABD* 4:379. See the discussion of חֶסֶד in chap. 3 (above) and in John C. Peckham, *The Concept of Divine Love in the Context of the God-World Relationship* (New York: Peter Lang, 2014), pp. 300-319.

[19]The *wāw* consecutive at the start of Deut 7:13 implies that verse 13 is likewise a result of Israel's appropriate response. Gottfried Quell notes that this verse indeed "links the love of God with blessing as a reward which Yahweh will give for covenant faithfulness. Hence the thought of love unintentionally acquires a note of *Do ut des*" ("Love in the OT," *TDOT* 1:33).

[20]Thus God's "people could experience the blessing of God only when the covenant relationship, which involved reciprocal responsibilities, was properly maintained" (Peter Craigie, *The Book of Deuteronomy*, NICOT [Grand Rapids: Eerdmans, 1976], p. 180).

you, because you have loved [φιλέω] Me" (Jn 16:27). Both John 14:23 and John 16:27 explicitly depict divine love as conditional, as evidenced by the use of the terms "if" (ἐάν) and "because" (ὅτι), respectively.[21] Thus D. A. Carson comments that such texts "tell us that Christians remain in the love of God and of Jesus by obedience."[22] Likewise, Raymond Brown comments, "if one turns away from the Son, one forfeits God's love."[23] Fernando Segovia adds, "Whoever loves Jesus . . . can rest assured that the Father himself will love him in return; on the other hand, he who does not so believe is not loved by the Father." The Father's love is thus "contingent upon belief."[24] Even the Father's love for the Son is conditionally grounded. Christ states, "For this reason the Father loves [ἀγαπάω] Me, because I lay down My life so that I may take it again" (Jn 10:17; compare Jn 15:9-10). The phrase "for this reason" (διά τοῦτο) provides explicit testimony of the conditionality of God's love; the voluntary action of Jesus "is given as the reason for the Father's loving the Son."[25] However, the text does not say that this is the *only* reason the Father loves Jesus.[26]

The conditionality of divine love complements and is supported by the evaluative aspect of God's love (see chapter five). For example, the "way of the wicked is an abomination to the LORD, But He loves [אהב] one who

---

[21]"*He loves you because* is literally 'because.' . . . In 14.21, 23 the disciples are required to love Jesus and to obey his commands if they are to be loved by the Father. Here [16:27] they are to love Jesus and to believe in him if they are to experience the Father's love" (Barclay Newman and Eugene Nida, *A Handbook on the Gospel of John* [New York: UBS, 1993], p. 518).
[22]Carson, "Love," p. 648.
[23]Brown, *Gospel According to John XIII-XXI*, p. 641.
[24]Fernando Segovia, *Love Relationships in the Johannine Tradition* (Chico, CA: SBL/Scholars Press, 1982), p. 154. Compare James Moffat, *Love in the New Testament* (New York: Harper, 1930), p. 265; Ceslas Spicq, *Agape in the New Testament*, 3 vols. (St. Louis: B. Herder, 1963), 1:87-88.
[25]Leon Morris, *The Gospel According to John*, NICNT (Grand Rapids: Eerdmans, 1995), p. 456. Compare William Klassen, "Love in the NT and Early Jewish Literature," *ABD* 4:389. Some, however, seek to avoid this notion by reversing the idea. Thus Gerald L. Borchert, considering it "highly unlikely that either Jesus or John would have based the love of the Father for Jesus on the Son's causal willingness to die," states, "I would reverse the idea and read the text of 10:17 as, 'Because [*dia touto*] the Father loves me, that is the reason [*hoti*, therefore] I lay down my life'" (*John 1-11*, NAC 25A [Nashville: B&H, 2001], p. 336). Compare Köstenberger, *John*, pp. 307-8. However, "the first part of this verse reads literally 'because of this the Father loves me because I give up my life'" (Newman and Nida, *Handbook on the Gospel of John*, p. 332). Thus the text explicitly points to grounded divine love not unlike what is seen elsewhere in John (cf. Jn 14:23; 16:27).
[26]D. A. Carson puts it well when he states: Jesus "is now at pains to elucidate why the Father loves him. It is not that the Father withholds his love until Jesus agrees to give up his life on the cross and rise again" (*The Gospel According to John* [Grand Rapids: Eerdmans, 1991], p. 388).

pursues righteousness" (Prov 15:9; compare Ps 146:8). That is, God appraises, delights in and enjoys creatures. By its very nature, such evaluation is contingent and conditional on the particular state of affairs. Further, as noted in chapter six, the reception of divine mercy is frequently conditional on humans bestowing mercy to one another (Mt 5:7; 18:33, 35; compare Jas 2:13) or otherwise contingent (Lk 1:50; 1 Tim 1:13; Gal 6:16; Jude 21). Yet such mercy is undeserved and unmerited (Tit 3:5).

Likewise, friendship with Christ is conditional. Jesus said, "You are My friends [φίλος] if you do what I command you" (Jn 15:14; compare Mk 10:20-22).[27] Here, whereas God initiates the relationship (compare Jn 6:70; 15:16), "the ongoing relationship between Jesus and his disciples is characterized by obedience on their part, and thus is logically conditioned by it."[28] However, doesn't God love everyone? As explained in chapter eight, God bestows his foreconditional love on everyone (Jn 3:16). However, John 15:14 refers to a particular, intimate, relational love received only by those who respond to God's foreconditional love, much like God's evaluative love for the righteous (Ps 146:8) and the "cheerful giver" (2 Cor 9:7). As such, God's love is both prior to human love and yet responsive to and conditioned on human love, which is itself responsive to God's initiative. This is the foreconditionality of divine love.

Divine love may be forfeited. The conditionality of divine love is further apparent in that the benefits of divine love may be forfeited. God declares in response to his people's rebellion:

> All their evil is at Gilgal;
> Indeed, I came to hate [שׂנא] them there!
> Because of the wickedness of their deeds
> I will drive them out of My house!
> I will love [אהב] them no more. (Hos 9:15; compare Jer 11:15; 12:8; 14:10)[29]

Similarly, Jeremiah 16:5 states, "'I have withdrawn My peace from this people,' declares the LORD, '*My* lovingkindness [חסד] and compassion

---

[27]This notion of friendship with God is common elsewhere (2 Chron 20:7; Is 41:8; Jn 11:11; Jas 2:23; cf. also Ex 33:11; Jn 3:29). See the discussion in the following chapter.
[28]Carson, *Gospel According to John*, p. 503. Compare Köstenberger, *John*, p. 458; Morris, *John*, p. 599.
[29]God's love is here depicted as prior to conditions (and thus foreconditional), since God is said to have "found" his people in the wilderness (Hos 9:10). Yet they became as detestable as what they loved (Hos 9:10).

[רַחֲמִים]'" (compare Ps 89:49). Likewise, Paul speaks of "the kindness [χρηστότης] and severity of God; to those who fell, severity, but to you, God's kindness, if you continue in His kindness; otherwise you will also be cut off" (Rom 11:22).[30]

Christ adroitly depicts God's foreconditional love in the story of the unforgiving debtor. Therein a slave receives forgiveness of a massive debt from his lord who "felt compassion [σπλαγχνίζομαι]" for him, but that same slave then refuses to forgive the much smaller debt owed him by another slave (Mt 18:27-31). For this reason, the master removes his compassion and restores the original debt, saying, "Should you not also have had mercy [ἐλεέω] on your fellow slave, in the same way that I had mercy [ἐλεέω] on you?" (Mt 18:33).[31] Christ thus illustrates that while God's compassionate love is not merited and bestowed prior to conditions, it may be forfeited.

Accordingly, Jude exhorts Christians, "keep yourselves in the love [ἀγάπη] of God, waiting anxiously for the mercy [ἔλεος] of our Lord Jesus Christ to eternal life" (Jude 21).[32] Richard Bauckham notes that this "probably means that God's love for Christians requires an appropriate response. Without obedience to God's will, fellowship with God can be forfeited."[33] Likewise, D. A. Carson comments, "it is possible for Christians not to keep themselves in the love of God."[34] In much the same way, the frequent New Testament language of "abiding" suggests that the divine-human love relationship must be maintained by appropriate human response. Even as friendship with Christ is conditional (Jn 15:14), the same pericope emphasizes the closely

---

[30]The χρηστότης word group refers to goodness, kindness, often used in description of God's beneficence and love. See E. Beyreuther, "χρηστος," *NIDNTT* 2:105; Ceslas Spicq, "χρηστευσομαι, χρηστος, χρηστοτης," *TLNT* 3:511; Konrad Weiss, "χρηστος, χρηστοτης, χρηστευομαι, χρηστολογια," *TDNT* 9:487-88.

[31]The reception of compassion created a moral obligation to likewise show compassion. So Donald A. Hagner, *Matthew 1-13*, WBC 33A (Dallas: Word, 2002), p. 540.

[32]While it is grammatically possible that the "love of God" is an objective genitive referring to human love for God, it is most likely a subjective genitive corresponding to "the mercy of our Lord Jesus Christ." The term might also have subjective and objective connotations as a comprehensive or plenary genitive. See Thomas R. Schreiner, *1, 2 Peter, Jude*, NAC 37 (Nashville: B&H, 2007), p. 483.

[33]Richard Bauckham, *2 Peter, Jude*, WBC 50 (Dallas: Word, 2002), pp. 113-14.

[34]Carson, "Love," p. 648. Notably, the same ones who are told to keep (imperative) themselves in the love of God here are those who are "the called, beloved in God the Father, and kept for Jesus Christ" (Jude 1; cf. Jude 24).

related concept of abiding in God's love.[35] The father "has loved [ἀγαπάω]" the Son, and Jesus loves his followers in the same way. In turn, they are commanded "abide in My love," and Christ explains, "If you keep My commandments, you will abide in My love" (Jn 15:9-10; compare Jn 15:5, 7).[36] Carson comments, "The injunction to *remain* in Jesus' love . . . presupposes that, however much God's love for us is gracious and undeserved, continued enjoyment of that love turns, at least in part, on our response to it."[37] That God is love entails that those who would be in relationship with God must abide in love. "God is love, and the one who abides in love abides in God, and God abides in him" (1 Jn 4:16; compare 1 Jn 4:17-18).

Consider Jeremiah's striking presentation of the simultaneous continuance of God's love for his people and yet restriction from actively loving them. Because of his people's continual apostasy, even breaking the covenant (Jer 11:10), God will "not listen when they call" (Jer 11:14). Even though they are His "beloved" (יְדִיד) they lack the right to his house because of their "vile deeds" (Jer 11:15; compare Jer 8:5). In one sense, the people continue to be viewed as God's "beloved," yet the love relationship is ineffective and broken. Thus it appears that divine benevolence, which stems from God's foreconditional love, is maintained, while his beneficence is interrupted by the beloved's apostasy. In this way, foreconditional divine love is subject to conditions within the actual history of the relationship. God may, at least temporarily, "forsake" his inheritance by giving the "beloved" (יְדִידוּת) of his "soul" (נֶפֶשׁ) to her enemies (Jer 12:7), noting that he has actually "come to hate [שָׂנֵא] her" (Jer 12:8; compare Jer 15:1). Israel's continued disloyalty removes the divine blessing such that God has "withdrawn" his "peace" from the people, even his "lovingkindness and compassion" (Jer 16:5; compare Jer

---

[35]As Gerald Borchert notes, the "basic requirements" of "friendship . . . are exactly the same obedience requirements as those (15:10) for abiding in his love" (*John 12-21*, NAC 25B [Nashville: B&H, 2003], p. 149).
[36]See also 1 Tim 2:15; Heb 8:9; 1 Jn 2:5-6, 10, 17; 3:1, 9-17, 23-24, 35-36; 4:12, 16.
[37]Carson, *Gospel According to John*, p. 520. He qualifies, however: "Such texts do not tell us how people become Christians; rather, assuming that followers of Jesus are in view, they tell us that Christians remain in the love of God and of Jesus by obedience, in precisely the same way that children remain in their parents' love by obedience" (Carson, "Love," p. 648). As Peter H. Davids puts it, in Jn 15 and Jude "we have a situation in which the believers are already loved but still need to remain in that love," and "it is possible to depart from that love" (*The Letters of 2 Peter and Jude*, PNTC [Grand Rapids: Eerdmans, 2006], p. 96).

14:10). As F. B. Huey Jr. puts it, "There is a limit to God's mercy and patience."[38] However, "it is not God's decision to remove himself, but they have 'done this to' themselves."[39]

The reality of the forfeiture of divine love is further implied in the many statements that God will *again* love his people (Hos 14:1-4) and restore them (Jer 30:18; Ezek 39:25; Joel 2:12-14; Heb 8:9, 12). Moreover, one need only look at the numerous instances of divine hatred and abhorrence (Ps 5:5; 11:5; Jer 12:8; Hos 9:15 et al.) to dismiss the sentimental notion that God's love is monolithic, constant and unconditional. Indeed, all the divine angst proclaimed by the prophets over God's wayward people, the unrequited love, abandonment, separation and the hope of reconciliation, must be overlooked or dismissed if the divine-human love relationship is considered to be strictly unconditional.

God's love relationship with the world, then, is not dependent on God's will alone but takes into account human disposition and action. Likewise, the love relationship described in Scripture is not a necessary or essential relationship but contingent and thus may be forfeited. Nevertheless, divine love for humans is amazingly enduring, far surpassing all reasonable expectations (compare Ps 136; Rom 11:28). God is willing to forgive all those who come to him and genuinely repent in response to his foreconditional love (Jer 31:3). However, the opportunity to turn to God is not everlasting. For this reason, Scripture exhorts, "Today if you hear His voice, Do not harden your hearts" (Heb 3:15; 4:7; compare Ps 95:7-8). Although divine love is surpassingly enduring, steadfast and reliable, it is not thereby altogether constant.

GOD'S LOVE IS PRIMARY, UNMERITED AND MAXIMALLY GREAT

The examples above (among others) depict conditional, motivated and evaluative love. However, some object to the conditionality of divine love for various reasons. First, if God's love is conditional, human action might be mistakenly afforded primacy in the divine-human relationship. Second, the conditionality of divine love may depict divine love as something that could

---

[38] F. B. Huey Jr., *Jeremiah, Lamentations*, NAC 16 (Nashville: B&H, 1993), p. 157.
[39] Peter Craigie, Page Kelley and Joel Drinkard Jr., *Jeremiah 1-25*, WBC 26 (Dallas: Word, 1991), p. 33. Indeed, the people have gone so far that even if Moses and Samuel were there to intercede, God declares, "My heart [נַפְשִׁי] would not be with this people" (Jer 15:1).

be somehow merited or deserved. Third, some believe that any conditionality in divine love simply diminishes the greatness of God and his love. Each of these objections warrants careful consideration.

God's love initiates all love. Regarding the first objection, which rightly guards against Pelagianism and legalism, the foreconditional-reciprocal model unequivocally recognizes the absolute priority of divine love in the God-human relationship. "God is love," and "love is from God" (1 Jn 4:7-8, 16), and "We love, because He first loved us" (1 Jn 4:19; compare Jn 15:16; 1 Jn 3:1; 4:9-10). As Daniel Akin comments, "inasmuch as anyone has even the smallest capacity to love, this comes by the grace of God."[40] Karl Barth adds that the "presupposition of genuine love is the existence of a man who is free for it, and therefore—since he is not and cannot be this of himself—freed for it. The love of God is the liberation of man for genuine love."[41] Eberhard Jüngel comments further that "one learns to love by being loved and by letting oneself be loved. Thus one can love neither God nor the other if one has not *already* been loved by God and let oneself be loved by him."[42]

God is the primary source of love and draws humans toward himself prior to any human action and thus before any conditions.[43] "I have loved you with an everlasting love," declares the Lord, "Therefore I have drawn you with lovingkindness" (Jer 31:3; compare Rom 2:4). As such, God's love holds sole primacy, prior to any other love. Indeed, the "God of love" (2 Cor 13:11) so loved the world that he gave his beloved Son, seeking reciprocal relationship with each one (Jn 3:16).[44]

Oord's essential kenosis theology also suggests that "God lovingly acts first in each moment to provide agency, freedom, values, and relationship."[45] Moreover, "creatures could not love if our relational God were not the Lover who initially empowers, inspires, and beckons them."[46] However, Oord contends that "prevenient grace is necessary grace" that stems from "God's

---

[40]Daniel Akin, *1, 2, 3, John*, p. 177.
[41]*CD* IV/2, p. 777.
[42]Eberhard Jüngel, *God as the Mystery of the World* (Grand Rapids: Eerdmans, 1983), p. 327; emphasis original.
[43]As I. Howard Marshall states, "the source of all love is God" (*The Epistles of John*, NICNT [Grand Rapids: Eerdmans, 1978], p. 222).
[44]See chap. 8 (below).
[45]Oord, *Nature of Love*, p. 129.
[46]Ibid., p. 21.

eternal nature" such that God could not do otherwise than bestow it on creatures. On the other hand, the foreconditional view of love suggests that, while God's character is love, he does not need to love creatures but voluntarily extends the love relationship that was already enjoyed by the Trinity to creatures (see chapter four). Moreover, although God freely initiates love with creatures prior to conditions, humans are expected to respond to God's foreconditional love by loving God in return. Thus divine love is prevenient but not strictly unconditional. God implements conditions for the reception and continuance of his love.

God's prevenient and foreconditional love enables and expects humans to respond with love while God also mediates the imperfect loving response of humans (1 Pet 2:5; 1 Jn 4:19). God's love is thus prior and posterior to human response, in different respects. William Hendriksen rightly comments, "Why cannot God's love *both* precede and follow ours? That is exactly what it does, and that is the beauty of it: first, by *preceding* our love, it creates in us the eager desire to keep Christ's precepts; then, by *following* our love, it rewards us for keeping them!"[47] Human love, then, is neither primary nor meritorious; it is the requisite response to God's love (compare 2 Tim 4:8). As such, love is a real condition of relationship with God and at the same time only comes about because of God's prior, foreconditional gift of love that draws the Christian to freely respond to God's love (Jer 31:3; 1 Jn 4:7, 19). Human love is thus impossible without God's prior love, yet it does not bypass human agency. God's prevenient love is a necessary but not sufficient condition of human love.

God's love is unmerited. However, does such conditionality lead to the view that divine love is merited? Some scholars speak as though conditionality implies merit or desert. For example, Norman Snaith comments that God's "love for Israel was unconditioned by anything in Israel that was good. It was wholly unmerited. It was not in the least degree because of anything in Israel that was good, or beautiful, or desirable. . . . Such is the story of God's unconditioned love."[48] Conversely, Peter C. Craigie distinguishes

---

[47]William Hendriksen, *The Gospel According to John* (Grand Rapids: Baker, 1953), 2:281-82; emphasis original. See Lk 7:41-50.
[48]Snaith, *Distinctive Ideas of the Old Testament*, p. 137. Compare Morris, *Testaments of Love*, p. 148.

contingency and merit, explaining that divine blessings were "contingent upon obedience," but that "did not mean that obedience merited divine blessing."[49] Similarly, the foreconditional-reciprocal model sharply distinguishes between conditionality and merit. While it is true that God's love for Israel was wholly undeserved and exceedingly generous, unmerited love is not the same as unconditional love. That is, something may be conditional yet unmerited, contingent on response but not thereby earned or deserved when it is received. For instance, the winner of a lottery must fulfill certain minor conditions to receive the prize (such as presenting the winning ticket) but does not, by meeting those conditions, *earn* the money that will be awarded. Similarly, those who freely receive God's love do not thereby merit it. Even the ability to freely accept the gift of God has been granted by God (compare 1 Cor 4:7). As Tanner puts it: "One cannot congratulate oneself for doing what created powers enable since we are not responsible for the fact that we have those powers to begin with."[50]

Humans would not exist, let alone be the beneficiaries of divine love, but for the free decision of God to create and sustain us (see chapter four). Since divine love is a gift, creatures cannot earn it. Divine love toward humans is always undeserved. God did not love and choose Israel because they were "more in number than any of the peoples." Indeed, they were the "fewest of all peoples, but" God saved them "because the LORD loved" them (Deut 7:7-8) and their fathers (Deut 4:37; 10:15). However, God did not arbitrarily reject the occupants of the Promised Land: "Do not say in your heart . . . 'Because of my righteousness the LORD has brought me in to possess this land,' but *it is* because of the wickedness of these nations *that* the LORD is dispossessing them before you" (Deut 9:4; compare Deut 9:5). God's persistent love for his undeserving people was modeled by Hosea, who was commanded to "love a woman *who* is loved by *her* husband, yet an adulteress, even as the LORD loves the sons of Israel, though they turn to other gods and love raisin cakes" (Hos 3:1). Likewise, "God demonstrates His own love toward us, in that while we were yet sinners, Christ died for us" (Rom

---

[49]Craigie, *Deuteronomy*, p. 180. Walter Brueggemann notes, "Christianity has for so long represented itself as a religion of free grace, that we flinch from the thought that God's gifts are conditional" ("The Book of Exodus," *NIB* 1:878).
[50]Kathryn Tanner, *Christ the Key* (New York: Cambridge University Press, 2010), p. 81.

5:8; compare Lk 6:35). Indeed, the "kindness [χρηστότης] of God our Savior and *His* love for mankind [φιλανθρωπία] appeared," and God acted salvifically "not on the basis of [our righteous] deeds" but "according to His mercy" (Tit 3:4-5; compare Eph 1:4; 1 Tim 1:13-14).

In all this, God freely and graciously loves undeserving humans. Yet God's love is by no means indifferent or strictly unconditional. God is deeply concerned for his people (see chapter six) and expects appropriate love response (Hos 9:15; Rom 11:22-23). Moreover, God can and does reward appropriate (albeit imperfect) human response.[51] God's unmerited love, then, does not nullify conditions, evaluative judgment, justice or reciprocity (see chapter five). God's love is bestowed prior to conditions and is undeserved, yet there are conditions for its continuance.

Wouldn't unconditional love be greater? This brings us to the third objection: Wouldn't God's love be greater if it continued to reach even those who finally reject it? Oord contends that "God cannot not love us" and contends that this view provides assurance that is "unavailable to those who think God could stop loving us."[52] Does the foreconditional view of divine love, then, remove one's assurance of God's love or suggest that God's love is not faithful?

God is love and never arbitrarily decides to remove his love from anyone (1 Jn 4:8, 16). The removal of divine love is always in response to unrelenting human evil. Throughout Scripture, God's people repeatedly reject him, but God never arbitrarily rejects humans (compare Jer 15:6; Neh 9:19). When God finally cuts off those who have rejected him, it is only in response to their *final* decision to shut him out, when (insofar as he is committed to respecting their free will to love or not love) there is nothing more he could do (Is 5:1-7).[53] Those who finally reject God's loving overtures thereby forfeit

---

[51]The conditionality of blessing entails the reality of contingent reward. See Gen 22:16-18; 26:4-5; 32:25-28; Ex 19:5; 23:25; Lev 26:3-17; Deut 5:29; 11:26-28; Lk 6:35; 11:28; 14:14; Gal 3:9; Eph 6:24; Jas 1:25; 1 Jn 3:21-22. Such rewards even include salvation as the result of the eschatological, evaluative judgment (2 Tim 4:8; Jas 1:12; 5:11; cf. 2 Thess 2:10). However, the temporary and partial suspension of the consequences of judgment (see chap. 5 above) is also apparent in that humans often do not (immediately) receive their just deserts in this disordered world such that there is often no one-to-one correlation between behavior and the reception of blessings or curses in this life (cf. Job; Eccles 3:16-17; 8:12, 14; 9:2; Mt 5:45). The theology of (immediate) retribution is far too simplistic (see Lk 13:1-5). Full justice awaits the eschaton.
[52]Oord, *Nature of Love*, p. 132. Compare Sponheim, *Love's Availing Power*.
[53]See the discussion in chap. 9 (below).

the reception of God's love. Accordingly, we need not worry that God will arbitrarily remove his love. Divine love is conditional but not capricious. His love never runs out, but humans may refuse to receive it.

However, why doesn't God's love triumph such that everyone is ultimately reconciled to him within a perfect reciprocal love relationship?[54] One argument might go like this: God is all-powerful and all-loving, so it follows that he desires to save all, and he ought to be able to make it so that all enjoy eternal life and love relationship with him. Consider Thomas Talbott's universalistic view that if "God is love . . . expresses a truth about the essence of God, then it is logically impossible that the person who is God should fail to love someone."[55] From this premise, he argues that God's love must extend unto the salvation of everyone. Thus, "God's love is unlimited and his redemptive purposes are unthwarted" such that all will be saved.[56]

In some (but not all) accounts, universalism is predicated on the following two premises.[57] First, God desires and wills a reciprocal love relationship with every person. Second, God possesses the ability to effectuate

---

[54]Consider Rob Bell's recent provocative work, which created a stir by raising the possibility of universalism as the triumph of God's love, without committing dogmatically to that position. See *Love Wins: A Book About Heaven, Hell, and the Fate of Every Person Who Ever Lived* (New York: HarperOne, 2011).

[55]Thomas B. Talbott, *The Inescapable Love of God* (Parkland, FL: Universal, 1999), p. 113. See also the informative debate between Piper and Talbott in Thomas Talbott, "On Predestination, Reprobation, and the Love of God: A Polemic," *The Reformed Journal* 33, no. 2 (1983): 11-15; John Piper, "How Does a Sovereign God Love? A Reply to Thomas Talbott," *The Reformed Journal* 33, no. 4 (1983): 9-13.

[56]Talbott, *Inescapable Love of God*, p. 48. For other universalist conceptions consider John Hick, *Evil and the God of Love* (London: Collins, 1966); Gregory MacDonald, *The Evangelical Universalist* (Eugene, OR: Cascade, 2012).

[57]Unless otherwise specified, by *universalism* I refer to what Robin Parry and Christopher H. Partridge call "strong universalism," a range of views holding that all individuals will in fact be saved, which goes beyond "Arminian universalism," which is the view that God desires and intends that each individual be saved ("Introduction," in *Universal Salvation? The Current Debate*, ed. Robin A. Parry and Christopher H. Partridge [Grand Rapids: Eerdmans, 2003], pp. xvi-xvii). Further, Oliver Crisp distinguishes between "contingent universalism," which claims that "all human beings will be saved" (in this world but not necessarily every possible world), and "necessary universalism," wherein "all human beings must be saved" (that, is in every possible world) ("I Do Not Teach It, but I Also Do Not [Not] Teach It: The Universalism of Karl Barth," in *All Shall Be Well: Explorations in Universalism and Christian Theology from Origen to Moltmann*, ed. Gregory MacDonald [Eugene, OR: Cascade, 2011], p. 307). Some other theologians might be described as hopeful universalists, that is, they hope that all will be saved without claiming that all will (or must) be saved. For a survey and discussion of various significant accounts of universalism throughout Christian history, see MacDonald, ed., *All Shall Be Well*.

a reciprocal love relationship with everyone.[58] However, are both of these premises valid? Determinism necessarily affirms the second premise, but many determinists reject the first.[59] As John Piper puts it, although "there is nothing beyond God's own will and nature which stops him from saving people ... there are people who are not objects of God's electing love."[60] That is, while God loves all in some respects, he chooses only some to irresistibly receive the benefits of divine love unto eternal life.[61] Humans do not possess the ability to choose to accept divine love or not.[62]

Why, then, does God not unilaterally determine that all humans accept his love? Why choose some and condemn others if the efficacious cause of the condemnation of those who are lost resides solely in God's decree? This is precisely Talbott's criticism of double predestination. If God is willing and able to determine that beings "love" him *and* he is altogether loving (compare 1 Jn 4:8, 16), then God should determine that everyone love him and not arbitrarily condemn anyone. Jerry Walls contends that if compatibilism is true, then God could determine "all to freely accept his love and be saved," but, inexplicably, he does not.[63] Conversely, some determinists say that

---

[58]Whether via determinism or via persuasion, God will (or must, depending on the account) bring it about that everyone will be saved. Talbott contends that God would not permit anyone to freely and irrevocably reject him. First, there is no "intelligible motive for such a rebellion" by a fully informed person, and a decision to reject God by one who is less than fully informed, misunderstanding the "true nature of God" or the "true import of union with God," is "less than fully free; hence, God should be able to remove these conditions ... without in any way interfering with human freedom" (*Inescapable Love of God*, p. 187). In the end, "we do not choose our own destiny," but God will save all because "no illusion can endure forever," and absent delusion, no one would reject God; thus "the end is foreordained" (ibid., p. 189). No one "could possibly hold out for an eternity against the love of God" (ibid., p. 186). William Lane Craig argues, on the contrary, that on a view of libertarian freedom such that God cannot determine that someone freely love him, there may be no "realizable" world wherein all freely accept salvation. See "Talbott's Universalism," *Religious Studies* 27, no. 3 (1991): 297-308. Compare the discussion in MacDonald, *Evangelical Universalist*, pp. 26-32. For Talbott, however, "even at the price of interfering with human freedom [were it required], a loving God would never permit his loved ones to reject him forever," for that would amount to "irreparable harm" (*Inescapable Love of God*, p. 183). Yet, if God were willing to override human free will at any point, one might wonder why God did not do so from the outset in order to exclude horrendous evils.

[59]See the discussion in chaps. 4 and 9.

[60]Piper, "How Does a Sovereign God Love?" p. 10.

[61]See J. I. Packer, "The Love of God: Universal and Particular," in *Still Sovereign: Contemporary Perspectives on Election, Foreknowledge, and Grace*, ed. Thomas R. Schreiner and Bruce A. Ware (Grand Rapids: Baker, 2000); Henry, *God, Revelation, and Authority*, 5:318.

[62]Compare chap. 8 (below).

[63]Jerry L. Walls, "Why No Classical Theist, Let Alone Orthodox Christian, Should *Ever* Be a Compatibilist," *Philosophia Christi* 13, no. 1 (2011): 96. As discussed previously, compatibilism

God's election is simply a matter of his inscrutable will. Martin Luther, for example, states, "If I could by any means understand how this same God, who makes such a show of wrath and unrighteousness, can yet be merciful and just, there would be no need for faith."[64] Others, however, contend that God wants to save everyone (in some sense) but desires to manifest his glory more, and thus some are damned to eternal fire.[65]

Karl Barth, on the other hand, proclaims regarding the doctrine of election that God's "first and last word is Yes and not No."[66] Alongside Barth's commitment to God's sovereign will as the prime cause to which all other causes are subordinate and his position that all are elect in Christ, some take this statement (and others) to amount to universalism. Yet Barth stated of universalism: "I do not teach it, but I also do not not teach it."[67] In this regard, Oliver Crisp has argued that Barth's doctrine of election either leads to "a form of necessary universalism" such that all humans *must* be saved, or it is "incoherent."[68] Crisp contends that defenders of Barth's consistency on this issue must "either affirm that election in Christ is conditional in some way" and thus Barth perhaps overstated his view of election, or "affirm with Barth that election in Christ [is] a completed matter" while coherently making sense "of Barth's assertion that he is not committed to universalism."[69] In response, David W. Congdon contends that "it is fully consistent for Barth to reject universalism even though his theology is indeed logically universalistic."[70] On Congdon's reading of

---

holds that God's unilateral determination of everything that happens is compatible with human freedom (defined as the absence of external compulsion). On this view, Thomas Schreiner maintains: "Those upon whom God set his covenantal love before creating the world are those he predestined to share the eschatological image of the Son"; his "chosen" thus "will surely persevere and attain to glorification" (*Romans* [Grand Rapids: Baker, 1998], p. 466).

[64]Martin Luther, *The Bondage of the Will*, trans. O. R. Johnston (Grand Rapids: Baker, 2003), p. 101.
[65]John Piper states, "God's will to save all people is restrained by his commitment to the glorification of his sovereign grace (Eph. 1:6, 12, 14; Rom. 9:22-23)" ("Are There Two Wills in God?" in Schreiner and Ware, eds., *Still Sovereign*, p. 130). See the further discussion in chap. 9 (below).
[66]*CD* II/2, p. 13. Compare *CD* III/3, p. 105.
[67]This statement is attributed to Barth in Eberhard Jüngel, *Karl Barth: A Theological Legacy*, trans. Garrett E. Paul (Philadelphia: Westminster Press, 1986), p. 44. Compare *CD* IV/3, pp. 477-78.
[68]Crisp, "I Do Not Teach It," p. 323.
[69]Ibid., p. 320.
[70]David W. Congdon, "*Apokatastasis* and Apostolicity: A Response to Oliver Crisp on the Question of Barth's Universalism," *SJT* 67, no. 4 (2014): 466. While many have defended Barth's assertion that he is not committed to universalism (cf. *CD* II/2, pp. 417-18; IV/3, pp. 477-78) by way of appeal to (their interpretation of) Barth's view of "God's freedom to save or not save

Barth, it is contingently and transcendently (but not immanently) necessary that all will be saved, "rooted in God's free and eternal self-determination," yet Barth is consistent in not affirming universalism because he "rejects all worldviews" and "denies that theology is ever a matter of describing what is objectively or generally the case regarding God and the world."[71] Accordingly, Barth's view does "necessarily involve universal salvation without permitting an abstract doctrine or theory of universalism."[72] On the other hand, T. F. Torrance agrees with Barth that God has elected all in Christ yet also believes that some say no to God.[73] "It is upon the Yes of God's eternal love for us that our salvation rests, but that Yes is also the judgment of those who perish."[74]

From a different standpoint, the foreconditional-reciprocal model also strongly affirms that God is all-loving. Indeed, God desires and wills that all enjoy love relationship with him. Numerous Scriptures declare that God desires the salvation of every human (e.g., Ezek 18:32; 33:11; 1 Tim 2:4-6; 2 Pet 3:9).[75] However, on the foreconditional-reciprocal model, a reciprocal love relationship between God and each individual cannot be unilaterally determined by God. This is not due to any divine defect or lack of power but due to the nature of love itself, which, according to this model, requires significant freedom (see chapter four).[76] If significant freedom is a necessary condition

---

certain individuals," Congdon views this as a "misreading" (Congdon, "*Apokatastasis*," p. 477). For other recent treatments of Barth's view of universalism, see George Hunsinger, "Hellfire and Damnation: Four Ancient and Modern Views," *SJT* 51, no. 4 (1998): 406-34; Bruce L. McCormack, "So That He May Be Merciful to All: Karl Barth and the Problem of Universalism," in *Karl Barth and American Evangelicalism*, ed. Bruce L. McCormack and Clifford B. Anderson (Grand Rapids: Eerdmans, 2011), pp. 227-49.

[71]Congdon, "*Apokatastasis*," p. 464. Barth states, "If we can speak of a necessity of any kind here [of God's will to reconcile the world to himself], it can only be the necessity of the decision which God did in fact make and execute" (*CD* IV/1, p. 213).

[72]Congdon, "*Apokatastasis*," p. 466.

[73]T. F. Torrance, "Universalism or Election," *SJT* 2, no. 3 (1949): 316-18. Torrance here responds to J. A. T. Robinson's piece, "Universalism—Is It Heretical," *SJT* 2, no. 2 (1949): 139-55. Compare Trevor Hart, "In the End, God . . . : The Christian Universalism of J. A. T. Robinson," in *All Shall Be Well*, pp. 355-81.

[74]T. F. Torrance, *The Christian Doctrine of God: One Being Three Persons* (New York: T & T Clark, 2001), p. 246.

[75]See chap. 9 (below) for a further discussion of these verses.

[76]On my commitment to significant freedom, see the discussion in chaps. 4 and 9 and the extensive discussion of God's will and human freedom in Peckham, *Concept of Divine Love*, pp. 204-35, 372-99, 494-502, 577-82.

of love, it is impossible for God to determine that all beings *freely* love him.[77] From this standpoint, determining another to love is impossible because it is nonsensical. As Vincent Brümmer puts it, "Love is necessarily free."[78]

In this regard, any contention that God's love *must* finally conquer all does not cohere with the consistent biblical portrayal of the voluntary and bilateral nature of love. Although God desires that humans love him, he grants humans the freedom to decide for or against the love relationship that he freely initiates while enabling humans to respond positively (see chapters four and eight).[79] As Brümmer states, "The fact that God allows us as persons to retain the ability to turn away from him, excludes any form of universalism which holds that God's love *must* triumph in the end and cause all to love him."[80] Further, to suggest that everyone *will* finally come to love God means that either God (1) determines that all love him or (2) everyone will freely choose to love him. The former rejects significant freedom, which this study considers to be embedded in the biblical concept of love, and thus contradicts the volitional nature of love, while I believe Scripture contradicts the latter.[81] Although universalism is not logically impossible, since God calls everyone to receive and respond to his love (see chapter eight), Scripture contends that, sadly, some do finally reject God

---

[77] As William Lane Craig puts it, "It is logically impossible to make someone freely do something" ("The Coherence of Theism: Introduction," in *Philosophy of Religion: A Reader and Guide*, ed. William Lane Craig [New Brunswick, NJ: Rutgers University Press, 2002], p. 211). See also Alvin Plantinga, *God, Freedom, and Evil* (Grand Rapids: Eerdmans, 1977).

[78] Vincent Brümmer, *The Model of Love: A Study in Philosophical Theology* (Cambridge: Cambridge University Press, 1993), p. 177. So, among many others, David Fergusson, "Will the Love of God Finally Triumph?" in Vanhoozer, ed., *Nothing Greater, Nothing Better*, p. 199; Stephen G. Post, *A Theory of Agape: On the Meaning of Christian Love* (Lewisburg, PA: Bucknell University Press, 1990), pp. 13, 108-11; Katharine Sakenfeld, *The Meaning of Hesed in the Hebrew Bible: A New Inquiry* (Missoula, MT: Scholars Press, 1978), p. 176; Hick, *Evil and the God of Love*, p. 266.

[79] God reaches out toward reciprocal love relationship with all humans, but some do not reciprocate God's love (Thomas C. Oden, *The Living God* [San Francisco: Harper & Row, 1987], pp. 120-21); Clark H. Pinnock, *Flame of Love: A Theology of the Holy Spirit* (Downers Grove, IL: InterVarsity Press, 1996), p. 74.

[80] Brümmer, *Model of Love*, p. 179. Fergusson adds: "Only a theology that recognizes the freedom finally to rebel against God can avoid the determinism of either double predestination or universalism" ("Will the Love of God Finally Triumph?" p. 196); compare Wolfhart Pannenberg, *Systematic Theology*, trans. Geoffrey W. Bromiley (Grand Rapids: Eerdmans, 1991), 1:438; Fritz Guy, "The Universality of God's Love," in *The Grace of God, the Will of Man: A Case for Arminianism*, ed. Clark H. Pinnock (Minneapolis: Bethany House, 1995), pp. 43-45; Torrance, "Universalism or Election," pp. 312-14.

[81] Moreover, the latter may overlook the corrosive impact and power of evil. Time alone will not heal the wounds of sin, only surrender to the living and loving God.

(Dan 12:2; Jn 3:18; 5:11-12, 28-29; 2 Thess 1:7-10; 2:10-12; Rev 20:12-15).[82]

The foreconditional-reciprocal model thus contends that the best explanation for why God does not save all is because some *finally* refuse to be saved. God allows humans the right of refusal because to do otherwise would rule out the possibility of reciprocal love relationship (see chapter four).[83] Since divine love can be forfeited, it cannot be strictly unmotivated, spontaneous or unconditional. This conditionality of love follows from and complements the volitional, evaluative and emotional aspects of love discussed in chapters four through six. Yet, according to the foreconditional-reciprocal model, there is a sense in which God's love is unconditional, to which we now turn.

THE CONDITIONALITY AND UNCONDITIONALITY OF DIVINE LOVE

If God's love is conditional, as explained above, how should we understand the many passages that speak of God's love as everlasting? For example, Jeremiah 31:3 states that God's love is an "everlasting love [אהבה]" (compare Rom 8:35, 39).[84] Elsewhere it is repeatedly asserted that God's "lovingkindness [חֶסֶד] is everlasting" (e.g., Ps 136).[85] On the other hand, we have seen that God's love might be forfeited, highlighted in God's own declarations: "I will love [אהב] them no more" (Hos 9:15), and "I have withdrawn My peace . . . *My* lovingkindness [חסד] and compassion [רחם]" (Jer 16:5;

---

[82]For a compelling biblical argument against universalism, see I. Howard Marshall, "The New Testament Does Not Teach Universal Salvation," in Parry and Partridge, eds., *Universal Salvation? The Current Debate*, pp. 55-76.

[83]What, then, about those who did not hear the gospel? Does God hold people accountable who had no opportunity to accept Christ? I personally believe that whereas salvation comes only through Christ (e.g., Acts 4:12), God holds each one accountable for their own response to the light that they encountered (however small) but not for light that was not available to them (Acts 17:30; cf. Lk 12:47-48; Jn 9:40-41). This inclusivist approach understands texts like Jn 1:9 (that Christ gives light to every person; cf. Jn 12:32) to mean that *some* divine light has shone on every human such that no one will be condemned due to (nonwillful) ignorance (cf. Jn 3:16-21). However, this view is not directly entailed by the foreconditional-reciprocal model.

[84]The phrase אַהֲבַת עוֹלָם, here translated "everlasting love," might also be translated "love of old" or "ancient love." However, the syntagm עוֹלָם + חֶסֶד seems to be thematically related to this syntagm, and the meaning "of old" applied to עוֹלָם in many such contexts does not fit (i.e., Is 54:8; cf. 2 Sam 22:51). If such a connotation were present, one would expect מֵעוֹלָם, so Ps 25:6. Divine חסד is elsewhere consistently depicted as "everlasting," unmistakably so in texts such as Ps 103:17. It seems best, then, to read this as a reference to "everlasting love."

[85]Beyond the repetition of this refrain in all 26 verses in Ps 136, it occurs in many other instances, including Jer 33:11; Ps 100:5; 106:1; 107:1; 118:1-4, 29; 1 Chron 16:34, 41; 2 Chron 5:13; 7:3, 7; 20:21.

compare Jer 12:7-8). If both those passages that speak of the everlasting nature of God's love and those that depict it as conditional and subject to forfeiture are taken seriously, as they are from the standpoint of my canonical approach, God's love must possess both an unconditional and conditional aspect.

This apparent tension has been recognized by many biblical scholars and dealt with in many ways. Some have maintained that there are at least two contradictory streams of tradition at work, one emphasizing God's unconditional love and the everlasting nature of his promises and the other (the Deuteronomist) emphasizing covenant obligations, presenting God's promises as conditional and potentially transient.[86] However, this kind of position is ruled out by the final-form canonical approach of the foreconditional-reciprocal model, which approaches the canon as a unified document and thus takes seriously the repeated presentation of the endurance of God's beneficence alongside the similarly recurrent predication of the continuance of such love and blessings on appropriate human response (both of which appear throughout the various parts of the canon).[87] Numerous other scholars, who contend that divine love is unconditional as rooted in unilateral election, nevertheless recognize some limited conditionality. For example, Norman Snaith asserts that God's love (אהב) is utterly "unconditioned" but recognizes conditionality by asserting that חסד is a "conditional" love, always within the context of covenant.[88] However, while it is true that

---

[86]In this view, the Deuteronomic historian(s) emphasized conditionality on faithfulness, while another strand, likely the Priestly, emphasized the unconditional "perpetual covenant" harking back to Abraham (Moshe Weinfeld, *Deuteronomy and the Deuteronomic School* [Oxford: Clarendon, 1972]); Weinfeld, "The Covenant of Grant in the Old Testament and in the Ancient Near East," *JAOS* 90, no. 2 (1970): 195; Sakenfeld, *Meaning of Hesed*, pp. 149, 237-39.

[87]John A. Davies points to such tension in the Davidic covenant: "The tensions which result may not be the result of careless redaction, but the necessary tensions in an account of a relationship which attempts to grapple with the conundrum of a persistent divine commitment and a meaningful human responsibility" (*A Royal Priesthood: Literary and Intertextual Perspectives on an Image of Israel in Exodus 19.6* [New York: T & T Clark, 2004], p. 181).

[88]Snaith, *Distinctive Ideas of the Old Testament*, p. 95. Elsewhere, however, he also states that "the chesed of God . . . is everlasting, determined, unshakable" (ibid., p. 102). Similarly, Hans-Jürgen Zobel suggests חסד is "characterized by permanence and reliability" ("חסד," *TDOT* 5:57). Yet D. A. Baer and R. P. Gordon acknowledge, "Numerous texts witness to at least the hypothetical possibility of losing God's חסד or of having it taken away" (*NIDOTTE* 2:215). Likewise, Sakenfeld notes that in some instances, "God's *ḥesed* is conditional, dependent upon the good repair of the covenant relationship that it is up to Israel to maintain" ("Love in the OT," *ABD* 4:379). For example, see Ex 20:6; Deut 7:9-12; 1 Kings 8:23; Dan 9:4; Ps 62:12.

there are numerous instances of conditional חסד, it is neither true that אהב is strictly unconditional (Hos 9:15) nor that חסד always operates within covenant.[89] Eugene Merrill, conversely, refers to divine lovingkindness (חסד) as "unconditional" and "the basis for covenant election" but within "relationship" as "part of a reciprocal process, a disposition conditioned upon . . . love (āhăbâ) and obedience."[90] Similarly, C. E. B. Cranfield contends that divine love is "spontaneous" and "not caused by any worth or attractiveness in its object" yet recognizes that while "God's love for Israel was spontaneous in origin, there is observable a tendency [in the OT] to understand its continuance as conditional on Israel's behaviour (e.g. Deut. 5.10, Exod. 20.6, Deut. 7.9-13), and the possibility of regarding it as a reward for human merit arises."[91] Walter Eichrodt, however, believes it "impossible to rationalize" the tension between Hosea's statements of the discontinuance (Hos 9:15) and continuance (Hos 14:4) of divine love.[92]

However, perhaps the key to the apparent tension appears in Psalm 103:17, which states that divine חסד is "from everlasting to everlasting *on those who fear him* [emphasis mine]." In this passage God's חסד is both everlasting and conditional, being directed specifically toward those who respond appropriately to God.[93] This illustrates the interpretive danger of absolutizing any one of the elements of divine love such that God's love is wholly uncondi-

---

[89]In fact, חסד is not restricted to a formalized relationship of any kind, and even within a covenant context may operate outside and/or above and beyond covenant restrictions. See Zobel, "חסד," *TDOT* 5:53, 61; R. Laird Harris, "חסד," *TWOT*, pp. 306-7; Sakenfeld, "Love in the OT," *ABD* 4:379; Stoebe, "חסד," *TLOT* 1:455, 60; Gordon R. Clark, *The Word "Hesed" in the Hebrew Bible* (Sheffield: JSOT Press, 1993), p. 192; Morris, *Testaments of Love*, p. 69. Frank Moore Cross (as many others) points to the more basic category of kinship, suggesting that not only אהב but also חסד "originally was a term designating the loyal and loving behavior appropriate to kinship relationship" (*From Epic to Canon: History and Literature in Ancient Israel* [Baltimore: Johns Hopkins University Press, 1998], p. 5). See the discussion of חסד in chap. 3 (above).

[90]Eugene H. Merrill, *Deuteronomy*, NAC 4 (Nashville: B&H, 1994), p. 148. Compare Post, *Theory of Agape*, p. 83. Although Merrill speaks of conditionality and reciprocality here, he adopts the compatibilist position that human love is itself determined and thus contends for "the absence of any conditionality" (Merrill, *Deuteronomy*, p. 128).

[91]C. E. B. Cranfield, "Love," *TWTB*, p. 132.

[92]Walter Eichrodt, *Theology of the Old Testament* (Philadelphia: Westminster Press, 1961), p. 253. Baer and Gordon also recognize this tension: "It may finally be impossible to square such agonized questioning with the frequent confident assertions that חסד is eternal. Perhaps this very tension reminds us of the relational core at the center of this concept" ("חסד," *NIDOTTE* 2:216).

[93]J. Clinton McCann Jr. suggests, "This contradiction, or better perhaps, tension, represents the inevitable dilemma for God, who both wills and demands justice and righteousness and yet who loves and is committed to relationship with sinful people" ("The Book of Psalms," *NIB* 4:1092).

tional or that God's love is merely a direct response to human actions; neither can be supported by examination of all of the evidence. The foreconditional-reciprocal model posits that the apparent tension between the conditionality and unconditionality of divine love is integral to understanding the God-world relationship and may be coherently understood by distinguishing between subjective and objective aspects of God's love. Divine love is everlasting in some respects, yet may nevertheless be discontinued in other respects.[94]

God's subjective and objective love. God's subjective love and objective love differentiate between that love which belongs to God's character independent of any external objects (his subjective love) and that which corresponds to, and is affected by, creaturely objects (objective love). In other words, God's subjective love is God's loving disposition, which is entirely grounded in himself as subject (his character of love) and thus not dependent on external factors, including any response or lack of response from humans. As such, it is prior to and not dependent on relationship with creatures and thus nonevaluative, unconditional and permanent. God's objective love, on the other hand, describes his (interactive) love relationship with creaturely objects and thus refers to that love which initiates relationship with creatures and evaluatively corresponds to, and is affected by, the disposition and/or actions of its object.[95] It is thus (fore)conditional and requires reciprocal love for its permanent continuance. The five aspects of divine love surveyed in this book (volitional, evaluative, emotional, foreconditional and ideally reciprocal) are descriptive of God's objective love, since they all refer to God's love in relationship to the world, whereas God's subjective love is prior to—and the unchanging and unconditional ground of—God's relationship to the world; it is the basis of his relational love, which reaches out to creatures via loving actions.

As prior to and not contingent on relationship, God's subjective disposition of love, which is unconditional, grounds God's foreconditional love toward everyone. God thus freely initiates love relationship with all persons

---

[94]Consider the congruity with John Walton's view of covenant jeopardy (*Covenant: God's Purpose, God's Plan* [Grand Rapids: Zondervan, 1994], pp. 94-107).

[95]This includes both God's universally relational love and particularly relational love, explained in the next chapter.

(God's universally relational love) and aims toward, but does not unilaterally cause, reciprocal love relationship (God's particularly relational love; see chapter eight). It is in the subjective sense that divine love and lovingkindness are described as eternal. God does not will to remove love but unceasingly desires love relationship with, and remains benevolent toward, all humans. However, humans possess the freedom to accept or spurn God's love. In this regard, God's love is unchanging and constant, whereas the objective aspects of God's love are relational and predicated on human response to God's prevenient (and always unmerited) love. God's love is thus unconditional in that his character of love is unchanging and he always wills to love all (subjective love), but conditional with respect to divine evaluation and relationship (objective love).

God never removes his love from anyone who wishes to receive his love. However, the object(s) of God's love may reject intimate relationship with God and, if persistent in such rejection, forfeit the reception of divine love altogether. In this way, while God's subjective love is itself everlasting and unconditional, it does not eternally benefit creatures, since humans may finally reject God entirely, thus forfeiting the love relationship beyond repair, having removed themselves from the sphere of God's loving actions (compare Jer 31:3; Hos 9:15; Jude 21). The removal of love relationship is always in response to the prior human rejection of God's love (Is 5:2-7; Heb 13:5). As John Goldingay comments, "Any breakdown in relationship between Yahweh and Israel is the responsibility of the latter, not the former" (compare Neh 9:33).[96] Accordingly, "there is a point when God abandons sinners to their wicked desires (cf. Rom. 1:28)."[97] If I *finally* spurn God's love, his love may continue to shine like the rays of the sun, but, by my own decisions, I am completely shaded from its light and warmth as if I have locked myself in a windowless basement.

Nevertheless, God's subjective love remains in God's disposition even after such forfeiture. Human rejection of God's love cannot quench God's subjective love but only prevents God's desire for love relationship from coming to fruition. Thus God's subjective love grounds God's longing for his people as well as elements of his compassion, sympathy and sorrow over

---

[96]John E. Goldingay, *Daniel*, WBC 30 (Dallas: Word, 1989), p. 242.
[97]Marten H. Woudstra, *The Book of Joshua*, NICOT (Grand Rapids: Eerdmans, 1981), pp. 337-38.

lost ones.[98] In this way, God's subjective love is everlasting (Jer 31:3; Rom 8:35, 39) and unconditionally constant, grounded in his eternal character of love (1 Jn 4:8, 16). There is no danger that God will voluntarily remove his love from anyone. However, although God continues to subjectively love his creatures for eternity, his subjective love is of no effect for anyone who has rejected the love relationship that God so desires.[99] God's character is love, and accordingly he will respect the final free decisions of humans (freedom being a necessary condition of love).[100] Divine love never runs out, but humans may refuse to receive and reciprocate it. "If you seek Him, He will let you find Him; but if you forsake Him, He will reject you forever" (1 Chron 28:9).

Corporate unconditionality and conditionality. Beyond the important distinction between God's subjective and objective love, God's love is also unconditional in a corporate sense. That God will love and save *some* people is unconditional. However, the identity of the specific recipients of that saving divine love is conditional. Humans can forfeit their place as beneficiaries in the relationship. This corporate unconditionality is apparent in the related themes of remnant and the so-called grant-type covenant.

The remnant theme itself implies unconditionality and conditionality.[101] That God's promises will come to fruition for God's people affirms corporate unconditionality, yet conditionality is manifested on the individual level with respect to who will be included in the remnant. As such, the very concept of "remnant" suggests that God's love does not endure forever unto all its intended objects. God's promises will come to fruition for God's

---

[98]God longs for relationship with his unresponsive lover, and this includes emotionality, which continues even after the rupture of the particular, relational love (cf. Mt 23:37; Lk 13:34). Yet the fullness of divine emotions, which include delight, pleasure and enjoyment of creatures, does not obtain once the intended object of God's love finally rejects God.

[99]Compare T. F. Torrance's insightful statement: "Why people may want to reject the love of God is quite inexplicable, but whether they believe in Jesus Christ as the incarnate love of God or refuse to believe in him, the love of God remains unchangeably what it was and is and ever will be, the love that is freely, unreservedly and unconditionally given to all mankind" (*Christian Doctrine of God*, p. 246).

[100]One might ask why God would *allow* someone to reject love relationship with him. The answer to this question hinges on the relationship between love and freedom. On the view of this book that love requires significant freedom (see chap. 4), God cannot determine that someone *freely* love him and, conversely, cannot prevent someone from not loving him.

[101]See Gerhard F. Hasel, *The Remnant: The History and Theology of the Remnant Idea from Genesis to Isaiah* (Berrien Springs, MI: Andrews University Press, 1972).

people, that is, those who respond to God as part of a faithful remnant (compare Is 65:8-9; Rom 9:6; 11:7, 22-23). As Post writes, divine love "may appear unconditional and therefore universal in its initial outreach, but eventually it requires that the recipient undergo a change of heart—a conversion grounded in the narratives and community that themselves sustain *agape* in the history of salvation."[102]

Consider, further, the unconditional covenant promises throughout the Old Testament, particularly as expressed in the so-called grant-type covenant. Generally speaking, a grant-type covenant includes a promise to a faithful servant of blessings that extends unconditionally to future generations. A particular generation may rebel and thus forfeit their covenant blessings and status, but future generations will still be privy to the covenant promise if they remain faithful.[103] Eugene Merrill puts it this way: "The pledge of redemption and conquest by Israel was a settled and nonnegotiable matter (the unconditional side of the covenant), but their reality in the experience of individual Israelites or even a generation of them was contingent on covenant faithfulness (the conditional side)."[104] In other words, such covenant promises are unconditional in general, but conditional with regard to who will or will not be the recipients of such promises.

These elements are prominent in a number of instances, especially in the Davidic covenant. Therein God promises blessings to David's descendants grounded, at least partially, in his faithfulness (1 Kings 3:6, 8; 15:4-5). The promises of the Davidic covenant are sometimes spoken of as everlasting and thus (in some sense) unconditional (2 Sam 7:13-16; 23:5; 1 Chron 17:12-14; Ps 89:38-39). However, there are conditions for receiving the promised blessings (1 Kings 9:4-9; 11:11, 33; 14:8; 1 Chron 28:9; 2 Chron 7:17-20).[105]

---

[102]Post, *Theory of Agape*, p. 83.

[103]The complexity of both ancient Near Eastern covenants and biblical covenants defies one-to-one correlation with the so-called covenant of grant (Gary Knoppers, "Ancient Near Eastern Royal Grants and the Davidic Covenant: A Parallel?" *JAOS* 116, no. 4 [1996]: 696). However, some parallels are striking and may shed light on the tension between conditionality and unconditionality regarding the divine-human relationship. See the further discussion in chap. 8 (below). Compare Weinfeld, "Covenant of Grant"; Scott Hahn, *Kinship by Covenant: A Canonical Approach to the Fulfillment of God's Saving Promises* (New Haven, CT: Yale University Press, 2009).

[104]Merrill, *Deuteronomy*, p. 173.

[105]Gary Knoppers compellingly argues that the Davidic covenant contains a "bilateral element" such that "David's descendants are not freed from their responsibility to obey Yhwh" (1 Chron-

Hence, "the lovingkindness of the LORD is from everlasting to everlasting on those who fear Him . . . To those who keep His covenant And remember His precepts to do them" (Ps 103:17-18; compare Lk 1:50). God's promises will reach his people corporately, but the individual objects of the covenant promise(s) are subject to conditions.[106] As John Oswalt comments, "On the one hand nothing could prevent God's promises to Abraham, Moses, and David from being realized," yet such "promises guarantee nothing to the individuals of any generation. If they sin, they will be punished; if they are righteous, they will be rewarded (Ezek. 18:1–24). Election promises made to the nation will not be participated in automatically by individuals."[107]

In many ways, Christ himself might be seen as the entirely faithful servant who warrants the bestowal of grant-type covenant promises by the Father; the antitypical David.[108] These promises mean that all his offspring are privy to God's kingdom, which will never pass away. However, particular individuals may choose to be part of God's people by adoption through Christ, or they may choose to reject God's intended blessings toward them and forfeit the love relationship that they could have enjoyed.[109] In this way, Christ stands as the ultimate guarantor of God's loving, covenant promises within this revelatory microcosm of God's loving relationship with the world.

CONCLUSION

In response to questions about whether God's love is strictly unconditional, conditional or something else, this chapter has explained that God's love is

---

icles 10-29, AB 12A [New York: Doubleday, 2004], p. 672). Compare J. A. Thompson, *1, 2 Chronicles*, NAC 9 (Nashville: B&H, 1994), p. 229.

[106]The foreconditionality of divine love complements the conditionality of covenant blessings and curses. God grants blessings to his people prior to conditions, but continued blessings are conditional (cf. Deut 7; Lev 26).

[107]John N. Oswalt, *The Book of Isaiah: Chapters 40-66*, NICOT (Grand Rapids: Eerdmans, 1998), pp. 90-91.

[108]The nature and content (dynasty, land, etc.) of covenant promises vary considerably throughout the OT. Without attempting to conflate these promises, the overall unconditionality that a remnant will be the beneficiary, while other potential beneficiaries may forfeit their place, may be recognized as a broad, overarching theme of the OT that, according to the NT, finds ultimate resolution in the eschatological kingdom that will be brought about by Jesus Christ. See Walton, *Covenant*, pp. 94-107.

[109]I am not suggesting univocity between the so-called grant-type covenant evident in the OT and these NT themes and concepts, but the overlap is striking and may present a helpful canonical model illuminating the foreconditionality of divine love.

foreconditional, complementing the volitional, evaluative and emotional aspects of divine love. God's foreconditional love means that God's love is initiatory, prior to any human action, love, merit or worth, while at the same time God implements conditions for the reception and continuance of that love (which is never merited). Appropriate human response is itself only possible because of God's prior love, which is the necessary but not sufficient condition of human love. Divine love is surpassingly enduring, steadfast and reliable, yet not altogether constant or unconditional. Although God's love is exceedingly long-suffering, the benefits of divine love may finally be forfeited (though they are never removed by God arbitrarily). Thus, whereas God's love is everlasting and unconditional with respect to God's character of love and his volition to love the world (God's subjective love), divine love is conditional with respect to evaluation and relationality (God's objective love). While God's subjective love never diminishes or ceases, God's objective love will eventually no longer reach the one who finally rejects it. Those who respond positively to God's love, however, enjoy everlasting reciprocal love relationship. To this ideally reciprocal aspect of divine love we now turn.

8

The Reciprocal Aspect of Divine Love

Is the God-world relationship unilateral, or can God be involved in a reciprocal (albeit asymmetrical) love relationship with humans? Bound up with this is the question of whether and to what extent God's love is universal and/or particular, including whether God loves everyone equally and, if not, why? The transcendent-voluntarist model proposes that God is the sole giver but never the receiver of love. Divine love for humans is purely the result of God's sovereign will and is thus unilaterally bestowed beneficence (thematic *agape*). In the immanent-experientialist model, conversely, love describes the essential God-world relation such that God's love is universal within necessarily reciprocal relationality. Both models, then, directly exclude the other's perspective, and there is considerable contemporary disagreement among theologians from various perspectives.[1]

My investigation of the canonical data concludes that divine love in relation to the world is ideally reciprocal, yet asymmetrical. That is, God desires reciprocal love relationship with every person but enters into and enjoys a particular, intimate relationship with only those who freely reciprocate his love. This (ideally) reciprocal love relationship is the framework that encapsulates and requires the volitional, evaluative, emotional and foreconditional aspects of divine love.

God's Love Is Ideally Reciprocal

Is divine love unilateral or reciprocal? On the one hand, God's love might be

---
[1]See chap. 1 (above).

unilateral such that God only bestows love but never enjoys it from creatures. Here, God's love relationship with the world is predicated on his will and results in overflowing beneficence toward the world, affirming God's sovereignty and self-sufficiency. On the other hand, God's love might be essentially relational such that God's love is his sympathetic relationship with all others, who are included in himself. Still others would suggest that divine love is reciprocal in a way that includes give and take, a bilaterally volitional relationship that is neither necessary nor the result of unilateral divine determination. My canonical investigation has led to this last view that God's love relationship with the world is *ideally* reciprocal. God desires and seeks mutual (though asymmetrical) love relationship with humans, yet divine love may be unreciprocated.

The reciprocal operation of divine-human love. God's triune nature undergirds the understanding that "God is love," since the Father, Son and Holy Spirit have eternally enjoyed love relationship (compare Jn 17:24).[2] As such, "God is eternally love prior to, and independently of, his love for us."[3] God's love relationship with creatures is predicated on God's free decision to create (and thus love) the world. Although God does not need relationship with any world, the biblical data consistently depict God as desiring and seeking reciprocal love relationship with humans.

Throughout Scripture, God expects that his love will be reciprocated by humans and responds with love to those who do so. Thus divine lovingkindness (חסד) is shown to the thousandth generation of those who love (אהב) God and keep his commandments (Ex 20:5-6 = Deut 5:10; compare Ex 34:7; Deut 7:9; Neh 1:5; Jer 32:18; Dan 9:4).[4] Such texts show "that covenant love or loyalty was to be reciprocal."[5] Likewise, David states of God,

---

[2]See the discussion of the multilateral circle of love below.
[3]C. E. B. Cranfield, "Love," *TWTB*, p. 135.
[4]As was seen in chap. 3 (above), חסד and אהב are the two primary OT terms of love and here describe reciprocal (but not symmetrical or identical) divine-human love. H. J. Stoebe sees a close (though not synonymous) association between their usage in the OT and states that "one could ask whether the formula 'to love with all your heart, etc.' (e.g., Deut 6:5; 10:12; 11:13; 13:4; 30:6) means to express the unreserved devotion implied by *ḥesed*" ("חסד," *TLOT* 1:460).
[5]Mervin Breneman, *Ezra, Nehemiah, Esther*, NAC 10 (Nashville: B&H, 1993), pp. 171-72. As Jeffrey H. Tigay puts it, "The Lord will faithfully reciprocate the devotion and obedience of the people" (*Deuteronomy* [Philadelphia: JPS, 1996], p. 67). Ronald E. Clements likewise comments, "There is to be a strong reciprocal bond of affection and commitment between Israel and the LORD as God" ("The Book of Deuteronomy," *NIB* 2:343).

"With the kind [חָסִיד] You show Yourself kind [חָסִיד], With the blameless You show Yourself blameless" (2 Sam 22:26 = Ps 18:25 [26]). Thus, "the fervent love of the godly man God requites with confiding love" such that "God's conduct to man is the reflection of the relation in which man has placed himself to God."[6] These and other instances of חסד (itself a basic grounding characteristic of God) convey reciprocal divine-human relationship. חסד is freely and voluntarily bestowed, unmerited (but not strictly unconditional), and continues or begins a relationship (often but not always covenantal) within which positive dispositions and/or actions will be reciprocated when/if occasion arises (even if חסד itself is not, or cannot, be).[7]

Likewise, in the New Testament, both God and Jesus respond with love toward those who love Jesus: "He who loves [ἀγαπάω] Me [Jesus] will be loved [ἀγαπάω] by My Father, and I will love [ἀγαπάω] him" (Jn 14:21; compare Jn 14:23). Further, the one who "loves [ἀγαπάω] [Jesus]," the "Father will love [ἀγαπάω] him," and both Father and Son will make their abode with that one (Jn 14:23). Likewise, the "Father Himself loves [φιλέω] you, because [ὅτι] you have loved [φιλέω] Me and have believed" (Jn 16:27).[8] This reciprocal love amounts to intimate friendship with Jesus (Jn 15:14). Thus objects of divine love are exhorted to "abide [μένω] in" Christ's "love," which is conditional on obedience (Jn 15:9-10).[9] Therefore, as D. A. Carson puts it, "the love for which we were created" is "a mutual love that issues in obedience without reserve."[10] Thus God engages in a bilateral love rela-

---

[6]Carl Friedrich Keil and Franz Delitzsch, *Commentary on the Old Testament* (Peabody, MA: Hendrickson, 2002), 5:162. Compare God's statement that "those who honor Me I will honor, and those who despise Me will be lightly esteemed" (1 Sam 2:30; cf. 1 Chron 28:9; 2 Chron 12:5). See also Judg 5:31; Ruth 1:8; Ps 36:10; 109:12; 122:6.

[7]See Gen 21:23; Josh 2:12-14; Ruth 2:20; 1 Sam 20:8, 14-15; 2 Sam 2:5; 2 Chron 24:22. Elsewhere, the חֲסִידִים are to love (אהב) God (Ps 31:23 [24]) and, likewise, God loves (אהב) justice and does not forsake the חָסִיד (Ps 37:28; cf. Ps 97:10). Similarly, but to a lesser extent, numerous instances suggest that אהב ought to be reciprocal, such as when it is lamented that love is repaid with hatred (Ps 109:4-5; cf. 2 Sam 19:6; 2 Chron 19:2; Job 19:19). Personified Wisdom even proclaims, "I love those who love me" (Prov 8:17). On this verse, Michael Fox comments, "Behind the concept of mutual love of wisdom and humanity may lie the theme of reciprocal divine-human love" (*Proverbs 1-9*, AB 18A [New York: Doubleday, 2000], p. 276).

[8]On the conditionality conveyed by ὅτι see chap. 7 (above).

[9]Similar conditional language of abiding (μένω) is prominent throughout the NT (e.g., Jn 15:7-10; 1 Tim 2:15; 1 Jn 2:5-6; 3:1, 9-17, 23-24; 4:12-16).

[10]D. A. Carson, *The Gospel According to John* (Grand Rapids: Eerdmans, 1991), p. 521.

tionship with humans, desiring and expecting that humans will reciprocate his love.

Reciprocal love in covenant and kinship relationships. The reciprocal aspect of divine-human love relationship is especially evident in the covenant relationship. God initiates covenant relationship through calling and election, yet the benefits of the relationship are conditional on appropriate response. While God loved Israel prior to their response, and thus elected them (Deut 4:37; 7:7-8; 10:15), the people are expected to "love" him in return and "always keep His charge, His statutes, His ordinances, and His commandments" (Deut 11:1; compare Ex 20:5-6).[11] The importance of reciprocal relationship is likewise evidenced by the blessings that correspond to the covenant fidelity of humans, including reciprocal love (e.g., Deut 7:12-13; 11:26-28; Lev 26:3-17; Ps 103:17-18).[12] "Love and keeping of the law are thus the two pillars on which the covenant rests."[13]

Some scholars, however, have maintained a distinction between so-called promissory and obligatory covenants in the Old Testament. In this view, promissory covenants describe those in which God's promises are independent of human response and thus unconditional, whereas obligatory covenants refer to those in which human response is required.[14] In this vein, some scholars have posited a sharp contrast between the supposedly promissory and unconditional Abrahamic and Davidic covenants, akin to the ancient Near Eastern grant-type covenant, and the so-called obligatory (on the vassal) and conditional Mosaic covenant, akin to the so-called ancient Near Eastern suzerain-vassal treaty type. However, close inspection of these covenants shows that, although the Mosaic covenant may place more emphasis on human obligations, and divine promise is more prominent in the Abrahamic and Davidic covenants, each includes elements of conditionality

---

[11]Indeed, humans are to love God with all their "heart" and "soul" (Deut 6:5; 10:12; 11:13; 13:3 [4]; 30:6; Josh 22:5).

[12]See chap. 7 (above), wherein it is also explained that a thoroughgoing theology of retribution does not cohere with the entirety of the canonical evidence.

[13]F. Charles Fensham, *The Books of Ezra and Nehemiah*, NICOT (Grand Rapids: Eerdmans, 1982), pp. 154-55.

[14]See Moshe Weinfeld, "The Covenant of Grant in the Old Testament and in the Ancient Near East," *JAOS* 90, no. 2 (1970): 184-85; George E. Mendenhall, "Covenant Forms in Israelite Tradition," *Biblical Archaeologist* 17, no. 3 (1954): 50-76. Weinfeld recognizes the conditionality apparent in many texts with regard to the Davidic covenant (e.g., 1 Kings 2:4; 8:25) but believes that these are the result of Deuteronomistic redaction ("Covenant of Grant," p. 195).

and unconditionality such that they are neither altogether promissory or obligatory, as recognized by many scholars (compare Gen 18:19; 22:16-18; 26:4-5; 1 Kings 2:3-4; 8:25; 9:4-9).[15]

Thus, as Frank Cross puts it, "there are no 'unilateral' covenants in a kinship-based society" (such as Israel), and missing this point has led to the "gross distortion" of viewing some biblical covenants as unilateral.[16] Accordingly, Gary Knoppers has effectively highlighted the insoluble problems related to positing a bifurcation between promissory and obligatory covenants in the Old Testament. By extensive reference to ancient Near Eastern parallels he contends that most covenants are bilateral such that "even in the most one-sided arrangements (e.g., Ulmi-Tesup; 2 Samuel 7, Psalm 89) there may be an element of reciprocity."[17] Thus covenant is not merely a one-sided oath but a "formal agreement involving two or more parties," that is, "inevitably bilateral."[18] As such, God's covenant relationship with humans is bilateral (though asymmetrical), including reciprocal love.

The bilateral nature of the covenant relationship is evidenced in many ways throughout Scripture but perhaps nowhere more so than the prevalent marriage and parent-child kinship metaphors.[19] Both metaphors model the give and take involved in the divine-human love relationship, demonstrating God's profound and extremely long-suffering love for his people as well as the expectations that he has for their love in return. In Ezekiel 16:8-13, God takes Israel as his bride, cares for her and lavishes her with gifts.[20] In Jeremiah 2:2, God fondly looks back at this time, recalling Israel's former, youthful devotion (חסד) and the love (אַהֲבַת) of her betrothals, and yet sorrows at what she has become (Jer 2:2; compare Jer 3;

---

[15] See Gary Knoppers, "Ancient Near Eastern Royal Grants and the Davidic Covenant: A Parallel?" *JAOS* 116, no. 4 (1996): 670-97.

[16] Frank Moore Cross, *From Epic to Canon: History and Literature in Ancient Israel* (Baltimore: Johns Hopkins University Press, 1998), pp. 14-15. Cross further contends that this view is dependent on extrabiblical presuppositions, including antinomianism (ibid., p. 15).

[17] Knoppers, "Ancient Near Eastern Royal Grants," p. 696.

[18] Ibid. Compare Scott Hahn, *Kinship by Covenant: A Canonical Approach to the Fulfillment of God's Saving Promises* (New Haven, CT: Yale University Press, 2009), p. 29.

[19] Covenant relationality is itself grounded in kinship language, rather than the other way around. See chap. 3 (above).

[20] God "entered into a covenant" so that she became his (Ezek 16:8) has parallels in the Elephantine marriage vow, "She is my wife and I am her husband" (R. Yaron, *Introduction to the Law of the Aramaic Papyri* [Oxford: Clarendon, 1961], p. 46).

Hos 1–2).²¹ Just as God is depicted as the husband of his people in the Old Testament, Jesus takes on the metaphorical role of the bridegroom who will wed his bride (the church), for whom he lovingly gave himself up (Mt 9:15; 25:1-10; Mk 2:19-20; Lk 5:34-35; Jn 3:29; Eph 5:23-27; 2 Cor 11:2; Rev 19:7; 21:9; compare Jas 4:4).

Further, God refers to his people as "My son, My firstborn" (Ex 4:22), "My dear son" and "delightful child" for whom "My heart yearns" (Jer 31:20). God has bestowed his great love on humans such "that we would be called children of God" (1 Jn 3:1), and he is thus the "Father" of those whom he loves (Jn 14:21, 23; 16:27; Rom 1:7) and who love him (Jn 8:42; 1 Jn 5:1). God "carried" his people "just as a man carries his son" (Deut 1:31) and discovered Israel as a foundling in the wilderness, took her even in her amniotic fluid, washed her and adopted her (Ezek 16:3-6; compare Deut 32:9-13).²² Similarly, God proclaims, "When Israel *was* a youth I loved him, And out of Egypt I called My son" (Hos 11:1; compare Hos 11:3-4). Here and elsewhere, though the parent-child metaphor freely alternates between language of adoption and of begetting/birth, the adoption imagery is especially significant, being descriptive of God's volitional kinship love (e.g., Deut 14:1-2; 32:6, 10; Rom 8:15-17; compare Ex 4:22).²³

The depth of God's affection is apparent in that his compassion for his people surpasses that of a mother for her infant (Is 49:15). Similarly, "just as a father has compassion on *his* children, so the LORD has compassion on those who fear Him" (Ps 103:13; compare Is 63:8-9). Accordingly, certain behavior is expected of God's children, and God disciplines Israel even as a "man disciplines his son" (Deut 8:5), a loving discipline which is ultimately for their "good" (Deut 8:16; compare 1 Cor 11:32) for "whom the LORD loves

---

²¹Some consider this to be a direct contradiction of the history (e.g., Jack R. Lundbom, *Jeremiah 1-20*, AB 21A [New York: Doubleday, 1999], p. 253), the so-called nomadic or desert ideal (see Michael V. Fox, "Jeremiah 2:2 and the 'Desert Ideal,'" *CBQ* 35 [1973]: 441-50). However, many scholars view the language as not merely wishful but also factual. Israel was briefly devoted, though inconsistent. See Michael DeRoche, "Jeremiah 2:2-3 and Israel's Love for God During the Wilderness Wanderings," *CBQ* 45 (1983): 364-76.

²²On language of adoption in Ezek 16, see Meir Malul, "Adoption of Foundlings in the Bible and Mesopotamian Documents: A Study of Some Legal Metaphors in Ezekiel 16:1-7," *JSOT* 46 (1990): 97-126.

²³See James M. Scott's exposition of the OT covenant background of the Pauline language of adoption in *Adoption as Sons of God: An Exegetical Investigation into the Background of huiothesia in the Pauline Corpus* (Tübingen: J. C. B. Mohr, 1992).

He reproves, Even as a father *corrects* the son in whom he delights" (Prov 3:12; compare Deut 4:36-37; Ps 89:30-32 [31-33]; Heb 12:6-8; Rev 3:19).[24]

Although God is the "Father of all" (Eph 4:6), status as born-again children of God is neither natural (as "children of wrath," Eph 2:3) nor automatic. Even "the sons of the kingdom" could be "cast out" (Mt 8:12). The Israelites were God's elect children, yet Paul proclaims they are not all "children because they are Abraham's descendants," for "it is not the children of the flesh who are children of God, but the children of the promise are regarded as descendants" (Rom 9:7-8; compare Rom 9:26-27; 1 Pet 3:6). Thus it is those who respond to God who may be "sons [υἱός] of God through faith in Christ Jesus" (Gal 3:26; compare Heb 3:6; Rev 21:7), and Jesus commands love toward enemies "so that you may be sons [υἱός] of your Father who is in heaven" (Mt 5:44-45; compare Mt 5:9; Lk 6:35; 20:36; Rom 8:14; 2 Cor 6:18). Likewise, "as many as received Him, to them He gave the right to become children of God" (Jn 1:12).[25] As such, "being a child of God" requires appropriate response, which "assumes that, in one sense, sinful people are not God's children, even though they are created by God, unless and until they believe in Jesus Christ (cf. 1 Jn 3:1-2)."[26]

On the other hand, humans can reject God as husband and/or parent and thus sever the kinship relationship. Both metaphors depict Israel's repeated and persistent unfaithfulness toward God wherein God is a devoted parent and/or faithfully loving husband, unjustly dishonored, scorned and grieved, whose overtures are rejected in a repetitive cycle of unrequited love.[27] Such repeated apostasy brings about the rupture of the special relationship between God and his people, who forfeit claim to special relationship as "wife" (Jer 3:1) or as God's children (Hos 1:6, 9; 2:4). Thus God sent his bride away and gave her a "writ of divorce" (Jer 3:8; compare Is 50:1; Hos 2:2).[28] His

---

[24]Indeed, the "comparison to a father's discipline indicates that the discipline, whether punitive or not, is administered with love" (Tigay, *Deuteronomy*, p. 93).

[25]Notably, God's initiative is primary since believers "were born, not of blood nor of the will of the flesh nor of the will of man, but of God" (Jn 1:13).

[26]Andreas J. Köstenberger, *John*, BECNT (Grand Rapids: Baker, 2004), p. 39.

[27]See, for example, Is 1:2-4; 30:9; 56:7-8; Jer 2:2-9, 24-25; 3:1-20; Ezek 16:15, 25-26; Hos 1-3; Mal 1:6; Mt 12:39; 23:37; Mk 8:38; Lk 13:34.

[28]This refers to the northern kingdom, Israel, and was intended to deter Judah from adultery, but it did not do so (Jer 3:8). Adultery should have incurred the death penalty (Deut 22:22), but God compassionately issued only a writ of divorce, which corresponds to something less than adultery (Deut 24:1). There has been some disagreement over whether God ever actually di-

"beloved" forfeited her place in his house by vile deeds (Jer 11:15). Therefore God gave the "beloved of [his] soul into the hand of her enemies" and even came to "hate her" (Jer 12:7-8; compare Hos 9:15). Likewise, Israel "acted corruptly toward" God and were thus "not His children, because of their defect" (Deut 32:5). They forgot the God "who begot" them, who gave them "birth" (Deut 32:18) and went after false gods, so he "spurned *them* Because of the provocation of His sons and daughters" (Deut 32:19). "The son thus disowns himself from his parent, just as the wife/Israel rejects her husband."[29]

Despite their apostasy, God graciously and lovingly maintains a heartfelt call for their repentance and return (Jer 3:12-14, 19, 22), on which restoration depends (Jer 4:1; compare Jer 3:19-22; 31:20-22; Hos 10:12; 14:1-3). The amazing endurance of God's love for his people, despite the enormity of their infidelity, is modeled in the command to Hosea to "Go again, love a woman *who* is loved by *her* husband, yet an adulteress, even as the LORD loves the sons of Israel" (Hos 3:1; compare Hos 2:2, 14). Those who return God "will love freely" (Hos 14:3-4 [4-5]), and with them He promises to make a new covenant (Jer 31:31-36; Ezek 16:60-62; Hos 2:19-20; Heb 9:15). God as "husband" will restore his people "like a wife forsaken" and "rejected," whom he briefly "forsook" but will gather in "great compassion" and with "everlasting lovingkindness" (Is 54:4-8; compare Is 62:4). However, although God's amazing love repeatedly works to draw his people back, he eventually gives those who reject him over to their choice, though it grieves him (Hos 9:15; 11:8; Mt 23:37; Lk 13:34). God's love always takes the initiative, but "it is only effective when there is a response."[30]

Divine-human love as freely reciprocal. Scripture thus depicts the ideal of reciprocal and loyal love, which assumes bilateral significant freedom.[31]

---

vorced Israel, especially considering the cryptic phrase in Is 50:1 where God asks, "Where is the certificate of divorce By which I have sent your mother away?" Some have taken this to mean that God never gave them a writ of divorce, while others see this as a reference to the fact that God did not abandon them but vice versa. Both interpretations could fit the meaning of Is 50:1 in isolation but, of the two, only the latter accords with Jer 3:8. Compare Francis I. Andersen and David Noel Freedman, *Hosea*, AB 24 (New York: Doubleday, 1980), pp. 220-24.

[29]Gale A. Yee, "The Book of Hosea," *NIB* 7:277. "By her faithlessness Israel [had] forfeited a father-child relationship and an inheritance" (F. B. Huey Jr., *Jeremiah, Lamentations*, NAC 16 [Nashville: B&H, 1993], pp. 77-78).

[30]Andersen and Freedman, *Hosea*, p. 264.

[31]Bilateral significant freedom refers to the freedom of both God and humans to will otherwise than they do. See chaps. 4 and 9.

That is, these biblical models of relationship support (by their description as well as their internal logic) that God does not unilaterally determine human love. Rather, the covenant and kinship descriptions of the divine-human relationship depict a freely reciprocal divine-human love relationship. Indeed, both marriage and adoption are voluntary, rather than natural, relationships. As Cross highlights, "Adoptive sonship places obligations of kinship on the father, as is generally recognized, and also on the son, which is often forgotten. Kinship obligations are necessarily mutual."[32] God deeply desires and works toward a reciprocal love relationship wherein humans freely love God in response to his prior love, but there is always the possibility of unrequited love and, finally, forfeited relationship.[33] As such, though God is the prime agent and initiator of the God-human love relationship, God's love relationship with the world is not unilaterally caused by God.

Since divine love is sometimes not reciprocated, the God-world love relationship is *ideally* reciprocal. As Thomas Oden puts it, "God's love for humanity, like all love, is reciprocal. God prizes the world, and values especially human creatures, who have the freedom and imagination to respond to God and to share with God consciousness and compassion."[34] Vincent Brümmer adds that "love must by its very nature be a relationship of free mutual give and take, otherwise it cannot be love at all."[35] Accordingly, love always "entails a desire for reciprocation" though it may be "unrequited."[36] The foreconditional-reciprocal model, then, contrasts with both the transcendent-voluntarist and immanent-experientialist models in that the former posits that the God-human love relationship is unilaterally deter-

---

[32]Cross, *From Epic to Canon*, p. 14.
[33]If love assumes freedom, as contended in chap. 4 (above), then by definition a reciprocal love relationship could not be unilaterally determined. Many theologians, like Vincent Brümmer, believe that "love is necessarily free" (*The Model of Love: A Study in Philosophical Theology* [Cambridge: Cambridge University Press, 1993], p. 177).
[34]Thomas C. Oden, *The Living God* (San Francisco: Harper & Row, 1987), p. 121.
[35]Brümmer, *Model of Love*, p. 161.
[36]Ibid., p. 155. So Oden, *Living God*, p. 120. Numerous other theologians, from various perspectives, also recognize the reciprocal aspect of human love. See, among many others, Stephen G. Post, *A Theory of Agape: On the Meaning of Christian Love* (Lewisburg, PA: Bucknell University Press, 1990), pp. 10-12, 27; Jürgen Moltmann, *The Trinity and the Kingdom: The Doctrine of God*, trans. Margaret Kohl (San Francisco: Harper & Row, 1981), p. 203; Clark H. Pinnock, "Constrained by Love: Divine Self-Restraint According to Open Theism," *Perspectives in Religious Studies* 34, no. 2 (2007): 149.

mined by God's sovereign will, whereas the latter posits that the God-world love relationship is necessary and essential, rather than volitionally reciprocal, thus denying the possibility that love could be unrequited.[37]

In all this, the reciprocal aspect of divine love complements and is complemented by the volitional, evaluative, emotional and foreconditional aspects of love. The volitional aspect of the reciprocal divine-human relationship is apparent in that such relationship is bilaterally voluntary rather than necessary. At the same time, deep and intense affection is evident in the description of the God-world relationship, especially by way of kinship metaphors. Further, the evaluative and emotional aspects of divine love are apparent in that God delights in the love of his people and, conversely, mourns when that love relationship is ruptured (Hos 9:15; 11:8; Mt 23:37; Lk 13:34). God bestows love on his people foreconditionally but also desires and expects them to love him in return. Thus, "God's activity is love, which looks for men's reciprocal love (1 Jn. 4:8, 16)."[38]

The Multilateral Circle of Love

Throughout Scripture God enjoys numerous kinds of love relationships, which constitute a multilateral circle of love, including (1) love between the persons of the Trinity, (2) love from God to humans, (3) love from humans to God and (4) love from believers to one another (which amounts indirectly to love toward God). Love between the persons of the Trinity consists of a reciprocal love relationship that predates creation and models the ideal nature of all love relationships (Jn 17:24).[39] The Father loves the Son (Mt 3:17;

---

[37]Recall that on Charles Hartshorne's model, love is the description of the essential and internal social relationship of which all reality consists. Therefore, whereas all minds possess indeterministic freedom, love on this account is not the result of will, and neither is it predicated on it.

[38]W. Günther and H. G. Link, "αγαπαω," *NIDNTT* 2:542.

[39]One might wonder regarding the role of the Holy Spirit in such love. Though theologians have made various suggestions, there is less information in this regard than that regarding the love of the Father and Son. Paul speaks of the "love of the Spirit" (Rom 15:30), an ambiguous genitive. Note also reference to the Colossians' "love in the Spirit" (Col 1:8). The "love of God is shed abroad in our hearts by the Holy Ghost" (Rom 5:5 KJV), and love is itself a fruit of the Spirit (Gal 5:22). The "fellowship of the Holy Spirit" is placed in parallel with "the grace of the Lord Jesus Christ" and "the love of God" in a trinitarian formula (2 Cor 13:14; cf. Phil 2:1), and it is further implied that the Spirit loves humans since the Spirit manifests love toward humans in action (not leastwise in Rom 8:26). Likewise, the Spirit comes as the "comforter," thus replacing Christ on earth (Jn 14:16). As such, it is implied that the Spirit should likewise be seen as a partner in such love relationship, both intratrinitarian and divine-human. Scripture reveals the Trinity

Jn 3:35; 5:20; 10:17; 15:9-10; 17:23-24, 26), and Christ loves the Father and does exactly what the Father commands (Jn 14:31).[40] The Father and Son also love humans. Thus the Son loves his followers intimately (Jn 13:1; compare Jn 11:5; 13:34; 14:21; 15:9, 12; 21:7, 20). Likewise, the Father "loved" Christ's followers "even as" he "loved" Christ (Jn 17:23; compare Jn 14:21, 23). Significantly, God's love is itself reciprocally responsive to human love toward God (compare Ex 20:6; Deut 5:10; 7:9; Neh 1:5; Dan 9:4; Jn 14:21, 23; 16:27).

Divine reciprocation of human love implies the validity and value of human love toward God, which some have questioned. The Bible further depicts the validity and value of human love in exhortations and explicit statements. Humans are frequently commanded to love God: "You shall love the LORD your God with all your heart and with all your soul and with all your might" (Deut 6:5; compare Mt 22:37-38).[41] This exhortation, along with the many others like it, manifests God's desire to enjoy reciprocal love relationship with his creatures and demonstrates the potential for valuable human love toward God. The reality of human love toward God is also evident, appearing by way of each of the most prominent Old Testament and New Testament terms for love.[42] Many such instances include the prospect of reward. For example, God has prepared things beyond imagining for "those who love Him" (1 Cor 2:9; Jas 2:5; compare Rom 8:28), and the "crown of life" is "promised to those who love" God (Jas 1:12; compare 2 Tim 4:8; Heb 6:10). Likewise, God "keeps all who love Him" while the wicked are destroyed (Ps 145:20; compare Ps 70:4 [5]; 91:14).[43] Such instances of

---

progressively such that even the Father-Son love relationship is not explicitly revealed until the NT and, even then, the most explicit statements about Father-Son love come in John, which many consider to be among the last NT books written. Since the Spirit is revealed most explicitly in the NT in relation to the church, it is not surprising that there is minimal data regarding the Spirit's role in the multilateral love relationship.

[40]Notice, however, that the Father-Son love relationship during Christ's early ministry is asymmetrically reciprocal. As Kathryn Tanner notes, "The Son prays to the Father, but the Father does not pray to the Son" (*Christ the Key* [New York: Cambridge University Press, 2010], p. 219).

[41]See also Deut 10:12; 11:1, 13; 13:3 [4]; 30:6; Josh 22:5; 23:11; Ps 31:23 [24]; Mk 12:30; Lk 10:27.

[42]Human love toward God appears in the OT by the terms אהב (Ex 20:6; Deut 5:10; 7:9; 1 Kings 3:3; Ps 91:14; 97:10; 116:1; Neh 1:5; Dan 9:4), חסד (Jer 2:2; cf. Neh 13:14), רחם (Ps 18:1 [2]) and חשק (Ps 91:14). Despite the claims of some, then, there are instances of human חסד and רחם toward God. See chap. 3 (above). In the NT, human love toward God likewise appears by ἀγαπάω (Lk 7:47; Jn 14:21, 23; Rom 8:28; 1 Cor 2:9; Jas 2:5) and φιλέω (Jn 16:27; 21:15-17).

[43]On the other hand, the one who "does not love [φιλέω] the Lord . . . is to be accursed" (1 Cor 16:22; cf. Deut 7:10).

promised reward signify the value of human love toward God and imply that humans have the freedom not to love God (hence the reward).[44]

Finally, because of God's love, believers "ought [ὀφείλω] to love one another" (1 Jn 4:11; compare Jn 15:12, 17; 1 Jn 3:16).[45] Moreover, human love toward humans indirectly amounts to love toward God (1 Jn 4:7-12, 20-21; 5:1-2; compare Mt 25:40). Thus, by responding to God's love with love for others, one is reciprocating God's love within the multilateral circle such that love reaches "perfection" (1 Jn 4:17-18). As Ethelbert Stauffer puts it, "The love that is ready to help even the least of brethren is equivalent to readiness to help the Son of Man, whereas lovelessness is the same as contempt for him. Both will be judged by the Son of Man in his day."[46]

Issues regarding human reciprocation of divine love. Most theologians agree that humans may love God, as the biblical texts above demonstrate. However, numerous issues have been raised regarding the nature of this love, including the view that this love is deficient and/or the result of God's unilateral action. If human love is deficient, then humans cannot truly reciprocate divine love but "love" God in a lesser manner. Further, if human love is the result of God's unilateral action, then humans are not free to reciprocate divine love (or not).[47]

First, if one understands "reciprocal" to refer to equality of relationship, then God and humans could not enjoy reciprocal relationships, since God and his love are immeasurably greater. In the foreconditional-reciprocal model, however, the term *reciprocal* does not mean that God's love is equal

---

[44]Some might argue that "reward" is possible without significant freedom, but that case is difficult to make without obfuscation of the basic concept of reward. Elsewhere the primary Greek word for "reward" (μισθός) is often used of eschatological reward (Mt 5:12; Lk 6:23, 35; Rev 22:12), and the term itself literally and consistently refers to dues paid for labor, wages or the natural reward for work. See Ernst Würthwein, "μισθός," *TDNT* 4:698-702.

[45]Notably, ὀφείλω always refers to a moral obligation in the NT, specifically that which one owes or ought to do but might not do (e.g., 1 Jn 2:6; 3:16; 3 Jn 8). The expectation that believers love one another is well represented (Jn 13:34-35; 1 Thess 4:9; 1 Pet 1:22; 1 Jn 3:11, 23; 2 Jn 5).

[46]Ethelbert Stauffer, "αγαπάω, αγάπη, αγαπητός," *TDNT* 1:48. Compare Stephen S. Smalley, *1, 2, 3 John*, WBC 51 (Dallas: Word, 2002), p. 257.

[47]Anders Nygren promoted both of these views, which can still be seen in whole or in part in various recent works. As Nygren puts it, human love is itself deficient (*eros*), but a human may love (*agape*) God "because God's unmotivated love has overwhelmed him and taken control of him, so that he cannot do other than love God. Therein lies the profound significance of the idea of predestination: man has not selected God, but God has elected man" (*Agape and Eros*, trans. Philip S. Watson [London: SPCK, 1953], p. 214).

to, or symmetrical with, that of creatures but refers to a relationship wherein God's love is responded to positively such that humans become conduits of divine love. For example, Christ's followers may enjoy the reciprocal love relationship of friendship with him, but that friendship is manifestly asymmetrical, since it requires obedience from them (Jn 15:14). Likewise, the God-human covenant relationship expects humans to reciprocate God's love, but, nevertheless, God is the Lord, while the human covenant partner fulfills the vassal role. The divine-human relationship is thus ideally reciprocal but always asymmetrical.

Furthermore, there is a sense in which all love is the result of God's love. As explained previously, God is the originator of love, and it is only because he freely bestowed love that any creatures even have existence, much less the capacity to reciprocate love: "We love, because He first loved us" (1 Jn 4:19). However, while humans could not love without God's prior love and corresponding action, humans possess the divinely granted freedom to reciprocate or reject God's love. Thus, in the foreconditional-reciprocal model, divine love is the necessary but not sufficient ground of human love.

This position is taken in accord with the many exhortations to love God and statements of human love toward God, which manifest God's desire to enjoy reciprocal love relationship with humans and demonstrate the potential for significantly free and valuable human love toward God. In my view, the divine exhortations for human love would be superfluous and misleading if human love were unilaterally determined by God such that those who do not love God could not love God. Likewise, the numerous instances where reward is presented as a direct consequence of human love toward God strongly imply genuine contingency and significant human freedom. The canonical evidence suggests, then, that human love toward God is an active, significantly free response to God's prior love.

This brings us back to the issue of the bilaterally volitional aspect of love (see chapter four). The ongoing conflict between theologians, including those who share a high regard for Scripture, shows that the debate between deterministic and indeterministic viewpoints will not be easily settled in a way that convinces those committed to either side.[48] However, in my view,

---

[48]Indeed, some of the most excellent evangelical scholars are committed to determinism; many posit an exclusivist kind of compatibilism wherein human love for God is the efficacious result

the weight of the evidence in favor of the significant freedom of humans, especially relative to the God-world love relationship, is overwhelming. Indeed, the biblical data regarding the divine-human love relationship in this and previous chapters strongly support the view that God grants all humans the freedom to reciprocate his love or to choose not to do so, and are difficult to explain otherwise.[49] Thus, the foreconditional-reciprocal model posits that, while humans would not have the ability to love God apart from his prevenient action, humans do possess the ability to reciprocate God's love or not, due to God's bestowal of significant freedom.

Peter's threefold affirmation of love for Jesus in John 21:15-17 is especially significant in this regard. If Peter's love for Christ were divinely determined and/or merely divine love flowing through a passive human agent, it is difficult to make sense of Christ's repeated question to him, "Do you love me?"[50] As G. Johnston puts it, if human love is only God's love, unilaterally determined by God, then "it is not really the believer's love at all! This is to evacuate Christian love of any value."[51]

What about the view that human love is deficient and thus less than reciprocal? In one sense, it seems obvious that humans, being imperfect and finite

---

of God's unilateral election. See Thomas R. Schreiner and Bruce A. Ware, eds., *Still Sovereign* (Grand Rapids: Baker, 2000). This should not be confused with other forms of compatibilism such as that represented by Karl Barth, whose doctrine of election pertains to Christ, in whom all humans are elect. Conversely, some evangelicals take the indeterminist perspective that humans have libertarian freedom not to respond to God's overtures. See David Lewis Allen and Steve Lemke, eds., *Whosoever Will: A Biblical-Theological Critique of Five-Point Calvinism* (Nashville: B&H Academic, 2010).

[49]As discussed previously, the most prominent determinist explanation is compatibilism, in the exclusivist version of which elect humans respond to God's love but that response is itself determined by God's decree of unconditional election. So Douglas Moo, *The Epistle to the Romans*, NICNT (Grand Rapids: Eerdmans, 1996), pp. 530-31; Thomas Schreiner, *Romans* (Grand Rapids: Baker, 1998), pp. 450-51. However, as briefly laid out in chap. 4 (and 9) and supported in subsequent chapters, I believe a canonical approach to this and other questions leads to a rejection of determinism, especially in light of the considerable biblical evidence that God's will is sometimes unfulfilled (e.g., Lk 7:30; 13:34). For a more extensive treatment of the issue of human freedom in Scripture, see the analysis of God's will and election (including considerable attention to Romans 9–11) in John C. Peckham, *The Concept of Divine Love in the Context of the God-World Relationship* (New York: Peter Lang, 2014), pp. 204-35, 372-99, 577-84; compare John C. Peckham, "Does God Always Get What He Wants? A Theocentric Approach to Divine Providence and Human Freedom," *AUSS* 52/2 (2014): 195-212.

[50]See chap. 3 (above) for a discussion of the alternating use of ἀγαπάω and φιλέω in these verses.

[51]G. Johnston, "Love in the NT," *IDB*, p. 173. Ceslas Spicq adds that, contra Nygren and others, true "*agape* can ascend from man to God" (*Agape in the New Testament*, 3 vols. [St. Louis: B. Herder, 1963], 1:105).

by nature, would also love imperfectly. If one refers to the deficiency of human love in this sense, then all who recognize human finitude and sinfulness (as I do) would agree. However, some have made a claim that goes far beyond these deficiencies, treating human love as so deficient as to be of no value (or worse) and, as such, altogether different from divine love. Yet such a claim does not appear to accord with the canonical evidence (compare Eph 6:24).

First, this claim is often grounded in the *agape-eros* dichotomy, most prominently asserted by Anders Nygren, which posits that *agape* is the highest love, descriptive of God's love, whereas all others (*eros, philia,* etc.) are lesser, deficient loves. That is, only God's love is truly *agape,* beneficent and altogether gratuitous and disinterested, whereas human loves are desirous and acquisitive (thematic *eros*).[52] However, the discussion of the evaluative aspect in chapter five has shown that even God's love includes appropriate desire and the enjoyment of value, demonstrating that desire and enjoyment do not require any deficiency of the recipient and that God values human love toward himself and others. Moreover, chapter three has shown that the semantics of love as used in Scripture, particularly with regard to the ἀγαπάω word group, do not posit a kind of love that is unique to God.[53] God's love is unique (at least) in the sense that it is never deficient and always perfect, whereas human love (including ἀγαπάω) might be misdirected (2 Tim 4:10) or worse, even being used in the LXX to refer to rapacious lust (2 Sam 13:15).

Thus a distinction with regard to the quality and perfection of God's love over and against all others is warranted, whereas a dichotomy between divine and human love is misleading. As D. A. Carson states, "Doubtless God's love is immeasurably richer than ours, in ways still to be explored, but they belong to the same genus, or the parallelisms could not be drawn."[54] It is not surprising, then, that the canon depicts strong semantic and thematic correspondence between divine love and virtuous human love.[55] Accord-

---

[52]See Nygren, *Agape and Eros,* pp. 213-18.
[53]As explained in chap. 3 (above), "The Greek Bible does not support the common assumption that *agape* should be defined in a way that stands in contrast to ordinary human love" (William E. Phipps, "The Sensuousness of Agape," *Theology Today* 29, no. 4 [1973]: 371).
[54]D. A. Carson, *The Difficult Doctrine of the Love of God* (Wheaton, IL: Crossway, 2000), p. 48.
[55]As seen earlier in this chapter, each of the prominent OT and NT terms of love is used of human love toward God.

ingly, the various love relationships of the multilateral circle are depicted as alike in nature (though not necessarily equal or symmetrical). Even as the Son loves the Father and the Son loves humans, humans are to love God and love one another within the multilateral circle of love.[56]

However, one might ask, does this view overemphasize the human will to the detriment or devaluation of God's work in loving and saving us? Is grace, then, no longer grace? In the foreconditional-reciprocal model, the freedom of humans to respond to God does not mean that humans merit God's love or in any way earn the right to relationship with him; the positive human response to God's love is no more meritorious than the acceptance of a gift from a benefactor (see chapter seven). While it is true that fallen human beings are incapable of bringing any value to God, such as truly loving him apart from God's prior and sustaining action, God reaches out to humans and enables a love response that grows progressively greater as one draws closer in intimate relationship with God while divine mediation makes up for the preglorification deficiency of human love (see chapter five). In this way, through God's initiating action and mediation, humans can truly and freely reciprocate divine love by reflecting (albeit imperfectly) God's immeasurably greater love.[57] Thus human love toward God may be reciprocal but never symmetrical, imperfect yet not wholly other.

---

[56]Believers are to obey Christ just as (καθώς) Christ has obeyed the Father and thus abide (μένω) in his love even as Christ thereby abides (μένω) in the Father's love (Jn 15:9-10; cf. Jn 10:17; 17:26). Likewise, just as (καθώς) the Son loves his followers, they are to love one another (Jn 13:34; 15:12), and the Ephesian Christians are to "walk in love, just as [καθώς] Christ also loved" them (Eph 5:2). As Carson puts it, humans "love and obey Jesus, and he loves them, in exactly the same way that he loves and obeys his Father, and the Father loves him," and the "love with which they learn to love is nothing less than the love amongst the persons of the Godhead" (Carson, *Gospel According to John*, pp. 503, 70). Compare Jordan Wessling's argument for the univocity of love ("Colin Gunton, Divine Love, and Univocal Predication," *JRT* 7 [2013]: 94). See also Colin Gunton, *Act & Being: Towards a Theology of the Divine Attributes* (Grand Rapids: Eerdmans, 2002), p. 70. Rather than claiming that such loves are in every respect *exactly* the same, however, one might more tentatively state that the text here depicts them as holding considerable correspondence to one another while being asymmetrical (among other dissimilarities).

[57]The view that humans are "beloved" unilaterally because they are elect overlooks and/or sterilizes the force of the exhortations to the beloved and the warning of future evaluative judgment (see chap. 5 above). Conversely, to say that humans are "beloved" merely due to their response to God would miss the essential divine initiative that makes such response possible (Phil 2:12-13; Jude 1, 21).

The Universality and Particularity of Divine Love

The instances surveyed above highlight the importance of the divine-human relationship *qua* relationship. However, what do we make of the nature of God's ideally reciprocal love as it relates to humans universally and/or particularly? Does God love all equally, and if not, why not and in what way? Theologians posit various answers to these questions. For instance, some critics of Scripture contend that the God of the Bible does not love everyone but shows unjust favoritism to his elect and thus promotes xenophobia.[58] Christian theologians, however, generally agree that God does in fact love all humans, but theologians remain divided as to the nature of God's universal love. The immanent-experientialist model posits that God's love is universal sympathy, descriptive of the necessary God-world love relationship such that God's love reaches everyone in an undifferentiated manner.[59] Others advocate various forms of universalism such that God's love will finally amount to the salvation of everyone.[60] Many theologians, however, distinguish between the universality and particularity of God's love, which entails that God does not love all equally. The transcendent-voluntarist model posits that God's love is universal in the sense of God's common love but particular in that God's love unto salvation (and other benefits of the love relationship) only reaches those whom God has chosen as his elect. On the other hand, in the foreconditional-reciprocal model, aligned with those who posit the significant freedom of humans, God loves everyone in a way that desires and seeks reciprocation, but only some respond and thus enter into a particular love relationship with God.

God's love as universal, yet also particular. In the foreconditional-reciprocal model, the reciprocation of divine love amounts to a particular relationship of divine love, which is universally available but not universal since not all reciprocate divine love. Such relationships between God and humans are only possible because of God's prior, foreconditional bestowal of love on everyone. This conception may be best understood by addressing the following questions: (1) Is God's love actually universal according to Scripture? (2) If so, what about the data regarding the particularity of divine love?

---

[58]See the discussion below.
[59]See chap. 1 (above).
[60]See chap. 7 (above).

With regard to the first question, there is an abundance of biblical data that posits the universality of divine love. Perhaps the most famous verse of Scripture states, "For God so loved the world, that He gave His only begotten Son, that whoever believes in Him shall not perish, but have eternal life" (Jn 3:16).[61] Likewise, God is the father of all (Mal 2:10; Eph 4:6; compare Ps 68:5 [6]), and the entire "earth is full of the lovingkindness of the LORD" (Ps 33:5; compare Ps 117:1-2; 119:64). Likewise, God is "good to all, And His mercies [רַחֲמִים] are over all His works" (Ps 145:9; compare Ps 16; 100:1, 5). As such, God is not "partial" (Deut 10:17-18; Acts 10:34-35; compare Deut 1:17; Gal 2:6) but bestows blessings on all his creatures, though not always equivalently (compare Mt 5:44-45; Lk 6:35-36; Acts 14:17), and does not want anyone to perish (2 Pet 3:9; compare Ezek 18:32; 33:11; Jn 12:32; 1 Tim 2:4-6; Tit 2:11).[62]

However, what about election? Does God have favorites, such as Israel, his elect? What about the particularity of the covenant and kinship relationships? In this regard, some critics of the Bible contend that the God of Scripture (particularly in the Old Testament) does not love everyone but is xenophobic.[63] In contrast to this claim, whereas the Bible does contain ex-

---

[61]Gerald Borchert comments, "Undoubtedly God's desire is that all might be saved (e.g., Acts 17:30-31; 22:15-16; 1 Tim 2:6), but because of human freedom or choice ('whosoever,' 3:16), all of humanity does not respond in believing acceptance of the Son (e.g., Jn 1:11-13; Rom 1:5; 10:16; 1 Tim 4:10)," and "the rejection of God's love brings judgment or condemnation (Jn 3:17)" (*John 12-21*, NAC 25B [Nashville: B&H, 2003], p. 184).

[62]Some contend that these texts do not teach that God actually desires that everyone will be saved, claiming that terms such as *anyone* and *all* may be referring to all kinds of people rather than every single individual, or that such terms may simply be referring to specific addressees. See Richard Bauckham, *2 Peter, Jude*, WBC 50 (Dallas: Word, 2002), p. 313; Douglas J. Moo, *2 Peter and Jude* (Grand Rapids: Zondervan, 1996), p. 188. However, some of the texts that suggest God's desire to save everyone do not leave room for that kind of interpretation, such as Ezek 18:32, where God states, "I have no pleasure in the death of *anyone* who dies.... Therefore, repent and live" (emphasis mine). Thus Peter H. Davids states that God wants "'everyone'/'all' to come to repentance.... God's will may not be done, but it will not be for lack of trying on his part" (*The Letters of 2 Peter and Jude*, PNTC [Grand Rapids: Eerdmans, 2006], p. 281). Compare Eric Fuchs and Pierre Reymond, *La deuxième Épitre de Saint Pierre. L'épitre de Saint Jude* (Neuchâtel, Switzerland: Delachaux & Niestlé, 1980), pp. 115-16. Likewise, some of the foremost determinist interpreters believe 1 Tim 2:4 and others describe God's genuine desire for the salvation of all. See John Piper, "Are There Two Wills in God?" in *Still Sovereign*, p. 108; Thomas R. Schreiner, *1, 2 Peter, Jude*, NAC 37 (Nashville: B&H, 2007), p. 382. Compare chap. 4 (above).

[63]This is a particularly popular claim of the so-called new atheists. For a compelling response to this and other criticisms of God's moral character, see Paul Copan, *Is God a Moral Monster? Making Sense of the Old Testament God* (Grand Rapids: Baker, 2011). Some critical scholars have, further, sought to relegate the numerous texts that demonstrate God's universal love and concern, such as Is 56, to a minority opinion of late authors. Conversely, John Oswalt points out, "the passages that are usually quoted as examples of narrow Jewish exclusivism (Ezek. 44:6-9;

tensive evidence of God's particular love (see below), it does not exclude or contradict his universal love. For instance, though God entered into a particular love relationship with Israel via covenant, that relationship did not exclude God's love for other peoples. Indeed, the Abrahamic covenant was intended for universal blessing (Gen 12:3; 22:18; 26:4; Is 42:1; Jer 4:2). Accordingly, the covenant blessings were conditionally available to foreigners (Is 56:4-8; compare Gen 17:14). Therefore, although Israel was graciously chosen to be a particular people in love relationship with God, "this choice does not limit God's rule on earth to this small people, but comes within the framework of God's plan for the whole world" such that "Israel's choice is for the purpose of mission."[64]

Indeed, God anticipates an ultimate gathering of the nations to himself, declaring that "many nations will" be joined with him and "become My people," and God "will dwell in [their] midst" (Zech 2:11; compare Is 66:18-22; Hos 14:5-7 [6-8]; Zeph 3:8-9).[65] Accordingly, God promises to "have compassion on" foreign peoples and "bring them back" each to their land, and then, "if they will really" learn the ways of his people, they will be built up, while the alternative is destruction (Jer 12:15-17). Patrick Miller comments that this "text betrays a powerful universalistic impulse. The Lord invites and welcomes all the 'neighbors' into the community of faith that is constituted by Israel. The invitation is real."[66] Furthermore, Jack Lundbom states that this is "nothing less than a conditional, Sinai-type covenant offered to the Gentiles. Yahweh's compassion is not conditional upon them learning his peoples' ways, but conditions will come afterward."[67] Thus there is evidence that God also loved the nations outside Israel foreconditionally.

That God's love extends beyond the elect to outsiders is also apparent in

---

Ezra 4:1–3)" refer to those "who are either open in their unbelief or are masquerading as believers," as in Is 57:3-13; 65:1-7 (*The Book of Isaiah: Chapters 40-66*, NICOT [Grand Rapids: Eerdmans, 1998], p. 457).

[64]Emile Nicole, "בחר‎," *NIDOTTE* 1:641.

[65]This language in Zech 2:11 is strikingly reminiscent of divine language of covenant making with Israel: "I will take you for My people, and I will be your God" (Ex 6:7).

[66]Patrick Miller, "The Book of Jeremiah," *NIB* 6:680.

[67]Lundbom, *Jeremiah 1-20*, p. 663. God's larger intention in covenant relationship was the adoption of other peoples through Israel. Indeed, God's reference to Israel as his "firstborn" (Ex 4:22), along with other OT data, implies that he has, or intends to have, other children. Beyond the texts above, see also Deut 2:5, 9, 19; 32:8; Is 19:19-25; 42:1-6; 49:6; Jer 4:2; Amos 9:7, 12; Lk 14:23; Acts 13:17; Rom 1:5; Gal 3:28; 1 Tim 4:10.

other instances. God "shows His love for the alien" and commands his people to do the same (Deut 10:18-19). Likewise, Christians are exhorted to have "love for one another, and for all people" (1 Thess 3:12). Furthermore, divine lovingkindness and/or compassion extends beyond the covenant people in numerous examples, such as the case of Nineveh (Jon 4:2, 11; compare Ruth 1:8; 2 Sam 15:20).[68] Accordingly, those who are outsiders may become party to God's insider love (Jn 3:16; Rom 5:8-10; 9:25-26; 2 Cor 5:19; Eph 2:3-5; compare Mk 10:21-22; Acts 10:34-35; 17:30-31). Hence God calls those who were not his people "My people" and "sons of the living God," and makes "beloved" those who were not his beloved (Rom 9:25-26). On the other hand, some who were once insiders may become outsiders, since such status is contingent on appropriate response (Rom 11:22-23; 2 Thess 2:10-15). As H. Wildberger recognizes, "Election does not have such permanence that it cannot be called into question by the improper behavior of the elect."[69] In the absence of appropriate response, one will eventually forfeit insider relationship (see chapter seven).

Particular, insider love in Scripture. The canonical evidence repeatedly suggests that God's love applies in a special sense to those who are (freely) involved in reciprocal love relationship with him (Jn 14:21-23; 16:27), while those outside this relationship are not loved in this particular sense (1 Cor 16:22). This might be called insider love, that is, love that is specially directed toward an individual or a group and goes beyond God's universal love.

The particularity of divine love for persons or groups is pervasive throughout Scripture and integral to understanding the God-world relationship. Many of the earlier cited examples of reciprocal love require some kind of particular love relationship. For example, God "keeps all who love Him," while the wicked are destroyed (Ps 145:20; compare Ps 37:28; 70:4 [5]; Judg 5:31), and the Father loves those who love the Son (Jn 14:21, 23; 16:27). Regarding these verses, Gustav Stählin comments, "To this love of the disciples for Jesus corresponds the reciprocal love of God for the disciples . . . which is obviously different from His love for the world."[70]

---

[68]Notably, God even has compassion for the animals (Jon 4:10-11).
[69]H. Wildberger, "מאס," *TLOT* 2:654. Consider the cases of Saul (1 Sam 15:23; cf. 1 Sam 13:13-14) and Judas (Mt 26:24; Jn 6:70). Compare chap. 4 (above).
[70]Gustav Stählin, "φιλεω, καταφιλεω, φιλημα," *TDNT* 9:133.

Various other depictions of God's insider love demonstrate that insider relationship with God requires reciprocation. For example, whereas God is the father of all as Creator (Mal 2:10; Eph 4:6) there is also a special, intimate fatherhood that is reserved for those who respond to God's overtures (Mt 5:9; Lk 6:35-36; Jn 1:12; Rom 9:7-8; Gal 3:26; Rev 21:7) and have thus been adopted (Rom 8:14-17, 23; Eph 1:5). Thus, "all are his [the Father's] sons in the sense that he made them and that he provides for them. But people are his sons in the full sense only as they respond to what he does for them in Christ."[71] God is thus "the Father of those who believe."[72] Likewise, as seen earlier, the repeated descriptions of God's people as his bride manifest particular love relationship that requires reciprocation.

The very concept of covenant also describes a particular relationship.[73] Thus God's elect are consistently differentiated from others, enjoying a particular love relationship with God along with attending benefits (Deut 4:37; 7:7-13; 10:15; Is 41:8-9; Mal 1:2; Mt 24:22; Lk 18:7). Although the elect are not recipients of God's love *because* they love God (God's love was bestowed foreconditionally), they will not continue to be elect if they refuse to reciprocate God's love (Rom 11:22; 1 Cor 16:22).[74] Accordingly, Scripture often depicts divine election as conditional and contingent (e.g., 2 Kings 23:27; Is 14:1; Jer 33:24; Zech 1:17; 2:12 [16]; Ps 78:67-68; Mt 22:3-14; Rom 10:9-13; 11:22-23; 2 Pet 1:10). Further, as seen above, peoples from other nations could become privy to elect status, and in the New Testament elect status is explicitly open to all peoples (Mt 22:14; Acts 10:34-35). Those who enjoy this particular love relationship with God are also referred to as God's "beloved" (ἀγαπητός; e.g., Rom 1:7; 11:28; 1 Pet 2:11; 4:12; 2 Pet 3:14; Jude 3).[75] Those

---

[71] Leon Morris, *The Gospel According to John*, NICNT (Grand Rapids: Eerdmans, 1995), p. 87.

[72] Robert Mounce, *Romans*, NAC (Nashville: B&H, 2001), p. 64. Christians are therefore "brethren" of one another and of Christ (through Christ) and should love one another (e.g., Mt 12:50; 1 Thess 4:9).

[73] Consider the distinction between the "inclusive" and "special" covenant relationships in Scripture posited in Joseph L. Allen, *Love & Conflict: A Covenantal Model of Christian Ethics* (Lanham, MD: University Press of America, 1995), pp. 39-45.

[74] Consider the biblical concept of a faithful remnant, which dovetails considerably with the canonical notion of insider love (e.g., Is 10:20-22; 37:32; 65:8-15; Zeph 3:17; Rom 9:6, 30-32). See Gerhard F. Hasel, *The Remnant: The History and Theology of the Remnant Idea from Genesis to Isaiah* (Berrien Springs, MI: Andrews University Press, 1972).

[75] Compare the special status of God's "beloved" (יָדִיד) in the OT, especially in Jer 11:15; compare Deut 33:12; Ps 60:5 [7]; 127:2.

who are finally among the "beloved" are "those who love" God (Jas 2:5; compare Eph 5:1-2; Phil 2:12; 1 Jn 4:7-11).[76]

Furthermore, humans are also spoken of as friends of God (Is 41:8; 2 Chron 20:7; Jn 3:29; 11:11; 15:13-14; Jas 2:23; compare Ex 33:11; Mt 11:19; Lk 7:34; 12:4).[77] Significantly, friendship with Christ is explicitly predicated on obedient and loyal love; they are his "friends" if they do his commands (Jn 15:14), whereas "friendship with the world is hostility toward God" (Jas 4:4). Thus friendship with God signifies a particular (rather than universal) and mutual (though asymmetrical) relationship that is grounded in reciprocal love and obedience. Likewise, whereas God loves "the world" (Jn 3:16), he loves some particularly. Thus God "loved" Solomon (2 Sam 12:24-25; compare Neh 13:26; 1 Kings 3:3), and Scripture refers to the disciple "whom Jesus loved" (Jn 13:23; compare Jn 19:26; 20:2; 21:7, 20) and Christ's "own" (ἴδιος) whom he loved to the end (Jn 13:1) in distinction from the "world" who does not love them but "would love its own" (ἴδιος; Jn 15:19).[78] Carson thus states, "With the connection between obedience and love so explicit, it should be self-evident that the circle of love in view embraces all of Jesus' true disciples, but not the 'world,' which falls within a rather different and more extended circle of love."[79] Mounce adds, "God loves the entire human race (Jn 3:16), but those who respond to him in faith are loved in a special way."[80]

Insider love is thus apparent in numerous descriptions of reciprocal love, complementing rather than excluding the universality of divine love. That God is not partial (Deut 10:17-18), then, does not mean that God does not enjoy particular relationship with some on the basis of their

---

[76]As seen in chap. 4 (above), divine election is conditional and often associated, but not to be conflated, with divine love.

[77]Although it is possible that the *qal* participle in Is 41:8 and 2 Chron 20:7 only denotes Abraham's love toward God, it is clear elsewhere that God loved Abraham (cf. Deut 4:37; 7:7-8; 10:15). Moreover, the NT explicitly refers to Abraham as the "friend [φίλος] of God," and this friendship is itself predicated on Abraham's belief (Jas 2:23) and thus conditioned on his appropriate response to God (cf. Gen 15:6; 22:9). So Stählin, "φιλεω, καταφιλεω, φιλημα," *TDNT* 9:169.

[78]The use of the term "own" (ἴδιος) implies belonging or membership in a close-knit group (particularity), and it "is of the nature of this love for one's own, for what belongs, to be reciprocal" (Stählin, "φιλεω, καταφιλεω, φιλημα," *TDNT* 9:130).

[79]Carson, *Gospel According to John*, p. 503.

[80]Mounce, *Romans*, p. 64.

response: "God is not one to show partiality, but in every nation the man who fears Him and does what is right is welcome to Him" (Acts 10:34-35).[81] As such, "God does not discriminate on the basis of race or ethnic background," but God "does discriminate between those whose behavior is acceptable and those whose attitude is not acceptable. Those who reverence God and practice what is right are acceptable to him."[82] Thus, while God satisfies the desires of "every living thing" (Ps 145:16), in a special way he "will fulfill the desire of those who fear Him" (Ps 145:19; compare Ps 65:2, 4 [3, 5]).[83] As Robert Bergen astutely observes, God "does not treat all people alike—to do so would demonstrate a moral indifference that is not found in the biblical view of God."[84] Scripture, then, consistently points to the universality and particularity of divine love, the latter requiring reciprocation.

GOD'S UNIVERSALLY RELATIONAL AND PARTICULARLY RELATIONAL LOVE

The canonical data surveyed above demonstrate that God loves everyone but also has particular love relationships with some, which can be forfeited and are thus foreconditionally reciprocal. This complexity regarding the universality and particularity of divine love can be understood by differentiating between what might be called God's universally relational love and his particularly relational love.

God's universally relational love. God loves the entire world. Divine love for everyone is foreconditional and universally relational, the undeserved and unprompted initiating love that God bestows on each human prior to any human response. As such, it flows unilaterally to all humans toward drawing them into a freely reciprocal love relationship by graciously bestowing prevenient love prior to any conditions, with the goal of eliciting a human response of love. The foreconditional-reciprocal model distinguishes between God's

---

[81]The word *welcome* translates δεκτός, which often connotes that which is evaluatively acceptable. See chap. 5 (above).

[82]John B. Polhill, *Acts*, NAC 26 (Nashville: B&H, 2001), p. 260.

[83]Likewise, God loves the righteous (Ps 146:8; cf. Ps 87:2), the pursuer of justice (Prov 15:9; cf. Prov 3:12) and the "cheerful giver" (2 Cor 9:7). On the other hand, God "hates" those who do evil, destroys those who speak falsehood, and "abhors the man of bloodshed and deceit" (Ps 5:4-6 [5-7]; cf. Ps 11:5; 106:40). See chap. 5 (above).

[84]Robert Bergen, *1, 2 Samuel*, NAC 7 (Nashville: B&H, 1996), p. 458.

universal love in general and his universally *relational* love that is bestowed foreconditionally on humans, because there is a sense in which God's universal love is prior to and independent of relationship with the world. This was explained in the previous chapter as God's subjective love (i.e., God's unconditionally and eternally loving disposition), which is grounded in himself as subject and not dependent on the response (or lack thereof) from humans. God's subjective disposition of love grounds God's loving actions toward all creatures (God's universally relational love), aimed at the goal of reciprocal love relationship.[85] God's subjective love is thus the universal and impartial ground of God's universally relational love, which extends to all humans foreconditionally. Whereas God's subjective love is not dependent on the dispositions and/or actions of creatures and is thus permanent, God's universally relational love can finally be rejected and thus forfeited.

God's universally relational love is manifest in all of his actions that pertain to the initiation of relationship with people (including creation, election, maintenance of the covenant and other manifestations of divine providence). Desiring the salvation of all and not wanting any to perish, God loves everyone foreconditionally for the purpose of loving them particularly and intimately, employing various actions to draw all humans into reciprocal love relationship (e.g., Ezek 18:23, 32; 33:11; Jn 3:16; 12:32; 1 Tim 2:4-6; Tit 2:11; 2 Pet 3:9; compare Acts 10:34-35; Rom 1:5; 1 Tim 4:10).

God's particularly relational love. Whereas God's universally relational love is the undeserved and unprompted initiating love that God bestows on each human prior to any response, God's particularly relational love refers to God's special and intimate kind of love for those who respond to him and thus enter into reciprocal love relationship. God's particularly relational love is thus the result of God's initiating and enabling love *as well as* appropriate human response (Jn 14:21-23; compare 1 Cor 16:22). Reciprocal love relationship is universally available, but not all accept and respond to God's foreconditional, universally relational love.[86]

---

[85]God's subjective love is thus the ground of God's universally relational love; the latter is itself categorized under God's objective love (that is, his initiating and interactive love relationship with creaturely objects). See chap. 7 (above).

[86]The universal opportunity to enjoy a saving love relationship with God is evident in the clause "whoever believes" in Jn 3:16; compare Acts 10:34-35; 1 Tim 4:10; 2 Tim 4:8; 1 Jn 2:2. On competing explanations of this verse, and an argument for the view that God's love reaches out to

Positive human response is itself only possible because of God's prevenient action(s) of universally relational love such that "while we were yet sinners, God died for us" (Rom 5:8; compare 2 Cor 5:19; Eph 2:3-5). Through Christ, then, outsiders may become insiders (Rom 9:25-26). However, those who do not love God remain (or become) outsiders, not privy to the intimate, particular divine-human love relationship that God intends for them (Jn 3:19; compare Rom 11:22-23; 2 Thess 2:10-15). With those who respond positively to God's loving overture, God enters into particular and intimate love relationship, which amounts to a reciprocal but asymmetrical love relationship. The difference is that those privy to God's particularly relational love allow God to love them forever, while the others reject him and thus forfeit divine love. Those who finally reject God's love need not have done so; they could have been insiders, but they were not willing (Mt 22:14; Lk 13:34).[87] As Shawn Floyd describes it, "While God's love is intensely felt for all, not everyone will reciprocate it and, as a result, preclude themselves from enjoying the goods that would otherwise be available to them."[88]

According to the foreconditional-reciprocal model, then, God desires and seeks particular, intimate relationship with all but enjoys such relationship only with those who respond appropriately to his foreconditional love. God's universally relational love is manifest in the universal invitation to the divine-human love relationship (Jn 3:16; 1 Tim 2:4; 2 Pet 3:9). God's particularly relational love is the result of God's initiating and enabling love as well as appropriate human response. God's love, then, is neither constant nor altogether unconditional and does not reach all of its objects equally, but

---

save everyone, see Jerry L. Walls and Joseph Dongell, *Why I Am Not a Calvinist* (Downers Grove, IL: InterVarsity Press, 2004), pp. 50-55. Compare Allen and Lemke, eds., *Whosoever Will*. However, many in the world love darkness and reject God's will (e.g., Jn 3:19; 14:24), coming to hate God (Ex 20:5; Deut 5:9; Ps 68:1; Rom 1:30), rejecting his love (Jn 5:42; 8:42) and making themselves his enemy (Jas 4:4).

[87]As Jerry L. Walls puts it, "God extends his love to such persons in such a way that they are truly enabled to respond," and God gives each one "'optimal grace,' which means they have every opportunity to accept the gospel and be saved. Despite this, some may resist grace decisively and be lost" ("Why No Classical Theist, Let Alone Orthodox Christian, Should *Ever* Be a Compatibilist," *Philosophia Christi* 13, no. 1 [2011]: 98).

[88]Shawn Floyd, "Preferential Divine Love: Or, Why God Loves Some People More Than Others," *Philosophia Christi* 11, no. 2 (2009): 371. He explains: "Even amongst people I love, I cannot maintain fellowship with them if they are unwilling to return my affection or behave in ways that promote a common life" (ibid.).

is evaluatively and conditionally responsive to the actual dispositions and/or actions of humans.

Why does God love some more than others? The transcendent-voluntarist and foreconditional-reciprocal models are on common ground in rejecting both the contention of universalism that all will finally be saved and the immanent-experientialist model's view that the reciprocal God-world love relationship is essential to God in a universal and undifferentiated sense.[89] Moreover, both the transcendent-voluntarist and foreconditional-reciprocal models recognize a distinction between universality and particularity of divine love. However, the two models differ when it comes to the crucial issue of *why* God's love is particular, that is, why doesn't God include everyone in eternal love relationship?

In the transcendent-voluntarist model, those whom God sovereignly predestines as his elect are loved unto salvation, while those who are not chosen by God benefit from God's universal common love but do not enjoy God's particular salvific love. As J. I. Packer explains, "God loves all in some ways" in that "everyone whom he creates, sinners though they are, receives many undeserved good gifts in daily providence," and he "loves some in all ways" in that "in addition to the gifts of daily providence he brings them to faith, to new life, and to glory according to his predestinating purpose."[90] Thus, in this model, the differentiation between those who receive God's particular salvific love and those who do not is predicated solely on God's sovereign will (exclusivist compatibilism).[91]

The foreconditional-reciprocal model agrees that Scripture differentiates between the universality and particularity of divine love. However, the foreconditional-reciprocal model believes that God's universal love calls all humans to a particular love relationship with God and gives each human the ability to respond positively and reciprocate God's love or to choose

---

[89]For an interesting discussion of whether it is even conceivable that God extend benevolence to all equally see Paul Helm, "Can God Love the World?" in *Nothing Greater, Nothing Better: Theological Essays on the Love of God*, ed. Kevin J. Vanhoozer (Grand Rapids: Eerdmans, 2001), pp. 168-85.

[90]J. I. Packer, "The Love of God: Universal and Particular," in *Still Sovereign*, pp. 283-84. Compare John Piper, "How Does a Sovereign God Love? A Reply to Thomas Talbott," *The Reformed Journal* 33, no. 4 (1983): 10. See also the debate between Dave Hunt and James R. White on this issue in *Debating Calvinism* (Sisters, OR: Multnomah, 2004), pp. 255-80.

[91]See the discussion of compatibilism in chaps. 7 and 9.

not to do so (significant freedom). Thus those who do not enjoy God's particularly relational love are excluded by their own decision rather than on the basis of God's will.[92]

Determinists generally see divine predestination in a positive light as the manifestation of God's "amazing" and "gratuitous" love to the undeserving.[93] Accordingly, they contend that God remains just in condemning the lost, since all are sinners and no one deserves God's salvific love. In this view, God should be praised for graciously saving any sinners at all and not questioned regarding those whom he does not save. However, many Christian theologians do raise questions in this regard, especially: If God can do so (as exclusivist compatibilists suppose), why does God not unilaterally determine that all humans reciprocate his love and thus be saved?[94] In this regard, Jerry Walls contends that to say that God loves those whom he has unilaterally chosen not to save is to use "the concept of love in a deeply idiosyncratic sense."[95] Roger Olson agrees: "God's love is simply incompatible with unconditional election or irresistible grace within a nonuniversalistic scheme."[96]

The foreconditional-reciprocal model contends that God wills and works to save every human. God does not desire that any perish but makes his particular, salvific love universally available (Jn 3:16; 12:32; 1 Jn 2:2) and will award the "crown of righteousness" to "all who have loved His appearing" (2 Tim 4:8; compare Acts 10:34-35; 1 Tim 4:10; 2 Tim 4:8). As Fritz Guy states, "It is unthinkable that the divine love is restricted to a fortunate part of creation and that another (perhaps even larger) part is excluded." God loves all

---

[92]Compare Oden, *Living God*, p. 118; Floyd, "Preferential Divine Love." Others who advocate for God's universal love with significant freedom include: H. Ray Dunning, *Grace, Faith, and Holiness: A Wesleyan Systematic Theology* (Kansas City, MO: Beacon Hill, 1988), pp. 196-97; Fritz Guy, "The Universality of God's Love," in *The Grace of God, the Will of Man: A Case for Arminianism*, ed. Clark H. Pinnock (Minneapolis: Bethany House, 1995), pp. 31-49; Mildred Bangs Wynkoop, *A Theology of Love: The Dynamic of Wesleyanism* (Kansas City, MO: Beacon Hill, 1972); Walls and Dongell, *Why I Am Not a Calvinist*, pp. 50-55; Brümmer, *Model of Love*, p. 175; Thomas Jay Oord, *The Nature of Love: A Theology* (St. Louis: Chalice, 2010), pp. 20, 121.

[93]Packer, "Love of God: Universal and Particular," p. 284.

[94]Indeed, if compatibilism is true, God could determine "all to freely accept his love and be saved" (Walls, "Why No Classical Theist," p. 96). See chaps. 7 and 9.

[95]Ibid., p. 98. He adds that "temporal blessings cannot begin to underwrite a sober claim of divine love for persons who are determined to damnation by God's unconditional choice" (ibid.).

[96]Roger Olson, *The Westminster Handbook to Evangelical Theology* (Louisville: Westminster John Knox, 2004), p. 169.

and intends "the eternal salvation—of every person."[97] Thus God grants, through the universal bestowal of prevenient love to everyone, the opportunity and capacity to be friends of God unto redemption. In this way God truly desires and does everything he can do within the bounds of bilateral significant freedom in working toward the salvation of all (e.g., Ezek 18:23, 32; 33:11; 1 Tim 2:4-6; Tit 2:11; 2 Pet 3:9). As such, God's particularly relational, intimate and preferential love is not arbitrary or groundless but conditional and evaluative. Consequently, some are loved by God more intimately than others but not because God decides to exclude anyone from such relationship. Those who are *finally* lost could have been insiders, but they were not willing (Mt 22:14; Lk 13:34).[98]

Eventually, the one who rejects God will neither enjoy God's particularly relational nor his universally relational love. However, God continues to bestow universally relational love on each human until they finally reject him. Prior to final judgment, God is "kind" even to "ungrateful and evil *men*" (Lk 6:35; compare Mt 5:45) and exhorts his children to therefore love their enemies (Mt 5:44-46; Lk 6:27-36; Rom 12:14-21). God's universally relational love thus extends even to those who hate God, as it works to draw all into reciprocal love relationship (Rom 5:8-10) but, eventually, those who resolutely make themselves God's enemies will forfeit divine love altogether (Jas 4:4), much to the grief of God (e.g., Ezek 33:11; Hos 11:8-9).[99] Conversely, the fullness of the divine-human love relationship is reserved until complete reconciliation in the eschaton. Then God and those who love him will forever enjoy intimate and reciprocal love relationship within the harmonious, multilateral circle of perfect love (1 Cor 2:9), much to God's delight (Zeph 3:17; Lk 15:7).

Conclusion

This chapter has addressed two crucial questions. First, can God be involved

---

[97]Guy, "Universality of God's Love," p. 36.

[98]What of those who seemingly did not have opportunity to accept God's love? Here, again, I personally affirm inclusivism of the kind that God holds humans accountable only for the light they encountered. Beyond this, I take it on faith that God will be supremely fair to each one (cf. Gen 18:25; Ps 19:9; Jer 12:1; Rev 15:3; 16:7).

[99]Accordingly, divine and human love toward enemies does not nullify evaluation or the biblical ideal of justice and reciprocality, and neither does it rule out intimate friendship, but it is part of the partial and temporary suspension of the consequences of evaluative judgment. See chap. 5 (above).

in a reciprocal (albeit unequal) love relationship with humans? Second, is God's love universal and/or particular, and in what way? The foreconditional-reciprocal model posits that divine love in relation to the world is ideally reciprocal, yet asymmetrical. God desires and persistently seeks reciprocal love relationship with all by foreconditionally bestowing universally relational love on every person, enabling reciprocal response. With those who freely reciprocate his love, God enjoys a particular and intimate love relationship within the context of the multilateral circle of perfect love.

This reciprocal divine-human love relationship is itself bound up with and encapsulates the volitional, evaluative, emotional and foreconditional aspects. That is, according to the foreconditional-reciprocal model, the reciprocal divine-human love relationship entails that God's love is (1) voluntary but not based solely on his will, (2) evaluative and deeply interested in the world, (3) profoundly emotional and passible, (4) foreconditional, but not unmerited, and (5) ideally reciprocal, that is, love relationship is universally available yet particularly enjoyed by those who freely reciprocate God's love. We now turn to some implications of the foreconditional-reciprocal model for divine ontology and the God-world relationship, toward a continuing dialogue on the nature of the God who loves.

9

WHO IS THE GOD WHO LOVES?

The impact of underlying ontological and metaphysical views on the dominant theological conceptions of love is difficult to overstate. The transcendent-voluntarist and immanent-experientialist models take widely divergent views of divine ontology and, unsurprisingly, come to mutually exclusive views of divine love. The transcendent-voluntarist model posits that God is necessary and self-sufficient, perfect, simple, timeless, immutable, impassible, omniscient and omnipotent, and thus divine love is sovereignly willed, unconditional, unmotivated and unmerited, freely bestowed beneficence. The immanent-experientialist model, conversely, posits that God is the world-inclusive universal subject, infinitely sensitive most moved mover and self-surpassing surpasser of all, and thus divine love is essential, universal, immediate and undifferentiated sympathy.[1] Both models derive their conception of divine love from a preexisting divine ontology. This study of divine love, however, has reversed this customary approach by first undertaking canonical investigation of the nature of divine love in relationship to the world while intentionally leaving the questions of divine ontology open to shaping by the findings. The conclusions arrived at in the foreconditional-reciprocal model of divine love point toward significant tensions and sometimes contradictions with the underlying ontologies supposed by the transcendent-voluntarist and immanent-experientialist models. This is not surprising since, as Kevin Vanhoozer states, any "new

---

[1] See chap. 1 (above) for a brief overview of the respective ontologies and conceptions of divine love.

paradigm for contrasting the love of God entails nothing less than a revision of the God-world relationship itself."[2] Accordingly, this chapter turns to the question: If God loves in this way, what must God be like?

Potential Implications for a Canonical Theo-ontology

According to the foreconditional-reciprocal model of divine love, God's love in relation to the world is: (1) volitional, (2) evaluative, (3) emotional, (4) foreconditional and (5) ideally reciprocal. First, divine love is volitional but not merely volitional. It includes a free, volitional aspect that is neither essential nor necessary to God's being yet also not arbitrary. Second, divine love is evaluative. This means that God is capable of being affected by, and even benefitting from, the disposition and/or actions of his creatures. Third, God's love is profoundly emotional, though not to the exclusion of volitional and evaluative aspects. Fourth, divine love is foreconditional, not altogether unconditional. That is, divine love is undeserved and prior to all other love and conditions but not exclusive of conditions. Fifth, God's love is ideally reciprocal. God desires and works toward bilateral love relationship with each human via his universally relational love but does not unilaterally determine that anyone love him in response. Those who reciprocate God's love enjoy particular love relationship with God for eternity. Each of these five aspects of divine love in relationship to the world fits together within the context of give-and-take relationality, pointing toward significant, though tentative, implications with regard to divine ontology and the metaphysics of the God-world relationship.

The five aspects of divine love in the foreconditional-reciprocal model are bound up with significant ontological issues, including (1) the relationship of divine love to God's essence/character, (2) the nature of divine perfection and/or self-sufficiency (dependence, independence or other), (3) the sovereignty of the divine will, especially as it relates to human freedom, (4) the acceptance, rejection or qualification of immutability and impassibility, and (5) the extent of the use of divine power (determinism/persuasion/other). Relative to these issues, this chapter will introduce some *tentative* facets of

---

[2]Kevin J. Vanhoozer, "Introduction: The Love of God—Its Place, Meaning, and Function in Systematic Theology," in *Nothing Greater, Nothing Better: Theological Essays on the Love of God*, ed. Kevin J. Vanhoozer (Grand Rapids: Eerdmans, 2001), p. 3.

a canonical ontology that are suggested by the foreconditional-reciprocal model of divine love.[3] Since these ontological suggestions rely on extrapolations from the canonical data regarding divine love, the proceeding outline of tentative ontological implications does not attempt to provide a comprehensive or dogmatic answer to these issues of divine ontology. However, insofar as this model of divine love accurately accords with the canonical data, a canonical ontology of God must account for the volitional, evaluative, emotional, foreconditional and ideally reciprocal facets of divine love.

The Ground of God's Love for Creatures

Is love itself God's essence, as many have posited?[4] First, the essence of God includes a great deal of mystery, and as such one should be careful regarding dogmatic assertions on this difficult topic. Theologians may mean many different things when they identify God's essence with "love."[5] Since the definition of *love* itself differs widely, this should be no surprise. In my view,

---

[3]These facets are tentative for at least four reasons. First, the foreconditional-reciprocal model of divine love presented in this book is itself tentative and open to revision based on further canonical investigation and systematic inquiry. Second, it could be misleading to attempt to derive a divine ontology from one divine characteristic, even one as major as divine love. Third, addressing the full scope of divine ontology is well beyond the scope of this volume. Fourth, other outlines of divine ontology may also be able to harmonize with this model of divine love and should continue to be sought.

[4]This is the view of the immanent-experientialist model whereas, for the transcendent-voluntarist model, Carl Henry comes close to positing love as God's essence but denies equating the two in order to avoid obscuring the other divine characteristics, which he considers equally essential to the purely simple divine essence (*God, Revelation, and Authority*, 6 vols. [Wheaton, IL: Crossway, 1999], 6:341, 48, 5:81-82, 135). Many classic theists and others, however, assert that God's essence is love, without denying other divine characteristics. For example, Martin Luther states: "God is nothing else than love" (LW 30:300). So also Thomas Aquinas, *Summa Theologica* 2.2.23.2; Augustine, *The Trinity* 9.2.2 (*NPNF* 3:235). Compare D. A. Carson, *The Difficult Doctrine of the Love of God* (Wheaton, IL: Crossway, 2000), p. 39; Leon Morris, *Testaments of Love: A Study of Love in the Bible* (Grand Rapids: Eerdmans, 1981), p. 136; Michael Horton, *The Christian Faith: A Systematic Theology for Pilgrims on the Way* (Grand Rapids: Zondervan, 2011), p. 265; Thomas Jay Oord, *The Nature of Love: A Theology* (St. Louis: Chalice, 2010), p. 139. Bruce McCormack affirms an actualist conception wherein "'God is love' is a statement which describes the nature and meaning of the act in which God gives himself his own being" ("The Actuality of God: Karl Barth in Conversation with Open Theism," in *Engaging the Doctrine of God: Contemporary Protestant Perspectives*, ed. Bruce L. McCormack [Grand Rapids: Baker Academic, 2008], p. 216). Compare *CD* II/1, p. 279; Alan Torrance, "Is Love the Essence of God?" in Vanhoozer, ed., *Nothing Greater, Nothing Better*, p. 137. From a universalist perspective, Thomas Talbott also asserts that God is essentially love and argues that proponents of limited election who assert that God's essence is love are contradicting themselves ("The Love of God and the Heresy of Exclusivism," *Christian Scholar's Review* 27, no. 1 [1997]: 101).

[5]For example, compare the widely divergent views of Morris, Oord, Talbott and McCormack.

the canonical data are underdeterminative regarding the precise nature of the divine essence, and I believe a complete understanding of God's essence is beyond human cognizance. I am thus reticent to make assertions regarding the precise nature of the divine essence and existence. Nevertheless, a few things may be said here without making dogmatic claims regarding the relationship between God's love and his essence.

First John declares that "God is love" (1 Jn 4:8, 16). However, many scholars contend that this statement does not require the view that love is God's essence, especially in consideration of the fact that John also states that "God is Light" (1 Jn 1:5) and "God is spirit" (Jn 4:24), not to mention other predications of God such as "God is a consuming fire" (Deut 4:24).[6] In this way, the question of whether love *is* God's essence cannot be settled by this singular statement in 1 John 4. Yet, whatever else may be said with regard to the relationship between God's essence and love, since the text proclaims that "God is love," all that God *is* and *does* must be understood as congruent with divine love.[7] That is, God's character is itself love, and God is essentially loving. The members of the Trinity have always been involved in a love relationship (compare Jn 17:24). Intratrinitarian love is thus essential to God, a product of God's trinitarian, essentially related nature. However, if God's character is love, and God is essentially loving, does that mean that God loves of necessity? Is God, ontologically or morally, bound to love the world?

---

[6]So Colin G. Kruse, *The Letters of John*, PNTC (Grand Rapids: Eerdmans, 2000), p. 157. Similarly, I. Howard Marshall, *The Epistles of John*, NICNT (Grand Rapids: Eerdmans, 1978), pp. 212-13. On the other hand, Daniel L. Akin is representative of those who take this to mean "his very nature is love" (*1, 2, 3, John*, NAC 38 [Nashville: B&H, 2001], pp. 178-79).

[7]Thomas Talbott contends: "If loving-kindness is an essential property of God, then it is logically impossible for him to act in an unloving way" ("On Predestination, Reprobation, and the Love of God: A Polemic," *The Reformed Journal* 33, no. 2 [1983]: 13). He argues from this premise to universalism. However, I believe that the fact that God is essentially loving does not require that he finally save all humans. As will be explained later in this chapter, even the destruction of those who finally reject God may be the most loving action he could take for those who intractably reject love. The scope of this book does not allow me to do justice to the complex debates and sincere disagreements over the biblical view of final judgment and the effects of divine condemnation. However, I personally believe that conditionalism (also known as annihilationism) best fits all of the canonical data. Those who finally and intractably reject God's love, on this view, sever the relationship with him that sustains them and thus lose their own existence. For an introduction to the debate over conditionalism, see Edward Fudge and Robert A. Peterson, *Two Views of Hell: A Biblical & Theological Dialogue* (Downers Grove, IL: InterVarsity Press, 2000). Compare John Stott's brief but insightful summary of his tentative case for annihilationism in David L. Edwards and John R. W. Stott, *Evangelical Essentials: A Liberal-Evangelical Dialogue* (Downers Grove, IL: InterVarsity Press, 1989), pp. 312-20.

According to the foreconditional-reciprocal model, the essential intratrinitarian love relation does not extend to creatures. Rather, the canonical data affirm that God's love *for creatures* is voluntary, not necessary to his being (see chapter four and the discussion of bilateral significant freedom below). God's love *for creatures* is not essential to his nature, because the very existence of human beings is contingent on God's free decision to create and sustain them. Thus God is not ontologically obligated to love creatures. God is both essentially and voluntary loving, in different respects. God is essentially loving as Trinity and in that his character is love. God is voluntarily loving in that God did not need to create any world and involve himself in relationship with creatures but did so freely. Karl Barth puts it this way: "God's loving is necessary" as "the essence and nature of God," yet "it is also free from every necessity in respect of its object." That is, "He would still be One who loves without us and without the world" and thus "needs no other" to be "the One who loves."[8]

This manifests a fundamental difference between the biblical conception of love and the "essential relations" of process panentheism wherein some world is necessary to God's being and Oord's essential kenosis theology wherein God "cannot not love us."[9] For process panentheism and essential kenosis, God is ontologically bound to the world and, though the most influential agent, he lacks the power to effect his will such that his freedom is limited to persuasion.[10] Moreover, God's essentially loving nature restricts him from not loving anyone or anything.[11] Oord posits that God is necessarily loving but free to choose between various actions only on the basis of his view that God lacks "exhaustive foreknowledge" and thus does not "know

---

[8]*CD* II/1, p. 280. Compare *CD* II/2, p. 166, IV/1, p. 213; Kevin Vanhoozer, *Remythologizing Theology: Divine Action, Passion, and Authorship* (New York: Cambridge University Press, 2010), p. 151. Recall, however, the ongoing discussion over whether (the mature) Barth viewed the God-world relationship as contingently necessary.

[9]Oord, *Nature of Love*, p. 132. Compare Jürgen Moltmann's panentheism wherein God also cannot not love on the view that it would be a divine self-contradiction (cf. 2 Tim 2:13; *The Trinity and the Kingdom: The Doctrine of God*, trans. Margaret Kohl [San Francisco: Harper & Row, 1981], p. 53).

[10]Similarly, Daniel Day Williams maintains a form of panentheism alongside the view that God is a free and contingent being. "God is the supreme instance of freedom to love. He never refuses to love, but the specific action of his love lies within the mystery of his being which no ontological analysis can fully penetrate or exhaust" (*The Spirit and the Forms of Love* [New York: Harper & Row, 1968], p. 127).

[11]Compare Charles Hartshorne's divine ethical immutability.

with certainty which single option is the most loving."[12]

The foreconditional-reciprocal model departs from these panentheistic conceptions by contending that God does not need any world and is not ontologically bound to love creatures, maintaining a far stronger sense of divine freedom. God voluntarily creates and sustains the world, freely initiating love relationship with creatures, and such loving action is grounded in his wholly loving character. As Alvin Plantinga has compellingly reasoned in this regard, dependence does not require control.[13] As such, God's will may depend on his essentially loving nature without his will being controlled by that essentially loving nature such that his character of love impels rather than compels him.[14] In this way God's will may be loving as dependent on his essentially loving nature but not determined by his nature. God retains moral freedom in the sense that what he does is not strictly necessary (ontologically or morally).[15] Thus God possesses freedom to do otherwise than he does while knowing with perfect adequacy which actions would yield the best results (in some

---

[12]Oord, *Nature of Love*, pp. 139-40. On foreknowledge, see the discussion later in this chapter.

[13]Alvin Plantinga, *Does God Have a Nature?* (Milwaukee: Marquette University Press, 1980).

[14]Moreover, it is helpful to keep in mind that with regard to God's loving action, moral obligation is often forfeited by human sin. God's love for humans is operating on the basis of grace. The canonical data frequently suggest that God maintains his love, compassion and mercy for creatures far beyond what is required or even reasonable and may also remove the same (cf. Ex 32–34; Hos 9:15), though he never does so arbitrarily. This dovetails with the nearly ubiquitous praise of God for his active goodness and love throughout the canon (Gen 24:27; Ps 98:3). Since many moralists contend that one may not be rightly praised or blamed for an action if one could not will otherwise, would not the axiological force of such praise be compromised if God could not will otherwise than he does? Compare Bruce R. Reichenbach, "Freedom, Justice, and Moral Responsibility," in *The Grace of God, the Will of Man: A Case for Arminianism*, ed. Clark H. Pinnock (Minneapolis: Bethany House, 1995), pp. 296-97; Richard Swinburne, *The Coherence of Theism* (Oxford: Clarendon, 1993), p. 147; Jerry L. Walls, "Why No Classical Theist, Let Alone Orthodox Christian, Should *Ever* Be a Compatibilist," *Philosophia Christi* 13, no. 1 (2011): 84, 87-88.

[15]Consider in this regard the view of David Baggett and Jerry Walls wherein God is the ultimate exemplar of the good and in this way God is *the* Good (without making God a universal; he is the particular exemplar par excellence; *Good God: The Theistic Foundations of Morality* [New York: Oxford University Press, 2011], p. 104). They contend that while God is essentially good, God retains libertarian freedom such that what he does is not determined by his goodness (without saying that he could do evil). This they refer to as "a version of voluntarism when it comes to moral obligations" (ibid., p. 37). Their "axiological theory (of moral goodness) is distinctly nonvoluntarist [rejecting Ockhamism], but" their "deontic theory (of moral obligation) is not.... Something can be morally good without being obligatory; moral duties, in contrast, are not voluntary, but required" (ibid., pp. 104-5). Accordingly, as shall be taken up with regard to divine self-limitation below, I do believe that God imposes "soft" moral obligations on himself by creating agents that possess significant freedom and by making promises.

situations various divine actions might yield equally good results).[16] As such, while God's character is love and he is always loving, the specific objects of God's love and the form and operation that love takes need not be determined by his essence.[17]

Whatever else is said about the correspondence between God's essence and love, one should not imply that love rules out the other divine characteristics that are prominent in the canon or vice versa, especially divine freedom. Concurrently, it is important to avoid asserting a false dichotomy between God's will and essence. Here there is mystery on which the canonical data investigated for this book appear to shed little light.[18]

Divine Perfection, Self-Sufficiency and Sympathy

The foreconditional-reciprocal model agrees with the transcendent-voluntarist and immanent-experientialist models that God is perfect. However, it departs from both models regarding the implications of divine perfection, since the foreconditional-reciprocal model is predicated on a canonical methodology that rejects an extracanonical way of eminence, on which both classic theism and process theism build in mutually exclusive directions. Indeed, the conflict between the two models manifests the fatal flaw in the way of eminence. Different theologians find different attributes and characteristics to be descriptive of perfection and/or defect.[19] For example, the transcendent-voluntarist model finds divine enjoyment of the world to be

---

[16]As shall be discussed below, the foreconditional-reciprocal model is not dependent on assent to divine foreknowledge, but for other biblical reasons I do affirm divine foreknowledge.

[17]However, I wonder whether what is revealed is sufficient to ground this or other conclusions regarding the precise nature of the interrelationship between God's will and essence as it relates to divine love, and I am reticent to place confidence in conclusions that are not grounded in divine revelation. I currently find the canonical data underdeterminative in this regard. I do not mean to imply, however, that such questions should not be asked and explored in ways that go beyond what is derivable from the canonical text. Yet, in my view, such theological extrapolations should be taken with a grain of salt.

[18]As such, I am not prepared to assent to the Thomistic identity of divine essence and existence since it seems to me that this *might* exclude significant divine freedom. Perhaps there is a coinherence of God's essence and his existence, including volition, in some manner. Possibilities abound and demand further, careful, canonical investigation.

[19]The *via negativa* (way of negation, i.e., apophatic theology) is likewise problematic, since one does not know with specificity which characteristics should be excluded, and thus runs the risk of excluding characteristics that seem inappropriate to God from our limited perspective but that God may possess analogically, or regarding which God is able to humble himself in order to experience in relation to the world.

defective, whereas the immanent-experientialist model contends that the lack of divine enjoyment of the world is a defect.[20]

In contrast to the immanent-experientialist model's conception of divine perfection as perfect adequacy within essential sympathetic relationship with the world, the foreconditional-reciprocal model agrees with the transcendent-voluntarist model that God is ontologically independent from the world as its Creator and self-sufficient. As such, God is complete without the world and has no need of anything. God is love and enjoys eternal intra-trinitarian love relationship, independent of any world. Further, God is wholly good and without moral fault, and is not becoming greater or lesser ontologically.

However, the foreconditional-reciprocal model departs from the transcendent-voluntarist conception of perfection and aseity by asserting that while God is self-sufficient in that he needs no world, God also takes enjoyment in the goodness of the world and displeasure in evil because he has voluntarily bound his own interests to the best interests of creatures.[21] In this way, God binds the quality of his own life to the course of creaturely history.[22] This is not due to any divine deficiency but results from God's overflowing love and willingness to absorb the profound cost to himself for the sake of love relationship with creatures. Yet God is not thereby passive; he exerts enormous power in providentially guiding and affecting, but not unilaterally determining, history toward his ultimate end. As Paul Gavrilyuk states, "God must be more than a Whiteheadian 'fellow-sufferer who under-

---

[20]See Charles Hartshorne, *Man's Vision of God and the Logic of Theism* (Hamden, CT: Archon, 1964), p. 163; Carl F. H. Henry, *God, Revelation, and Authority*, 6 vols. (Wheaton, IL: Crossway, 1999), 5:292.

[21]Vincent Brümmer contends that "the view of divine perfection which was put forward by Plato and was self-evident for a vast number of theologians in the Christian tradition, including Augustine and Nygren . . . turns God into a quietist who avoids vulnerability and suffering by renouncing all desires. Such a God could be infinitely beneficent toward us, but as we have argued at length, he cannot be the God of love" (*The Model of Love: A Study in Philosophical Theology* [Cambridge: Cambridge University Press, 1993], p. 227). As Jürgen Moltmann adds, "The justifiable denial that God is capable of suffering because of a deficiency of being may not lead to a denial that he is incapable of suffering out of the fullness of his being, i.e., his love" (*The Crucified God: The Cross of Christ as the Foundation and Criticism of Christian Theology*, trans. R. A. Wilson and John Bowden [New York: Harper & Row, 1974], p. 230).

[22]Compare Karl Barth's view that "God in His love elects another to fellowship with Himself. First and foremost this means that God makes a self-election in favour of this other. He ordains that He should not be entirely self-sufficient as He might be" (*CD* II/2, p. 10).

stands." A God who is merely a fellow-patient cannot help those who suffer."[23] Accordingly, "the Weeping One did not just stand at the tomb of Lazarus and continue weeping for all eternity, as some passibilists imagine. He has also raised Lazarus from the dead," and one day "God will wipe away every tear from the sufferers' eyes (Rev. 7:16), as he had wiped away the tears of Mary and Martha by raising Lazarus from the dead."[24]

In all this, the foreconditional-reciprocal model posits that God is interested in his creatures and can be affected by, and even the beneficiary of, human disposition and/or action. This requires a theo-ontology that allows for reciprocity (though not symmetry or equality) between God and creatures. Indeed, such a theo-ontology is hinted at by the intratrinitarian love relationship, three coeternal persons (centers of consciousness) in love relationship with one another who equal the one God (Jn 17:24). Moreover, since God loves others *and* himself as Trinity, the complementary nature of proper self-love *and* other-love is essential to the trinitarian conception itself.[25] However, the volitional, foreconditional and reciprocal aspects of divine love suggest that God's relationship with creatures is *not* essential to his being. Indeed, if divine love is conditional on human response and may be forfeited, it cannot be necessary. Rather, God freely enters into reciprocal relationship with those who willingly respond to his loving overtures (human response itself made possible by God's prior action). This supposes the bilateral freedom of God and humans, to which we now turn.

SIGNIFICANT FREEDOM OF GOD AND CREATURES

The foreconditional-reciprocal model of love suggests the ontological independence and significant freedom of God as well as the significant, albeit

---

[23]Paul L. Gavrilyuk, "God's Impossible Suffering in the Flesh: The Promise of Paradoxical Christology," in *Divine Impassibility and the Mystery of Human Suffering*, ed. James Keating and Thomas Joseph White (Grand Rapids: Eerdmans, 2009), p. 145.
[24]Ibid.
[25]Consider Jerry Walls's excellent and sustained reasoning for proper self-interest in light of "Trinitarian love" as "the deepest reality," over and against "the notion of altruism as ultimate sacrifice with no expectation of compensation.... At worst, the notion that such utter disinterest represents a higher or more admirable standard is pagan hubris" (*Heaven: The Logic of Eternal Joy* [New York: Oxford University Press, 2002], p. 191). See also Kathryn Tanner's view that the Trinity is a "paradigmatic" instance of a "community of mutual fulfillment in which the good of one becomes the good for all" (*Christ the Key* [New York: Cambridge University Press, 2010], p. 235). Compare ibid., p. 246.

limited, freedom of humans. As has been seen, Scripture consistently depicts God's freedom to act otherwise than he does, including as it relates to his love for creatures (the volitional aspect). Kevin Vanhoozer comments that "God is already love in himself," and "it is only thanks to a free act that God wills to relate in love to those who are not God."[26] Barth adds, "God does not owe us either our being, or in our being His love."[27]

God not only bestows his love on creatures but also gives each creature the significant freedom to reciprocate that love or refuse to do so. The evaluative and emotional aspects of divine love suggest that humans may act in ways that actually impact God, suggesting that he himself is not the only causal agent. The foreconditional and reciprocal aspects further assume that humans can (due to God's prevenient action) positively or negatively respond to God's loving overtures. This ability of humans to accept or reject divine love requires that the divine will is not unilaterally efficacious but that significantly free beings actually affect the course of history, often in ways that are not in accordance with God's ideal desires. That is, insofar as God's love is conditional and contingent on human response, human response must itself be contingent. In this way, God's logically and ontologically primary decision to create other beings is the necessary (but not sufficient) condition of the divine-human love relationship.

Human beings possess significant freedom and have exercised that freedom such that God's ideal will is not always done. God's ideal will refers to what would take place if all agents acted in perfect accordance with God's wishes. This is to be distinguished from God's effective will, which refers to God's will that has already taken into account all factors, including the wills of significantly free creatures.[28] As such, it includes not only the active

---

[26]Vanhoozer, *Remythologizing Theology*, p. 151. So John W. Cooper, *Panentheism, the Other God of the Philosophers* (Grand Rapids: Baker Academic, 2006), p. 328. Compare Robert Jenson's view that "the biblical God cannot be the object of knowledge that secures us against historical contingency. We do not so know God as thereby to make ourselves secure against his future; God always remains free with us" (*Systematic Theology* [New York: Oxford University Press, 1997], 1:210).

[27]*CD* II/1, p. 281. Michael Horton argues that "God is not free to decide whether he will be merciful and gracious," yet he further maintains an exclusivist perspective wherein God "is free to decide whether he will have mercy on some rather than others" and does, in fact, decide to have salvific mercy on only some (*The Christian Faith: A Systematic Theology for Pilgrims on the Way* [Grand Rapids: Zondervan, 2011], p. 267).

[28]In other words, it is what God evaluatively wills in accordance with the wider matrix of creaturely freedom. This distinction is similar to the Arminian distinction between antecedent and

divine will but also what might be called his permissive will, what God allows.[29] For instance, God did not want Adam and Eve to sin. However, while God's ideal will was that Adam and Eve not disobey him, God also desired the kind of reciprocal divine-human love relationship that is predicated on the significant freedom of both parties (see chapter four). God could not unilaterally effect both desires (because they were not compossible) and therefore permitted Adam and Eve to depart from his ideal will in favor of allowing significant freedom. Yet God's unfulfilled desires do not amount to ontological need, lack or deficiency but refer to his voluntary identification with the best interests of the world.[30]

To take another example, Scripture states that God was "pleased to crush" the Messiah (Is 53:10). At the same time, God has no pleasure in the death of anyone (Ezek 18:23, 32; 33:11). God did not sadistically delight in, or ideally desire, the crucifixion of his Son. He "does not afflict willingly" (Lam 3:32-33). Rather, it was God's "pleasure" or will in the wider context of the plan of salvation.[31] That is, because of his love for his creatures and because the death

---

consequent wills. I have elected not to use these terms in order to avoid unintended connotations, especially with regard to the operation of the divine will as it relates to providence (including regarding the theoretical order of the divine decrees). For a discussion of Arminius's view of the antecedent and consequent wills of God and their implications for divine sovereignty see Roger E. Olson, *Arminian Theology: Myths and Realities* (Downers Grove, IL: IVP Academic, 2006), p. 123. See also the discussion of what Arminius called the twofold love of God (for himself/justice and creatures) and the further distinction between God's "antecedent love [which] is for the salvation of all," and "after sin, his saving love [which] is consequently directed toward those who are in Christ through faith" (Keith D. Stanglin and Thomas H. McCall, *Jacob Arminius: Theologian of Grace* [New York: Oxford University Press, 2012], pp. 185-86). Compare Alvin Plantinga's distinction between weak and strong actualization in favor of the significant freedom of creatures *and* divine omnipotence and omnibenevolence (*The Nature of Necessity* [Oxford: Clarendon, 1974], pp. 172-73).

[29]On God's ideal and effective wills, see John C. Peckham, "Does God Always Get What He Wants? A Theocentric Approach to Divine Providence and Human Freedom," *AUSS* 52/2 (2014): 195-212; John C. Peckham, "Providence and God's Unfulfilled Desires," *Philosophia Christi* 15, no. 2 (2013): 453-62.

[30]God never desires anything that would make himself ontologically greater, since he has no ontological lack or need. Likewise, divine existence is in no way dependent on creaturely wills.

[31]Here it should be noted that God possesses the power to create other beings that then themselves possess the freedom and power to act in ways that he does not ideally will, such that what God "creates, as the effect of a truly transcendent causality, possesses its own being, and truly exists as other than God" (David Bentley Hart, "Impassibility as Transcendence: On the Infinite Innocence of God," in Keating and White, eds., *Divine Impassibility and the Mystery of Human Suffering*, p. 308). That is, in "the act of creation . . . God imparts to the creature its own dependent actuality" such that "they are able to impart actuality to potentialities proportionate to their powers" (ibid.). Indeed, though we cannot "describe the 'mechanism' by which he does" so (just

of his Son was the means of their redemption, God was "pleased to crush Him" (Is 53:10).[32] Ideally, there would have never been sin and thus no occasion for such redemptive suffering. As Stephen Post states, divine love "takes on the form of self-sacrifice out of necessity rather than preference due to the tolerance of human freedom."[33] The contrast between God's ideal and effective wills, then, is the result of a sinful, disordered world, which is itself the result of creaturely rebellion against God's ideal will. In the eschaton, God's ideal will shall perfectly correspond to God's effective will since all creaturely wills will be freely subjected to the perfect will of the omniscient (e.g., Ps 147:5; 1 Jn 3:20) and omnibenevolent God (e.g., Ps 100:5; 145:9).

While Scripture presents a robust picture of God's will and intervention in human affairs, the language related to the divine will and election suggests in numerous places that God's will is not unilaterally efficacious, that is, God's desires are sometimes unfulfilled.[34] For example, God "called, but no one answered," and he "spoke, but they did not listen. And they did evil in [his]

---

as we cannot explain *creatio ex nihilo*), "it is no more contradictory to say that God can create—out of the infinite wellspring of his own freedom—dependent freedoms that he does not determine, than it is to say that he can create—out of the wellspring of his being—dependent beings that are genuinely somehow other than God" (ibid., p. 314). Thus God's permissive will may function in accordance with wide principles (put in effect ontologically at creation) of the extent of freedom afforded to creaturely agents. However, it is well beyond the scope of this work to delve more deeply into this issue of divine providence. Consider, for a brief overview of these issues of divine providence, Fernando Canale, "Doctrine of God," in *Handbook of Seventh-day Adventist Theology*, ed. Raoul Dederen (Hagerstown, MD: Review and Herald, 2000), pp. 118-20. Compare Randall G. Basinger, "Exhaustive Divine Sovereignty: A Practical Critique," in Pinnock, ed., *The Grace of God, the Will of Man*, pp. 191-205; Dennis W. Jowers, ed., *Four Views on Divine Providence* (Grand Rapids: Zondervan, 2011).

[32]In this way, strong statements of divine sovereignty may be reconciled with statements that assert that God's will is unfulfilled. That God does "whatever he pleases" does not mean that everything that happens pleases God or is unilaterally determined by his will (Ps 115:3; 135:6; cf. Job 23:13). Rather, what occurs is what God allows and/or wills in the greater interest of the kind of real, relational love that requires creaturely freedom.

[33]Stephen G. Post, *A Theory of Agape: On the Meaning of Christian Love* (Lewisburg, PA: Bucknell University Press, 1990), p. 33.

[34]Significantly, the OT and NT usage of the primary terms of volition, the חפץ, θέλω and βούλομαι word groups, suggests that these word groups do not necessarily refer to a unilaterally efficacious will, as is sometimes claimed. חפץ often refers to divine desire and delight, respectively, as well as what is wanted or willed (whether fulfilled or unfulfilled). The θέλω word group relates to what is willed, desired, wanted, taken pleasure in or even liked. It may be related to the fulfilled or unfulfilled wish of its agent. The βούλομαι word group similarly relates to what is wanted, desired, willed, intended and/or planned, whether of volition or inclination, often with the connotation of deliberation. Thus both may be used of God's fulfilled or unfulfilled will (Mt 23:37; Lk 7:30; 13:34; cf. 2 Pet 3:9; 1 Tim 2:4). See John C. Peckham, *The Concept of Divine Love in the Context of the God-World Relationship* (New York: Peter Lang, 2014), pp. 236-41, 372-78.

sight And chose that in which [he] did not delight [חפץ]" (Is 66:4; compare Is 65:12; Jer 19:5). Further, the rejection of God's will is explicit when the "Pharisees and the lawyers rejected God's purpose [βουλή] for themselves, not having been baptized by John" (Lk 7:30; compare Mk 7:24). Most poignantly, Jesus laments, "Jerusalem, Jerusalem, who kills the prophets and stones those who are sent to her! How often I wanted [θέλω] to gather your children together, the way a hen gathers her chicks under her wings, and you were unwilling [θέλω]" (Mt 23:37; compare Lk 13:34; Jn 5:40; Deut 5:29; Ezek 3:7).[35] This echoes God's lament in Psalm 81:11-14: God called his people,

> But My people did not listen to My voice,
> And Israel did not obey Me.
> So I gave them over to the stubbornness of their heart,
> To walk in their own devices.
> Oh that My people would listen to Me,
> That Israel would walk in My ways!
> I would quickly subdue their enemies
> And turn My hand against their adversaries.

Thus, insofar as humans possess the ability to reject God's ideal will, God may have unfulfilled desires (compare Is 30:9, 15-19; Lam 3:32-33).

This brings us to perhaps the most crucial point in contrast to divine determinism. The determinist view maintains that "God's holy will is accomplished in love." It is an act of God's will "requiring no creaturely element as a cooperating cause." As such, there is "no possibility that . . . opposition on the part of the creature will somehow constitute a genuine threat to the consecrating will of God."[36] Yet God has no pleasure in the death of the wicked (Ezek 18:23, 32; 33:11; compare Is 30:18). He wills (βούλομαι) that none would perish (2 Pet 3:9) and "desires [θέλω] all men to be saved" (1 Tim 2:4; compare 1 Tim 2:6; Tit 2:11).[37] However, not all will be saved, but God

---

[35]By the same verb (θέλω) Christ's will is directly opposed by the will of humans. Notice how bilateral significant freedom and passibility dovetail in this instance of human rejection of God's love.
[36]John B. Webster, "The Holiness and Love of God," *SJT* 57, no. 3 (2004): 264, 266.
[37]It is sometimes argued regarding texts such as 2 Pet 3:9 and 1 Tim 2:4 that the terms *anyone* and *all* may simply be referring to the addressees of the letter. Compare Richard Bauckham, *2 Peter, Jude*, WBC 50 (Dallas: Word, 2002), p. 313; Douglas J. Moo, *2 Peter and Jude* (Grand Rapids: Zondervan, 1996), p. 188. Thomas Schreiner, while adopting determinism, recognizes that such a restriction is unsatisfactory, saying: "By extension we should understand 2 Pet 3:9 in the same way as Ezek 18:32. It refers to God's desire that everyone without exception be saved"

eventually gives people over to their persistent desires (e.g., Jn 3:18; Rom 1:24, 26, 28; 2:4-12; 1 Jn 2:17).[38] If God desires to save everyone and yet not every person will be saved, God's ideal will does not always come to pass.

Some exclusivist determinists deal with this issue by distinguishing between God's "desired will" and "decretive will" so that "God genuinely desires in one sense that all will be saved," while at the same time "he has not ultimately decreed that all will be saved."[39] In this view, God (in some sense) desires that all be saved but nevertheless decrees solely on the basis of his unilaterally efficacious will that some will be damned. However, this raises an insoluble difficulty. If God's will is unilaterally efficacious *and* God wants to save everyone, why does he not do so? According to the determinist perspective of compatibilism, God's unilateral determination of all events and human freedom are compatible.[40] It should follow from this that "God could

---

(1, 2 Peter, Jude, NAC 37 [Nashville: B&H, 2007], p. 382). Moreover, the wider canonical theology, including Ezek 18:32, suggests that this indeed refers to a desire for universal salvation, against determinism. So Anton Vögtle, *Der Judasbrief, der 2. Petrusbrief* (Düsseldorf: Benziger Verlag, 1994), pp. 231-32; Eric Fuchs and Pierre Reymond, *La deuxième Épitre de Saint Pierre. L'épitre de Saint Jude* (Neuchâtel, Switzerland: Delachaux & Niestlé, 1980), pp. 115-16. Compare D. Müller, "θελω," *NIDNTT* 3:1020; Peter H. Davids, *The Letters of 2 Peter and Jude*, PNTC (Grand Rapids: Eerdmans, 2006), p. 281.

[38] Universalism is excluded by the view that humans can (and some will) finally reject God's love, which supports the significant canonical material that speaks of those who are finally lost. See I. Howard Marshall, "The New Testament Does Not Teach Universal Salvation," in *Universal Salvation? The Current Debate*, ed. Robin A. Parry and Christopher H. Partridge (Grand Rapids: Eerdmans, 2003), pp. 55-76. See the discussion of various forms of universalism in chap. 7 (above).

[39] Schreiner, *1, 2 Peter, Jude*, pp. 381-82. For a further defense of this view of double predestination see Thomas R. Schreiner and Bruce A. Ware, eds., *Still Sovereign* (Grand Rapids: Baker, 2000), especially John Piper's essay, "Are There Two Wills in God?" This is akin to Luther's view of God's "hidden" will, which created a dilemma that he could not resolve: "If I could by any means understand how this same God, who makes such a show of wrath and unrighteousness, can yet be merciful and just, there would be no need for faith" (*The Bondage of the Will*, trans. O. R. Johnston [Grand Rapids: Baker, 2003], p. 204). In my view, this is a dogmatic assumption that goes against the preponderance of canonical evidence and is beholden to a prior commitment to the idea that salvation must be the result of unconditional election. See John C. Peckham, "An Investigation of Luther's View of the Bondage of the Will with Implications for Soteriology and Theodicy," *JATS* 18, no. 2 (2007): 274-304.

[40] However, David Bentley Hart argues that "freedom lies not in an action's logical conditions, but in the action itself; and if an action is causally necessitated or infallibly predetermined, its indeterminacy with regard to its proximate cause in no way makes it free" ("Impassibility as Transcendence," p. 309). David Baggett and Jerry Walls, accordingly, consider the (exclusivist) compatibilist account of divine love to rely on euphemistic, evasive and misleading use of language, stating, "It's only the elect who can actually receive salvation, so no offer of salvation to the non-elect is a genuine offer.... To describe such an empty offer as a genuine one is worse than euphemistic" (*Good God*, p. 72). See the discussion in ibid., pp. 67-73.

have created a world in which all persons freely did only the good at all times."⁴¹ Indeed, God ought to be able to determine every individual "to freely accept his love and be saved."⁴² From this vantage point, it seems that God must not really want to save everyone after all. As I. Howard Marshall comments, proposing that God's will is always done "in such deterministic terms is inconsistent with the freedom which the Bible itself assigns to God's children, and it wreaks havoc upon the biblical idea of the personal relationship which exists between God and his children."⁴³

The foreconditional-reciprocal model's distinction between God's ideal and effective will, conversely, requires no position that God's revealed will is different from his "hidden" will, while also recognizing that God's will is neither simple nor monolithic. God, in accordance with his universal love, genuinely wants to save those who are finally lost, but they were not willing (Is 66:4; Mt 23:37; Lk 13:34). In this way, the canonical analysis comes to the conclusion, shared by many scholars, that the "fact that all are not saved can be attributed to the stubbornness of the human will rather than to the weakness of the divine intent."⁴⁴ God does not irresistibly determine humans to be saved because doing so would undercut another element of his ideal will, the existence of reciprocal love relationship, which itself requires the responsive love of significantly free beings.⁴⁵

DIVINE CONSTANCY AND PASSIBILITY

In accordance with bilateral significant freedom and divine emotionality, the foreconditional-reciprocal model of divine love suggests that God is affected by the dispositions and/or actions of his creatures and therefore not impas-

---

⁴¹Walls, "Why No Classical Theist," p. 82.
⁴²Ibid., p. 96. "To put the point most bluntly, if compatibilism is true, it is all but impossible, in the actual world, to maintain the perfect goodness of God, and altogether impossible to do so if orthodox Christianity is true" (ibid., p. 80). Walls adds that it is surpassingly evil and "perverse if a being determines a being to perform evil actions and then holds him accountable, and punishes him for those actions" (ibid., p. 88). This echoes Antony Flew's contention: "Certainly it would be monstrous to suggest that anyone, however truly responsible in the eyes of men, could fairly be called to account and punished by the God who had rigged his every move" ("Divine Omnipotence and Human Freedom," in *New Essays in Philosophical Theology*, ed. Antony Flew and Alasdair C. MacIntyre [New York: Macmillan, 1964], p. 163).
⁴³I. Howard Marshall, *Epistles of John*, p. 245.
⁴⁴Thomas D. Lea and Hayne P. Griffin Jr., *1, 2 Timothy, Titus*, NAC 34 (Nashville: B&H, 2001), p. 89.
⁴⁵"God never imposes His love by overriding human will" (Craig Blomberg, *Matthew*, NAC 22 [Nashville: B&H, 2001], p. 350).

sible. If God feels emotions, as many theologians agree, *and* God does not unilaterally determine the course of history, God is passible insofar as his emotions are responsive to what he did not unilaterally will.[46] Indeed, if the volitional aspect of love requires significant freedom (as argued in chapter four), then love must be freely given and received but cannot be taken. Thus, one who receives love must be passible (capable of being affected) at least in this basic sense.[47] Accordingly, since divine evaluation consists of appraisal of the actual state of its object(s), and divine emotions are consistently depicted as prompted by world occurrences, the evaluative and emotional aspects of divine love entail that God is impacted by the free actions of creatures. That is, insofar as divine love is both evaluative and responsively emotional, a canonical theo-ontology must recognize that God is capable of emotional affection, enjoyment and the recognition and appreciation of value in the world.[48] John Stott comments that love "is inevitably vulnerable to pain, since it exposes itself to the possibility of rejection and insult."[49] He

---

[46]As seen previously, those who maintain that God's love is unaffected and nonevaluative contend that instances of emotion and/or delight are simply the result of God's causally determinative will and not prompted by the object(s) as such. See Morris, *Testaments of Love*, p. 93. Yet this does not exclude a qualified kind of divine emotions. As Henry notes, "The world does not alter God ontologically," but "that is hardly to say that God is indifferent to the created universe. . . . Nor does God's immutability dwarf the fact that the incarnation of the Logos conjoins human nature enduringly to the Son of God" (*God, Revelation, and Authority*, 5:292). Yet, although Henry allows that God's "love is wounded" at Israel's disobedience, God is the one who sovereignly decreed that disobedience such that passibility of the kind that includes God being affected by what he does not causally determine is excluded (ibid., 6:345). Compare Carson, *Difficult Doctrine of the Love of God*, pp. 59-60.

[47]This may suggest intratrinitarian (analogical) passibility, as might also be suggested by the apparent passibility manifest in the Father's evaluative delight in the incarnate Son (Mt 3:17; Jn 10:17). However, it is beyond the scope of this work to take on these wider trinitarian issues, especially the implications this might hold with regard to the complex debates over conceptions of the economic and immanent Trinity. Insofar as one finds current understanding of the canonical data to be insufficient, such issues should be approached nondogmatically since there is considerable mystery regarding intratrinitarian relationality.

[48]Many scholars have come to reject the notion of divine impassibility, so much so that Ronald Goetz has stated that "the rejection of the ancient doctrine of divine impassibility has become theological commonplace" ("The Suffering God: The Rise of a New Orthodoxy," *Christian Century* 103, no. 13 [1986]: 385). On the other hand, Rob Lister notes an ongoing "miniature resurgence" of "impassibilism" (*God Is Impassible and Impassioned: Toward a Theology of Divine Emotion* [Wheaton, IL: Crossway, 2013], p. 148). Compare Paul Gavrilyuk, *The Suffering of the Impassible God: The Dialectics of Patristic Thought* (Oxford: Oxford University Press, 2004); Keating and White, eds., *Divine Impassibility and the Mystery of Human Suffering*. See also the discussion in chap. 6 (above).

[49]John R. W. Stott, *The Cross of Christ* (Downers Grove, IL: InterVarsity Press, 2006), p. 323.

goes on: "In the real world of pain, how could one worship a God who was immune to it?"[50]

However, whereas God does love creatures in such a way that they affect his experience, his passibility in relation to the world is not essential to him (as in many passibilist conceptions), since God freely chose to create a world that affects him.[51] That is, God is not passible to this (or any) world by nature but by his choice to condescend by creating a world to which he has bound his own interests.[52] Thus divine passibility as understood in the foreconditional-reciprocal model does not mean that God is ontologically vulnerable or could be overpowered. Rather, God is the transcendent, omnipotent and omniscient Creator over all, who willingly subjects himself to experiences impacted by other beings in love (see chapter six and the discussion of omnipotence and omniscience below).[53]

---

[50]Ibid., p. 326.

[51]The foreconditional-reciprocal model also departs from the view of some passibilists that "Christ's death on the cross acts . . . out of time back into the divine eternity" such that the "pain of the cross determines the inner life of the triune God from eternity to eternity" on the basis of Rahner's rule that the "economic Trinity *is* the immanent Trinity" (Moltmann, *Trinity and the Kingdom*, pp. 159-61). Jung Young Lee contends that the "eternal Cross" represents "the inner experiences of divine love" such that Christ's death on the cross points to "the eternal suffering and death of God on the eternal cross" (*God Suffers For Us: A Systematic Inquiry into a Concept of Divine Passibility* [The Hague: Martinus Nijhoff, 1974], p. 56). However, I agree with Gavrilyuk that "perpetual divine suffering" only serves to "eternalize evil" while "the destructive nature of suffering is trivialized and falsely romanticized" ("God's Impassible Suffering," p. 145). Christ suffered on the cross once and for all historically (Heb 10:10), and the Father and Spirit also suffered in their own fashion as they witnessed the suffering of Christ. It is not, however, essential to God's nature to suffer the grief and agony of the cross (or any negative emotions at all), but he willingly took on himself those experiences in order to conquer and eradicate them. This understanding rejects the utter atemporality of God and adopts the canonical view that God may experience temporal events in a fashion analogous but not univocal to that of human experience. See the brief discussion of God and time further below.

[52]Karl Barth may intend to assert something like this distinction between God being necessarily passible to this (or any) world and God's choice to open himself up to others, stating, "In giving Himself to this act He ordained the surrender of something, i.e. of His own impassibility [*Unangerührtheit*] in the face of the whole world" (*CD* II/2, p. 163). God "could have remained satisfied with Himself and with the impassible [*unangerührten*, i.e., unmoved] glory and blessedness of His own inner life. But He did not do so" (ibid., p. 166). Bruce McCormack notes that *unangerührten*, translated "impassible" above, is "more literally" translated as "'unmoved'" ("Divine Impassibility or Simply Divine Constancy? Implications of Karl Barth's Later Christology for Debates over Impassibility," in Keating and White, eds., *Divine Impassibility and the Mystery of Human Suffering*, p. 155).

[53]*Transcendence* here refers to God's ontological independence from creaturely limitations as the all-powerful Creator of all. However, God is also immanent in the world by choice, and as seen in the incarnation, God can even willingly humble and subject himself to creaturely limitations.

Those who assert divine impassibility of the kind that supposes that God cannot be affected by the world often appeal to passages such as Mal 3:6, "For I, the LORD, do not change; therefore you, O sons of Jacob, are not consumed."[54] However, attention to the immediate and wider context of this passage (and others like it) suggests that it does not assert immutability in the sense that God cannot experience history and respond to it but, rather, refers to God's changelessness of character.[55] That God does not change is presented here as a characteristic that preserves Israel from immediate judgment and is, as such, already in the context of reciprocal relationship. The wider context of Malachi repeatedly depicts give-and-take relationality; human actions directly affect God's responsive actions.[56]

With regard to the wider canon, William Klassen points out that "a God who does not care whether people respond is hardly the God portrayed in Hosea or in the New Testament image of Jesus weeping over Jerusalem."[57] As discussed in chapter six, the interpretive maneuver of explaining such strongly emotive language of God as merely anthropopathic does not hold up to close scrutiny and lacks a consistent and compelling *canonical* rationale for determining which biblical data accurately depict God's nature and which canonical data are to be dismissed as merely accommodative language.[58] On the contrary, since humans were created in the image of

---

[54]As discussed in chap. 6 (above), there are no biblical texts or passages that assert divine impassibility. It is a corollary of a particular conception of divine immutability and self-sufficiency. As Trent Pomplun writes, "Satisfied that God was immutable (Mal. 3:6) and invariable (Jas 1:17), theologians took it for granted that the Most High was impervious to any pathos external to his own nature" ("Impassibility in St. Hilary of Poitiers's *De Trinitate*," in Keating and White, eds., *Divine Impassibility and the Mystery of Human Suffering*, p. 187).

[55]See Bruce A. Ware, "An Evangelical Reexamination of the Doctrine of the Immutability of God," (PhD diss., Fuller Theological Seminary, 1984), pp. 431-46. Compare Robert B. Chisholm Jr., "Does God 'Change His Mind'?" *BSac* 152, no. 608 (2007).

[56]Likewise, 1 Sam 15:29 and Num 23:19 are frequently referred to in order to claim that divine relenting (נחם) is merely metaphorical or the term is "anthropopathic" and thus "from man's limited, earthly, finite perspective it only appears that God's purposes have changed" (Wilson, "נחם," *TWOT*, p. 571). Yet twice elsewhere in 1 Sam 15 God is said to נחם. As such, the statements in 1 Sam 15:29 and Num 23:19 should not be taken as universal statements but as statements with regard to the constancy of God's character and the reliability of his promises. See the discussion in chap. 6 (above). See also John C. Peckham, "The Passible Potter and the Contingent Clay: A Theological Study of Jeremiah 18:1-10," *JATS* 18, no. 1 (2007): 130-50.

[57]William Klassen, "Love in the NT and Early Jewish Literature," *ABD* 4:385.

[58]However, as noted in chap. 6 (above), hermeneutical approaches do exist that provide a rationale for interpreting much or all of the biblical language of divine emotion as anthropopathic while also recognizing divine passibility. Compare Eberhard Jüngel, *God as the Mystery of the*

God (Gen 1:26-27), Vanhoozer suggests that "perhaps the Bible's depiction of divine suffering is less a matter of anthropopathic projection than it is a case of human suffering being theopathic (God-like)," such that, in an analogical rather than univocal sense, "human capacities to know, will, and love are themselves theomorphic."[59]

The consistent witness of Scripture presents God as active and reactive, calling out to human beings and responding to them, affecting the world and being affected by it, pleading with humans to turn to him and being entreated to mercy, calling for human repentance and himself relenting in accordance with human action, showing undeserved mercy and feeling compassion prompted by the actual state of affairs, bestowing love foreconditionally and enjoying love that is reciprocated by his people. The divine compassion exhibited throughout Scripture presents God as affected and thus passible (in the sense qualified here and in chapter six).[60] Douglas Stuart comments, "The idea that God would not shift direction or adjust his plans in response to prayer is foreign to the Bible but unfortunately at home with some forms of deterministic theology."[61] Thus, in contrast to the transcendent-voluntarist model, the foreconditional-reciprocal model's re-

---

World (Grand Rapids: Eerdmans, 1983), pp. 258, 373. Indeed, Jüngel maintains, on the basis of "the word of the cross," that "absoluteness," "apathy" and "immutability" are "unsuitable axioms for the Christian concept of God" (ibid., p. 373). Compare McCormack, "Divine Impassibility or Simply Divine Constancy?"; T. F. Torrance, *The Christian Doctrine of God: One Being Three Persons* (New York: T & T Clark, 2001), pp. 239, 254.

[59]Vanhoozer, *Remythologizing Theology*, pp. 64, 77-78. Moisés Silva adds: "Our human qualities are themselves but a reflection of God's person and attributes" (*God, Language, and Scripture: Reading the Bible in the Light of General Linguistics* [Grand Rapids: Zondervan, 1990], p. 22). On the other hand, A. B. Caneday cautions: "The fallacy is to forget that we are analogues of God and to regard ourselves as the fundamental reference point for ascriptions concerning God" ("Veiled Glory? God's Self-Revelation in Human Likeness—A Biblical Theology of God's Anthropomorphic Self-Disclosure," in *Beyond the Bounds: Open Theism and the Undermining of Biblical Christianity*, ed. John Piper, Justin Taylor and Paul Kjoss Helseth [Wheaton, IL: Crossway, 2003], p. 153).

[60]A similar case can be made with regard to divine passion/jealousy and many other divine emotions depicted throughout the canon (see chap. 6 above).

[61]Douglas Stuart, *Exodus*, NAC 2 (Nashville: B&H, 2006), p. 672. The impassibility advocated by David Bentley Hart, however, rejects determinism, maintaining that God is impassible in that he utterly transcends the cause and effect of the world order and, as such, also does not determine the events of the world. In his view, "divine *apatheia* is not merely the opposite of passibility; it is God's transcendence of the very distinction between the responsive and unresponsive" as "not situated within any kind of ontic continuum with the creature" such that he transcends "even the traditional metaphysical demarcations between the transcendent and the immanent" ("Impassibility as Transcendence," pp. 301-2, 307).

jection of impassibility suggests that God may be affected by the state of the affairs of the world, which he does not causally determine. Thus God is not immune to spatio-temporal activity. As Walter Brueggemann states, the "immutable God" of "scholastic theology" that maintains God's utter imperviousness to being affected by the world "stands in deep tension with the biblical presentation of God."[62]

At the same time, a proper concept of divine immutability may be affirmed if by that one means (1) that ontologically God is not becoming greater or lesser and (2) that God's character of love is constant such that God does not break his promises and always acts in the most loving way possible.[63] As Kenneth Matthews puts it, God is "incomparably affected by, even pained by, the sinner's rebellion. Acknowledging the possibility (emotions) of God does not diminish the immutability of his promissory purposes."[64] Divine passibility as suggested by the foreconditional-reciprocal model, then, does not deny divine immutability (understood as divine constancy) but does conflict with any conception of immutability that rules out the ability of God to engage the world in genuinely reciprocal relationship (that is, one with bilateral, significant freedom).[65]

However, the passibility depicted in Scripture departs from many of the ontological tenets adopted by recent and contemporary passibilists. Scripture treats both divine passible emotion *and* volition as complementary aspects of divine love. This stands in stark contrast to the view of Charles Harts-

---

[62]Walter Brueggemann, "The Book of Exodus," *NIB* 1:932. Gene M. Tucker adds that God is "both affected and determined by human actions, if only in response. This God is by no means immutable" in the Aristotelian sense ("The Book of Isaiah 1-39," *NIB* 6:161). Compare Terence E. Fretheim, *The Suffering of God: An Old Testament Perspective* (Philadelphia: Fortress, 1984); Abraham Heschel, *The Prophets* (New York: Perennial, 2001), pp. 285-357.

[63]A number of evangelicals hold to a qualified kind of immutability that breaks from the Thomistic conception of God as pure act. Thus Bruce Ware contends that God is "relationally mutable" such that God may "'change' in relation to" human action "in ways called forth by his immutable character and promise" (*God's Greater Glory* [Wheaton, IL: Crossway, 2004], p. 28). In keeping with Ware's view, Rob Lister states, "God as *actus purus* (or pure actuality), while seemingly guaranteeing that God is never passive, also ensures that God is never, properly speaking, responsive either" (*God Is Impassible and Impassioned*, p. 157).

[64]Kenneth A. Mathews, *Genesis 1-11:26*, NAC 1A (Nashville: B&H, 1995), p. 344.

[65]See Swinburne, *Coherence of Theism*, pp. 219-23. For classic critiques of the traditional doctrine of immutability see further Norman Kretzmann, "Omniscience and Immutability," *Journal of Philosophy* 63 (1966): 409-21; Nicholas Wolterstorff, "God Everlasting," in *Contemporary Philosophy of Religion*, ed. Stephen M. Cahn and David Shatz (New York: Oxford University Press, 1982), pp. 77-98.

horne, wherein divine love is purely passive and experiential "sensation" or "experience which is neither thought nor *volition*, neither meaning nor action, but qualitative feeling."[66] In the foreconditional-reciprocal model, conversely, God is passible but not passive. Divine volition is always operative and active, though the precise interrelationship of divine volition and emotion is not entirely clear. God voluntarily and evaluatively identifies with the *best* interests of creatures and exerts enormous power in providentially guiding and affecting, but not unilaterally determining, history toward his ultimate end.[67] God possesses the power to overrule all other wills but has chosen not to do so (see the discussion below). In this way, he need not be affected by creatures.

However, that God takes upon himself the joys and sufferings of the world (evaluatively and volitionally but not essentially) manifests his greatness in a way that expands divine majesty rather than reducing it. The one who is incapable of empathy is not a greater individual but an impoverished figure. God shoulders all the pain and suffering of the world without being overwhelmed by it, even unto the cross. Thus, whereas the transcendent-voluntarist model posits that God cannot be affected by others and the immanent-experientialist model posits that God cannot *not* be affected by others, the canonical model of divine love suggests that God is affected by others because he voluntarily opens himself up to others by creating and bestowing significant freedom on them, while at the same time maintaining ontological independence from the world.

DIVINE OMNIPOTENCE, OMNISCIENCE, SELF-LIMITATION AND THEODICY

If God grants bilateral significant freedom and is affected by human response, then it follows that he does not use his power to effect his will

---

[66]Hartshorne, *Man's Vision of God*, p. 199. Indeed, Hartshorne contends that God *immediately* feels all the feelings of the world (ibid., p. 163). However, Henry Simoni-Wastila questions whether universal immediate feeling is in fact possible. For instance, how could God sympathize with the feelings of temporary life and finitude when the divine life is eternal? Moreover, "The idea of God being able to fully appreciate ignorance seems categorically impossible" ("Is Divine Relativity Possible? Charles Hartshorne on God's Sympathy with the World," *Process Studies* 28, nos. 1-2 [1999]: 99).

[67]Recall that divine love is evaluative rather than essentially indiscriminate such that God does not delight in the "delight" of the sadist but despises it.

omnicausally. God is omnipotent (Jer 32:17; Rev 19:6); he possesses the power to do anything (excluding, of course, logical or semantic absurdity).[68] However, the possession of all power (omnipotence) does not require the exercise of all power (omnicausality). God, being omnipotent, freely grants power to other agents whose choices he does not unilaterally determine. In doing so, God has voluntarily limited himself by bestowing significant freedom on other beings, thus creating the possibility of reciprocal love relationship. Divine self-limitation is apparent in that God makes promises and invariably keeps them. That is, since God would never break a promise, his engagement with the world in a way that includes promise-making entails limits on divine action.[69] As Terence Fretheim states: "For God to promise never to do something again, and to be faithful to that promise, entails self-limitation regarding the exercise of divine freedom and power."[70] Such divine self-limitation in no way limits God's power itself, or otherwise restricts God ontologically, but merely limits the avenues, applications and uses of his power insofar as he voluntarily keeps his word.[71]

---

[68]On the semantic and logical challenges to omnipotence and why they do not hold up to scrutiny, see Swinburne, *Coherence of Theism*, pp. 151-66; P. T. Geach, "Omnipotence," in Cahn and Shatz, eds., *Contemporary Philosophy of Religion*. Barth once stated: "Loyally binding Himself to this work [of 'creation, reconciliation and redemption'] He does not cease to be omnipotent in Himself as well as in this work" (*CD* II/1, p. 527). McCormack, however, finds these to be part of the "residue of classical metaphysics" that "had to be eliminated," particularly the "speaking of a surplus of power which passes beyond the limits of what God actually willed to do" (McCormack, "Actuality of God," p. 236).

[69]Michael Horton comments that God "has bound himself to us . . . by a free decision to enter into covenant with us" such that "God is not free to act contrary to such covenantal guarantees" (*Lord and Servant: A Covenant Christology* [Louisville: Westminster John Knox, 2005], p. 33). Barth affirms a more profound kind of divine self-limitation in keeping with his view of God's eternal act of self-determination, saying, "God has limited Himself to be this God and no other" (*CD* II/1, p. 518). "God has bound and still binds Himself to us" as the one who is able to do so "because primarily He is not bound" (ibid., p. 527). On McCormack's reading of Barth: "In that God chooses to be God for us in Christ, he is giving himself the being he will have for all eternity" (McCormack, "Election and the Trinity: Theses in Response to George Hunsinger," in *Trinity and Election in Contemporary Theology*, ed. Michael T. Dempsey [Grand Rapids: Eerdmans, 2011], p. 135). Paul Molnar sees Barth's view of God binding himself to us as "an expression of divine freedom and not a curtailment of it" ("The Trinity, Election, and God's Ontological Freedom: A Response to Kevin W. Hector," in *Trinity and Election in Contemporary Theology*, p. 47). Compare *CD* II/1, pp. 526-27.

[70]Terence E. Fretheim, "The Book of Genesis," *NIB* 1:396. On divine self-limitation see further Jack W. Cottrell, "The Nature of the Divine Sovereignty," in Pinnock, ed., *The Grace of God, the Will of Man*, pp. 107-10; Olson, *Arminian Theology*, pp. 123-24.

[71]This is what I have called a soft obligation (chap. 3 above), which refers to a kind of "obligation" where the agent is ontologically free to will otherwise yet morally obligated to respond, in dis-

Moreover, the interactive responsiveness of divine love in relation to the world suggests that God truly (though analogically) experiences the events of history, such that he might be thought of as analogically temporal, experiencing history but also transcending it as Creator (compare Ps 90:2; 102:25-27; 103:15-17).[72] However, that God has bestowed significant freedom on his creatures does not require the rejection of divine foreknowledge, as is supposed in open theism.[73] Although the foreconditional-reciprocal model of divine love itself does not require it, I believe exhaustive divine foreknowledge best accounts for the data regarding divine love and election, especially in light of Rom 8:28-30.[74] The foreconditional-

---

tinction from a hard obligation, which refers to some kind of compulsion (internal or external). As Katharine Sakenfeld puts it with regard to חסד, "because the person is acting faithfully within a relationship initiated by God there is a clear sense that God should exercise responsible care for that person. God is free not to act on the person's behalf; he alone is powerful, so there is no recourse if he does not act" (*The Meaning of Hesed in the Hebrew Bible: A New Inquiry* [Missoula, MT: Scholars Press, 1978], p. 107).

[72]The debate regarding the relationship of God and time is ongoing, and the complexity of the issues cannot be addressed in this brief treatment. Suffice it to say that the canonical material appears to contradict any notion of divine timelessness that renders God entirely atemporal, that is, immune or impervious to entering into and experiencing the history of the world. For an introduction to prominent views on God and time see Gregory E. Ganssle, ed., *God & Time: Four Views* (Downers Grove, IL: InterVarsity Press, 2001). For a brief but excellent discussion of the historicity of God and foreknowledge in relation to free will see Canale, "Doctrine of God." For a more extended critique of timelessness and one view of God's historicity and analogical temporality see Fernando Canale, *A Criticism of Theological Reason: Time and Timelessness as Primordial Presuppositions* (Berrien Springs, MI: Andrews University Press, 1987). Compare William Lane Craig, *Time and Eternity: Exploring God's Relationship to Time* (Wheaton, IL: Crossway, 2001). Consider also Robert Jenson's emphasis on narrativity leading to a concept of God's "eternity" that is "not immunity to time" (*Systematic Theology*, 1:210) and McCormack's actualist reading of Barth, by which he "tease[s] out of his mature Christology" a "postmetaphysical doctrine" that Barth "never elaborated directly" wherein he claims the timelessness and impassibility of classical metaphysics are coherently overcome and "rendered completely untenable," substituting "the living God of the Bible for a timeless, impassible deity" (McCormack, "Actuality of God," pp. 240, 222). In contrast, consider Paul Helm's Calvinist and David Bentley Hart's Eastern Orthodox depictions of their respective views, more akin to traditional classical metaphysics in this regard. See David Bentley Hart, *The Beauty of the Infinite* (Grand Rapids: Eerdmans, 2003), especially pp. 159-67; Paul Helm, "Classical Calvinist Doctrine of God," in *Perspectives on the Doctrine of God: Four Views* (Nashville: B&H Academic, 2008), pp. 5-52.

[73]For an introduction to the ongoing contemporary debate on foreknowledge and free will see James K. Beilby and Paul R. Eddy, eds., *Divine Foreknowledge: Four Views* (Downers Grove, IL: InterVarsity Press, 2001). Compare Robert Kane, ed., *The Oxford Handbook of Free Will*, 2nd ed. (Oxford: Oxford University Press, 2011).

[74]Notice the priority of divine foreknowledge to divine "predestination" as described in Rom 8:28-30 and strongly implied elsewhere (cf. 1 Pet 1:1-2). See, in this regard, Canale, "Doctrine of God," pp. 113-15. Compare William G. MacDonald, "The Biblical Doctrine of Election," in Pinnock, ed., *The Grace of God, the Will of Man*, p. 226.

reciprocal model of love suggests that divine omniscience (1 Jn 3:20), however it functions, is neither identical with, nor the unilateral result of, the divine will.[75] At the same time, the divine will remains logically and ontologically prior to all other wills since God's will is the necessary condition of all other agencies.

Yet why would God choose to limit himself in order to bestow significant freedom on creatures? This dovetails with the question of theodicy: if God is good, all-powerful and all-knowing, and hates evil, why is there evil in the world? Adequate treatment of this question is far beyond the scope of this book, and I do not pretend to do justice to the magnitude of the issue of theodicy, or the various perspectives on it, by the following excursus. However, I do believe that the outline of theodicy suggested in accordance with the foreconditional-reciprocal model has considerable advantages over and against the responses of the immanent-experientialist and transcendent-voluntarist models.

On the one hand, Carl F. H. Henry affirms the determinist view that

---

[75]In this view, God knows who will finally be "elect" not because they are necessarily such and could not will otherwise but because he has infallible knowledge of their future free decisions. Many reject this view based on the belief that exhaustive foreknowledge and libertarian free will are incompatible. Open theism and process theism resolve the supposed incompatibility by denying exhaustive foreknowledge, whereas deterministic compatibilists remove "libertarian" free will in favor of "free will" in the sense that the "will" is not externally "compelled" but is nevertheless controlled by the unilaterally efficacious divine will (compatibilism). On the former see William Hasker, *God, Time, and Knowledge* (Ithaca, NY: Cornell University Press, 1989); Clark Pinnock, Richard Rice, John Sanders, William Hasker and David Basinger, *The Openness of God: A Biblical Challenge to the Traditional Understanding of God* (Downers Grove, IL: InterVarsity Press, 1994); Hartshorne, *Man's Vision of God*, p. 98. On the latter see Henry, *God, Revelation, and Authority*, 5:282; Millard J. Erickson, *What Does God Know and When Does He Know It?* (Grand Rapids: Zondervan, 2003).

However, more than one model of how divine foreknowledge and libertarian freedom might be compatible has been proposed. To take just a couple of examples, Richard Land has utilized Boethius's view that God is eternally present and posits that election is timeless, taking into account God's universal experience of all that "will" happen. This he calls "congruent election" ("Congruent Election: Understanding Salvation from an 'Eternal Now' Perspective," in David Lewis Allen and Steve Lemke, eds., *Whosoever Will: A Biblical-Theological Critique of Five-Point Calvinism* [Nashville: B&H Academic, 2010]). However, this view may be criticized for qualifying (or even denying) the strong language that depicts God as experiencing the events of history (at least to some degree). See Canale, *Criticism of Theological Reason*. William Lane Craig has made a strong case for a view that utilizes middle knowledge (Molinism) to show that divine foreknowledge and libertarian free will are compatible. See Craig, *Divine Foreknowledge and Human Freedom: The Coherence of Freedom* (New York: Leiden, 1991). Further, perhaps God's knowledge of future free events transcends time in a way that we do not understand such that God's knowledge is caused by the future free decisions themselves or otherwise.

God predestines all history, yet "does no evil."[76] Since God is entirely good, God is the "ultimate cause" but not the "author" of evil.[77] On this view, God's "foreordination of an evil act is not itself evil, since God need not will what he wills for the reasons others may will them."[78] Nevertheless, while it is important to understand that the determinist perspective adamantly denies that God himself does evil, I fail to see *how* the determinist perspective successfully avoids making God culpable for evil.[79] How could God be good if he could have unilaterally and effectively willed to prevent all evil without hindering his purpose? If God arbitrarily determines every event, such that everything happens in accordance with his desires, then God must desire evil *somehow* and, therefore, would not be infinitely and wholly good.[80] To suggest that this manifests God's glory does not resolve the issue since, on compatibilistic determinism, God could have unilaterally determined that he be fully glorified in the sight of all creatures without evil.[81]

In Charles Hartshorne's process panentheism, on the other hand, the problem of evil is avoided by denying divine omnipotence. God is not responsible for evil because God could not prevent it. Rather, God administers

---

[76] Henry, *God, Revelation, and Authority*, 5:283. God "does not even stimulate evil desires in man" (ibid., 6:86). Compare Carson, *Difficult Doctrine of the Love of God*, p. 56.

[77] For Henry, "the sovereign God in some sense creates sin. But to say that God commits sin is unthinkable"; it is "abhorrent to him" (Henry, *God, Revelation, and Authority*, 6:294).

[78] Ibid., 5:315.

[79] David Bentley Hart contends that if God "has eternally, infallibly, irresistibly, 'permissively' decreed that the creature will [intend and] commit this sin and suffer this damnation, not on account of any prevision of the creature's sins, but solely on account of his own predetermining act of reprobation" such that the "creature is incapable of availing himself of 'sufficient' grace . . . then moral evil is as much God's work as is any other act of the will" ("Impassibility as Transcendence," p. 310).

[80] Henry suggests that, in the eschaton, "God's providential purpose and presence in history and experience subordinate all the pain and suffering of regenerate believers to a higher good," yet in the meantime, God's purpose is "partially revealed yet somewhat inscrutable" (ibid., 6:304, 296). John Piper similarly suggests that God wills evil for the higher purpose of his glory (Piper, "Are There Two Wills in God?" pp. 124, 130). However, this does not resolve the issue but raises the question: why would a God who unilaterally determines all events *need* evil for his glory? See Thomas McCall's criticism of Piper in this regard, in "I Believe in Divine Sovereignty," *TJ* 29 (2008): 205-26.

[81] Indeed, as Jerry Walls puts it, "If freedom and determinism are compatible, God could have created a world in which all persons freely did only the good at all times" ("Why No Classical Theist," p. 82). Compare Stephen T. Davis, "Universalism, Hell, and the Fate of the Ignorant," *Modern Theology* 6, no. 2 (1990): 190; David Fergusson, "Will the Love of God Finally Triumph?" in Vanhoozer, ed., *Nothing Greater, Nothing Better*, p. 190.

"a maximal ratio of chances of good to chances of evil."[82] Theodicy is merely a "false problem" that stems from "a faulty or non-social definition of omnipotence."[83] This is because conflict, suffering and evil are inevitable due to the pan-indeterministic nature of social reality. "Tragedy is thus inherent in value," and evil will never be eradicated.[84] Thomas Jay Oord's essential kenosis theology similarly attempts to resolve the issue by also contending that "God does not essentially possess all power," cannot coerce creatures, and is thus not responsible for evil.[85] Yet, if God lacks the power to prevent or eliminate evil, what assurance is there that evil will finally come to an end? In my view, this is a severely impoverished view of God and his love. Oord goes further, however, asserting that, in order to be good, God *must* lack the power to prevent evil since "if God does not care enough to prevent genuinely evil occurrences while having the power to do so, God is not love."[86] That is, a "voluntarily kenotic God is culpable for failing to prevent evil."[87]

However, much to the contrary, I believe that God's voluntary allowance (but not determination) of evil actually testifies to the nature of God's love.[88] God never desired evil, but the very allowance of evil is itself because of God's love. As explained in chapter four, by definition love must be free and cannot be unilaterally determined. Thus it is impossible to determine that all beings *freely* love God, because it is nonsensical to say that love is determined.[89] This means that the necessary context for love requires the possibility that God's ideal will may be rejected and, consequently, the possibility of evil. God allowed evil, while passionately despising it, because to exclude its possibility would exclude love. Thus, as Stephen Post states, "God

---

[82]Charles Hartshorne, *Reality as Social Process* (New York: Hafner, 1971), p. 107.
[83]Ibid., p. 41.
[84]Ibid., pp. 107, 190.
[85]Thomas Jay Oord, "Matching Theology and Piety: An Evangelical Process Theology of Love" (PhD diss., Claremont Graduate University, 1999), p. 314.
[86]Ibid., p. 345.
[87]Oord, *Nature of Love*, p. 124.
[88]As such, the foreconditional-reciprocal model contradicts the transcendent-voluntarist model in proposing that God's power is not omnicausal yet also rejects the immanent-experientialist model's view that God lacks the power to coerce.
[89]God "wills that the dependent freedom of the creature be joined to his absolute freedom; but an indispensable condition of what he wills is the real power of the creature's deliberative will to resist" God's work of grace (David Bentley Hart, "Impassibility as Transcendence," p. 316).

refuses to eliminate human freedom, because a divine determinism would preclude the realization of communion, of which freedom is a constitutive principle."[90] As already noted, by granting humans significant freedom, God has limited the exercise of his own power.[91] God need not have limited himself, but if love is genuine only if it is freely given (as in the foreconditional-reciprocal model), then the possibility of reciprocal love relationship is "contingent upon God's willing to enter into such a relation in the first place, to place himself under certain relational constraints, to be limited in his freedom by the existence of a genuinely free other."[92]

Evil is thus alien to God's original creation and his ideal will. God created the world "very good," but evil resulted from creaturely disobedience (Gen 1; 3; Rom 5:12). Jesus masterfully depicted this in his parable of the wheat and tares, in which a landowner sowed only good seeds in his field. However, tares, representing evil, sprang up among the wheat. His servants do not understand how the field could have tares if the owner sowed only good seed (Mt 13:27), but the master replies: "An enemy has done this!" (Mt 13:28). That is, evil is the result of the action of an enemy of God.[93] The servants then inquire why the tares are not immediately removed (Mt 13:28), that is, why not eradicate evil immediately? The master replies that gathering up the tares prematurely will include uprooting the wheat (Mt 13:29). God passionately hates evil, as he should, and he will finally put an end to evil, but he allows it for a time. He allows it initially because to do otherwise would eliminate freedom and, with it, love. Further, God continues to allow evil

---

[90]Post, *Theory of Agape*, p. 26.

[91]As Clark Pinnock comments, "God, although he could control everything, chooses not to do so but restrains himself for the sake of the freedom that love requires" ("Constrained by Love: Divine Self-Restraint According to Open Theism," *Perspectives in Religious Studies* 34, no. 2 [2007]: 149). Although I do not agree with the rejection of foreknowledge (see the earlier discussion), Greg Boyd's warfare theodicy contains many excellent insights that complement this view. See *God at War: The Bible & Spiritual Conflict* (Downers Grove, IL: InterVarsity Press, 1997); *Satan and the Problem of Evil: Constructing a Trinitarian Warfare Theodicy* (Downers Grove, IL: InterVarsity Press, 2001).

[92]Trevor Hart, "How Do We Define the Nature of God's Love?" in Vanhoozer, ed., *Nothing Greater, Nothing Better*, p. 109. Compare Wolfhart Pannenberg, *Systematic Theology*, trans. Geoffrey W. Bromiley (Grand Rapids: Eerdmans, 1991), 1:438; Thomas C. Oden, *The Living God* (San Francisco: Harper & Row, 1987), p. 75.

[93]I do not mean to suggest that this resolves the problem of evil, but it does seem to me to point in a direction that might helpfully be pursued in the realm of theodicy, and I plan to develop this in future work.

because if he were to destroy it prematurely, creatures would not understand why he did so and serve God out of fear rather than love.

Thus, bilateral significant freedom, possibility, and divine self-limitation to the exclusion of omnicausality individually and collectively illuminate how God can be love despite the fact that there is so much evil in the world. God voluntarily created a world that he remains ontologically independent from, and yet, by choosing to create a world wherein creatures possess genuine freedom, he consequently chooses not to exercise the full extent of his power, manifesting "a form of love that lets the creatures have their own existence."[94] Thus God is omnipotent, omnibenevolent *and* passionate, always desiring and working toward the ultimate good of all, but allows other wills to impact history (positively and negatively) because love requires significant freedom as its context. Since love assumes bilateral significant freedom, which cannot be selectively removed, and significant freedom thereby assumes that God does not exercise all of his power but limits his own action on the basis of his prior commitment to the freedom that love relationship requires, history does not progress in accordance with God's ideal will. By allowing evil to continue temporarily, the depth of evil is manifested. All of God's creatures may, in turn, understand that God is love, that all of his commands have always been, and always will be, out of love, intended toward the ultimate happiness of all.[95] Finally, God will make an utter end of evil and "wipe away every tear," and "there will no longer be *any* death; there will no longer be *any* mourning, or crying, or pain," for those former things will have passed away (Rev 21:4).[96]

In the meantime, Paul assures us that ultimately all this will be worth it since "the sufferings of this present time are not worthy to be compared with the glory that is to be revealed" (Rom 8:18; compare 2 Cor 4:17). Though creatures suffer immensely due to evil, God himself suffers most of all,

---

[94]Pannenberg, *Systematic Theology*, 1:438.

[95]Moreover, the divine self-limitation assumed by a genuine, reciprocal, give-and-take, divine-human relationship adds complexity such that the world as a whole, because of the entrance of evil in opposition to God's ideal will, does not operate in a way in which blessing/curses correspond universally to human disposition and/or behavior. Thus the "righteous" often suffer while the wicked temporarily prosper (cf. Job; Jer 12:1; Eccles 7:15; Lk 13:1-5).

[96]If God were to remain in a love relationship with those who finally reject him, having chosen evil over good, they would be allowed to continue not only to hurt God but the rest of his creatures continually. A truly loving God cannot allow such evil to continue forever.

having done everything he could do within the context required for genuine love relationship (compare Is 5:1-7; Mt 21:33-40), even subjecting himself to death on a cross (Phil 2:8). By so doing, he demonstrated that he considered *this* world, despite evil, to be worth the cost to himself, while also demonstrating his righteousness (Rom 3:25-26) and love (Rom 5:8). The final answer to evil, the ultimate theodicy, will only be fully known in the eschaton. In the meantime, the voluntarily suffering God on the cross unequivocally demonstrates the depth of God's love. If there had been any other way to ensure that the universe would continue in unceasing love and uninterrupted goodness, would he not have chosen it? There is no greater love than God's giving of himself in love for us (Jn 3:16; 15:13; Rom 5:8). God is love (1 Jn 4:8, 16).

Conclusion

Overall, then, God's love is volitional, evaluative, emotional, foreconditional and ideally reciprocal within the context of the God-world relationship. First, divine love is volitional but not merely volitional. It includes a free, volitional aspect that is neither essential nor necessary to God's being, yet also not arbitrary. The divine-human love relationship is neither unilaterally deterministic nor ontologically necessary to God but bilaterally (though not symmetrically) volitional and contingent. Second, divine love is evaluative. This means that God is capable of being affected by, and even benefitting from, the disposition and/or actions of his creatures (due to God's prior action). Third, God's love is profoundly emotional and passible (in that God is affected by creaturely actions, which he does not causally determine), though not to the exclusion of volitional and evaluative aspects. Fourth, divine love is foreconditional, not altogether unconditional. That is, divine love is prior to all other love and conditions but not exclusive of conditions. Divine love in relation to the world is unconditional with respect to God's volition (subjective love), but conditional with respect to the ongoing God-world relationship (objective love). Finally, divine love is ideally reciprocal. God universally seeks a relationship of reciprocal love but enters into particular, intimate relationship only with those who respond appropriately.

If God loves in this way, what must God be like? This canonical model of divine love suggests that God possesses significant freedom and bestows it on his creatures toward the goal of reciprocal love relationship. Accordingly, God is not omnicausal but creatures may affect history. God is omnipotent but voluntarily limits the use of his power to allow significant freedom such that creaturely decisions impact history. God is passible, being profoundly affected by and concerned about the world he has created, yet not essentially bound to it nor passive. God has voluntarily bound his own interests, including his joy on the one hand and suffering on the other, to the best interests of the world. Yet, independent of any relationship with the world, God is perfect and self-sufficient, meaning that he is not growing and neither does he need this or any world, but he nevertheless desires a reciprocal love relationship with each person. God's character is love, and all that God does is loving. God does not need to love humans, or any creatures, but he voluntarily creates beings on whom he bestows his love, which is grounded in his wholly loving character, and enjoys a reciprocal love relationship with all who positively respond. "For God so loved the world, that He gave His only begotten Son, that whoever believes in Him shall not perish, but have eternal life" (Jn 3:16).

Author Index

Ackerman, Susan, 79
Adamson, James B., 145
Akin, Daniel, 200
Allen, Joseph L., 239
Allison, Gregg, 55
Alson, William P., 173, 174, 176, 182-83
Andersen, Francis I., 226
Aquinas, Thomas, 19-20, 21, 132, 168, 173, 178
Aristotle, 18, 19, 74, 173
Arminius, Jacob, 259
Augustine, 18-19, 21, 132, 256
Ayres, Lewis, 18
Badcock, Gary, 22, 124, 130, 193
Baer, D. A., 83, 84, 210, 211
Baggett, David, 254, 262
Baloian, Bruce, 159
Barr, James, 74
Barstad, H. M., 119
Barth, Karl, 33, 39, 61, 62, 90-93, 97, 100, 135, 168, 192, 200, 206-7, 232, 253, 256, 258, 265, 270, 271
Barth, Markus, 121, 142
Basinger, David, 30
Bergen, Robert, 241
Bernard, J. H., 76
Block, Daniel I., 157, 185
Bloesch, Donald, 39, 167, 168
Blomberg, Craig, 110, 132, 263
Borchert, Gerald L., 159, 195, 198, 236
Botterweck, Johannes G., 120
Boyd, Gregory, 275
Bray, Gerald, 165
Breneman, Mervin, 155, 220
Brown, Raymond, 195
Bruce, F. F., 137, 142
Brueggemann, Walter, 202, 268
Brümmer, Vincent, 15, 18, 34, 36, 37, 42-43, 113, 129, 167, 208, 227, 256
Brunner, Emil, 36, 97, 135

Bultmann, Rudolf, 86, 87
Burnaby, John, 18, 19, 42
Caird, G. B., 163, 184
Calvin, John, 162, 164
Campbell, William, 108
Canale, Fernando, 47, 56, 57, 58, 260, 271
Carr, G. Lloyd, 149
Carson, D. A., 25, 38, 41, 56, 77, 127, 138, 160, 170-71, 193-94, 195, 196, 197, 198, 221, 233, 234, 240
Chardin, Pierre Teilhard de, 17
Childs, Brevard, 46, 49, 57
Clark, Gordon R., 82
Clayton, Phillip, 41, 193
Clements, Ronald E., 106, 220
Clendenen, E. Ray, 43, 104
Coenen, L., 109, 110, 121
Congdon, David W., 91-92, 206-7
Cooper, John W., 41, 90, 162, 170, 193
Cooper, Lamar Eugene, Sr., 106
Coppes, Leonard J., 157
Craig, William Lane, 24, 205, 208, 272
Craigie, Peter C., 124, 126, 158, 160, 194, 199, 201, 202
Cranfield, C. E. B., 71, 148, 211, 220
Creel, Richard, 169, 170, 177
Crisp, Oliver, 204, 206
Cross, Frank Moore, 80, 223, 227
Culpepper, Gary, 169, 177
D'Arcy, Martin Cyril, 36
Davids, Peter H., 142, 198, 236, 262
Davidson, Richard M., 50, 156
Davies, John A., 210
Davis, Stephen T., 44
Delitzsch, Franz, 120, 221
DeWeese, Garrett, 62
Dorner, Isaak, 135
Dunning, H. Ray, 33, 36, 43, 131

Eichrodt, Walter, 211
Elliott, John, 144
Emery, Gilles, 168, 178
Erickson, Millard, 24, 36, 129, 130-31, 163, 171
Esser, H. H., 86
Evans, C. Stephen, 188
Farber, Marvin, 45
Fee, Gordon, 111, 121, 127, 134
Fensham, Charles, 222
Fergusson, David, 114, 208
Flew, Antony, 263
Floyd, Shawn, 243
Fox, Michael, 221, 224
Frame, John, 168
France, R. T., 139, 152
Freedman, David Noel, 49, 52, 226
Frei, Hans, 52
Fretheim, Terence, 119, 183, 185, 270
Gadamer, Hans-Georg, 54
Garrett, Duane A., 124, 164
Gavrilyuk, Paul L., 165, 170, 171, 178-79, 256-57, 265
Geisler, Norman, 24, 25, 38, 134-35, 170
Glueck, Nelson, 82, 83
Godet, Frederic, 106
Goldingay, John E., 86, 151, 213
Gordon, R. P., 83, 84, 210, 211
Gowan, Donald, 82, 86, 151
Green, Joel B., 4, 50
Griffin, Jeffery D., 184
Grondin, Jean, 54
Groningen, Gerhard Van, 125
Grudem, Wayne, 39, 167
Guelich, Robert A., 122
Günther, W., 64, 152, 228
Guy, Fritz, 245-46
Hagner, Donald A., 110
Hahn, Scott, 80
Harris, Murray J., 124
Harris, R. Laird, 80, 107
Hart, David Bentley, 148, 180, 259, 262, 267, 271, 273, 274

Hart, Trevor, 114, 275
Hartshorne, Charles, 17, 22, 26-31, 32, 35, 37, 40, 42, 46, 134, 138, 166, 188, 193, 228, 256, 268-69, 273-74
Hasel, Gerhard F., 54, 239
Hasker, William, 272
Hector, Kevin W., 33, 91
Helm, Paul, 23, 163, 169, 170, 244, 271
Hendriksen, William, 201
Henry, Carl F. H., 22-26, 32, 34, 35, 37-38, 40, 42, 46, 129, 138, 144, 177, 192, 251, 264, 272-73
Herrera, Max, 38, 170
Hick, John, 34, 97, 204
Holmes, Stephen, 61
Horton, Michael, 40-41, 168, 192, 258, 270
House, H. Wayne, 38, 170
House, Paul, 157
Huey, F. B., Jr., 199, 226
Humboldt, Wilhelm von, 175
Hunsinger, George, 91, 92-93
Husserl, Edmund, 46, 57
Jacob, Edmund, 81, 102, 149
Janzen, J. Gerald, 151
Jenni, Ernst, 105, 127
Jenson, Robert, 52-53, 61, 93, 179, 258, 271
Johnston, G., 64, 71, 75, 140, 232
Joly, Robert, 74
Josephus, 77
Jüngel, Eberhard, 60, 63, 70, 71, 92, 133, 137, 164, 167, 172, 200, 267
Kant, Immanuel, 172
Keil, Carl Friedrich, 120, 221
Klassen, William, 70, 266
Knoppers, Gary, 215, 223
Konkel, A. H., 127
Köstenberger, Andreas, 161, 225
Köster, Helmut, 152
Lane, Tony, 125, 127
Lapsley, Jacqueline, 80, 103, 149, 150
Larue, Gerald, 83
Lee, Jung Young, 265
Link, H. G., 64, 152, 228
Lipinski, E., 104, 125
Lister, Rob, 38, 40, 57-58, 161, 163, 164, 165, 166, 169-70, 172, 177, 178, 179-80, 183, 187, 264, 268
Longman, Tremper, III, 156
Lundbom, Jack, 224, 237
Luther, Martin, 20-21, 62, 71, 163, 206, 251, 262
Maier, Gerhard, 48, 58
Marcus, Joel, 150
Marshall, I. Howard, 52, 200, 209, 262, 263
Martin, D. Michael, 111
Mathews, Kenneth, 158, 268
McCall, Thomas, 259, 273
McCann, J. Clinton, Jr., 211
McCormack, Bruce, 32, 33, 39, 61, 62, 63, 39, 61, 63, 90-92, 93, 165-66, 168, 251, 265, 270, 271
Merrill, Eugene H., 78, 102, 103, 211, 215
Miller, Patrick, 153, 158, 160, 237
Moffat, James, 42, 111, 158
Molnar, Paul D., 91, 92, 93, 270
Moltmann, Jürgen, 36-37, 39, 123, 129, 166, 253, 256, 265
Moo, Douglas J., 106, 107, 108, 110, 126, 144
Moran, William L., 78, 103
Morris, Leon, 25, 26, 36, 41, 42, 64, 71, 73, 100, 101, 124, 138, 143, 148, 188, 192, 195, 239, 251
Motyer, J. A., 126, 151
Mounce, Robert, 107, 239, 240
Nash, Ronald, 17, 23
Newlands, George M., 15
Newman, Barclay Moon, 108, 195
Ngien, Dennis, 20
Nicholson, Ernst W., 80
Nicole, Emile, 237
Nida, Eugene Albert, 108, 195
Noble, Paul R., 49
Nolland, John, 131, 152
Nygren, Anders, 21-22, 36, 70, 71, 72, 101, 129, 140, 230, 232, 233, 256
O'Brien, Peter, 132
Oden, G. S., 99
Oden, Thomas C., 36, 37, 42, 43, 123, 124, 129, 135, 141, 208, 227
Olson, Dennis T., 153, 155
Olson, Roger, 245, 259
Oord, Thomas J., 16, 17, 33, 36, 39, 41, 43, 45, 65, 98, 131, 166, 193, 200, 203, 253-54, 274
Osborne, Catherine, 36, 130, 135
Osborne, Grant, 51, 52, 54, 58, 70
Oswalt, John N., 121, 153, 161, 216, 236
Outka, Gene H., 21, 136
Packer, J. I., 33, 43, 205, 244, 245
Pannenberg, Wolfhart, 34, 114, 276
Parry, Robin, 204
Partridge, Christopher H., 204
Parunak, H. Van Dyke, 185
Peels, H. G. L., 157
Petersen, David L., 105
Philo, 172
Pinnock, Clark, 17, 45, 114, 275
Piper, John, 36, 118, 205, 206, 273
Plantinga, Alvin, 254, 259
Plato, 18, 256
Platt, David, 29
Post, Stephen G., 41, 131, 136, 189, 215, 260, 274-75
Przywara, Erich, 172
Quell, Gottfried, 80, 86, 149, 194
Reuter, E., 156, 186
Rice, Richard, 94, 167, 189
Richards, Jay Wesley, 57
Ridderbos, Herman N., 149
Robertson, O. Palmer, 120
Robinson, J. A. T., 72-73, 149, 207
Rolnick, Philip A., 176
Ruprecht, E., 120
Sakenfeld, Katharine D., 83, 84, 194, 210, 271
Sanders, James, 46
Sauer, G., 157
Schleiermacher, Friedrich, 38, 93, 127, 135, 144, 163
Scholz, Heinrich, 21, 71
Schreiner, Thomas, 64, 108, 110, 143-44, 145, 206, 261-62
Schrenk, Gottlob, 110, 111, 112,

Author Index   281

121, 127, 142
Scott, James M., 224
Seebass, H., 121
Segovia, Fernando, 195
Seitz, Christopher, 54
Silva, Moises, 267
Simoni-Wastila, Henry, 269
Simundson, Daniel, 160
Singer, Irving, 17, 20, 21, 97, 98
Smith, Duane, 80
Snaith, Norman H., 78, 155, 192, 201, 210
Spicq, Ceslas, 73, 74, 85, 88, 122, 130, 139, 152, 232
Stählin, Gustav, 73, 74, 238, 240
Stanglin, Keith D., 259
Stauffer, Ethelbert, 78, 100, 122, 230
Stein, Robert H., 110
Stoebe, H. J., 86, 87, 151, 153, 154, 220
Stott, John, 252, 264
Stuart, Douglas, 267
Stumpff, Albrecht, 171-72
Talbott, Thomas, 34, 97, 204, 205, 251, 252
Talley, David, 119, 120, 123

Tanner, Kathryn, 61, 62, 63, 132, 133, 135, 136, 137, 202, 229, 257
Tarelli, C. C., 74
Thiselton, Anthony, 47, 53, 63, 143
Tigay, Jeffrey, 81, 188, 220, 225
Torrance, Alan, 20, 64
Torrance, Thomas F., 41, 64, 93, 94, 98, 133, 134, 135, 137, 141, 168, 207, 214
Treier, Daniel J., 48, 52, 55, 56
Trench, Richard, 74, 75
Vacek, Edward Collins, 135, 136, 138
Vanhoozer, Kevin J., 15, 19, 40, 45, 46, 48, 49, 50, 51-52, 53, 54, 55, 56, 57, 59, 60, 61, 90, 100, 164, 167, 181, 182-83, 187, 249-50, 258, 267
Vischer, Wilhelm, 186
Walker, Norman, 119
Wallis, Gerhard, 158
Walls, Jerry L., 141, 205, 243, 245, 257, 262-63, 273
Walton, John H., 106, 212
Ware, Bruce, 266, 268

Warnach, Viktor, 122
Watson, D. C. K., 159
Webster, John B., 261
Weinandy, Thomas, 38, 165, 169, 170, 177
Weinfeld, Moshe, 80, 81, 156, 157, 210, 222
Wenham, Gordon, 159
Wessling, Jordan, 173, 174, 175, 234
Westphal, Merold, 183
Whitehead, Alfred North, 17
Wildberger, H., 109, 238
Williams, Daniel Day, 32, 39, 159, 166, 253
Williams, Thomas, 173, 174
Wolterstorff, Nicholas, 48, 53, 128-29, 130, 148, 182
Wood, Leon J., 119, 120
Woodbridge, John D., 56
Woudstra, Marten H., 213
Wuest, Kenneth, 72
Yaron, R., 223
Yeago, David, 48, 49, 55, 57
Yee, Gale A., 226
Zobel, Hans-Jürgen, 82, 83, 84, 210

Subject Index

abhorrence, divine, 103, 118, 199, 241
abiding, in God's love, 197-98, 221
acceptability, 119, 121, 123, 141-43, 241
actus purus, 170, 268
adoption, 95, 99, 216, 224, 227, 237, 239
adultery, spiritual, 202, 225-26
agape
    Greek root, 69-77
    thematic, vs. *eros*, 18, 21-22, 34-36, 69-73, 233
altruism, 21, 31, 36-37, 71, 129, 138, 171, 257
analogia entis, 19, 172, 173
anger, divine, 95, 154, 157-61, 181, 186
animosity. See hatred, divine
aseity. See self-sufficiency
beloved, 72-73, 111, 121-22, 137, 139, 157, 158, 197-98, 200, 226, 238-40
bilateral significant freedom. See free will
blessing. See love, beneficent
calling, 65, 101, 108-12, 197, 222
canonical theological method, 45-67, 69-70, 128, 172, 176, 182, 186-87, 251, 255
caritas, 18, 20, 21
character of God, 15, 25, 82-83, 86-87, 96, 100-101, 107, 156, 188-89, 201, 212-14, 252-55, 268, 278
classic theism, 15, 17, 22-24, 39-40, 90, 170, 255-57
comfort, 73, 88, 154, 185
compassion. See love
compatibilism, 20, 24, 113, 180, 205-6, 211, 231-32, 244-45, 262-63
condescension, divine, 47, 62-64, 265

contingency/necessity of God-world relationship, 32-34, 90-100, 193, 202, 206-7, 212, 251-55, 258, 275
covenant
    Abrahamic, 107, 216, 222, 225, 237
    bilateral, 215, 222-23
    Davidic, 210, 215-16, 222-23
    grant, 214-16, 222
    kinship, 80, 211, 223, 227-28
    Mosaic, 99, 216, 222
    New, 226
Creator-creature distinction, 24, 58, 93, 171-81, 239, 256, 265, 271
delight. See love, evaluative
desires, unfulfilled divine, 258-63, 274
determinism, 19-20, 24, 32, 34, 43, 66, 101, 106-8, 110, 112, 171, 180, 205, 208, 231-32, 245, 250, 256, 261-64, 272-75
deuteronomist, 79-80, 210, 222
discipline, 56, 65, 76, 224-25
Edom, 104, 105, 107
election, 25, 32-33, 42-43, 67, 71-72, 78-79, 89, 91-112, 121, 127, 139, 142, 206-7, 216, 222, 225, 230, 235-39, 244-45
epoché, 45, 55, 57-58
eros, 18, 21-22, 34-36, 69-71, 73-74, 77-78, 233
evil, problem of. See theodicy
foreknowledge, 17, 24, 112, 253, 255, 271, 272
forsakenness, 137, 198, 214, 221, 226
free will, 24, 82, 89, 99-100, 110, 112-13, 180, 203, 205, 208, 214, 226-27, 230-31, 246, 257-64, 272-76
    libertarian, 24, 92, 112, 205, 232, 272

significant freedom, 112-14, 207-9, 226-28, 231-32, 244-46, 257-63
grief, divine, 154, 157, 185, 187, 225-26, 246, 265
hatred, divine, 19, 73, 79, 81, 104, 105, 107, 124-27, 139, 149, 158, 178, 186, 196, 198-99, 226
heart. See seat of emotions
Hellenization thesis, 39, 165-66, 172
hermeneutical spiral, 51, 53-54, 57-59
hesed, 79, 81-86, 96, 210, 220, 271
immanent-experientialist model, 15, 26-32, 34, 37, 40, 42, 44, 89, 93, 98, 171, 219, 227, 235, 244, 249, 255, 256, 269, 272, 274
immutability, 17-19, 20, 23-24, 26, 29-30, 33, 35, 37-39, 165, 168-69, 213-14, 266, 268
impassibility. See passibility, divine 38, 161, 169, 170, 178, 180
incarnation, 23, 41, 60, 62-64, 91, 93, 133, 135, 137, 170, 172, 179, 214, 264, 265
independence. See self-sufficiency
jealousy. See love, passionate
joy. See love, evaluative
judgment, divine, 26, 35, 105, 124, 127, 129, 140-41, 143-45, 186, 203, 246
justice, divine, 26, 32, 35, 43, 65, 67, 82-83, 85, 106-7, 144, 156-57, 159, 203, 245, 277
kindness. See *hesed*
kinship metaphors
    husband-wife (marriage), 66, 95, 99, 126, 128, 157, 189, 202, 223-27, 239
    parent-child, 66, 86, 95,

99, 128, 134, 153, 186, 198, 223-27, 236-39
language
  accommodative, 66, 128, 162-64, 266
  analogical, 162, 172-77, 181-87, 255, 267, 271
  anatomical, 66, 162, 183-84
  anthropomorphic/ anthropopathic, 60, 92, 162-64, 171, 183, 186, 266-67
  equivocal, 172-74, 176-78
  univocal, 62, 172-76, 181, 183, 185, 187, 267
libertarian free will. *See* free will, libertarian
love
  acquisitive, 18, 21, 69-70, 71, 233
  affectionate, 16, 72-73, 75, 77, 81, 86-87, 102, 120, 122, 126, 149, 150, 152, 154, 178, 188, 220, 224, 228, 264
  attachment, 103, 120
  attraction, 20, 73, 103, 149
  belonging, 73, 240
  beneficent, 16, 18-22, 25, 32, 34, 36-37, 42, 65, 70-72, 86, 89, 97, 130, 153, 194, 197, 202, 210, 215, 219, 222, 233-34, 236-37, 249
  benevolent, 19, 25, 40, 70, 134, 198, 213
  bestowal, 18, 20, 25, 32, 36-37, 83, 89, 94-96, 99, 101, 107, 118, 129, 134, 140-41, 188, 196-97, 201, 203, 219-21, 224, 228, 231, 235, 241-42, 246, 258, 272
  bilateral. *See* love, reciprocal
  circle of, 220, 228-30, 234, 246, 247
  commanded, 78-79, 81, 140-41, 188, 196, 198, 202, 226, 229, 238, 240
  compassionate, 26, 64, 66, 67, 73, 82-83, 85-88,
  95-96, 98-99, 107, 149-50, 153-54, 156, 159, 164, 178, 184, 187-89, 196-99, 203, 209, 213, 224, 226-27, 237-38, 267
  conditional. *See* love, foreconditional
  covenantal, 41, 78, 80-81, 82-84, 90, 103, 157, 193-94, 198, 211-12, 214-16, 221-23, 227, 231, 236-37, 239
  desirous, 18-21, 25, 30, 36-37, 65-66, 69, 70-72, 78, 81, 103, 113, 119, 121, 149, 213-14, 220, 227-29, 231, 233, 235, 243, 246-47
  devotion, 78, 81, 84, 99, 149, 155, 220, 223
  disinterested, 34, 36, 131, 233
  divine essence, 20, 25, 41-42, 89-90, 94, 98, 130, 204, 220, 251-57
  emotional, 31, 38, 66, 82, 85-86, 101-4, 120-21, 139, 147-89, 228, 247, 250, 258, 263-64, 268-69
  enemy, 140-41, 225, 246
  evaluative, 34, 66-67, 72-73, 76, 79, 81, 103-4, 108, 117-45, 149, 159, 189, 195-96, 228, 233, 246-47, 264, 269
  everlasting, 65, 79, 83-84, 186, 200, 209-17, 226
  foreconditional, 41, 66, 72, 79, 84, 111, 141, 191-217, 221, 228, 237, 239, 241-43, 247, 257-58, 267, 277
  friendship, 18-20, 66, 70, 73-74, 76, 78, 96, 196-98, 221, 231, 240, 246
  insider, 76-77, 238-40, 243, 246
  intratrinitarian, 25, 94, 132, 228, 252-53, 256-57
  long-suffering, 65, 73, 83, 88, 96, 140, 184, 199, 217, 223
  loyal. *See* hesed
  merciful. *See* love, compassionate
  misdirected, 72, 76, 77, 79
  mutual. *See* love, reciprocal
  non-coercive, 30, 83, 274
  objective, 212-14, 217, 277
  passionate, 76, 80-81, 103, 119, 149, 151, 156-57, 159, 169, 177-78, 181, 186-88, 267
  preferential, 43, 65, 72, 76-77, 246
  reciprocal, 19-21, 42-43, 73-74, 79, 84, 141, 178, 189, 204, 205, 207-8, 219-47, 250
  relational. *See* love, reciprocal
  steadfast. *See* hesed
  subjective, 212-14, 217, 242, 277
  unconditional, 22, 25-26, 40-41, 67, 69, 71, 78, 191-93, 199-203, 209-14, 216-17
  universal, 26, 42, 43, 44, 87, 97, 140, 215, 235-38, 240-44, 246-47
  unmerited, 25, 83, 95, 99, 103, 107, 124, 139, 140-41, 155, 196-98, 200-203, 213, 217, 221, 234, 241-42, 245, 247
  unrequited, 42, 66, 157, 199, 225, 227, 228
  unselfish. *See* self-interest; love, bestowal
  volitional, 25, 32, 34, 66, 71, 78, 83, 89-115, 188-89, 220, 231
lovingkindness. *See* hesed
lust, 72, 77-78, 233
mediation, 66, 140, 141-43, 201, 234
necessity of God-world relationship. *See* contingency/necessity of God-world relationship
obedience, 41, 74, 81, 95, 111, 123-24, 139, 193, 195-98, 202, 211, 215, 220-21, 231, 234, 240
omnibenevolence, 187, 204-7,

259-60, 276
omnipotence, 17, 23-24, 29, 33, 62, 172, 179-80, 204, 249, 253, 256, 265, 269-78
omniscience, 23-24, 28-29, 31, 35, 62, 179, 180, 249, 260, 265, 272
open theism, 17, 94, 271
other-interest. *See* self-interest
panentheism, 15, 17, 24, 27-30, 41, 130, 188, 193, 253-54, 273
panpsychism, 27, 30
passibility, divine, 18-20, 23-26, 31, 37-40, 61, 66, 86, 118, 128, 134, 148-50, 154, 156-58, 161-72, 177-81, 184-89, 212, 249-50, 257, 263-69
patience. *See* love, long-suffering
perfection. *See* self-sufficiency
phenomenological exegesis, 45, 56-59
philos, 73-77, 126, 194-96, 221
pleasure. *See* love, evaluative
predestination, 22, 24-25, 33, 100, 107, 110, 205-6, 230, 244-45, 273
prevenient grace, 141, 200, 232
providence, 112, 242, 244, 256, 260, 269
remnant, 127, 214, 215, 239
repentance, divine, 153-55, 185
reward, 111, 141, 144-45, 203, 211, 229-31, 245
righteousness. *See* justice
seat of emotions, 81, 86, 87, 125-26, 128, 149, 151-52, 154, 157-58, 162, 184, 198-99, 220, 222, 224, 226, 229, 261
self-abnegation, 129, 134-35
self-interest, 30-31, 69, 118, 130-34, 157, 257
selfishness. *See* self-interest
self-love, 129, 131-34
self-sacrifice, 37, 70, 130-32, 134-38
self-sufficiency, 16-21, 23-25, 34, 40, 90, 98, 191, 220, 249-50, 256, 278
significant free will. *See* free will, significant freedom
simplicity. *See* classic theism
soft obligation, 83, 270
sorrow. *See* grief
soul. *See* seat of emotions
suffering. *See* passibility
sympathy, 26-27, 29-32, 35, 37, 40, 51, 85-87, 89, 118, 152, 154, 178, 185, 188, 191, 193, 213, 220, 249, 256
theodicy, 272-77
theological interpretation of Scripture, 56
timelessness, 17, 23-24, 61, 160, 170, 249, 265, 271
transcendent-voluntarist model, 15, 22-26, 32-35, 37, 40, 44-45, 89-91, 93, 97, 191, 219, 244, 249, 255, 274
universalism, 34, 97, 100, 204-8, 235, 244
way of eminence, 186, 255
way of negation, 255
wills, God's ideal and effective, 226, 258-63, 274-76
wrath, 26, 35, 65, 103, 159, 206, 225

Scripture Index

Old Testament

Genesis
1, *275*
1:26-27, *140, 172, 267*
2:24, *133*
3, *275*
6:5-6, *184*
6:6, *185*
6:6-7, *154, 157*
6:8, *144, 184*
6:11, *144*
7:1, *144*
12:2-3, *106*
12:3, *95, 106, 237*
14:20, *184*
15:6, *52, 240*
15:16, *105*
17:14, *237*
18:18, *95*
18:22-32, *153*
18:25, *186, 246*
19:19, *83, 85*
20:13, *84*
21:23, *84, 221*
22:9, *240*
22:16-18, *203*
22:18, *237*
24:12, *83*
24:27, *83, 254*
24:49, *84*
25:23, *107*
26:4, *237*
26:4-5, *203, 223*
27:4, *76, 150*
27:9, *76, 150*
27:14, *76, 150*
29:31, *104*
29:33, *104*
32:5, *184*
32:10, *83*
32:25-28, *203*
34:2-3, *72*
34:3, *78, 81, 120*
34:8, *81, 103, 120*
37:3-4, *76, 77*
37:4, *81, 125*
43:30, *86, 162*
47:29, *84*
49:24, *184*

Exodus
3:1-15, *47*
3:14, *99*
4:22, *150, 224, 237*
5:21, *144*
6:6, *184*
6:7, *237*
10:11, *184*
15:26, *144*
17:14, *53*
19:5, *203*
19:5-6, *122*
20:1, *47*
20:5, *156*
20:5-6, *81, 157, 220, 222, 243*
20:6, *73, 79, 81, 82, 84, 85, 194, 210, 211, 229*
21:5, *79*
23:25, *203*
27:17, *103*
28:37, *119*
31:18, *47*
32-34, *96, 99, 254*
32, *83*
32:1-14, *153*
32:10, *155*
32:12, *154, 155*
32:12-13, *106*
32:14, *154*
32:26, *99*
32:26-30, *154*
33:5, *155*
33:11, *196, 240*
33:12-34:10, *153*
33:14, *184*
33:19, *85, 86, 87, 96, 98, 99, 107, 154, 155*
34:6-7, *154, 156*
34:6, *82, 83, 85, 86, 87, 153, 184*

34:7, *83, 85, 160, 220*
34:14, *156*
35:29, *95*
38:17, *103*
38:28, *103*

Leviticus
1:3, *144*
1:3-4, *119*
7:18, *119*
19:5, *119*
19:17, *125*
19:18, *113, 131*
22:19-27, *119*
22:29, *119*
23:11, *119*
26, *216*
26:3-17, *203, 222*

Numbers
21:4, *154*
23:19, *154, 165, 185, 266*
25:11, *157*

Deuteronomy
1:17, *236*
1:31, *150, 224*
2:5, *105, 237*
2:9, *237*
2:19, *237*
4:22, *157*
4:23-24, *81*
4:24, *156, 252*
4:25, *158*
4:31, *152, 156*
4:36-37, *225*
4:37, *73, 78, 79, 80, 100, 102, 103, 202, 222, 239, 240*
5:9, *156, 243*
5:9-10, *81, 157*
5:10, *79, 84, 211, 220, 229*
5:29, *203, 261*
6:5, *79, 81, 113, 188, 189, 220, 222, 229*

6:15, *81, 156*
6:18, *144*
7, *216*
7:6, *122*
7:6-8, *95*
7:7, *100, 102, 103*
7:7-8, *102, 109, 112, 120, 202, 222, 240*
7:7-13, *78, 95, 239*
7:9, *79, 84, 85, 104, 112, 194, 220, 229*
7:9-12, *210*
7:9-13, *109, 211*
7:10, *194, 229*
7:11-12, *112*
7:11-13, *104, 112*
7:12, *84, 194*
7:12-13, *79, 194, 222*
7:13, *79, 194*
8:3, *184*
8:5, *150, 160, 224*
8:16, *150, 160, 224*
9:4, *107, 202*
9:4-5, *105, 112*
9:5, *202*
10:12, *79, 220, 222, 229*
10:13, *81*
10:15, *78, 79, 81, 95, 100, 102, 103, 120, 202, 222, 239, 240*
10:15-16, *109*
10:16, *104, 112*
10:17, *106*
10:17-18, *236, 240*
10:18, *106*
10:18-19, *140, 238*
11:1, *79, 222, 229*
11:13, *79, 81, 220, 222, 229*
11:26-28, *203, 222*
12:31, *122*
13:3, *79, 81, 222, 229*
13:4, *220*
13:17-18, *87*
14:1-2, *224*
14:2, *122*

15:16, *79*
16:22, *105*
21:11, *103*
21:14-15, *120*
21:15-17, *104*
22:13, *104*
22:16, *104*
22:22, *225*
23:21-22, *157*
24:1, *225*
24:3, *104*
26:18, *122*
28:63, *122*
29:20, *157*
30:2-3, *87*
30:6, *79, 81, 220, 222, 229*
30:9-10, *120*
30:15-16, *113*
30:19-20, *113*
31:9, *53*
31:12, *53*
31:17-18, *184*
32:4, *65*
32:5, *226*
32:6, *224*
32:8, *237*
32:9-13, *224*
32:10, *100, 224*
32:10-11, *153*
32:16, *158*
32:18, *226*
32:19, *226*
32:21, *157*
32:21-22, *156*
32:36, *154*
33:12, *239*

Joshua
1:8, *53*
2:12-14, *84, 221*
22:5, *79, 81, 222, 229*
23:6, *53*
23:11, *79, 229*
24:19, *156*

Judges
2:12, *158*
2:18, *153, 154*
5:31, *79, 221, 238*
8:35, *83*
10:13, *155*
10:16, *153, 154, 160*
14:16, *104*
15:2, *104*
16:16, *154*

Ruth
1:8, *82, 221, 238*
2:20, *221*
4:15, *79*
18:3, *80*
18:22, *79*
20:17, *79*

1 Samuel
2:30, *221*
7, *223*
8:3, *186*
8:8, *155*
10:24, *109*
13:13-14, *109*
15, *266*
15:6, *84*
15:11, *154, 185*
15:22, *122*
15:23, *109, 238*
15:29, *155, 185, 266*
15:35, *154, 185*
18:22, *81, 120*
20:8, *84, 221*
20:14-15, *84, 221*

2 Samuel
1:26, *79*
2:5, *84, 221*
3:8, *84*
5:8, *125*
7:13-16, *215*
7:15, *83*
9:1, *84*
9:3, *84*
9:7, *84*
12:24-25, *240*
13:1, *78*
13:4, *78*
13:13-14, *238*
13:15, *72, 74, 78, 81, 104, 158, 233*
14:19, *184*
15:11, *110*
15:20, *82, 238*
16:17, *84*
19:6, *221*
21:14, *154*
22:2, *87*
22:21-28, *122*
22:26, *81, 84, 85, 221*
22:51, *209*
23:5, *215*
24:14, *152*
24:16, *154*
24:25, *154*

1 Kings
1:41, *110*
1:49, *110*
2:3, *53*
2:3-4, *223*
2:4, *222*
3:3, *79, 229, 240*
3:6, *215*
3:8, *215*
3:26, *86, 162*
8:23, *84, 210*
8:25, *222, 223*
8:50-53, *154*
9:1, *103*
9:2-9, *109*
9:4-9, *215, 223*
9:19, *103*
10:9, *120, 122*
11:11, *109, 215*
11:33, *109, 155, 215*
14:8, *215*
14:9, *158*
15:4-5, *215*
19:10, *157*

2 Kings
19:16, *184*
21:6, *158*
21:15, *158*
22:17, *155, 155-56*
23:27, *239*

1 Chronicles
7:12-14, *215*
16:34, *209*
16:41, *209*
21:13, *152*
21:15, *154*
22:13, *109*
28:7, *109*
28:9, *109, 214, 215, 221*
29:17, *73, 122*

2 Chronicles
5:13, *209*
6:14, *84*
6:16, *109*
6:42, *83*
7:3, *209*
7:7, *209*
7:14, *153*
7:17-20, *109, 215*
8:6, *103*
9:8, *120, 122*
12:5, *221*
19:2, *221*
20:7, *79, 196, 240*
20:21, *209*
24:22, *84, 221*
30:9, *87, 153*
31:14, *95*
32:32, *84*
33:6, *159*
35:26, *84*
36:15-16, *155*
36:16, *105*

Ezra
4:1-3, *237*
10:1, *119*

Nehemiah
1:5, *79, 84, 220, 229*
8:8-18, *53*
9, *96*
9:3, *53*
9:7-33, *155*
9:17, *153, 154*
9:19, *153, 203*
9:27, *153*
9:31, *153, 154*
9:33, *213*
13:14, *84, 229*
13:26, *240*

Esther
6:9, *73, 122*

Job
10:12, *82*
19:19, *221*
23:13, *260*
30:27, *153*
40:9, *184*

Scripture Index

Psalms
5:4, *122*
5:4-6, *126, 241*
5:5, *124, 125, 199*
5:5-6, *105*
5:11, *79*
7:9, *143*
11:5, *81, 105, 124, 125, 199, 241*
11:7, *79, 122, 126*
16, *236*
18:1, *87, 229*
18:25, *81, 85, 221*
19:9, *246*
22:15, *153*
23:4, *154*
25:6, *83, 209*
25:7, *83*
25:10, *84*
25:19, *127*
30:5, *160*
31:23, *79, 82, 85, 221, 229*
32:10, *84*
33:5, *79, 82, 122, 236*
34:12, *79, 81, 120*
35:19, *126*
36:10, *83, 221*
37:22, *123*
37:28, *79, 82, 85, 122, 123, 221, 238*
37:34, *123*
37:38, *123*
40:6, *122*
45:7, *125*
47:4, *78, 100, 103*
51:1, *153*
51:6 [LXX 50:8], *73, 119, 122*
51:16 [LXX 50:18], *121*
60:5, *239*
62:12, *210*
65:2, *241*
65:4, *241*
68:1, *243*
68:5, *236*
69:4, *126*
69:16, *153*
69:36, *79*
70:4, *229, 238*
71:21, *154*
77:8, *83*
78, *96*
78:38, *160, 186*
78:40-41, *158*
78:58, *157, 158, 186*
78:58-59, *103, 158*
78:67, *103*
78:67-68, *239*
78:68, *78, 100, 103*
79:9, *131*
81:11-14, *261*
85:10, *82, 83*
86:15, *153, 154*
86:17, *154*
87:2, *241*
88:11, *83*
89, *223*
89:14, *82, 83*
89:30-32, *225*
89:38-39, *215*
89:49, *83, 155, 197*
90:2, *271*
90:13, *154*
91:14, *103, 229*
94:19 [LXX 93:19], *73, 122*
95:7-8, *199*
95:9-11, *158*
97:10, *79, 85, 221, 229*
98:3, *254*
100:1, *236*
100:5, *186, 187, 209, 236, 260*
101:14, *87*
102:17, *85, 153*
102:25-27, *271*
103:8, *153*
103:13, *86, 150, 155, 224*
103:15-17, *271*
103:17, *84, 209, 211*
103:17-18, *216, 222*
103:21, *119*
104:31, *120*
106:1, *83, 209*
106:7, *83*
106:8, *131*
106:40, *125, 241*
106:45, *83, 154*
107:1, *83, 209*
107:8, *83*
107:15, *83*
107:21, *83*
107:31, *83*
109:4-5, *221*
109:12, *221*
109:17, *79, 81, 120*
109:21, *106*
110:4, *185*
111:4, *153*
112:4, *152*
115:3, *119, 260*
116:1, *79, 229*
117:1-2, *82, 236*
118:1-4, *209*
118:29, *209*
119:47, *81*
119:64, *82, 236*
119:76, *154*
119:82, *154*
119:132, *153*
119:167, *81*
122:6, *221*
127:2, *239*
129:5, *105*
132:11-14, *109*
135:6, *260*
135:14, *154*
136, *83, 199, 209, 209*
138:8, *83*
139:14, *140*
139:21-22, *127*
143:2, *125, 140*
143:10, *119*
143:11, *106, 131*
145:8, *83, 153*
145:8-9, *82*
145:9, *87, 236, 260*
145:16, *241*
145:19, *241*
145:20, *79, 229, 238*
146:8, *124, 140, 196, 241*
146:8 [LXX 145:8], *73, 79*
147:5, *260*
147:10 [LXX 146:10], *121*
147:10-11, *119, 122, 123*
148:5-6, *94*
149:2, *94*
149:4, *122, 150*

Proverbs
1:7, *47*
3:3-4, *84*
3:11-12, *150*
3:12, *79, 81, 120, 122, 160, 225, 241*
3:31, *157*
5:1, *184*
8:17, *76, 77, 221*
10:20, *121*
11:1, *122*
11:15, *127*
11:17, *85*
11:20, *120, 122, 124, 125*
12:2, *120*
12:10, *86*
12:22, *120, 122*
14:20, *125*
14:29, *184*
15:8, *119, 122*
15:8-9, *120, 126*
15:9, *79, 196, 241*
16:4, *94*
16:7, *122*
16:13, *79, 81, 120*
19:7, *127*
19:17, *85*
20:6, *85*
21:17, *76, 77*
25:17, *127*
27:6, *125*
28:22, *85*

Ecclesiastes
3:8, *125*
3:16-17, *203*
5:4, *123*
7:15, *276*
8:12, *203*
8:14, *203*
9:2, *203*
9:6, *81, 158*

Song of Solomon
1:3-4, *79*
1:7, *79*
3:1-4, *79*
5:4, *153*

Isaiah
1:2-4, *225*
1:11, *122*
1:14, *105, 122, 126, 186*
1:24, *154*

5:1-7, *155, 203, 277*
5:2-7, *213*
5:7, *73, 122*
6:1-3, *47*
8:16, *53*
8:20, *52, 53*
9:17, *120, 123, 155*
10:20-22, *239*
12:1, *154*
14:1, *239*
16:5, *82*
16:11, *153*
19:19-25, *237*
26:11, *157*
27:11, *87, 155*
30:9, *225, 261*
30:15, *161*
30:15-18, *113*
30:15-19, *261*
30:18, *87, 156, 160, 261*
30:18-19, *161*
30:19, *153, 156*
37:32, *239*
38:17, *103*
40:6, *84*
40:28, *186*
41:8, *78, 79, 100, 103, 196, 240*
41:8-9, *239*
42:1, *100, 103, 139, 237*
42:1-6, *237*
42:21, *119*
43:4, *79, 122*
43:7, *94*
43:10, *94*
43:18-19, *47*
43:19-21, *94*
44:1-2, *100*
44:28, *119*
46:10, *119*
48:9-11, *131*
48:10, *109, 121*
48:14, *120*
49:6, *237*
49:10, *153*
49:13, *87, 154*
49:15, *86, 151, 153, 178, 186, 224*
50:1, *226*
51:3, *154*
51:12, *154*
51:16-17, *81*

51:19, *81, 154*
52:9, *154*
53:3, *184*
53:10, *119, 259, 260*
54:4-8, *226*
54:7-10, *160*
54:8, *209*
54:11, *154*
55:7, *87*
55:8, *181, 185*
55:11, *119*
56, *236*
56:4-8, *237*
56:7-8, *225*
56:10, *76*
57:3-13, *237*
57:6, *154*
57:17-18, *154*
60:15, *120*
61:2, *154*
61:8, *79, 122, 125*
62:4, *120, 150, 157, 226*
62:4-5, *128*
63:7, *83, 153*
63:8-9, *224*
63:9, *81, 150, 153*
63:10, *158*
63:15, *86, 151, 153, 155*
64:6, *140*
65:1-7, *237*
65:3, *158*
65:8-9, *215*
65:8-15, *239*
65:12, *113, 119, 123, 261*
65:19, *120, 128*
66:4, *113, 119, 123, 261, 263*
66:13, *150, 154*
66:18-22, *237*
66:19, *120*

Jeremiah
1:16, *155*
2:2, *79, 82, 84, 150, 157, 223, 229*
2:2-9, *225*
2:24-25, *225*
3, *150, 223*
3:1, *225*
3:1-12, *157, 161*

3:1-20, *225*
3:8, *225, 226*
3:8-10, *99*
3:12, *85*
3:12-14, *226*
3:13-14, *100*
3:19, *100, 226*
3:19-22, *226*
3:20, *99*
3:22, *226*
4:1, *226*
4:2, *237*
4:19, *153, 184*
4:28, *155, 185*
7:18-19, *158*
8:5, *198*
9:23, *82, 83*
9:24, *122*
11:10, *198*
11:14, *198*
11:15, *155, 196, 198, 226, 239*
11:20, *143*
12:1, *246, 276*
12:7, *158, 198*
12:7-8, *210, 226*
12:8, *105, 125, 126, 158, 196, 198, 199*
12:15, *87*
12:15-17, *237*
14:10, *155, 196, 198-99*
15:1, *155, 198, 199*
15:6, *155, 203*
16:5, *83, 87, 96, 155, 196, 198, 209*
18:1-10, *108, 185*
18:7-10, *96, 154, 185*
19:5, *261*
20:16, *185*
26:19, *154*
30:18, *199*
31:3 [LXX 38:3], *73, 79, 82, 141, 199, 200, 201, 209, 213, 214*
31:13, *154*
31:20 [LXX 38:20], *86, 122, 151, 153, 171, 178, 183, 184, 224*
31:20-22, *226*
31:31-36, *226*
32:17, *270*
32:18, *220*

32:41, *120, 128*
33:11, *83, 209*
33:24, *239*
42:12-16, *87*
44:4, *105*
49:25 [LXX 30:31], *73, 120, 122*
50:1, *225*

Lamentations
1:2, *74, 125*
1:20, *153, 184*
2:11, *153*
2:15, *120*
3:22, *152*
3:32-33, *160, 259, 261*
3:33, *113*
4:10, *86*
4:22, *105*

Ezekiel
3:7, *261*
5:11, *155*
5:13, *154*
8:17, *158*
16, *150, 157*
16:1-6, *100*
16:3-6, *224*
16:8, *223*
16:8-13, *223*
16:15, *225*
16:25-26, *225*
16:26, *158*
16:33-37, *81*
16:60-62, *226*
18:1-24, *216*
18:23, *113, 119, 242, 246, 259, 261*
18:25, *106*
18:32, *113, 140, 207, 236, 242, 246, 259, 261, 262*
20:9, *106, 131*
20:14, *106, 131*
20:22, *106, 131*
20:28, *158*
20:39-42, *128, 142*
20:44, *106*
23, *150, 157*
24:14, *185*
25:12-13, *105*
25:12-14, *105*

33:11, *113, 119, 140, 207, 236, 242, 246, 259, 261*
34:10-11, *128*
34:11, *141*
34:13, *128*
34:16, *141*
35:15, *105*
36:5, *105*
39:25, *157, 199*
44:6-9, *236*

Daniel
9:4, *79, 84, 210, 220, 229*
9:18, *153, 155*
9:23, *122*
12:2, *209*

Hosea
1–2, *224*
1–3, *150, 157, 225*
1:6, *225*
1:6-7, *87*
1:9, *225*
2–3, *99*
2:2, *225, 226*
2:4, *87, 225*
2:14, *226*
2:19, *82, 156*
2:19-20, *226*
2:25–3:1, *86*
3:1, *79, 81, 150, 202, 226*
4:1, *84*
6:4, *84, 186*
6:6, *84, 122*
8:13, *126*
9:1, *79*
9:4, *122*
9:10, *79, 196*
9:15, *79, 96, 105, 125, 126, 127, 155, 158, 196, 199, 203, 209, 211, 213, 226, 228, 254*
10:12, *84, 226*
11:1, *73, 81, 100, 150, 224*
11:1-9, *81*
11:3-4, *150, 224*
11:4, *81*
11:8, *154, 184, 226, 228*
11:8-9, *81, 160, 161, 162, 163, 164, 183, 184, 185, 246*
11:9, *181*
12:6, *84*
12:14, *158*
13:14, *154*
14:1-3, *226*
14:1-4, *199*
14:3-4, *86, 226*
14:4, *78, 95, 113, 127, 211*
14:5, *81*
14:5-7, *237*

Joel
2:12-14, *199*
2:13, *153, 154*
2:13-14, *153, 154*
2:18, *157*
2:18-19, *156*
3:19, *105*

Amos
1:9, *105*
1:11, *105*
5:15, *79*
5:21, *105*
5:21-22, *122*
6:8, *105, 125*
7:3, *154*
7:6, *154*
9:7, *237*
9:12, *237*

Obadiah
10, *104*
10-14, *105*

Jonah
2:8, *85*
3:9, *96*
3:9-10, *153, 154*
3:10, *185*
4:2, *82, 96, 153, 154, 185, 238*
4:10-11, *238*
4:11, *238*

Micah
6:7-8, *122*
6:8, *84*
7:18, *122*

Nahum
1:2, *156*

Zephaniah
3:5, *65*
3:8-9, *237*
3:17, *79, 81, 120, 128, 150, 239, 246*

Zechariah
1:13, *154*
1:14-17, *157*
1:17, *154, 239*
2:11, *237*
2:12, *239*
7:9, *84*
8:2, *150, 157*
8:14, *185*
8:17, *79*
11:8, *154*

Malachi
1, *100*
1:2, *104, 239*
1:2-3, *81, 104, 105, 106*
1:3, *104, 107*
1:3-5, *104*
1:4, *105*
1:6, *225*
1:9-10, *155*
1:10, *126*
2:10, *236, 239*
2:11, *105*
2:17, *185*
3:6, *105, 165, 185, 266*
3:12, *128*

New Testament

Matthew
2:15, *139*
3:17, *73, 76, 121, 122, 139, 228, 264*
5, *140*
5:7, *86, 155, 196*
5:9, *225, 239*
5:12, *230*
5:43-44, *73*
5:44, *140*
5:44-45, *140, 225, 236*
5:44-46, *246*
5:45, *203, 246*
5:45–6:6, *141*
6:5, *76, 150*
6:24, *72, 125*
7:1-2, *140*
7:12, *131*
7:24, *53*
7:26, *53*
8:12, *225*
9:13, *86*
9:15, *224*
9:36, *152, 153*
10:31, *122, 123*
10:37, *76*
11:19, *77, 240*
12:7, *86*
12:12, *122, 123*
12:18, *100, 122, 139, 149*
12:39, *225*
12:50, *239*
13:27, *275*
13:28, *275*
13:29, *275*
14:14, *152, 153*
15:32, *152, 153*
17:5, *73, 76, 122, 139*
18:13, *128*
18:26-33, *140*
18:27, *152, 153, 155*
18:27-31, *196, 197*
18:33, *155, 197*
18:35, *155, 196*
20:34, *152*
21:13, *159*
21:33-40, *277*
22:3-4, *109*
22:3-14, *239*
22:8-9, *109*
22:14, *110, 239, 243, 246*
22:37, *188, 189, 214, 260*
22:37-38, *229*
22:37-39, *113*
22:39, *131*
23:6, *76*
23:37, *113, 156, 225, 226, 228, 261, 263*
24:22, *239*

24:24, *102*
25:1-10, *224*
25:40, *230*
26:24, *238*
27:46, *137*

Mark
1:11, *122, 139*
1:41, *152, 189*
2:19-20, *224*
3:5, *152, 158*
6:34, *152*
7:24, *261*
8:2, *152*
8:38, *225*
9:7, *139*
9:22, *152*
9:24, *142*
10:20-22, *196*
10:21, *73, 150, 152*
10:21-22, *238*
12:30, *229*
13:22, *102*

Luke
1:32-35, *139*
1:50, *85, 155, 196, 216*
1:54, *153*
1:58, *64, 85*
1:78, *85, 86, 87, 88, 152, 153*
2:49, *139*
3:22, *122, 139*
5:34-35, *224*
6:13, *125*
6:23, *230*
6:27-36, *246*
6:31, *131*
6:31-37, *141*
6:35, *203, 225, 230, 246*
6:35-36, *140, 203, 236, 239*
6:36, *73, 88*
6:37, *140*
7:13, *152*
7:30, *113, 232, 260, 261*
7:34, *77, 240*
7:47, *73, 229*
9:35, *139*
10:26, *53*
10:27, *229*
10:33, *85, 152*

10:37, *85*
11:28, *203*
11:43, *72*
12:4, *240*
12:6-7, *122, 123*
12:24, *122*
12:47-48, *209*
13:1-5, *203, 276*
13:34, *160, 214, 225, 226, 228, 232, 243, 246, 260, 261, 263*
14:14, *203*
14:16-24, *109*
14:23, *237*
15:7, *128, 246*
15:10, *128*
15:20, *152*
15:20-24, *128*
15:24, *128*
16:15, *122*
18:7, *239*
19:10, *141*
19:41, *153*
20:35, *143, 144*
20:36, *225*
20:46, *76*
22:15, *76*
23:12, *125*
24:27, *53*
24:44, *53*

John
1:1-3, *139*
1:1-14, *47*
1:9, *141*
1:11-13, *236*
1:12, *225, 239*
1:13, *225*
1:14, *61*
2:17, *157*
3:16, *73, 90, 106, 110, 125, 137, 138, 159, 161, 196, 200, 236, 238, 240, 242, 243, 245, 277, 278*
3:16-21, *209*
3:17, *236*
3:18, *209, 262*
3:19, *72, 243*
3:29, *196, 224, 240*
3:35, *73, 76, 229*
5:11-12, *209*

5:20, *64, 76, 229*
5:28-29, *209*
5:40, *261*
5:42, *243*
6:44, *112, 141*
6:70, *109, 196, 238*
8:29, *123, 139*
8:35, *63*
8:39, *63*
8:42, *224, 243*
8:58, *139*
9:40-41, *209*
10:17, *72, 139, 195, 229, 234, 264*
10:17-18, *96, 137*
11:5, *76, 229*
11:11, *196, 240*
11:33-38, *152*
11:36, *76, 150*
12:25, *76, 125, 132*
12:26, *144*
12:32, *112, 141, 209, 236, 242, 245*
12:43, *72*
13:1, *73, 76, 149, 229, 240*
13:23, *76, 240*
13:34, *113, 229, 234*
13:34-35, *230*
14:9, *61, 63, 152*
14:21, *72, 73, 76, 194, 195, 221, 224, 229, 238*
14:21-23, *242*
14:23, *72, 76, 194, 195, 221, 224, 229, 238*
14:24, *243*
14:26, *228*
14:31, *73, 229*
15, *198*
15:5, *198*
15:7, *198*
15:7-10, *221*
15:9, *64, 229*
15:9-10, *72, 195, 198, 221, 229, 234*
15:10, *198*
15:11, *137*
15:12, *229, 230, 234*
15:13, *74, 96, 135, 161, 277*
15:13-14, *77, 240*

15:14, *74, 109, 112, 126, 196, 197, 221, 231, 240*
15:14-15, *76*
15:16, *109, 141, 196, 200*
15:17, *76, 230*
15:17-19, *77*
15:19, *76, 100, 109, 125, 240*
15:25, *126*
16:27, *76, 195, 221, 224, 229, 238*
17:5, *94*
17:12, *109*
17:13, *137*
17:23-24, *229*
17:23, *229*
17:24, *94, 139, 220, 228, 252, 257*
17:26, *229, 234*
19:26, *240*
20:2, *76, 240*
21:7, *229, 240*
21:15, *76*
21:15-16, *76*
21:15-17, *75, 229, 232*
21:16, *76*
21:17, *76*
21:20, *229, 240*
21:25, *186*

Acts
2:42, *53*
4:12, *209*
5:41, *143*
8:26-39, *53*
10:9-17, *47*
10:17, *72*
10:34, *106*
10:34-35, *106, 236, 238, 239, 241, 242, 245*
10:35, *126*
13:1, *72*
13:17, *237*
14:17, *236*
17:3, *140*
17:11, *53*
17:25, *94*
17:30, *209*
17:30-31, *236, 238*
22:15-16, *236*
24:14, *53*

Scripture Index

Romans
1:5, *236, 237, 242*
1:7, *111, 224, 239*
1:24, *262*
1:26, *262*
1:28, *213, 262*
1:30, *243*
2:4, *200*
2:4-12, *262*
2:11, *106*
3:10, *125, 140*
3:20, *144*
3:22, *107*
3:23, *125, 136*
3:25-26, *277*
4, *52*
4:3, *53*
4:11, *107*
4:24, *107*
5:5, *94, 228*
5:8, *64, 72, 90, 95, 96, 138, 202-3, 243, 277*
5:8-10, *238, 246*
5:12, *275*
6:13, *143*
8:1, *141*
8:8, *123*
8:14, *225*
8:14-17, *239*
8:15-17, *142, 224*
8:18, *276*
8:23, *239*
8:26, *228*
8:28, *111, 145, 229*
8:28-29, *110*
8:28-30, *271*
8:28-39, *64*
8:32, *95, 133, 137*
8:35, *64, 209, 214*
8:39, *64, 209, 214*
9, *100*
9–11, *108, 232*
9:6, *107, 215, 239*
9:6-14, *107*
9:7-8, *225, 239*
9:11-12, *107*
9:11-13, *100*
9:13, *88, 101, 104, 106*
9:15, *86, 88, 107*
9:15-16, *154*
9:15-18, *96, 98*
9:21, *108*
9:22-23, *206*
9:25, *101*
9:25-26, *238, 243*
9:26-27, *225*
9:30-32, *239*
10:9, *110, 111*
10:9-13, *107, 239*
10:12, *111*
10:12-13, *110*
10:13, *106, 110*
10:16, *236*
11:7, *215*
11:22, *155, 197, 239*
11:22-23, *107, 110, 111, 203, 215, 238, 239, 243*
11:28, *100, 199, 239*
12:1, *143*
12:1-2, *123, 142*
12:2, *123, 143*
12:10, *74*
12:13, *77*
12:14-21, *246*
13:9, *131*
14:18, *122, 123*
15:3, *123*
15:30, *228*

1 Corinthians
2:9, *111, 145, 229, 246*
3:13, *143*
4:5, *140*
4:7, *142, 202*
6:16, *133*
7:32, *123*
8:3, *73, 111, 145*
10:5, *123, 127, 158*
11:28, *143*
11:32, *224*
13, *138*
13:4, *73*
13:4-13, *72*
13:5, *133, 135*
13:12, *177*
15:51-56, *144*
16:22, *76, 229, 238, 239, 242*

2 Corinthians
1:3, *153*
2:14-15 *142*
4:4, *61*
4:14, *143*
4:17, *276*
5:9, *123*
5:9-10, *143, 144*
5:19, *238, 243*
6:18, *225*
8:9, *137*
8:12, *142-43*
9:7, *72, 124, 196, 241*
10:18, *143*
11:2, *150, 157, 224*
13:5-6, *143*
13:5-7, *143*
13:7, *143*
13:11, *200*
13:14, *94, 228*

Galatians
1:6, *112*
1:8-12, *53*
1:10, *123*
2:6, *236*
2:20, *96*
3:9, *203*
3:26, *225, 239*
3:28, *237*
5:13, *112*
5:22, *73, 94, 228*
6:16, *85, 196*

Ephesians
1, *108*
1:4, *203*
1:4-5, *100*
1:4-6, *142*
1:5, *121, 239*
1:6, *206*
1:9, *121*
1:12, *206*
1:14, *206*
2:3, *225*
2:3-5, *238, 243*
2:4, *73, 85, 153*
4:1, *112*
4:6, *225, 236, 239*
5:1-2, *64, 240*
5:2, *137, 142, 234*
5:10, *123*
5:23-27, *224*
5:25, *96, 133*
5:28, *132*
5:28-30, *133*
5:29, *131*
5:33, *132*
6:24, *111, 203, 233*

Philippians
1:8, *87, 88*
1:15-16, *73, 122*
2:1, *73, 88, 228*
2:3, *136*
2:3-4, *135*
2:5-8, *136, 137*
2:8, *277*
2:9-11, *136*
2:12, *240*
2:12-13, *234*
2:13, *121*
4:18, *123, 142*

Colossians
1:8, *228*
1:10, *122, 123*
1:15, *94*
1:22, *143*
1:28, *143*
2:9, *61, 139*
3:12, *88, 100, 111, 112*
3:19, *76, 149*
3:20, *122, 123*

1 Thessalonians
1:3-4, *103*
1:4, *100, 111*
1:13, *196*
2:4, *123, 143*
2:7, *149*
2:12, *112, 123*
2:13, *47, 53, 163*
2:15, *123*
3:12, *238*
4:1, *122, 123*
4:4, *108*
4:7, *112*
4:9, *77, 230, 239*
5:13, *72*

2 Thessalonians
1:5, *123, 143, 144*
1:7-10, *209*
1:11, *112, 143*
2:10, *111, 203*

2:10-12, *209*
2:10-15, *238, 243*
2:12, *111*
2:13, *111*
2:13-15, *103, 112*
2:14, *111*
2:15, *53*
2:16, *64*
3:14, *53*

1 Timothy
1:13, *85*
1:13-14, *203*
2:3, *144*
2:4, *110, 113, 236, 243, 260, 261*
2:4-6, *207, 236, 242, 246*
2:6, *110, 236, 261*
2:15, *198, 221*
3:2, *77*
3:10, *143*
4:10, *236, 237, 242, 245*
5:4, *123, 144*
6:12, *112*
6:11-12, *112*

2 Timothy
1:2, *85*
1:13, *53*
2:2-4, *143*
2:4, *123*
2:13, *253*
2:15, *143*
2:16, *73*
2:20-21, *108*
3:2-4, *132*
3:4, *76*
3:16, *47, 53*
4:8, *73, 201, 203, 229, 242, 245*
4:10, *72, 76, 233*

Titus
1:9, *53*
2:9, *123*
2:11, *110, 236, 242, 246, 261*
3:4-5, *153, 203*
3:5, *85, 155, 196*

Hebrews
1:2-3, *61*
1:3, *61*
1:9, *72, 139*
2:18, *152*
3:6, *225*
3:8-10, *158*
3:15, *199*
4:7, *199*
4:15, *152, 153*
5:8, *152*
6:10, *73, 229*
8:9, *155, 199*
8:12, *156, 199*
9:15, *226*
9:26, *137*
10:5-10, *142*
10:8, *121, 122*
10:10, *265*
10:27, *157*
10:38, *121, 122, 139*
11:8, *109, 110*
11:5, *122, 123*
11:6, *123, 144*
12:2, *137*
12:6, *76, 122, 160*
12:6-8, *225*
12:23, *144*
12:28, *142*
13:2, *77*
13:5, *213*
13:15-16, *142*
13:16, *123, 124*
13:21, *123, 142*

James
1:12, *73, 111, 122, 145, 203, 229*
1:17, *266*
1:25, *203*
2, *52*
2:3, *76*
2:5, *100, 111, 145, 229, 240*
2:13, *86, 155, 196*
2:23, *126, 196, 240*
4:4, *76, 125, 126, 150, 158, 224, 240, 243, 246*
5:11, *88, 153, 203*

1 Peter
1:1-2, *271*
1:3, *85, 153*
1:7, *143*
1:15, *112*
1:22, *72, 77, 149, 230*
2:3, *64*
2:4, *139*
2:4-5, *142*
2:5, *141, 201*
2:6, *139*
2:9, *112, 142*
2:11, *239*
2:21, *112*
3:4, *122, 144*
3:6, *225*
3:9, *112*
4:8, *72, 149*
4:12, *143, 239*
5:7, *153*
5:10, *112*

2 Peter
1:3, *112*
1:10, *111, 112, 239*
1:17, *122, 139*
1:20-21, *47*
2:15, *72*
3:9, *113, 140, 160, 207, 236, 242, 243, 246, 260, 261*
3:14, *112, 239*
3:17, *111, 112*
8:19, *198*

1 John
1:5, *252*
1:9, *106*
2:2, *242, 245*
2:5-6, *198, 221*
2:6, *230*
2:10, *198*
2:15, *72*
2:17, *198, 262*
3:1, *97, 141, 198, 200, 221, 224*
3:1-2, *225*
3:2, *144*
3:9-17, *198, 221*
3:11, *230*
3:16, *137, 230*
3:20, *260, 272*
3:21-22, *142, 203*
3:22, *122, 123*
3:23, *230*
3:23-24, *198, 221*
3:35-36, *198*
4, *252*
4:7, *201*
4:7-8, *200*
4:7-11, *240*
4:7-12, *230*
4:8, *203, 205, 214, 228, 252, 277*
4:9, *61*
4:9-10, *137, 141, 200*
4:11, *230*
4:12, *198*
4:12-16, *221*
4:16, *198, 200, 203, 205, 214, 228, 252, 277*
4:17-18, *198, 230*
4:19, *141, 200, 201, 231*
4:20-21, *230*
4:24, *252*
5:1, *224*
5:1-2, *230*
5:2, *145*
5:3, *73*

2 John
3, *85*
5, *230*
9-10, *53*

3 John
2, *77*
5, *77*
8, *230*
11, *77*
14, *77*

Jude
1, *111, 112, 197, 234*
2, *85*
3, *53, 239*
21, *72, 85, 111, 194, 196, 197, 213, 234*
24, *197*

Revelation
2:6, *124, 125*

3:9, *76*
3:19, *76, 160, 225*
4:11, *94*
5:2, *140*
5:4, *140*
5:9, *139, 140*
5:12, *139, 140*

7:16, *257*
12:11, *72, 76*
15:3, *65, 246*
16:7, *246*
17:14, *111*
19:6, *270*
19:7, *224*

20:12-15, *209*
21:4, *276*
21:7, *225, 239*
21:9, *224*
22:12, *230*
22:15, *76*

Works Outside the Protestant Canon

Odes 9:18, *86*
2 Esdras 8:3, *110*
2 Esdras 8:41, *110*
Wisdom 4:10, *123*

Finding the Textbook You Need

The IVP Academic Textbook Selector
is an online tool for instantly finding the IVP books
suitable for over 250 courses across 24 disciplines.

www.ivpress.com/academic/